LANGUAGE IDEOLOGIES

Language Ideologies

Critical Perspectives on the
Official English Movement

Volume 2
History, Theory, and Policy

Edited by

ROSEANN DUEÑAS GONZÁLEZ

University of Arizona, Tucson
National Center for Interpretation Testing, Research and Policy

with

ILDIKÓ MELIS

University of Arizona, Tucson

National Council of Teachers of English
1111 W. Kenyon Road, Urbana, Illinois 61801-1096

LEA

Lawrence Erlbaum Associates, Inc.
10 Industrial Avenue, Mahwah, New Jersey 07430

Staff Editor: Bonny Graham
Interior Design: Jenny Jensen Greenleaf
Cover Design: Carlton Bruett

NCTE Stock Number: 26790-3050

Lawrence Erlbaum Associates, Inc. ISBN 0-8058-4054-0

It is the policy of NCTE in its journals and other publications to provide a
forum for the open discussion of ideas concerning the content and the teaching of English and the language arts. Publicity accorded to any particular
point of view does not imply endorsement by the Executive Committee, the
Board of Directors, or the membership at large, except in announcements
of policy, where such endorsement is clearly specified.

Library of Congress Cataloging-in-Publication Data

Language ideologies: critical perspectives on the official English movement
/ edited by Roseann Dueñas González with Ildikó Melis.
  p. cm.
  Includes bibliographical references and index.
  Contents: v. 1. Education and the social implications of official language
  ISBN 0-8141-2667-7 (pbk.)
    1. Language policy—United States. 2. Language and education—
  United States. 3. English language—Study and teaching—United States.
  4. English language—Political aspects—United States. 5. Pluralism
  (Social sciences)—United States. I. González, Roseann Dueñas.
  II. Melis, Ildikó.
P119.32.U6 L358 2000
428'.0071'073—dc21
                                                    00-055887

v. 2. History, theory, and policy
ISBN 0-8141-2679-0

I dedicate this book to my mother, Maria Luisa Sazueta Dueñas, who believed in all the languages of knowledge. She prayed in her eloquent Spanish, read the Bible in English and Spanish, listened to the Mexican radio station, watched gothic novelas on Spanish television, read her favorite literature in Spanish, baby-talked to my children in Spanish, read the newspaper and health books in English, scolded me in Spanish, and read the English dictionary for fun! In her beautiful Spanish and broken English, she instilled in me my fundamental belief in social justice and taught me, by example, that we are all accountable for our actions toward each other, and that doing the right thing is always the most difficult thing to do.

Roseann Dueñas González
Tucson, Arizona, October 2000

CONTENTS

Contents

FOREWORD

English Only and the Crisis of Memory, Culture, and Democracy

HENRY A. GIROUX
Pennsylvania State University

> *Throughout human history, the apostles of purity, those who have claimed to possess a total explanation, have wrought havoc among mere mixed-up human beings. Like many millions of people, I am a bastard child of history. Perhaps we are, black and brown and white, leaking into one another, as a character of mine once said, "like flavours when you cook."*
>
> SALMAN RUSHDIE, *Imaginary Homelands: Essays and Criticism 1981–1991*

The rise of the English Only movement in the last decade signals a deepening crisis of historical memory, culture, and democracy in U.S. society. Within the discourse of this movement, cultural difference rather than bigotry becomes the overriding threat to American life. Culture becomes the primary sphere for mobilizing moral panics about the alleged threat of minorities to the American way of life, and the call for national unity becomes a thinly veiled excuse for waging an attack on multiculturalism, bilingual education, affirmative action, or welfare reform. While its attempts to eliminate bilingual education programs and enforce policy-mandated language restrictions are self-evident specific attributes and policies of the English Only movement, its political, cultural, and economic significance can be more readily grasped as part of a broader assault on the basic tenets of democracy.[1]

Central to understanding and struggling against the English Only movement is the recognition that it must be engaged as part of a wider ideological and policy-oriented attack against the democratic foundations of the public good. The undemocratic nature of this movement is revealed, in part, through its attempts to exclude those viewed as "linguistically" and racially "other" from public life while simultaneously abstracting the meaning of critical citizenship from the discourse of equity and social justice. The nature of this assault is marked by right-wing attempts to eliminate or diminish all those public spheres in which cultural differences might flourish, such as schools, the arts, and urban youth services. By rendering such spheres either obsolete or dysfunctional, movements such as English Only and the Council of Conservative Citizens present any notion of critical democracy as obsolete and attempt to undermine the value of citizenship by defining its obligations within a racially coded politics of exclusion and discrimination. Underlying this assault on public life is the tacit assumption that public space is white and middle class. Also missing from this notion of citizenship are those discourses aimed at developing nonmarket identities and noncommodified values such as love, trust, fidelity, compassion, and justice. While it is frequently argued that many minorities are fervent advocates of the English Only movement, such assertions merely reflect the truth that social identity is no guarantee of a particular political position, and that even with the best of intentions people may support causes that are undemocratic and repressive. Moreover, such conservative response usually serves to utterly individualize racism by reducing it to a matter of personal preference. In doing so, this approach has little to say about the various ways in which racism becomes institutionalized and embedded in dominant social structures and the machineries of everyday life. Lost from this analysis is the power of racism both as a signifying system and as a system of material production that informs and locates social subjects (Goldberg 1993).

The English Only movement represents more than simply another example of American xenophobia or an accelerated war on the role of schools as democratic public spheres. It is also an embodiment of a growing movement on the part of the evangelical right, neo-liberals, and others who now attempt to expunge the notions of cultural difference, multicultural democracy, and redistributive justice from the language of citizenship, schooling, and public life. Democracy at its best requires an ongoing struggle to expand social equality, to eliminate systemic domination and subordination, and to develop public spheres in which citizens can participate in meaningful dialogue and debate across linguistic and cultural differences. These are dangerous presuppositions to those who believe there is little room in a society for dissent, multiple forms of literacy, social justice, and citizens who inhabit a variety of subject positions—citizens whose identities leak into each other, challenging the possessive investment in whiteness that has so powerfully shaped this country's destiny and history (Lipsitz 1995).

Since the emergence of the Reagan administration in the 1980s, we have witnessed a full-fledged attempt on the part of the government, corporate interests, and conservative think tanks to rewrite the history of the civil rights movement and to reverse whatever legislative, educational, and economic gains have been made by various groups struggling against segregation, inequality, and racism. The traumatic and effective deployment of historical memory, particularly memories of slavery, struggles over school desegregation, and the fights for decent health care and services for the poor have been either rendered invisible by many conservatives, liberals, and right-wingers, or such historical memories have been rewritten to serve politically retrograde policies. The full-fledged assault on historical narratives that depict minorities of color and class as agents in the struggle for human rights and democracy can be seen in the attempts by conservatives such as Denish D'Souza, Robert Bork, and Charles Murray to associate minorities with a culture of poverty, a culture reduced to pejorative associations with high crime and illegitimacy rates, welfare dependency, and inferior modes of communication. For conservatives such as D'Souza, this means rewriting the history of slavery and its legacy of institutional racism by arguing that the legacy of such racism is no longer operable. But more is at stake than disavowing a history of racist exclusion. For D'Souza and his conservative colleagues, history is being rewritten so that it can be appropriated in order to reinvent its most sordid racist legacies. Hence D'Souza's public call for the repeal of the Civil Rights Act of 1964 and the passing of legislation that "allows private actors to be free to discriminate as they wish" (Toler 1999, 14–15).

The growing movement to implement English Only laws, eliminate bilingual education from the schools, and end affirmative action mandates is rooted in a complex legacy of racism that has reasserted itself with great vigor since the election of Ronald Reagan and the Republican revolution that began in the 1980s. In part, the success of this resurgence of antidemocratic fervor and politics is due to its ability to suppress those "dangerous" memories and subordinate forms of knowledge in which the subaltern not only speaks, but also plays an active role in shaping history. Fashioning history as a series of erasures suggests more than the distortion of the past or the rewriting of history from the vantage point of dominant groups. It also offers up a powerful challenge to progressives to make history part of the process of social change and a crucial resource in waging battle against the enemies of a multicultural democracy. Any attempt on the part of progressive educators, parents, and communities to resist antidemocratic forces, including the English Only movement, will have to contextualize such movements within the sordid history of repression and racism that constitutes their legacy, while simultaneously making visible alternative historical struggles and narratives that have challenged in word and action such repressive and dangerous movements. This is a crucial pedagogical and political move because it provides an opportunity for the public to understand that those who join and speak in support of the English Only movement often appeal to a notion of patriotism that is rooted in the legacy of white supremacy. Making this legacy visible is all the more important because its racist sentiments are often hidden within a racially coded language that appeals to emotionally charged terms such as "single nation," "American character," "common people," "common culture," and "national identity." Yet, as Stanley Fish points out, this politically correct and sterilized discourse cannot go unchallenged given the blatantly racist narrative it presents about "the American character and the necessity of preserving it, and the threat it faces from ethnic upsurges: a story that continues in every respect, from words and phrases to large arguments, a tradition of jingoism, racism and cultural imperialism" (Fish 1992, 64).

Culture and questions of identity have become central to some of the most intense battles facing people of color in the last twenty years. This lesson has not been lost on conservatives. Recognizing that culture is a site of permanent education and struggle over what it means to be an "American" and to fashion a sense of national identity and citizenship, conservatives have been enormously successful in making the political more pedagogical and, in doing so, have reasserted the importance of a cultural politics in which issues of politics and power are connected to the domain of meaning and communication. Reinventing the notion of public pedagogy, conservatives and right-wing extremists have breathed new life into the assumption that the most important forms of learning now take place within the mass media and popular culture (Messer-Davidow 1997). Using the traditional technologies of radio and television, along with the new electronic media such as the Internet and e-mail, the Right has waged a powerful educational campaign suggesting that the greatest threat to U.S. culture comes from minorities of class and color. Within this discourse, Euro-American cultural capital becomes the model for the culture of civility, and those whose culture is different from this "norm" are represented as a threat to U.S. unity, identity, and citizenship. Capitalizing on the very real fears that many people have over growing inequalities of wealth and income; the loss of viable jobs; the flight of the middle class to the suburbs; rising police repression; and shrinking federal, state, and city services, the right wing has been able to spread its messages of hatred and bigotry with great success through a range of public media, buttressed by ample funding from highly influential conservative foundations such as the Olin Foundation, the American-Enterprise Institute, the Intercollegiate Studies Institute, the Manhattan Institute, and the Scaife Foundation. Not only has the right wing waged a war against cultural difference by asserting a powerful role in shaping public memory through the mass media, but it has also created potent educational institutions for training its own public intellectuals. (For a commentary on such funding, see Solomon 1998, 14–16.)

The outcome of this activity is evident in the public presence of such conservative-backed intellectuals as Linda Chavez, Stephan Thernstrom, Abigail Thernstrom, Christina Hoff Summers, Charles Murray, and George Gilder, all of whom are against bilingual education and have relentlessly pursued the assumption that minorities who are poor inhabit a culture of poverty and suffer from a crisis of character (Herman 1999). At stake here for progressives is the recognition that questions of power have important cultural and ideological dimensions that need to be addressed in order to challenge the right-wing attack on bilingualism, democratic identities, and the expansion of democratic social relations into all spheres of public life. As Angela Davis (1996) points out, any progressive form of multiculturalism "that does not acknowledge the political character of culture will not . . . lead toward the dismantling of racist, sexist, homophobic, economically exploitative institutions" (47). But if movements such as English Only are to be challenged by progressives, educators, artists, and others, we need to take the issue of culture seriously in both political and pedagogical terms, and begin to reimagine what it means to engage in pedagogical struggles, not just in the schools, but in all of those sites where ideas are being produced and distributed in the ongoing struggle over diverse forms of identification. In opposition to the culturally dogmatic pedagogies that support the English Only approach to learning, progressives must reassert the argument that too many students of color cannot find their lives represented in classrooms and schools across the United States. Not only does this conservative, exclusionary approach to pedagogy silence minorities of class and color, but it also eliminates opportunities for all students to engage their differences with one another and to address the essential issue of what it means for identities to be structured in a multicultural, democratic society.

For too many progressives, culture is seen as either a hindrance or irrelevant to political struggles. As well as being self-defeating, such a position effectively turns the crucial spheres of mass and popular culture over to conservatives. The fight over what it means to be a citizen, to live in a democracy, and to participate in the shaping of the future must be waged from many sites, and progressives need to think seriously about the implications of forging a new form of cultural politics and pedagogy in order to carry on such a struggle both within and outside of the schools. Culture has a determinate relation to the practices of power and politics, and must be engaged as part of an ongoing attempt to name history, experience, knowledge, and the meaning of everyday life in one's own terms, or, at the very least, from a position of struggle and resistance. The struggle over questions of representation is at stake, as well as the more important struggle to link a critical and democratic politics of cultural justice to broader institutional practices and social structures. Struggles over language and culture might be more successfully engaged as part of a wider campaign (1) to define the conditions necessary to produce social subjects and institutional arrangements from a variety of pedagogical and political sites that view cultural difference as essential to any substantive democracy, (2) to resist repressive and hierarchical social relations, and (3) to eliminate modes of authority that silence dissident traditions, voices, and histories. In short, such a struggle cannot be divorced or understood outside of broader struggles for democracy and social justice that are taking place around a number of related issues such as the attack on public schooling, homophobic legislation, the dismantling of the welfare system, the backlash against civil rights and affirmative action, and the ongoing attempts to pass anti-immigration legislation.

The English Only movement can be best understood and challenged as being deeply antithetical to the values and relations of a democratic society. The attack on bilingual education can be best grasped in its complexity when it is engaged as part of the ongoing struggle against public education and broader efforts by various social movements to extend democracy into all spheres of society. In this context, language rights would be defended as part of a struggle on behalf of literacy projects that would affirm the right of students and others to speak and learn from the context of their specific cultures and histories. Such rights would also be understood as an essential condition for people to write, speak, and act from a position of agency, one that provides opportunities, pedagogically and politically, in which students can exercise self-representation through the choices available to them within a proliferation of discourses, cultural identities, and social relations. Language in this context provides the symbolic and material resources for the production of multiple discourses and performative literacies that infuse public life with identities and cultures, opening up differences to new connections, knowledge, identities, social relations, and forms of individual and social empowerment. Within this context, democracy celebrates rather than closes down the multiple selves and cultures that constitute the public spheres and construct the meaning of citizenship and democracy in a global context.

Democracy demands what June Jordan (1985) calls a legitimate American language, "a language including Nebraska, Harlem, New Mexico, Oregon, Puerto Rico, Alabama, and working-class life" (30). Of course, what advocates of English Only want is the enforcement of language policies that omit or deny the truth of many peoples' lives—the legitimization of English as a language that makes minorities of color and class the object rather than the subject of the sentence. Jordan is unsparingly correct about the undemocratic implications of such language policies:

> I am talking about majority problems of language in a democratic state, problems of a currency that someone has stolen and hidden away and then homogenized into an official "English" language that can only express non-events involving nobody responsible, or lies. If we lived in a democratic state our language would have to hurtle, fly, curse, and seeing, in all the common American names, all the undeniable and representative and participating voices of everybody here. We would not tolerate the language of the powerful and, thereby, lose all respect for words, *per se*. We would make our language conform to the truth of our many selves and we would make our language lead us into the equality of power that a democratic state must represent. (30)

What is so crucial about Roseann Dueñas González and Ildikó Melis's excellent two-volume book is that it offers a wide spectrum of critical analysis for understanding both the promise and the challenges of living in a multicultural democracy, along with the crucial roles that culture, power, politics, and language play in fashioning the different terrains on which diverse identities are shaped and democratic struggles occur. In addition, *Language Ideologies: Critical Perspectives on the Official English Move-*

ment repeatedly and insightfully stresses the ways in which pedagogy is always the outcome of particular struggles and how the production of school knowledge, values, desires, and social relations are always implicated in power. Pedagogy is always about the specificity of place: how power shapes and is reinvented through the prisms of culture, politics, and identity. The struggle against the underlying ideologies of the English Only movement is fundamentally about the struggle over the meaning of political agency, citizenship, and empowerment, and how these get either closed down or expanded in the schools and larger society. The conflicts over language occupy a primary role in these struggles because it is through language and the realm of the symbolic that individuals become responsible as critical agents, disrupt the continuity of common sense, and challenge strategies of domination. But if the struggle against English Only is to be successful, it must define itself first and foremost as part of a much broader struggle for social justice and human rights, and progressives who take up such a cause must be willing to enter into alliances with others who are also struggling to expand the values and social relationships necessary for a vibrant democracy.

Note

1. Two excellent sources for such critical analysis are Crawford (1992) and Macedo (1994).

Works Cited

Crawford, James. 1992. *Hold Your Tongue: Bilingualism and the Politics of English Only*. Reading, MA: Addison-Wesley.

Davis, Angela. 1996. "Gender, Class, and Multiculturalism: Rethinking 'Race,' Politics." In Avery Gordon and Christopher Newfield, eds., *Mapping Multiculturalism*. Minneapolis: University of Minnesota Press. 40–49.

Fish, Stanley. 1992. "Bad Company." *Transition* 56.

Goldberg, David Theo. 1993. *Racist Culture: Philosophy and the Politics of Meaning*. Oxford: Blackwell.

Herman, Edward S. 1999. "All the Book Reviews Fit to Print." *Z Magazine* [Online]. Available: http://www.zmag.org/Zmag/articles/april99herman.html

Jordan, June. 1985. "Problems of Language in a Democratic State." In June Jordan, *On Call: Political Essays*. Boston: South End Press.

Lipsitz, George. 1995. "The Possessive Investment in Whiteness: Racialized Social Democracy and the 'White' Problem in American Studies." *American Quarterly* (47)3: 369–88.

Macedo, Donaldo. 1994. *Literacies of Power: What Americans Are Not Allowed to Know*. Boulder, CO: Westview Press.

Messer-Davidow, Ellen. 1997. "Whither Cultural Studies?" In Elizabeth Long, ed., *From Sociology to Cultural Studies: New Perspectives*. Malden, MA: Basil Blackwell. 489–522.

Rushdie, Salman. 1991. *Imaginary Homelands: Essays and Criticism 1981–1991*. London: Penguin Books.

Solomon, Norman. 1998. "Writers of the Right Unite." *Extra!* (March/April): 14–16.

Toler, Deborah. 1999. "Slouching towards Bigotry: AEI's Racial Fellows." *Extra!* (March/April): 14–15.

ACKNOWLEDGMENTS

This book grew out of three interests. First, in my work as director of the National Council of Teachers of English (NCTE) Commission on Language from 1993 to 1996, we struggled with the misconceptions surrounding the English Only controversy held by many educators—that it was no longer a threat, that it was an old story, that it had no real effects on the lives of students and teachers. Often sessions concerning the English Only movement planned by the Commission were not as well attended as we had hoped. But all of this changed when California Propositions 187 and 227 passed, and it became clear that English Only had begun to affect teachers' and students' lives in California in a very real way. We were stunned by the inhumanity of these events and concerned that this was a national trend that could spread to other states with large language-minority populations. The Commission sponsored panels and wrote resolutions opposing these hostile propositions directed against minority children, and as a group we immediately recognized the pressing need for a new volume on English Only. *Not Only English: Affirming America's Multilingual Heritage,* NCTE's first book on the English Only controversy, is now nearly a decade old, and a new volume seems essential to explore the path this virulent movement took in the 1990s. When I stepped down as director, I took the project with me to work on. I would like to thank the Commission on Language for its constant encouragement and dedication to the completion of *Language Ideologies: Critical Perspectives on the Official English Movement,* which resulted in two volumes of excellent essays, proving that such a collection was indeed timely.

Second, the Conference on College Composition and Communication's (CCCC) Language Policy Committee, chaired by Geneva Smitherman, University Distinguished Professor of

English at Michigan State University, had been working steadily for many years to explore the sociolinguistic and sociopolitical dimensions of the official language movement and to counter its monolingual, monolithic perspectives through the development and dissemination of an inclusive language policy that embraces the natural language of all groups in the United States. Five of the essays in this collection emanate from that panel's work in 1997. I am very grateful to Geneva Smitherman for her cooperation and assistance on this project and to another member of the CCCC Language Policy Committee, Gail Okawa, assistant professor of English at Youngstown State University, who kindly collected the papers given at that panel for my review.

Third, this book is born out of my own experience. For a Chicana who grew up in the '50s in Arizona, the English Only movement conjures up a nightmare of the bad old days that many of us desire to forget but cannot entirely put out of our minds. Being a Mexican American child in Phoenix in the '50s meant understanding my family's and my place in the world; knowing that, for whatever reason, we were often not welcome in the majority milieu; knowing that there were certain places we could and could not go; and knowing that our Spanish language (and even our brand of English) was suspect and a constant object of attack. I quickly realized that "Sorry, I don't speak Mexican" was a polite cover for "Mexicans aren't served here," a familiar refrain from my youth.

I knew from my earliest moment that my family and I were different. It wasn't just that Santa Claus didn't come in the morning as he did for all the other kids (he must have come some time during *Misa de Gallo* [Midnight mass] because when we came home from mass at about 1:30 A.M. and ate our *tamales,* our presents were already under the tree). It wasn't just that we looked different, especially me—I had black hair and wore two big braids tied in bright ribbons woven in and out. It wasn't just that I didn't celebrate birthdays with a dozen classmates, party hats, and favors. All my aunts and uncles came over, and Mama served *menudo* or *tostadas* while my cousins and I played together and the grown-ups listened to their Spanish *boleros* and *cumbias,* danced, and drank *cuba libres.* There was no "pin the tail on the donkey"; instead, we had a beautiful *piñata.* And it also wasn't that we were called "dirty Mexicans" a few times in school or at the park. I think our most important difference was that we spoke Spanish and our own brand of English. My dad spoke only Spanish (except for swear words in English, as well as construction terms that he learned to survive on his job). Being a hod carrier didn't give him a lot of English practice, especially since he worked with a primarily Spanish-speaking crew, and laboring eight to twelve hours in the sun didn't leave him much energy to attend English class either. He left that to Mama.

And Mama did that with a vengeance. By the time I was five, Mama faithfully attended English classes at the Friendly House, a nonprofit agency in Phoenix that assisted immigrants to become citizens, offering citizenship and ESL classes. That's what she did on Tuesday and Thursday afternoons. She took off her apron and her housedress, put on her fancy downtown clothes, walked to the corner, got on the bus, and headed downtown for two hours of English oral practice, reading, and writing. She had waited years for the opportunity since the classes had always been full. And she had also waited for me to be old enough to stay with my older sisters and brother. Every day Mama did her homework, which consisted of writing out English sentences and doing assigned readings. On top of that work, Mama assigned herself the job of reading the newspaper. I watched her, every morning, spread the *Arizona Republic* on the kitchen table and begin reading it voraciously, looking up every word she didn't know in the huge, navy blue, 1948 unabridged *Webster's* that I sometimes used as a stool. She read every article, every column, every obituary, every comic—often asking me to listen so that I could tell her why it was funny. I was five then and knew enough English to help Mama read. Why did I know English? Because my teenage brothers and sisters did, because my friends in the neighborhood did, and because Mama tried her best to speak only English to me, so that, in her words, I wouldn't be mistreated in school the way her other children had been. She was doing her best to protect me by forcing me to become proficient enough in English to enter the culture of the school without the harassment and hostility my sisters and brother had encountered there.

My two older sisters and my brother had been corporally and verbally punished for speaking Spanish in school—spanked, rapped on the knuckles, made to pay fines, put in the corner, kept in from lunch, and ridiculed by both students and teachers (besides being forcibly sprayed for lice). My sisters and brother were all put into 1C, the infamous "English Only" isolation classroom for Mexicans who didn't know English. In this class, all content learning was prohibited. The purpose of the class was to teach English in English to a group of wide-eyed and confused Mexican children who didn't understand a word the teacher was saying until quite late in the year. The problem was that most children didn't get out of 1C in a year, or even two. Some children stayed there for three years, stuck in a holding tank until they had learned to speak English well enough to be mainstreamed. For one to three long years, these children lost the opportunity to learn in all of the conceptual areas of knowledge that they were biologically and mentally ready to learn at that age, had they been given the chance to learn in their own language. The educational outcome for my brother and sisters and for most other children treated in this manner was grim. It was no wonder that Hispanic/Latino children dropped out long before eighth grade and that graduation from high school was considered a wondrous achievement. English Only 1C was the wholesale discriminatory approach to educating Hispanics/ Latinos that the Bilingual Education Act of 1968 sought to remedy—providing educational access for Hispanic/Latino and other language-minority children to help them begin learning immediately in the language they knew so that their school experience would be enriching rather than disabling. For good reason, this educational approach embraced Spanish and the Mexican American culture rather than shunning it or ignoring it completely.

Despite the fact that there has never been an adequate number of bilingual education programs, there has been an improvement in the educational achievement of language minorities, among them the many fortunate Hispanic/Latino children who have been saved from the pain of facing a new language and culture on the first day of school—who have been given the chance to learn in the code they know best and to master English as they progress in their education. For many socioeconomic and sociopolitical reasons, Hispanic/Latino children are still near the bottom of the educational ladder in the United States. If the only assistance they receive in the way of bilingual education is taken away, however, our society will regress to the bad old days of English Only, when blatant and subtle exclusion was intimately linked with the suppression of language.

For all of these reasons, I felt compelled to develop this collection and am grateful to a number of people who so graciously helped along the way. First, I would like to thank Agnese Nelms Haury, a local philanthropist and friend who assisted us financially in the preparation of the manuscript. I am deeply grateful for her deep and abiding commitment to social justice and the variety of projects in which she has shown an interest throughout the years.

I thank my son, Roberto José González, Truman Scholar and first-year law student at Stanford University, for his astute and critical readings of many of the articles in process and my introduction. His wide reading and intellectual curiosity about the radicalized politics of the language wars both inspired and aided me in my work. My daughter Marisa, A.B. Duke Scholar and sophomore at Duke University, I thank for her special insight and pride in her culture and language, and to my husband Bob, thank you especially for all the support and understanding during the many hectic months of work on this collection.

Many thanks go to Julie Gray, our technical assistant and proofreader extraordinaire, for her critical contribution in the preparation of the manuscript. Without her expert work, we would not have been able to finalize this project. I would also like to thank Patty Mathews for her helpful comments and suggestions, and John Bichsel, Jonathan Levy, and Paul Gatto for their careful manuscript reading and editing. I am also indebted to my staff at the National Center for Interpretation Testing, Research and Policy for their great support in many important arenas—unlocking attachments we could not open; retyping tables that could not be transferred electronically; and delivering paper, disks, and toner for our voluminous drafts. Thanks to Socorro Hurtado and Armando Valles.

We also appreciate the thoughtful contributions of our authors, who took the time to produce articles that have special meaning for this volume. Their responsiveness to our suggestions and questions was heartening and truly made this otherwise formidable task pleasant. We extend our most sincere thanks to all of our contributors for their great cooperation, collaboration, and faith in us. I am honored to have worked with such a stellar group of scholars.

We are exceedingly grateful for the support and encouragement from Michael Greer, former NCTE Senior Editor of Books, and Karen Smith, former NCTE Associate Executive Director, both of whom remained excited about and committed to this volume despite our roving deadlines. Since putting such an extensive work together required a lot of time, we also had the pleasure of working with Zarina Hock, current Senior Editor at NCTE. We would also like to thank Bonny Graham, Staff Editor, for her meticulous attention to the details of this book. NCTE is fortunate to have staff members who are so committed to equity and social justice and do the work of the Council so thoughtfully.

To my co-editor, graduate student, research assistant, and dear friend Ildikó Melis, I express my deepest thanks for making a tremendous commitment of time and energy to this project and for doing a magnificent job of library research and editing, working with authors, proofreading, and providing insightful comments on all the essays and my introduction in process. One of my greatest pleasures has been to renew my friendship with Ildikó. After her initial stay in the United States in 1988 as a student in the ESL graduate program and my teaching assistant at the University of Arizona, she returned from Hungary in 1996 to the University of Arizona to pursue a doctorate degree in rhetoric and composition. Her intensity, depth, and breadth of cross-disciplinary reading and her insight as a reader are remarkable, and her dedication to this project was pivotal to its completion. I am honored to count Ildikó Melis among the colleagues and friends I most respect and admire—she is a true scholar dedicated to discovering and revealing truths for the purpose of bettering the world we live in.

INTRODUCTION

ROSEANN DUEÑAS GONZÁLEZ
University of Arizona

*It is not a question of eliminating the inequalities among
men but of widening them and making them into a law.*
RENAN, FRENCH PHILOSOPHER, quoted in
Discourse on Colonialism, Aimé Césaire

Since the publication of the last NCTE volume on Official English in 1992, an onslaught of unfair and restrictive language policies and initiatives have limited the ability of linguistic minorities to speak their own language. These legislative proposals attacking the rights of linguistic minorities, often cloaked in misleading double-speak, reflect a prevailing hostility and an embedded set of power relations dedicated to marginalizing certain members of our society. My ambition in writing this introduction is to shed some light on the current English Only discussion, framing it in a larger sociopolitical context, which is of crucial interest to all Americans. Further, by examining two relevant court cases and analyzing exactly how an English Only initiative is being played out in Arizona, I hope to provide some empirical evidence in a discourse often filled with euphemisms and vague, emotional appeals. In this way, legislators, educators, and academics especially may address these issues in a more level-headed and fair-minded manner than the current discourse would allow.

I share the concern of other educators, activists, and citizens about the general level of hostility, ignorance, and illogic that pervades the English Only movement and the rapidity with which it is spreading nationally. As many contributors to both volumes of *Language Ideologies* point out, English Only is often a politically acceptable mask for intolerance toward Hispanics/Latinos,[1] immigrants, and racial/ethnic minority groups in general, a symptom perhaps of fear of the future status of current dominant groups in general. The history of the United States has been marked by periods in which brands of hatred come into fashion and go out again, are let loose and reined in. We are currently experiencing a particularly hostile period. Recent polls reveal that 53 percent of Americans agree that Blacks and Hispanics/Latinos are less intelligent than Whites, and a majority believes that they are lazy, violent, welfare dependent, and unpatriotic (Williams 1997, 49). These beliefs are promulgated by the discourse of English Only; anti-immigrant and anti-affirmative action initiatives; as well as the steady drone of what Patricia J. Williams, author of *The Rooster's Egg: On the Persistence of Prejudice,* characterizes as a White male discourse of a "constantly bunkered sense of transgressed rights" (69). She reminds us that the larger discourse of racism has grown considerably in the last decade and is at an all-time high, promoted mainly through right-leaning radio and television programs, such as Rush Limbaugh, who commands an audience of twenty million. Williams (1997) further states that this

> crude, in-your-face racism, sexism, anti-Semitism, and homophobia have become commonplace, popularly expressed, and louder in volume than at any time since the beginning of the civil rights movement. . . . Blaring the battle hymn of the First Amendment, these radio programs enshrine a crude demagoguery. . . . I feel more and more surrounded by megawatted expressions of hate and discrimination—the coded epithets, the mocking angry glee, the endless tirades filled with nonspecific, nonempirically based slurs against "these people" or "those minorities" or "liberals" . . . or "foreigners." (44)

Williams concludes that "[t]he polemics of right-wing radio are putting nothing less than hate onto the airwaves, into the market place, electing it to office, teaching it in schools, and exalting it as freedom" (51).

As the history of English Only conflicts demonstrates, these movements invariably emerge at times when social tension is high and minorities become an easy target for veiled attacks. Although the U.S. economy was prosperous during the 1990s, the gap between the rich and the poor grew, and the relative position of many social groups deteriorated. In 1967 those who belonged to the highest fifth of the average income earned six times as much as those who belonged to the lowest fifth. In 1994 the difference between the same income groups was tenfold (U.S. Bureau of the Census 1998). The poverty rate fell from 13.3 percent in 1997 to 12.2 percent in 1998, but it remained "statistically the same as its 1989 level of 13.1 percent" (Weinberg 1999, 1). At the same time, the influx of legal and illegal immigrants, especially across the southern border, was constant and unprecedented. In 1998 the average per capita income of Hispanics/Latinos was less than half the average income of non-Hispanic/Latino Whites.

These tensions are further compounded as we move from an industrial to a technology-based society. Computer technology is beginning to dominate almost all fields of work, and working- and middle-class Americans are finding that the traditional areas of employment and success are no longer as predictable as they once seemed to be. The inevitable contacts with new cultures and technologies result in social anxiety, creating perceived threats to social stability—great enough to generate hostile sentiments against "outsiders" and easy-to-scapegoat newcomers.

The Official English/English Only discourse is not a discourse about the need to protect English or to ensure that non-English-speakers learn English; it is a discourse of "neo-racism" in which the category of Official English or English Only has replaced the offensive terms involving biological differentiation and genetic inferiority. As Phillipson (1992) holds, "It seems highly likely that in many neo-colonial contexts linguicism has taken over from racism as an ideology which legitimates an unequal division of power and resources" (318). "Linguicism" is a construct that has been evolved to explain the "relationship between the language of the dominant group and dominated (idigneous [sic] and immigrant) groups" (318). Obviously, it is much less problematic in our society to talk about the officialization of English in the United States and about initiating antibilingual education legislation than it is to talk about race, and the persistent introduction of Official English initiatives in state after state over the past twenty years by U.S. English and other groups has successfully promoted this seemingly unproblematic discourse on a state and national level, driving a wedge between the mainstream population and Hispanic/Latinos as well as other linguistic minority groups.

Critical to a complete understanding of the English Only agenda is locating it in the larger dynamics of power, especially as articulated in Michel Foucault's concept of the "micro-physics" of power (Foucault 1977, 209). This model argues that institutions of power seek to exert control at every level, down to the most everyday interactions between individuals and the individuals' construction of their own identity. That is, the public discourse on English Only, along with the anti-immigration discourse, serves as a mechanism to discipline the Hispanic/Latino community and other language-minority populations. It reminds all Latinos/Hispanics that they can be defined as illegitimate members of the larger population. In this way, the public discourse becomes a mechanism of control by instilling in Hispanics/Latinos the societal power relationships—relationships that relegate Hispanics/Latinos to a less powerful status than that of the dominant social groups. This explains the mysterious yet intense interest of persons like Ron Unz, the California millionaire who has no tie to bilingual education and who knows nothing about education, to the English for the Children movement in California and now in Arizona. Enacting legislation that does away with bilingual education and the rights of minorities to keep their language while learning English is a powerful way for him and his associates to maintain domination over growing Latino and other linguistic minority populations, and their increasing political presence.

In fact, the discourse of English Only has already caused division between members of the Hispanic/Latino community, often between members of the same family. To the extent that the powerless or subordinate group adopts the hegemonic discourse—anti-immigrant, anti-dark-skinned, anti-Spanish-language or anti-any-other-language, antibilingual education, antinative cultural values—it begins to engage in autocolonization. In the process of autocolonization, members of subordinate social groups try to harmonize with the values of the dominant groups by adopting the dominant discourse values. This makes them feel more American and more accepted in society—a psychologically understandable reaction. Autocolonization helps to explain why some Hispanics and other language minorities voted for the English Only, anti-affirmative action, anti-immigrant, and antibilingual education initiatives in California and elsewhere. These voting data have been egregiously misrepresented by the media as evidence of the extent to which the issues such as bilingual education required reform—it must be bad if "even Hispanics" voted against it.

Another trend of major concern is that the number of court cases involving language issues has grown by astonishing proportions in the last decade. To my mind, the sheer number of states, agencies, schools, and private employers trampling on the rights of linguistic minorities brings the collective issue to the level of human rights violations. These legal challenges to language policy have been provoked because the language needs of persons in a variety of settings and situations have been ignored. These cases involve parents who feel that their children's language needs are not being met by the schools; individuals whose personal and business language use on the job is restricted; employees who are required to take unreasonable language tests that exclude them from various rights and privileges, such as buying, owning, and operating franchised businesses (*American Civil Liberties Union Investigation of Ching v. UNOCAL* 1996; Gonzalez 1997a); bilinguals whose language skills are used but not rewarded on the job; bilinguals who are restricted from normal job progression because their bilingual skills are needed in certain positions; and people whose access to various social services and governmental functions such as obtaining a driver's license is barred because of language. Two quintessential examples of current language discrimination cases—*Sandoval v. Hagan* (1998) and *Yang v. O'Keefe* (2000)—will be discussed later in this writing.

Finally, it is vital that current and future educators understand English Only within its various historical and theoretical contexts and recognize how language figures into the scale and scope of the social, political, and demographic changes that have shaped our school culture in the United States for the past de-

cade. Teachers and other professions involved in public education must understand that language policy, both in the classroom
and in society, has an impact on the academic achievement and
future of every student. I am hopeful that the essays in this volume, along with those in Volume 1, will help school communities respond to the needs of language minority students by
adopting fair language policies in school and by supporting state
and federal policies that provide fair and equal treatment to linguistic minorities in society. One of the problems we face is the
generation gap—the fact that younger generations of Americans,
including teachers and academics, have forgotten that the Bilingual Education Act of 1968 is a part of a set of civil rights legislative initiatives created to help non-English-speakers gain access
to four principal institutions: schools, courts, the voting booth,
and the workplace.

Now, only thirty years later, with a larger than ever need for
bilingual education as a result of high immigration rates in the
past two decades, we are faced with the closing down of systems
that were just beginning to make our democracy real for everyone, not just English speakers. English Only initiatives threaten
bilingual voting ballots, interpretation and translation for government services, bilingual teaching methods for transitioning
into English, and the opportunity to work without being sanctioned for lack of English-language skills or for speaking a native
language on the job, if the job does not require English skills for
its performance. (The chapters by Juan Perea and Guadalupe
Valdés presented in this volume discuss in more detail the English Only trend of the courts in relation to language conflicts in
employment.)

These hostile and pervasive movements have spurred renewed
scholarly interest in language issues in the workplace and in other
public and private settings. As a result, the issue of the rights of
individuals who speak a minority language, an unpopular variety of English, or English as a second language is being revisited.
The recurrent conflicts over language have motivated scholars from
a wide range of disciplines to examine language-related phenomena as symptoms of deeper societal anxieties and fears. Linguists
and scholars are examining not only the use and control of language by various social groups, but they are also inquiring into

the origins of language conflict within the larger context of shifting socioeconomic, racial, ethnic, and power relations.

I am hopeful that emerging research in such areas as postcolonial, feminist, and cultural studies will shed new light on this complex issue previously in the domain of linguists and language teaching experts. Volume 2 offers the reader a rich backdrop against which to better understand the current political agenda embroiled in both state and national English Only and related initiatives. Jane Hill's insight into "language panics," as she labels these language conflicts, is invaluable in uncovering the less than noble intentions of official language mobilizers. (See also Alastair Pennycook's more historical approach to understanding the use of language in the colonial process.)

The essays in this collection should alert us to the underlying power and status conflicts at the root of the English Only ideology so that we can decode the intended message from the transmitted ones. Likewise, a thoughtful consideration of the evidence and analysis presented in these essays can help us retrieve the egalitarian spirit, empowering assumptions, and progressive ideologies that led to the birth of bilingual education and other language access/language rights policies in the United States during the late '60s and early '70s such as the Bilingual Education Act, the Voting Rights Act, and the Court Interpreters Act. I have faith that these chapters will inspire in readers a concerted effort to protect these important language policies by taking the English Only movement seriously as citizens, academicians, researchers, teachers, and activists and combating its divisive and pernicious intentions. A national English Language Amendment, passed at the federal level either as a statute or an amendment to the Constitution, would render these linguistic civil rights protections void. State English Only policies that restrict the use of native languages should also be taken seriously and fought on a more unified, political level. Local and institutional language policies should be examined for their equity. Agencies, schools, and classrooms should have transparent language policies that encourage the use of native languages and include opportunities for bridging linguistic barriers among students, teachers, and parents. As the essays in this volume help us all better understand, the English Only movement is polite racism, a useful colonial strategy of the past and the present that demands a subtle understanding so that it can be deconstructed and fought. Often, as in instances of institutionalized racism, agents of restrictive language policies—thus racist policies—are unaware of their engagement and are only carrying out the status quo or unquestioned agency tradition. Therefore, self-examination is of particular importance. I am confident that after reading these authors' excellent explorations of issues of language and society both inside and outside the context of the United States, readers will be able to see the divisive and exclusionary ideology offered by English Only and come away with a renewed wish to use language in an equitable way to make our democracy real for all persons.

In the comments that follow, I present brief summaries of two important language discrimination cases to illustrate the ongoing language service needs of our changing U.S. population. These two cases exemplify how damaging institutionalized responses are to the simple human needs of working adults who are struggling to provide for their families. I also focus on Arizona and its English for the Children proposition because this is only the latest example of local English Only initiatives that deserve national attention in the escalating conflicts over language. These propositions, along with other debates surrounding language issues such as Ebonics, serve as lightening rods for other racist sentiments and are having devastating effects on the discourse surrounding education and equality, largely because they distract attention from legitimate concerns about public education. Hopefully, a presentation of facts supporting bilingual education will clarify its validity as a method of instruction.

Language Discrimination Cases: Institutional Attempts to Control Language-Minority Populations

The overwhelming fear instigated by the hateful discourse of English Only and its associated topics must be at the root of language policies so mean-spirited that they go otherwise unchallenged. Yang and Sandoval are quintessential examples of the language discrimination cases that are becoming endemic in our country. *Yang v. O'Keefe* (2000) is a class action suit brought against the Minnesota Department of Human Services (MDHS) by Hmong, Spanish, and Somali persons who have lost their health care and other human services because of their inability to speak, understand, and read English. Even though the demographics of Minnesota have significantly changed since 1980 because of a tremendous influx of refugee and other immigrant groups, MDHS maintains an English Only policy and does not offer interpretation assistance, nor does it provide translated forms for obtaining medical services or benefits of any kind. The agency's Household Report Forms and the Health Care Programs Application place the responsibility on the applicant to have the forms translated if they have difficulty comprehending them.

These fifteen-page questionnaires are written at a college level of reading complexity and contain many instances of difficult, formal, and frozen language that would require a skilled translator with subject-matter expertise to effectively communicate. The language of the forms includes a number of specialized vocabularies from the domains of medical, legal, insurance, kinship, and banking discourse. Additionally, questions containing these special vocabularies are conceptually difficult as well as contextually bound and would require a caseworker to explain their specialized meanings according to the culture of the agency. Non-English-speakers, however, have no access to caseworkers because there are none who could serve them in their native languages. Furthermore, even if translated forms were available, applicants would need to be able to discuss their particular cases and problems face to face with a caseworker who knows their language, or at least has a competent translator or correctly translated form available.

Families with children who were dependent on these services have lost their benefits because of this exclusionary language rule. The agency stands by its language access policy, however, and will not translate forms or provide language services so that those who are in need and have limited English proficiency can complete their applications or make emergency requests.

Yang v. O'Keefe asserts that MDHS treats non-English-speakers differently from all other applicants. In my expert report to the court, I argued that the agency's policy severely limits the ability of limited- or non-English-speakers (LEP or NEP) to access welfare and health services in Minnesota and is not consistent with the policy of equal access for all citizens to these services (González 2000). Policies that provide services only in English create barriers to access to services for individuals who do not have the requisite English proficiency. This English Only policy and practice also places symbolic barriers before any LEP or NEP client who desires to apply for or to continue to receive benefits. MDHS's failure to provide translated forms, interpreter services, or bilingual agency assistance causes LEP and NEP clients to be alienated and stigmatized. Most important, policies that require written or oral communication in English perpetuate and institutionalize the historical stigmatization of minority populations, the majority of whom are LEP and NEP speakers in the first and sometimes second generation.

Of course, stigmatized features of language are associated with low-status groups; that is, the lack of English proficiency "marks" the ethnic and linguistic minority as surely as skin color marks African Americans. This serves to signal the linguistically diverse (ethnic or racial minority) populations that they are second-class citizens by ensuring that it is more difficult for them to access the benefits and services offered by MDHS than it is for the "unmarked" population. It appears especially callous that birth into an ethnic or racial minority group—a condition not open to choice—is effectively being used to bar these applicants from equal access to welfare and health services. Lack of linguistic proficiency is a condition tantamount to a disability since these individuals are not able to remedy it in a short period of time and require assistance to overcome it. Without access to basic social services, many LEP and NEP speakers will be isolated in their own "linguistic ghettos," and this isolation will retard their movement to self-sufficiency, which is a broad goal of the Minnesota Department of Health Services. As of this writing, this case has not come to trial.

Another recent case that illustrates the sometimes petty but harmful nature of these language conflicts is *Sandoval v. Hagan* (1998). This is a class action lawsuit against the Alabama Department of Public Safety's English Only policy of requiring all persons in the state of Alabama to take their driver's license test in English. This condition made the tests inaccessible to a large number of LEP and NEP persons in Alabama. I argued that this rule serves no linguistically useful purpose and is in actuality counterproductive to Alabama's English Only Rule, which was enacted to promote the speaking of English. Withholding drivers' licenses by making testing inaccessible to limited- and non-English-speakers retards this group's ability to become mobile members of their community and acquire English through interaction (González 1997b)

I explained that sociolinguistic research has long established that the employment domain most significantly affects language acquisition and ultimately language shift (Fishman 1989). In other words, a job that requires some English proficiency encourages adults to learn more English. Yet better and more demanding employment opportunities were barred for these LEP and NEP speakers because they lacked a driver's license and quality public transportation. Without the possibility of better employment, English acquisition would be retarded; this population would not be able to achieve true integration into Alabama society and would probably end up depending on the state. The plaintiff in the lawsuit, Ms. Sandoval, could not read English well enough to pass the licensing test. And even though she drove in her native country, in Alabama she was forced to walk back and forth to work two hours a day until she developed a crippling foot condition, became severely disabled, and had to quit her employment. This situation led Ms. Sandoval to the Southern Poverty Law Center (SPLC), which took her case and tried to negotiate with the Alabama Department of Safety to allow her and others like her to take the test in their native languages. The Department of Safety refused, and the SPLC sued on the basis of national origin discrimination. The case was won, appealed, and upheld by a higher court. Adamant about discontinuing testing in languages other than English, however, Alabama has appealed the case to the Supreme Court of the United States, where it will be heard in January 2001. If this case is not upheld, it will deal a major blow to language discrimination cases.

This case is instructive in many ways for the general public and for students of language policy. The Alabama Department of Safety testified that it was not that expensive to test these persons in their native languages. Therefore, what is the problem? It is, unfortunately, a simple case of bigotry. The state of Alabama is sending a clear signal to Alabama language minorities: "You are not wanted here, but now that you are here, do as you're told and don't complain." Most of these language discrimination cases involve states and private businesses that want to be able to treat members of certain groups differently, with no consequences. Politicians call this "state's rights" and "local control," but these terms are often euphemisms for discriminatory, stigmatizing practices that block the fair and equal treatment of racial and language minorities. Dennis Baron's, Juan Perea's, and Guadalupe Valdés's chapters in this volume include more discussion of similar cases.

English Only Is Not about English *Only:*
The Big Picture on English Only Rhetoric

Anti-immigrant hostility manifests itself in many forms, not just through restrictive regulation of language use. California spawned the popular antibilingual education initiative Proposition 227—English for the Children—close on the heels of passing a string of anti-immigrant/anti-Hispanic/Latino legislation, beginning with Proposition 187, which curtailed government services for immigrants and undocumented persons residing in California, and Proposition 209, the anti-affirmative action legislation that undid the first steps being taken to level the playing field by permitting schools to "take account of race" as Supreme Court Justice Blackmun—the only dissenting justice on the *Bakke* case—suggested, in order to bring discriminatory practices to an end (*Regents of University of California v. Bakke* 1978, No. 76-811).

It is no coincidence that, at the same time that Arizona's antibilingual education proposition gains steam, the state has become a battlefield for a blatant and illegal fight against Mexican and other Latin American immigrants. Ranchers on the Southern Arizona border have taken up arms against impoverished, often dehydrated, and malnourished illegal immigrants who make the trek from Mexico and other parts of Latin America in search of jobs in the United States. Roger Barnett and several other Arizona ranchers pursue trespassers, arrest them at gunpoint, subject them to detention and other assaults, and then turn them over to the border patrol (Borden 2000, A4).

These anti-immigrant tensions are not restricted to the border areas. By 2025 the Hispanic/Latino populations of Arkansas, Delaware, Georgia, Kansas, Maryland, Nebraska, and North Carolina are expected to grow 70 percent or more, compared to the overall national growth rate of less than 20 percent. The growth of the Hispanic/Latino diaspora over the past ten years in the Midwest and South has exacerbated racial tensions and produced venomous Ku Klux Klan demonstrations and terrorist attacks. While employers recruit Hispanic/Latino employees to debone chickens and slaughter cattle and pigs, various groups including townspeople, local Ku Klux Klan leaders, and David Duke, former KKK grand dragon, implore townsfolk to "kick the illegal aliens out" (Yeoman 2000, 36). Sam van Resenburg, a leader of a neo-Nazi group called the National Alliance, held a rally in Siler, North Carolina, calling Hispanics/Latinos "mongrels" and "the sewer of immigration" (Yeoman 2000, 36). In Nashville, private security guards are accused of systematically terrorizing Hispanic/Latino residents, handcuffing them, holding guns to their heads, ransacking their belongings, and kicking residents in the ribs. In Lexington, Kentucky, citizens circulate a petition opposing efforts to make the city "a safe place for Hispanics" (Yeoman 2000, 36–37). These states have one thing in common: they all have passed restrictive English Only policies.

The Gap between Matters of English and Matters of English Only

While overt displays of racism are unnerving, no less important or virulent are the battles fought in the public schools. The English Only debate is not a matter of contrasting linguistic theories on language acquisition. The public discussions are increasingly interwoven with deep-rooted anxieties about status and dominance, with beliefs about the value of English and the social status of racial and linguistic minority people. Those of us old enough to remember sense a return to the intolerance and bigotry of the 1950s, as the overtly optimistic expectations about globalization are interrupted by undercurrents of exclusionary and isolationist rhetoric. What is especially frustrating about this movement for educators is the discrepancy between scholarly and popular views on how language works, how bilingual individuals function in a dominantly monolingual society, and how language can be most effectively learned. The popular campaign cites no data, no theory, and no explanation. It needs only to make an allegation. Data and evidence do not appear to be foundational to people's opinions. This irrational foundation for dismantling bilingual education reeks of racist underpinnings. Where there is no logic, there is usually a set of predetermined concepts about Hispanics/Latinos and other language minorities. This is the same phenomenon we witness in the larger political arena of the 2000 presidential campaign in which condescending words about change hold more weight than data that may or may not support them. This irrational mode is clearly a manifestation of unreasoned prejudice.

Expert opinions on language issues are not only largely unknown to the public, but they also remain relatively underrepresented in political debates for several reasons. First of all, research rarely finds such overwhelming support for a single method of teaching that could successfully counter the confident "commonsense" rhetoric of English Only advocates. For example, Hector Ayala, co-chair of the Arizona English for the Children, stated that although it might sound draconian to place children who do not speak English in a total English-immersion program, "we know that it works" (Tapla 2000b, A1). Language experts, on the other hand, can find only a few points of agreement, and even these points are conservatively phrased. What most language experts agree on is that at least some instruction in a child's first language helps the child learn both English and general content. In addition, language experts also agree that one year is not enough to master a second language, no matter how "mastering a second language" is defined. Research has established that five to seven years are required for a child to acquire enough English to be academically competitive (Collier 1987, 1989, 1992).

The Ebonics controversy is another good example of the discrepancy between expert and popular opinion. Labov's research almost fifty years ago clearly established the status of African American Vernacular English (AAVE) as a variety that is not inferior in its structures to any other language. Moreover, evidence from Labov (1969), Gates (1988), and Smitherman[2] strongly suggests that the difference of AAVE from standard English is not simply structural but rhetorical. In fact, the rhetorical style of signifying and the indirectness of evaluation in narratives are superior AAVE discourse strategies. Yet the public strongly resists the idea that this variety deserves respect. Teachers, educators, and often even successful African American public personalities argue that AAVE is "bad English," and they insist on total standardization and normalization. They are reluctant to admit that if a language is maintained so long in spite of continual discrimination and stigmatization, it must offer something to the community of its users that "correct" English does not provide. Namely, it must be an important component of its speakers' sense of expression, identity, and belonging. Consequently, public discourse would benefit from listening to the voices of those who are "tired of being always wrong" (Lippi-Green 1997, 11).

↞ The case of Spanish-language speakers is equally perplexing and clearly illustrates society's double standard on the value of language acquisition. For members of our society who speak English as their native language and value education as a bankable asset, learning a second language is clearly cultural capital. These students know that their efforts to learn another language will be encouraged and lauded. In fact, a considerable percentage of the U.S. school population spends a significant amount of time, money, and effort to learn a foreign language. In 1997, 89,742 college students studied abroad, providing evidence that for a particular stratum of elite, learning a second language is worth the investment of time and expense (Altbach and Peterson 1998, 38). Yet, for a linguistic minority individual, a heritage language such as Spanish has proven to be a definite liability, and maintaining or developing that language is of little interest to the general public. (See Frances R. Aparicio's chapter in Volume 1 for a deeper examination of these contrasting values of Spanish depending on the learner's status.) The "foreign" language that English-language learners bring from home is generally viewed as a source of error and confusion, something to be forgotten, extinguished, and replaced by English. In the cases of Ebonics and home Spanish, the topic of language serves a focal point around which other, often unpopular, opinions can be acceptably aired, resulting in indirect dialogues that cloud a number of important issues facing all students.

The Argument for Bilingual Education and Its Misrepresentation

Therefore, it is not merely a coincidence that today's English Only supporters avoid overtly anti-immigrant or racist slogans and present their dubious project in the sentimental, humanitarian, egalitarian rhetoric of English for the Children. After a two-year campaign, this approach worked in California, and now again in Arizona, and it may take root as well in other states that are watching the outcome before proceeding in the same vein. But those who read the papers and pay attention to publicized statistics know that children in Arizona are in need of many things: an alarming percentage of school-age children live in poverty. Arizona has the highest general population of children without health insurance—27 percent. Arizona's teen suicide rate is three times the national average. Arizona has the third highest dropout rate for grades 9 through 12 among all the states. In spite of years of systematic recruitment efforts, minorities are still underrepresented in the student body of the University of Arizona. For example, while 28 percent of the Arizona public high school population is Hispanic/Latino, this group makes up only 13 percent of the University of Arizona's undergraduates, and only 16 percent of these graduate (University of Arizona Office of Decision and Planning Support, 1999–2000). Many of these measures indicate that students are alienated from their school culture, which is one of the reasons why they do not stay in school or seek higher education, and that their near-segregated educational conditions are severely inadequate. It is difficult to understand how all these pressing socioeconomic and educational problems could be solved by denying these children a transitional bilingual education while they learn English.

As has been shown by many studies (see especially Stephen Krashen's work, and his essay in Volume 1), bilingual education programs work effectively to assist students to acquire the kind of English required for academic learning. Learning enough English to get by and play on the playgrounds or even be a nuisance is a difficult but not overwhelming task. But acquiring sufficient English to learn academic subjects and to be critical readers, writers, and thinkers requires learners to build a solid foundation in the native language and then transfer those skills to the second language. The dual-language approach not only produces quicker acquisition of English, but it also enhances learners' cognitive skills and enables them to perform significantly higher on certain assessment measures (Lambert and Tucker 1972). Such positive outcomes are also demonstrated by Arizona educational statistics. Although only 31 percent of the state's limited-English-speaking children were enrolled in bilingual education in the 1998–99 school year, their test scores have shown significant improvement since bilingual education was instituted nearly thirty years ago. Bilingual education expert James Crawford analyzed Arizona's Stanford 9 scores and demonstrated that in 1998–99, for the third year in a row, students learning English in bilingual education programs scored significantly higher in reading and language than students enrolled in "English only" programs. Furthermore, the Stanford 9 scores in Arizona demonstrated that students in three different types of bilingual education appeared to be doing well, including (1) transitional bilingual education in grades K–6, which teaches academic subjects partly in the native language while students are making the "transition" to English; (2) secondary bilingual education, grades 7–12, a transitional program for grades 7–12; and (3) bilingual, bicultural education, a dual-language development program in which both English and students' native-language skills are developed (Crawford 2000, 5).

Although English for the Children claims to be part of the solution, it is unmistakably clear that this movement is the problem. According to Toni Griego Jones, head of the University of Arizona College of Education teacher education department, there is a decline in the number of education students who graduate with a degree in bilingual education because students are worried that they may not have jobs if the one-year restriction on

English-transition programs proposed by the Arizona English for the Children passes (Tapla 2000b, A9). This decline adversely affects a system already rife with inadequacies. On a national level, more than half of all teachers have limited-English-proficient learners in their classes, but only one in five of these teachers is qualified to teach English as a second language. In Arizona, where there is a strong university program and a long history of bilingual education, 40 percent of bilingual or ESL teachers work without bilingual or ESL qualifications.[3]

The Arizona Language Education Council (2000) points out that the English Only initiative, instead of solving problems, would result in the following calamitous outcomes:

◆ elimination of parental choice and local option in favor of a "one size fits all" method

◆ dismantling of successful educational programs, including bilingual instruction—in both English and students' native languages—that has proved effective in numerous Arizona schools, bilingual programs which offer a valuable bonus in today's global economy: fluency in two languages

◆ further loss of Native American languages; all of the state's Native American languages are now in danger of dying out, at a great loss to Native communities and to Arizona as a whole

English for the Children threatens the existence of various forms of educational support provided for students whose first language is not English. The umbrella term "bilingual education" is often used to mask massive ignorance about the range, goals, and methods of programs that are available to English learners including dual language schools, ESL classes, and bilingual and immersion programs. Although immersion programs do not use the students' first language at all to assist them in the acquisition of English, this kind of instruction still requires expertise in language teaching methods. But bilingual education is often—and mistakenly—described as a costly and inefficient strategy based on pampering non-English-speakers in Spanish. As most teachers know, however, effective education is not simply a matter of Spanish or English, but a matter of using whatever language is available to teach kids some content and literacy skills. As one Arizona teacher explains, she "zigzags between Spanish and English days," using her red pen for English words and green for Spanish words as she tries to describe story plots or relay geographic facts about Germany (Tapla 2000b, A8).

All of these existing programs for English-language learners target transition from Spanish to English by using Spanish in different ways and to different degrees to assist students in acquiring English. "Maintenance," one of the goals of many bilingual education programs throughout the world, is heresy in the United States. It is obvious that the Spanish these students already possess is devalued and considered simply a source of errors in English rather than as an asset.

Bilingual education is not only incorrectly defined by its critics, but it is often blamed for deeper social problems as well. In both California and Arizona, many of the public schools serving predominantly Hispanic/Latino populations are located in high-poverty areas. While inadequate teaching methods and general lack of resources contribute to the poor academic performance of these students, these students' financial and sometimes emotional environments also contribute heavily to their lack of educational success. The use of Spanish as a temporary means of instruction in their schools does not. In general, an unfavorable combination of several factors can aggravate the disadvantage that LEP children bring to school. For example, LEP children tend to be placed in overcrowded classrooms in which unqualified teachers and teacher's aides work. Untrained and inexperienced, many of these teachers believe that English as a Second Language is like acne that will go away after a few sessions of treatment. In many of these schools, there is a shortage of adequate ESL and bilingual teaching materials, and tutoring programs are not available to serve the special needs of LEP students. Often these children are improperly tested and end up in special education classrooms which were not designed to meet their language needs, and which may stigmatize these LEP students for the rest of their educational careers.

The accumulated discriminatory effect of these shortcomings was recognized by Federal Judge Alfredo Marquez of Arizona in a court case filed originally against the Nogales Unified School

District by parents in 1992. Judge Marquez ruled that the state of Arizona discriminates against limited-English-proficiency students by failing to provide school districts with enough funding to educate them. In his January 1999 opinion, Marquez held that the Arizona state legislature's minimum base-level funding of $150 per LEP student was "arbitrary and capricious," and it has not been updated for inflation since 1987–88. This is a violation of the federal Equal Educational Opportunity Act, which directs states to "take appropriate action to overcome language barriers that impede equal participation by its students in its instructional programs" (*Flores v. Arizona* 1999; Combs 2000, 5).

The proponents of English Only and anti-bilingual education laws not only underestimate the adverse effects of these combined socioeconomic and political factors when they blame bilingual education for poor educational outcomes, but they also give credit to English Only policy for positive results that are instead achieved by the interplay of several factors. Aiding in the passage of the Arizona English for the Children initiative is premature and irresponsible media coverage such as a recent *New York Times* article, "Test Scores Rise, Surprising Critics of Bilingual Ban," celebrating the success of English for the Children in California. This flawed article assumes that bilingual education has actually been erased in schools where scores have gone up and ignores the fact that in many California schools parents have chosen to continue their students in bilingual education. The observations of Kenji Hakuta, professor of education at Stanford University, are carefully buried in this article, although they clearly point out problems with the triumphant accounts.

Hakuta states that few conclusions about bilingual education can be drawn from the published test scores alone because of the large number of variables simultaneously introduced into the California system. The *New York Times* also noted that it may be too early to measure precisely the effects of the law after two years; furthermore, it is "difficult to ascertain to what degree they [school districts] have been teaching their Spanish-speaking students in English." Finally, the numerous factors introduced into the system that might have contributed to the dramatic rise of test scores include the reduction of class sizes in lower grades to twenty from more than thirty, a change of teaching methods, and an infusion of financial aid (Steinberg 2000, Y16). As Hakuta concluded, "with so many variables introduced at once, . . . few conclusions about bilingual education could be drawn from the results " (Steinberg 2000, Y16). Hakuta also added that with all the renewed interest in standardized testing nationwide, many schools have been teaching to the exams and tests, which may also explain why the scores are high.

One more factor to consider is that test score reports are often not controlled for significant extraneous factors, and as James Crawford has pointed out, we cannot tell "whether children in bilingual and English Only programs were fully comparable—for example, in prior knowledge of English, parental education levels, and socioeconomic status—or whether they differed in ways that affected their scores" (Crawford 2000, 5)

Yet proponents of English for the Children such as Hector Ayala confidently claim that they do not need to explain how their program affects learning or what is wrong with bilingual education. "We don't feel like we need to specify," he said in the *Arizona Daily Star.* "We mean exactly what they [bilingual teachers] are doing" (Tapla 2000b, A8). Also, the emotional appeal of English for the Children is so overwhelming that it makes the public completely ignore how English Only would address the linguistic needs of adults or, for that matter, college students, who are just as, and in some regions even more, underserved as children. ESL classes are hard to find, and even in Arizona's community colleges, ESL students are often advised to see tutors because the teachers are simply not prepared to work with them. The "ESL is like acne" syndrome rules at the higher levels of education, too. Most instructors would like to see a solution that requires only a short and intensive period of treatment, after which no accent, no idiosyncratic language use, and no misunderstanding of cultural expectations remain.

Proposition 203 English for the Children

I believe that Arizona's case is symptomatic because of its strong current and historical Hispanic/Latino presence and its demonstrated conservative political leanings, refueled by California's bold, racist politics. (Arizona passed an Official English initiative in 1988, soon after California did in 1986). At present, several campaigns of intolerance coexist in Arizona. An English Only initiative, Proposition 203—English Language Education for Children in Public Schools—gathered enough public support to be placed on the November 2000 ballot and to win the support of 67 percent of the voters. The campaign for this initiative imported the rhetoric used in Proposition 227 in California, spurred by Ron Unz. Unz, a Silicon Valley millionaire, despite admitting he has never set foot in a bilingual school program, orchestrated the California initiative Proposition 227, and he also organized and provided campaign support of $56,000 in Arizona. Unz's seemingly sophisticated and popular message was hard to counter because in public he rarely uses the overtly hostile and intolerant tone that is revealed in an e-mail exchange with James Crawford, prominent chronicler of the English Only movement. While his public slogan "English for the Children" brings to mind a caring, thoughtful movement for allegedly victimized children, his private sentiments can be best characterized as irrational and mean-spirited. In an e-mail to Crawford, Unz calls academics "loonies" and confidently states that "[i]t looks increasingly likely that 'bilingual education' will be completely wiped out in California within seven months, and nationwide shortly thereafter" (Unz 1997). Anti–English Only proponents rightly feared that the same disarming slogans that swayed the Californian public and that conceal Unz's vicious project would succeed in distorting discussions of the value of bilingual education in Arizona as well, where one-third of the population is Hispanic/Latino and thousands of children are limited English speakers. The result is now two states setting a precedent, making it easier for Unz's campaign to succeed in the next targeted states.

Arizona's Proposition 203, Language Education for Children in Public Schools, like its California counterpart, does not offer an educational program that would assist language-minority children to achieve academic success and does not guarantee them an equal opportunity to a good education. Instead, it dismantles bilingual education and offers the simplistic dictum that "English is required for all public instruction." Proposition 203 places students who do not speak English into unspecified sheltered immersion classes for one year, and transfers those "who acquire good working knowledge of English" to mainstream classes. It is not clear what kind of instruction is meant by "sheltered immersion classes"; and proponents of this approach do not provide evidence from research to support their idea that any learner at any stage can acquire a "good working knowledge of English" in a year in the proposed sheltered immersion class (Tapla 2000a).

Because this proposed policy flagrantly ignores best research and practice while leaving unaddressed the known sociocultural and socioeconomic issues that surround the language-minority population in general and in the Southwest and Arizona in particular, its motivations beg questioning. From a pedagogical standpoint, this policy is not meant to be a solution to the educational problems of LEP students but a backlash against the Hispanic/Latino population that many fear is becoming politically formidable. It is not an oversimplification to associate Arizona's Proposition 203 with xenophobia and racism. We need to address the real educational and cultural problems that continue to deny language-minority students educational success. Most important, the language ideologies represented in English Only rhetoric require thorough analysis and questioning. The ESL and bilingual programs under attack belong to those public programs and institutions that were launched and funded in the 1960s but became abandoned, underfunded, or poorly implemented in many regions during the 1980s and 1990s. These programs, as Henry Giroux (1989) points out, have "never been given a chance at achieving their expected results" (xiii).

Are Alienation, Exclusion, and Revocation of Bad Memories Alternatives to Embracing and Empowering Difference?

The prematurely congratulatory *New York Times* article that reports the success of English for the Children in California and expects that these results will influence voters in Colorado, Massachusetts, and New York, where antibilingual forces are marshalling to put similar laws on the ballot, unwittingly ends with an anecdote that epitomizes one of the most tragic consequences of English Only. A child who recently came from Mexico now reports that "[w]hen my friends from Mexico come here, I don't understand what they're saying" (Steinberg 2000, Y16). This story was meant to provide a humorous ending to the article, and the child's alienation from her culture is simply termed by the journalist "an unforeseen consequence of Proposition 227" (Steinberg 2000, Y16). But the anecdote also eminently illustrates the underlying forces of elimination and division that motivate the celebration of such outcomes.

Bilingual education programs are based on a different idea. Instead of eradicating students' home culture and linguistic difference, these programs both preserve and develop the students' native language in the process of developing their English proficiency. This process may take an extra two years, but the outcome is superior in three ways, as has been validated in the research: the native language and culture are preserved, English is learned, and because of dual-language development, cognitive skills are increased, which ultimately leads to bilingual learners' greater academic success in general compared to their monolingual counterparts. You see this every day whenever a well-schooled European, Asian, or Latin American exchange student who speaks his or her own language plus English performs above average in U.S. schools. For whatever reason, U.S. society does not want to accept either this fact or the research results that support it.

The lack of respect for cultural and linguistic difference and the apparent eliminative overtones of antibilingual education legislation may cause anxiety in the language-minority communities that already have negative historical memories. Fearful of returning to the restrictive system that dominated schools before bilingual education was introduced in the mid-60s, members of the Hispanic/Latino community in Tucson and the rest of Arizona have found forums to express their distress. Some members of this community are concerned that English for the Children legislation will turn back the clock to the days when minorities were excluded from educational excellence and were forced to endure an inferior education "in English only," in special classes called 1C.

Community leaders, educators, and businesspeople remember the previous English Only system in which children were segregated and then kept in a classroom "until they were ready to move on in English." These children languished in 1C classes where they were forbidden to learn in their language of nurture and were forced to listen like mutes to a language that was both culturally and structurally unfamiliar to them. Consequently, their learning readiness in their native language was stymied. They were forbidden from progressing naturally from their Spanish-speaking and listening proficiency to gaining gradual proficiency in English. All their cultural and linguistic habits developed in Spanish were extinguished through strict disciplinary techniques such as verbal and corporal abuse. These dynamics in the classroom and on the playground, along with the children's and their families' unequal socioeconomic status, combined to make the educational experience unfavorably affect the self-concept of language minorities. As a result, language-minority students were denied the opportunity to perceive themselves as good learners. It is no wonder that from 1919 to 1967 only 40 percent of all Hispanic/Latino children in Tucson Unified School District graduated ("Turning Back the Clock" 2000, 1).

Not only did the children in 1C fail to learn English quickly, but they were also seriously behind in school. Many were severely cognitively and emotionally scarred by the time they emerged from their English Only instructional captivity in 1C. As the Arizona Language Education Council points out, the new English Only initiative would bring back a failed approach to teaching English, reinstating virtually identical programs that held back Hispanic/Latino and Native American children for decades and neglecting their academic needs. It would turn back the clock, returning Arizona to a time when these students were denied equal opportunities.

The Navajo Nation, the largest Native American nation in the United States, concurs. Navajo Nation President Kelsey A. Begay, in an impassioned address to the Navajo people, warned that Proposition 203 would detrimentally affect the Navajo way of life. It is unfortunate that many Navajo children begin their education with little or no Navajo language skills. In a broad sense, however, these children currently have the choice of using their native language because they have the option to learn the language in school. If enacted, Proposition 203 will take this

choice away from Navajo children. Begay summarizes the pernicious effects of this legislation on Navajo culture, emphasizing
that the enactment of this English-language bill will deny parents
the right to have their children excluded from the English Only
program and the right to get their children into any other language development program. The Resolution of the Navajo Nation Council clearly links English for the Children with
unfavorable historical precedence when it states that

> [t]he Navajo Nation experienced almost a hundred years of "En-
> glish only" education between the late 1860s and the late 1960s.
> Only with the inclusion of some Navajo language and culture in
> the schools did more Navajo students begin to succeed. Good
> Navajo-and-English bilingual education programs can and do
> work. (Resolution of the Navajo Nation Council 2000).

As the anxieties expressed by these groups demonstrate, the
educational system promoted by English Only supporters is a
potential vehicle for dividing the population and reopening the
scars of colonized territorial minorities in the United States instead of contributing to a healing and redeeming process. The
lives of these linguistic minorities have throughout history been
marked by a lack of choice and by the obligatory abidance to the
arbitrary decisions of privileged members of society. There is no
doubt that legislation recalling memories of past injustices is likely
to cause alienation and distrust. The official language movement
is an easy vehicle with which to stigmatize a population and to
retard rather than accelerate its assimilation into this nation. Those
who are truly interested in "the children" would ensure that the
best teachers, methodologies, and pedagogical approaches are
used in classrooms in which teachers and students are valued
and the physical and emotional environments are conducive to
learning. They would also ensure that schools have the financial
means to justly reward teachers and to provide an infrastructure
to aid students and their families faced with sociocultural and
economic challenges. They would, for example, provide adequate
funding for English as a Second Language. None of these considerations is attached to Proposition 203 or to any other English
Only initiative created to "save" linguistic minority children in
the name of English only.

Notes

1. All chapters in this book have been edited to conform to NCTE's house style for books, including editing the names of various racial and ethnic groups in the United States in accordance with sensitive and bias-free usage. We deviate from this practice only when the authors refer to specific studies, where changing the names would misrepresent results. In all other cases, names of racial and ethnic groups have been changed to comply with *The Dictionary of Bias-Free Usage* and NCTE's Policy Statement on people of Color, among other sources.

2. See a survey of the history of African American Vernacular English by Smitherman in this volume (pages 322–328).

3. Data were collected by the federal office of Bilingual Education and Minority Languages Affairs and by the State Department of Education's 1998–99 report and were published in the *Arizona Daily Star*, April 10, 2000.

Works Cited

Altbach, Philip G., and Patty McGill Peterson. 1998. "Internationalize American Higher Education? Not Exactly." *Change* (30)4: 36–39.

Arizona Language Education Council. 2000. *Academic Excellence for All Children*. Information Brochure. Oro Valley, Arizona.

Borden, Tessi. 2000. "Is Border Watch Crossing the Line? Ranchers, Officials at Odds in Detaining Illegal Immigrants." *The Arizona Republic,* May 8. A1, A4.

Césaire, Aimé. 1972. *Discourse on Colonialism*. New York: Monthly Review Press.

Collier, Virginia P. 1987. "Age and Rate of Acquisition of Second Language for Academic Purpose." *TESOL Quarterly* 21: 617–41.

———. 1989. "How Long? A Synthesis of Research on Academic Achievement in Second Language." *TESOL Quarterly* 23: 509–31.

———. 1992. "A Synthesis of Studies Examining Long-Term Language Minority Student Data on Academic Achievement." *Bilingual Research Journal* 16(1-2): 187–212.

Combs, Mary Carol. 2000. "*Flores v. Arizona:* Bilingual Education Is Seriously Under-Funded, Judge Rules." *ALEC [Arizona Language Education Council] Voices* 1(Spring): 5–6.

Crawford, James. 2000. "Stanford 9 Scores Show a Consistent Edge for Bilingual Education." *ALEC [Arizona Language Education Council] Voices* 1(Spring): 4–5.

Fishman, Joshua. 1989. "Language and Ethnicity." *Minority Sociolinguistic Perspective.* Bristol, PA: Multilingual Matters.

Foucault, Michel. 1977. *Discipline and Punish: The Birth of the Prison.* Trans. Alan Sheridan. New York: Vintage Books.

Gates, Henry, L. 1988. "The Signifying Monkey and the Language of Signifyin(g)." *The Signifying Monkey: A Theory of Afro-American Literary Criticism.* New York: Oxford University Press.

Giroux, Henry. 1989. "Introduction." In Henry Giroux and Peter McLaren, eds., *Critical Pedagogy, the State, and Cultural Struggle.* Albany: SUNY Press. xi–xxv.

González, Roseann D. 1997a. "An Evaluation of the Validity of UNOCAL's Use of the Test of English for International Communication (TOEIC) for Selection of Franchisee/Strategic Partners." A Report for the American Civil Liberties Union, San Francisco, California.

———. 1997b. "A Review of the Alabama Department of Public Safety English Only Rule." A Report for the Southern Poverty Law Center, Montgomery, Alabama.

———. 2000. "A Review of the Language Access Policy of the Minnesota Department of Human Services." A Report for the Mid-Minnesota Legal Assistance, Minneapolis, Minnesota.

Labov, William. 1969. "The Logic of Non-standard English." In J. Alatis, ed., *Georgetown Monographs on Language and Linguistics* 22: 1–44.

Lambert, W., and G. R. Tucker. 1972. *Bilingual Education of Children.* Rowley, MA: Newbury House.

Lippi-Green, Rosina. 1997. "What We Talk about When We Talk about Ebonics: Why Definitions Matter." *The Black Scholar* 27(2): 7–11.

Phillipson, Robert. 1992. *Linguistic Imperialism.* New York: Oxford University Press.

Resolution of the Navajo Nation Council. 2000. *ALEC [Arizona Language Education Council] Voices* 1(Spring): 9.

Steinberg, Jacques. 2000. "Test Scores Rise, Surprising Critics of Bilingual Ban." *New York Times,* Aug. 20. A1, Y16.

Tapla, Sarah Tully. 2000a. "English for the Children: The Debate over Whether to Teach in Spanish." *Arizona Daily Star,* Apr. 9. A16–17.

———. 2000b. "English for the Children: How Bilingual Students Learn." *Arizona Daily Star,* Apr. 10. A1, A8–9.

"Turning Back the Clock: Proposition 203 and English-Only Schooling in Arizona." 2000. Symposium held at the University of Arizona. Sept. 23. Flier.

Unz, Ron. 1997. E-mail response to James Crawford's language Web site. Nov. 7. Available: http://ourworld.compuserve.com/homepages/jwcrawford/unzmail.html

U.S. Census Bureau. 1998. "Income Inequality—Table 4." Available: http://www.census.gov/ftp/pub/hhes/income/incineq/p60tb4.html

Weinberg, Daniel H. 1999. "Press Briefing on 1998 Income and Poverty Estimates [Online]." U.S. Census Bureau. Sept. 30. Available: http://www.census.gov/ftp/pub/hhes/income/income98/prs99asc.html

Williams, Patricia J. 1997. *The Rooster's Egg: On the Persistence of Prejudice.* Cambridge, U.K.: Harvard University Press.

Yeoman, Barry . 2000. "Hispanic Diaspora." *Mother Jones* (July/August): 36–37.

I

UPDATE AND DOCUMENT

The emergence and reemergence of English Only movements in the United States has a cyclical pattern that lends itself to associations with either economic cycles or waves of immigration, international conflicts, and other sociopolitical phenomena that are likely to generate public expressions of suspicion and hostility toward the linguistic-minority populations of the United States. Although the cyclical nature of English Only suggests that every time it resurfaces we are faced with the "same old rhetoric," change in targets and agendas is just as significant. Dennis Baron's account of the "American language policy of the 1990s" covers both permanent and changing components. The most recent waves of "language legislation and language abuse" range from small and seemingly isolated local disputes or court hearings to new additions to pending national legislation. They spring up in age-old disputes over bilingual education, but new domains of debate over what English is are also generated in the process, as the flare-ups over Ebonics demonstrate. Finally, the issue of language penetrates the sites of ostensibly unrelated and sensitive political areas like the Puerto Rican statehood referendum. Baron's conclusion is that despite the fact that many regions of the United States may seem "like a foreign country" to some Americans, English is not a language in danger of disappearing, and "the United States, without an official language law, has had more success getting its population to speak a common language than any of the seventy-nine nations of the world with official language laws on their book" (p. 27).

But if English Only, as Geoffrey Nunberg (1997) also points out, is "a bad cure for an imaginary disease," and if, as Baron notes, it is an issue that "quickly disappears when more important issues loom," with bill proposals stalled in committees, what is it that deserves concern from the general public in this most recent phase of the official language cycles? A document compiled by Edward M. Chen, staff counsel of the American Civil Liberties Union (ACLU) of Northern California, is published in this volume to address this question. This chapter, which is a slightly modified version of the ACLU document submitted to a U.S. government committee, potently outlines those areas of civil rights and liberties that an official language policy will violate. Such laws, claims Chen, are not only unnecessary, but they would also adversely affect the provision of fundamental government services, bar language minorities from exercising their constitutional right to vote, and most likely discriminate against an already disadvantaged and powerless minority. In addition, the proposed official language laws foster bigotry and generally undermine the spirit of tolerance and pluralistic ideals that the U.S. Constitution embodies. This document is a valuable source for anyone who wants to study the history of English Only from a constitutional perspective. It is also an argument that constructs American values in terms of rights and liberties, tolerance and diversity, and points out the deficiencies of English Only's minimalist conception of American identity that is based solely on the ability to speak standard English.

Robert S. Williams and Kathleen C. Riley's study was selected to be part of the Update and Document section to represent a more specific view of language change. In a typical update scenario, we want to read about the recent changes in the manifestations of English Only ideologies, and we expect an overview of how they can be countered effectively. Both Baron's and Chen's writings stress that official language policy is unnecessary since English has been acquired by successive generations of new immigrants at record speed. Williams and Riley's longitudinal ethnographic study provides insight into the intricacies and complexities of this process by showing how, within one Franco-American family, English became the dominant language of all thirteen siblings, but especially of the last five. This study represents only a small slice of the actual processes of language shift, but it is a well-carved slice that illustrates the multidimensional influences of family structure, occupation, economic change, and the manifold roles played by various facilitators of language socialization including the church, school, media, family, and friends.

The study shows not only the spectacular speed of English acquisition, but it also demonstrates the rapid loss of the family's home language. English Only legislation, Williams and Riley conclude, "would . . . foster beliefs among minority cultures that speaking English and only English is the best marker of a patriotic American" (p. 87). The study also finds that although the examined family is shifting from bilingual to monolingual, members do not unanimously accept the English Only agenda, and still express "a rich and nurturing sense of their family's linguistic strengths and unique heritage" (p. 87).

Work Cited

Nunberg, Geoffrey. 1997. "Lingo Jingo: English-Only and the New Nativism." *American Prospect* 33: 40–47. Available: http://epn.org/prospect/33/33nunbfs.html. Accessed March 14, 1999.

CHAPTER ONE

Language Legislation and Language Abuse: American Language Policy through the 1990s

DENNIS BARON

University of Illinois at Urbana-Champaign

During the past two hundred years, there have been many attempts to make English the official language of the United States. While supporters of Official English have been successful in imposing English, on a symbolic or a functional level, in a number of cities and counties, in some twenty-three states, and even in some businesses, they have not been successful at the national level. Americans have shied away from proposed Constitutional amendments that would make English official, because the idea has always been closely associated with prejudice against people who do not speak the language, whether they are immigrants or natives, and because in the end, the vast majority of non-English-speaking Americans wind up speaking English after all, a situation which renders drastic Constitutional action unnecessary (Baron 1990).

Official English movements come in waves, cycles in which Americans become protective and look inward, avoiding foreign entanglements that seem threatening. The United States experienced such a cycle in the 1890s in response to increasing immigration, and again in the 1920s, after World War I. Official English reemerged as an issue in the 1980s in response to renewed immigration and to U.S. involvement both militarily and economically on the international scene, and accompanying the rapid spread of English around the physical and virtual globe. It would not be surprising if the new millennium were abetting concerns about keeping America for the Americans, something that Official English legislation promises to do.

In this essay, I look at this latest cycle of official English, which ranges from the very local—an Amarillo custody hearing and an insurance office dispute—to the national level, where legislation to make English the official language of the federal government has been pending for several years. Along the way, I consider as well the fate of bilingual education, the proposed Puerto Rican statehood referendum, and the Ebonics controversy. All of these recent manifestations of official English suggest that the United States is moving closer than it ever has to accepting some sort of formal language policy at the federal level. But that does not mean such a policy is inevitable. While language is a popular issue, in that it attracts attention and most people have an opinion on what language policy should be, it is also an issue that quickly disappears when more important matters loom. An election, an international incident, a political scandal, or a twitch in the economy quickly turns legislators away from language policy to an issue they see as having more meat, and the public is happy to follow that lead. Even so, Americans keep returning to what I have called the English Only question, feeling the need to protect a language that without formal protection has been more successful than any other language in human history

Spanish Abuse

In June 1995, an Amarillo, Texas, district court judge, ruling in a child custody suit, accused Martha Laureano of child abuse for speaking Spanish to her five-year-old daughter (Verhovek 1995). Judge Samuel C. Kiser ordered the mother to speak only English to the girl, who would enter kindergarten that fall. He warned that English was necessary for her daughter to "do good in school." Even worse, the judge added, without English the girl would be condemned to a life as a maid.

When the story broke at the end of August that summer, there was a national outcry against this overreaching and misdirected decision. Judge Kiser, sensing that some fence-mending might be appropriate, held a press conference and apologized to maids, insisting that he held them in high esteem. But he held resolutely to his English Only order.

The judge's own mastery of English grammar is not the issue here. Nor are the obvious free-speech concerns of the case or the fact that Kiser's equation of speaking Spanish with child abuse draws attention away from the serious forms of abuse that do warrant legal intervention. Judge Kiser reached his unwise decision, which I would characterize as language abuse, without even considering Martha Laureano's reason for speaking Spanish to her daughter. Laureano was in fact bilingual in English and Spanish, and she knew that once her daughter entered school she would quickly lose her Spanish. So the mother spoke Spanish at home to the child in an attempt—one she knew was probably doomed—to maintain some Spanish in the face of the inevitable transition to English that was soon to come.

It was Judge Kiser, not Martha Laureano, who was practicing a traditional American form of language abuse. For many years, young speakers of Spanish, Navajo, Chinese, and other minority languages in the United States were beaten, humiliated, or given detentions if they used their first language in classrooms or the schoolyard. Such punishments did not accelerate the students' adoption of English. As the average student chafing under a language requirement will attest, you cannot *make* someone speak a "foreign" language. Physical force and corporal punishment do even less to secure linguistic compliance.

Language abuse is common in the adult world as well. Workers are regularly disciplined or fired by employers for using languages other than English on the job or during breaks. In 1994 the Teamsters Union filed a class-action complaint against the Dolphin Hotel at Walt Disney World in federal court in Orlando, charging that the Dolphin's English Only policy discriminated against its Haitian and Hispanic/Latino housekeeping and laundry workers (Lewin 1994). The hotel denied having such a policy. A year after the Laureano case, a small Amarillo, Texas, insurance agency fired two women who were bilingual in English and Spanish and had been hired for their ability to speak Spanish to Hispanic/Latino customers (Verhovek 1997). The owner of the agency did not like the fact that these bilingual clerks spoke Spanish to one another as well as to customers. She asked them to sign a pledge making the agency "an English speaking office except when we have customers who can't speak our language." When they refused, she fired them. The clerks felt insulted. The owners felt the clerks were being rude, "almost like they were whispering to each other behind our backs" (A10). This is a common scenario: paranoid employers are certain their employees are talking about them if they use a language other than English, so they institute an English-only requirement. Federal law is vague when it comes to the regulation of language that is not specifically job related. The courts have not been particularly helpful here, either, sometimes ruling for the employer, sometimes for the employee.

Suppression of languages other than English has been a feature of U.S. language policy for the past 150 years. In extreme cases, banning foreign languages was tied to issues of national security. Soon after the United States entered World War I in April 1917, twenty-five states banned the teaching of German in the schools. In May 1918, the governor of Iowa forbade the use of any foreign language in the schools, on the streets, or on the telephone, a more public instrument then than it is now. German words that had entered English were targets for replacement: hamburgers became "liberty sandwiches," and sauerkraut was renamed "liberty cabbage." Superpatriots caught the "liberty measles" (*rubella*, the technical name for German measles, probably sounded suspiciously foreign as well). German street names in U.S. cities were similarly sanitized, many of them forever. In 1995 the Cincinnati City Council considered a request to rehabilitate the city's geographical past by displaying informational signs on twelve area streets which had lost their earlier German names (*Cincinnati Enquirer* 1995). Thus English Street would receive a 12" by 18" sign reading, "Formerly German Street, renamed April 9, 1918 because of the anti-German hysteria during WWI." Other renamed streets included Woodrow (formerly Berlin) Street, Republic (Bremen) Street, Connecticut (Frankfort) Avenue, Stonewall (Hamburg) Street, Panama (Vienna) Street, and Orion Avenue (Wilhelm Street).

Official English

The German language is no longer considered a threat in the United States. Spanish now has that honor, followed to a lesser degree by other minority languages such as Cantonese, Hindi, or Russian. When I ask people if they think English should be the official language of the United States, most of them respond, "You mean it isn't?" Then they think about it, briefly, and they add, "Sure, why not?" My mother, who spoke only Yiddish until she entered kindergarten, thinks English should be official.

When I tell people about the Illinois official language law, they laugh. In 1923, as the nation turned away from foreign entanglements after World War I, a group of Chicago Irish and Jewish politicians combined the postwar isolationist mood with their own unhappiness at British treatment of Ireland and Palestine and got a law passed making "American" the official language of the state of Illinois. The law had no real impact—other languages were still tolerated in Illinois, and English rather than American continued to be taught in the state's schools—so in 1969 it was quietly amended, and English became the state's official language. Even so, the Illinois official language law has had little more than a symbolic impact. My students liken it to the time, some twenty years ago, when Illinois elementary school pupils were asked to choose the state fossil.

The Illinois example amuses people. But then the language policy discussion becomes more serious, and someone mentions the public safety myth: What if a person who can't speak English has to call the police or the rescue squad? What if firefighters can't read an address because it's in Greek or Korean? Or someone recalls what it was like to visit Miami: "It was, like, a foreign country." Or they tell me about the vote in 1776, when German lost out to English as the language of the new United States by only one vote. Finally, though, someone remembers that calls to 911 are automatically traced and that the fire department can find any address. And I tell them that in 1997, the *Boston Globe* reported that there was a shortage of Spanish speakers in Miami. According to the story, "despite a high unemployment rate companies have to go outside the country to recruit bilingual em-

ployees because not enough local residents speak Spanish well
. . . . While Spanish is widely spoken in Miami, statistics indicate
that immigrants are learning English and that their children prefer English" (Mears 1997). Miami's director of bilingual education notes that 90 percent of elementary school students take
Spanish, but once it becomes an elective in middle school, they
drop it. Only 6 percent of Dade County students study Spanish
in high school (Mears 1997). It seems that, despite the perception of visiting Midwesterners, bilingual announcements at the
Miami airport and Cuban restaurants have not turned Miami
into a foreign country.

The "German vote" also turns out to be an illusion. Several
times a year I get questions about the legendary vote in which
German supposedly lost out to English. It is a vote that never
took place. A new story seems to be circulating in the Greek
American community that in the late eighteenth century, it was
Greek that was beaten by English by a mere one vote. These
stories are myths—nothing like them ever happened. In the supposed struggles between English, German, Greek, Native American languages, Chinese, and now Spanish, the outcome was never
in doubt, not for a second. English wins. Hands down. Every
time. End of story.

Language and the Puerto Rican Statehood Referendum

Still, supporters of Official English raise the specter not only of
Germany but also of Quebec. They look to Puerto Rico as one
area where language legislation will be critical. In 1998 Puerto
Rico observed its one-hundredth year as a possession of the United
States. Anticipating this, Congress considered a self-determina-
tion referendum for the Commonwealth, giving it the option to
choose independence, statehood, or continued commonwealth
status. When the House of Representatives debated this referendum in the summer of 1997, conservatives tried to amend the
bill to require English as Puerto Rico's official language. In a
letter to the *Washington Post,* one Official English supporter
warned that unless Puerto Ricans were required to accept English as their official language, statehood for the Commonwealth

would open the door to official national bilingualism for the rest of the United States and the divisiveness which that move was sure to entail. He concluded, "The cultural and linguistic apartheid that now exists in Canada should be a warning bell tolling loudly for congressional attention. With the racial and ethnic tensions this country already has, do we need to voluntarily create our own Quebec?" (Hopwood 1997, A20).

The House passed the Puerto Rican referendum measure by one vote, once Official English requirements were softened. As passed, the bill encourages Puerto Rico, under the heading "English Language Empowerment," to "promote the teaching of English" so that students "achieve English language proficiency by the age of 10." There was no Senate action on the bill in 1997, and the matter was revived in both houses the following year. In the 1998 version of the House bill, the language issue is left open, though the act hints at the possibility that the United States may in the future establish a more formal Official English policy, in which case Puerto Rico will get no special treatment:

> In the event that a referendum held under this Act results in approval of sovereignty leading to Statehood, upon accession to Statehood, the official language requirements of the Federal Government shall apply to Puerto Rico in the same manner and to the same extent as throughout the United States.

In addition, the bill seeks to promote English to facilitate interaction between state and federal levels; to give citizens "the language skill necessary to contribute to and participate in all aspects of the Nation"; and to allow "all citizens of Puerto Rico to take full advantage of the opportunities and responsibilities accorded to all citizens, including education, economic activities, occupational opportunities, and civic affairs" (H.R. 856 1997).

The Senate began considering the referendum bill during the summer of 1998. So far, the language question has not been revisited, but it is sure to resurface as the bill moves closer to a vote. If Puerto Rican voters do choose statehood, that statehood must then be approved by Congress. In the past, Congress has withheld statehood from areas where English was not the dominant language, including Michigan and, more recently, New

Mexico. Assuming Congress approves statehood for Puerto Rico, the referendum bill provides for a transition period of no more than ten years. Those ten years would provide yet another fascinating chapter in the history of U.S. language policy. In any case, the situation will be different from that in Quebec: for one thing, as the Québécois consider secession from Canada, the Puerto Ricans are contemplating the possibility of solidifying their ties with the mainland.

Official Language Goes to School

The possibility of Puerto Rican statehood is only one of several areas in which Official English comes into play. The issues of bilingual education, Ebonics, and the language of government all combine to make Official English the biggest issue in U.S. language policy today. While everyone seems to have an opinion on the Official English question, few people are well-informed about it. Consider, for example, the following excerpts from written student responses to the question. After reading a short news article on the Language of Government Act (see the section The 1995–1997 Language of Government Acts), transfer students taking a writing placement test at the University of Illinois were asked to write an essay supporting or opposing Official English legislation. Their essays reveal some of the confusion and misinformation surrounding current or proposed language policy:

◆ The (Official English) movement started as a way of keeping public doctors speaking English.

◆ The entire language would have to be given up because England started the language.

◆ Renaming every object with a foreign title would create numerous problems. . . . It is illogical to have one man living in Colorado and his next-door neighbor living in Colored.

◆ If one is going to be unfair, one may as well be unfair equally to everyone. I support the Official English movement on the basis that anything short of recognizing *all* foreign languages is selectively unfair.

◆ Officially recognized words should include all of what the average citizen can understand.

◆ In an English Only system, new words will not be accepted. New technology, techniques, diseases, and theories will not be properly named.

◆ The United States is built on foreign words and ideas. . . . U.S. government and society could not have been formed if communism, capitalism, calculus, bacteria, and so forth had not been discovered by foreign people.

◆ The immigrants are in the same position. They wanted to come to the United States just as I decided to transfer to the University of Illinois. I had to adapt to the way of life at this university.

◆ English Only will help ensure that the future immigrants who come here are dead serious about becoming productive members of our society.

On one level, the answer to the question of whether English should be official in the United States is a no-brainer: English has always been the language in which most of the country's business has been transacted, so as the last comment above indicates, it would make sense that knowing English might facilitate fuller participation in that business, might better enable people to enter into the governmental, economic, educational, and social mainstream. Indeed, most student responses touched on these points. But on another, more complex level, the answer to the English Only question is not simple at all. Knowing English is one thing; requiring it is another. Legislation supporting English often is— or appears to be—a way of telling non-English-speakers that they are not welcome. One international student taking the placement test picks up on this, writing, "The language is probably the only thing by which Americans can demonstrate their superiority towards us, foreigners. . . . Many foreign immigrants take away jobs from American people, and international students by far outsmart U.S. citizens."

Unfortunately, this response overestimates the success of immigrants both in the classroom and in the workforce. For example, a recent *New York Times* report reminds us that the stereotype of the overachieving, mathematically minded Asian immigrant is in need of revision. Not all Asian Americans fit the mold of the overrepresented "model minority." According to the 1990 census, nearly two-thirds of Hmong families from Southeast Asia live below the poverty line, compared with only 7 percent of Japanese Americans and 13 percent of the nation as a whole. Only 3 percent of Hmong and 6 percent of Cambodians in this country have college degrees, compared with 60 percent of Asian Indians and 40 percent of Chinese (Sengupta 1997).

School dropout rates for children with limited English proficiency may be high, but they have been high for most of this century. What supporters of Official English fail to acknowledge is that immigrants, not to mention women and minorities, have often found that even if they do master standard English, they are still denied access to the mainstream.

Official English legislation sends a negative message. It also sends an unnecessary one, since the English language is not under attack in this country. People who do not speak English want to learn it. There are not enough spaces in English-language classes to meet the demand. Census reports continue to underscore the fact that, while many people in this country speak other languages, 97 percent of U.S. residents claim to speak English well. Even if this is just a claim—that is, even if some of those responding to the question do not speak English particularly well—their answer clearly indicates that they know that speaking English well is desirable.

Apparently no one needs to encourage the children of non-English-speakers to switch to English: indeed, the concern of most non-Anglophone parents in the United States has always been that their children, in adopting English, all too quickly reject their first language and the cultural heritage that accompanies it. My college students routinely report how they hated going to Chinese School or Hindi School or Greek School or Korean School when they were younger, and how much they now regret the language loss that prevents them from fully engaging with their culture, makes speaking to grandparents difficult, or hinders communication when they visit the old country.

The official language question is frequently tied to the schools, particularly targeting programs in bilingual education. Federal official language bills proposed in Congress typically seek to eliminate bilingual ballots and bilingual education. California's Proposition 227, passed in 1998, required that all schools in the state immediately shift from multiyear bilingual education programs to one-year English immersion programs for its limited-English-speaking students.

It is not clear that immersion will work better, or worse, than bilingual education. The novelist Chang-rae Lee commented in the *New York Times* several years ago on his own immersion, as a young Korean speaker, in an English Only school, long before schools thought to do anything about their non-English-speaking students: "I had spent kindergarten in almost complete silence, hearing only the high nasality of my teacher and comprehending little but the cranky wails and cries of my classmates" (Lee 1996, A17). Somehow—not through the efforts of the school—Lee learned English, not an unusual story to hear from non-Anglophone immigrant children. Nowadays, at least, the schools feel the need to teach language, whether English or a foreign language. But adding to the complexity of the U.S. language policy situation is the fact that no one seems to know how to teach language very well. U.S. schools have failed miserably in their attempts to turn out students who can speak or read foreign languages with any degree of fluency. California's voters have forgotten that the failure of immersion programs was what led to bilingual education in the first place. Now, after twenty-five years of bilingual education, many people are convinced that schools do not teach English any better than they teach French, Spanish, German, or Latin. It may be that, except perhaps for the playground, school is not the best place to learn a language.

Arizona: A Punitive Law Struck Down

In the spring of 1998, the Arizona Supreme Court ruled that state's official language law unconstitutional. Arizona's Official English law, passed by 51 percent of the state's voters, was the most detailed and the most restrictive of any of the twenty-three state official language laws currently on the books, affecting all political subdivisions, departments, agencies, and organizations of the state, including municipal and township governments. It required all government officials and employees—from the governor down to the dogcatcher—to use English and only English during the performance of government business. The law was challenged in the federal courts by a state employee and defended by a private group, Arizonans for Official English. A U.S. district court found the law unconstitutional on free-speech grounds. That ruling was upheld by the U.S. court of appeals. But in 1997, the Supreme Court refused to rule on the case, returning it to the state courts on a technicality: the plaintiff in the case no longer worked for the state of Arizona. The Arizona Supreme Court found that the law "chills First Amendment rights" and violates the federal Constitution as well as the equal protection clause of the Fourteenth Amendment. This is the first official language law to be overturned by the courts since the 1920s, when the U.S. Supreme Court ruled in *Meyer v. Nebraska* that state laws prohibiting the teaching of foreign languages in schools were unconstitutional. The state court opinion emphasizes that it would not throw out less restrictive language laws, nor does its decision support the official use of Spanish or other tongues: "Nothing in this opinion compels any Arizona governmental entity to provide any service in a language other than English" (Davenport 1998). But the law's supporters have nonetheless vowed to appeal the state court decision to the U.S. Supreme Court.

Other states have weighed in, if briefly, on the official language question. In 1996 the county executive of Suffolk County, New York, vetoed a proposal that would have made English the official language of the county. Official English has not proved popular in the Northeast, at least on the state level, with only New Hampshire having an official language law on its books (Perez-Pena 1996). But at the local level, some towns in New York and New Jersey, where established residents fear that new immigrants will overwhelm them and turn the town into a "foreign country," have adopted new sign laws requiring that half of any commercial sign in a foreign language be in English (Lee 1996). Ironically, these older, established residents are themselves the descendants of immigrants who had an earlier generation of English Only sign laws directed against them in the early 1900s.

Other areas have seen Official English activity as well. In May 1998, the commissioner of Kootenai County, Idaho, urged the state's Republicans to adopt an Official English plank and pressed the state legislature to mandate that all state business and publications be done in English (Coddington 1998). Interest at the state Republican convention in June proved minimal, however, and the discussion was dropped. Advocates for Official English in Missouri garnered some new support in early 1998 when they added extra funding for English classes to their proposed law (unlike other states, Missouri does not give schools extra funding for ESL classes) and softened their tone by declaring English the "common language" rather than the "official language" of Missouri. Opponents of the measure fear that the bill will backfire, encouraging discrimination against the very people it seeks to help (Sanchez 1998).

Ebonics and Official English

An Official English backlash accompanied the Ebonics controversy in 1996. When the board of the Oakland, California, Unified School District passed a resolution on December 18 of that year declaring Ebonics the native language of its African American children—a separate language and not a dialect of English—the declaration was greeted by the nation as an act of linguistic secession.

The Oakland Resolution, which was later modified, is based on a recommendation by a panel charged with studying all the problems of the Oakland schools. That panel spent a long time trying to decide why Oakland's African American schoolchildren had lower grades and standardized test scores, and were more likely to be in remedial than advanced classes, compared to other racial or ethnic groups. The panel issued a detailed report calling for a number of changes, including remodeling classrooms, improving educational materials, decreasing student-teacher ratios, and improving teacher morale. In other words, their conclusion was that a lot of things besides language are "wrong" with the Oakland schools and need to be addressed before there will be any improvement in such things as graduation rates and reading scores.

Prodded by political activists in the community, however, the Oakland School Board seized only on the language issue in its resolution, and that in turn is what brought national attention to Oakland. The resolution—which some school board members later claimed they had not read—asserted that Ebonics or "African Language Systems are genetically based and not a dialect of English." In effect, the media seemed to say, Oakland was declaring Ebonics to be its official language. That in turn was perceived as downright un-American, so much so that the Oakland School Board had to immediately recant and insist, in a revised resolution issued on January 15, 1996, that it was only trying to emphasize the need to use second-language learning techniques to help Oakland's black students make the transition from Ebonics to standard English (Oakland 1995).

One striking absence from the Ebonics debate was an examination of why at least some people in Oakland felt the need to define Ebonics as a distinct language in the first place. Defining speech as a language or a dialect has political as well as grammatical implications, and taking control of language is one way to assert independence and exercise political power. But it was quickly made clear that a majority of Americans, including a significant number of middle-class African Americans, could support such independence only if it were couched in standard, "official" English.

Some legislators around the country quickly sought to outlaw Ebonics. A resolution was introduced in the Virginia legislature to that end, and a Michigan lawmaker hoped to make English the official language of that state in order to make it clear that there was no room for Official Ebonics (Cole 1997). One young African American commentator went even further, asking hopefully when African American students would be required to use only English in the classroom (Carter 1998). Carter, a journalism fellow at the conservative Heritage Foundation, expresses the sentiment of many middle-class African Americans, who think of Ebonics not as a separate language but as simply bad English. Carter adds:

> Elevating bad grammar and street slang to the status of a language is not the way to raise standards of achievement for our children. . . . There's nothing worse that a school board could do to ruin a child's self-esteem than to create a special language for

blacks. . . . I mean, it's one thing to "get black" with friends and family members in private and quite another to try to elevate a form of bad English, regardless of its origin, to the level of a language.

Responses to the Ebonics issue at the University of Illinois suggest that the view of language in the black community is more complex. While both African American faculty and students were clear in their insistence that the rights of Oakland's black children were endangered, they split on the issue of language. In a number of forums held on campus to discuss the question of Ebonics, a kind of generation gap made itself evident when African Americans commented on the situation. Many of the black faculty participating in these forums had come from working-class or rural backgrounds and were the first in their families to attend college. Many of them had also come of age during the civil rights era. They tended to support Ebonics, the viability of Black English as a medium of communication, and Oakland's initial radical stand. In contrast, many black students, particularly those from suburban middle- and upper-middle-class families, rejected the whole concept of Ebonics, insisting like Carter that they had been raised to believe there were no significant racial varieties of language, just good English and bad English. Ebonics to them was not the radical cause the faculty seemed to favor; instead, the students saw Ebonics at best as slang, at worst as what one student labeled "Leroy English," the stereotypical, incorrect English of the inner city whose celebration or exploitation they found embarrassing and essentially racist. To these students, more conservative than their faculty mentors, the inner city could have no viable official language separate from and equal to the official language of the whole country.

The 1995–1997 Language of Government Acts

Since the 1980s, the U.S. Congress has annually considered, and failed to act on, measures to make English the official language of the nation. Although close to half the states now have official language laws, most of them enacted in the past fifteen years, constitutional amendments making English official seem destined to die in legislative committee. A constitutional amendment was introduced once again in 1997 (H.J. Res. 37). It is a bit more detailed than previous amendment proposals, requiring English in some specific instances, and like other official language amendments, it is likely to die in committee:

> Section 1. The English language shall be the official language of the United States. As the official language, the English language shall be used for all public acts including every order, resolution, vote or election, and for all records and judicial proceedings of the Government of the United States and the governments of the several States.

> Section 2. The Congress and the States shall enforce this article by appropriate legislation.

Recently, supporters of Official English, who have kept up the pressure for legislation at the state level, have tried a second approach at the federal level, introducing bills in the House and the Senate designed to make English the official language not of the nation but of its government. Such laws require only a simple majority of the House and Senate, plus a presidential signature, whereas passage of a constitutional amendment requires a two-thirds vote in each house, followed by ratification by three-fourths of the states. These federal language bills have had various names, but they tend to be similar in content and intent. The 1996 Language of Government Act (LOGA), which passed the House on August 1 of that year but died for lack of action in the Senate, is a fair representative of the genre. It was reintroduced and passed again by the House in 1997.

The LOGA was first introduced by the late Representative Bill Emerson (R-MO) in 1995. Arguing that "it has been the long-standing national belief that full citizenship in the United States requires fluency in English," the bill provides that "the official language of the Federal Government is English." Its latest version notes as well that "English is the preferred language of communication among citizens of the United States" (H.R. 123 1996, 1). LOGA's supporters claim that 86 percent of citizens and 81 percent of immigrants want this bill: "The vast majority of citizens in this country are fed up with the present day situation which has fostered linguistic welfare."

But the LOGA goes beyond simply designating English the language of government—something it has clearly been for more than two hundred years. LOGA repeals the Federal Voting Rights Act of 1965, which provides for federal ballots in languages other than English under certain conditions. That repeal was strongly opposed by the Justice Department, which argued, "But our language alone has not made us a nation. We are united as Americans by the principles enumerated in the Constitution and Bill of Rights: freedom of speech, representative democracy, respect for due process, and equality and protection under the law" (U.S. Department of Justice 1996, 1).

The LOGA bans naturalization ceremonies in languages other than English. Further, it requires that federal employees use English when they conduct official business, and it asks them to promote the language as well: federal officials "shall have an affirmative obligation to preserve and enhance the role of English as the official language of the Federal Government" (H.R. 123 1996, §162). How they are to do this is not specified, but drafters of the bill clearly feared that the government might go so far as to create an environment hostile to English or its speakers, for they also added these provisions to the LOGA:

1. No person shall be denied services, assistance, or facilities, directly or indirectly provided by the Federal Government, solely because the person communicates in English.

2. Every person in the United States is entitled to communicate with representatives of the Federal Government in English; to receive information from or contribute information to the Federal Government in English; and to be informed of or be subject to official orders in English. (H.R. 123 1995, §163)

The bill's sponsors cite no instance of anyone ever being denied government services for communicating in English, nor do they demonstrate that anyone has ever been dissuaded from using English when communicating with the government. Moreover, all governmental orders and regulations have always been drafted in English. When regulations are translated from English to other languages, the English version has always been the only valid version should questions arise. In case the government fails to use English or discriminates against someone's use of English, however, the LOGA provides a remedy: "A person injured by a violation of this chapter may in a civil action . . . obtain appropriate relief" (H.R. 123 1996, §164).

LOGA recognizes some exceptions to its general rules. Foreign languages may be taught. Also excluded from the act are requirements under the Individuals with Disabilities Education Act, and actions required by national security, international relations, trade, or commerce. Languages other than English may be used to protect public health and safety or to protect the victims of crimes or criminal defendants. The Bureau of the Census may use other languages in carrying out its mission. And, to calm the fears of those representatives who wondered aloud whether foreign words would have to be removed from the national currency, LOGA permits using terms of art such as *habeas corpus* or phrases from languages other than English, for example *e pluribus unum*—a motto which, curiously enough, renders an important aspect of "full citizenship in the United States" in a language other than English. And finally, LOGA provides that federal officials may communicate orally in a language other than English while on official business if circumstances require it.

Hearings on the LOGA were held before the House Subcommittee on Early Childhood Youth and Families on October 18 and November 1, 1995, with only "friendly" witnesses permitted to testify (House Subcommittee 1995; academics were specifically excluded as witnesses). The majority report coming out of the hearings, written by the House Republicans on the committee, after a nod to diversity, declares, "throughout the history of the United States, the common thread binding individuals of differing backgrounds has been a common language. In order to preserve unity in diversity, and to prevent division along linguistic lines, the Federal Government should maintain a language common to all people." English, in the majority view, will empower immigrants, and any money saved through the adoption of the LOGA would go to teaching English to immigrants.

Supporters of the bill played on fears of immigration and overpopulation, arguing that over the past few decades, congressional action and inaction resulted in a balkanized national language policy. They complained that publishing government documents in languages other than English discourages immigrants from learning English. And they noted with alarm that the Bureau of the Census reports that over 320 different languages are spoken in the United States. In rebuttal, opponents of the bill reminded the committee that a General Accounting Office (GAO) investigation, ordered by the Republican majority on the committee whose line has consistently been that the government is wasting a phenomenal amount of money on translation, found a mere 265, or .06 percent of 400,000 federal documents, published in foreign languages. In the face of this evidence, the House Republicans on the committee promptly switched their attention away from numbers: "The point is not to quibble over facts and figures but rather to focus on the bigger policy: is America going to advocate policies like the learning of English to empower people to realize the American dream? Or, do we continue the trend toward the balkanization of languages, encouraging people to interact only with those of similar backgrounds?" (House Subcommittee 1995).

In their minority report, House Democrats produced an Alaskan language specialist who argued that "[t]he common thread has not been a common language but rather to 'promote the general welfare and secure the blessings of liberty to ourselves and to our posterity'. . . . Division along linguistic lines has only been created historically by Federal Government policy." Democrats further argued that even though Republicans have consistently opposed frivolous lawsuits, the LOGA would encourage such court-clogging suits by permitting anyone who felt wronged to sue in civil court.

The Senate Committee on Governmental Affairs also held a hearing on its version of the LOGA on March 7, 1996. At this hearing, Hawaiian and Native American groups argued that the bill should pass only if it is amended to "guarantee the revitalization and perpetuation of the indigenous languages of the United States" (Senate Committee 1996). Although the Navajo Nation opposed the LOGA, other Native American groups made support for their languages a condition of their support for the LOGA: "In recognizing English as the official language of the United

States, Congress must, at the same time, reaffirm Indian sovereign rights regarding the use of our own languages to protect an important part of Native American culture from becoming extinct." The statement of the National Congress of American Indians stressed that Native Americans are sovereign nations, not in the same class as the immigrants who are the target of the LOGA: "American Indian and Alaska Native people . . . are not simply 'ethnic groups.'"

As a result of the testimony of these Native American groups, the Senate bill was amended to read, "The official language of the Government of the United States is English *except for special provisions for Native American languages which are the national languages of the United States.*" The House version of the bill was similarly amended to read, "The act shall not limit the preservation or use of Native Alaskan or Native American languages."

English Plus

In addition to the various Language of Government acts, members of Congress have also been presented with a more user-friendly position in the English Plus Resolution, which recognizes both the importance of learning English and the need to learn other languages. In seeking to preserve the heritage of Native American, Hawaiian, and Alaskan languages, to strengthen the United States in the world political and economic arenas, and to protect those whose English is limited, the resolution reminds Americans of their historical diversity, promotes multilingualism as a valuable asset in the global economy, notes that English is spoken by 94 percent of U.S. residents, and warns that English Only measures

> violate traditions of cultural pluralism, divide communities along ethnic lines, jeopardize the provision of law enforcement, public health, education, and other vital services to those whose English is limited, impair government efficiency; . . . represent an unwarranted Federal regulation of self-expression, abrogate constitutional rights to freedom of expression and equal protection of the laws . . . and contradict the spirit of the 1923 Supreme Court case Meyer v. Nebraska, wherein the Court declared that "The

protection of the Constitution extends to all; to those who speak other languages as well as to those born with English on the tongue." (H. Con. Res. 4 1997)

Both the Language of Government Acts of 1997 and the English Plus Resolution remain in committee at this writing.

The Future of Official Language Legislation

It would be rash to predict what will happen to official language legislation in the United States in the future. To illustrate, California's Proposition 227 ending bilingual education was passed on June 2, 1998. It has already survived one major test in federal court, and opponents of the measure have appealed to the U.S. Court of Appeals for the Ninth Circuit. As I write, the public schools of Los Angeles, California, are scurrying to dismantle their twenty-five-year-old bilingual education system and implement an English immersion curriculum before the opening of the fall term less than a week from now, not even sure that what they come up with will be legal under Proposition 227. The law reads, in part, "all children in California public schools shall be taught English by being taught in English" (Anderson 1998). English immersion is mandated for a period "not normally intended to exceed one year," and mainstreaming is to occur once students achieve "a good working knowledge" of English, though the law does not specify what that may mean.[1]

At a recent meeting, school principals faced with structured immersion asked Los Angeles district officials how much non-English talk would be permitted in a classroom full of non-Anglophones? None? Ten percent? Twenty percent? And in what contexts? Introducing new material? Reviewing what students should already know? The law specifies that English-immersion classes conduct "nearly all" their business in English. The meeting produced no clear answers. Other school districts in California, including Oakland and San Francisco, have announced that they plan to ignore Proposition 227 and keep their bilingual programs until directed otherwise by the courts, while still other districts see no problem either making the switch to immersion or mainstreaming non-Anglophones after they have completed their one year of structured English immersion. The law does provide that parents may apply annually to have their children kept in bilingual programs, and state education officials have advised school districts that such petitions must be approved unless there is "substantial evidence" to deny them. In addition, any school with twenty or more approved petitions must offer bilingual education. The situation in California is currently fluid, or chaotic, depending on who is describing it. Supporters of Proposition 227 complain that the state has misinterpreted the law, and that local districts are going out of their way to subvert the will of the people, as expressed in the referendum. The state itself has said it will review its implementation decisions in four months to see what changes need to be made.

At the federal level, no one can tell if this will be the year for passage of a Puerto Rico statehood referendum. While the Speaker of the House, Newt Gingrich, on record in the past as favoring Official English, has openly begun to court southwestern Hispanic/Latino voters for his party, the Republican Senate majority leader, Trent Lott, has stated that there is no room on the calendar for a Senate vote on the Puerto Rico issue. The Language of Government Act continues to hover in the wings. President Clinton, who openly opposed Proposition 227, has indicated that he would not sign such a bill, if passed, though he did sign Arkansas's official language law when he was governor of that state.

What does remain clear is that official language legislation is not necessary. According to Dorothy Waggoner (1995), in her analysis of 1990 census data, although the foreign-born population of the United States increased between 1980 and 1990, the percentage of immigrants with difficulty speaking English who come from homes where languages other than English are spoken is actually declining. Waggoner concludes:

> People who speak languages other than English are less likely to have difficulty speaking English now than a decade ago. English-speaking difficulty is directly related to the length of time . . . spent in the United States. Native-born home speakers of non-English languages are less likely to have difficulty than immi-

grants and immigrants who have spent more than ten years here are less likely to have difficulty than their counterparts in 1980. (1995, 2)

Despite the fact that Miami or an urban emergency room may seem like a "foreign country" to some American visitors, all indicators confirm that English is alive and well in the United States. The United States, without an official language law, has had more success getting its population to speak a common language than any of the seventy-nine nations of the world with official language laws on their books. The languages in danger of disappearing are the minority languages, and it is imperative that the nation craft its language policy to address that problem rather than to protect an English language that is doing fine on its own.

Note

1. As expected, the California proposition found followers in other states, too. Arizona has Proposition 203 on the November 2000 ballot, and the issues are similar to California's Proposition 227. See more on this in the introduction.

Works Cited

Anderson, Nick. 1998. "Proposition 227 Speaks the Language of Uncertainty." *Los Angeles Times* [Online], July 29. Available: http://www.latimes.com. Also available: http://www.nabe.org/press/reprints/980729f.htm.

Baron, Dennis. 1990. *The English-Only Question: An Official Language for Americans?* New Haven: Yale University Press.

Carter, Stefani. 1998. "Ebonics." *Nando Times* [Online], July 28. Available: http://www.nando.net

Cincinnati Enquirer. 1995. July 19. B1.

Coddington, Brian. 1998. "GOP Talking English Only." *Spokane Spokesman-Review* [Online], May 2. Available: http://www.spokesman review.com

Cole, Kenneth. 1997. "Lawmaker: Make English Official State Language." *Detroit News* [Online], Jan. 24. Available: http://www.detnews.com

Davenport, Paul. 1998. "Arizona Court Strikes Down English-Only Law." *Arizona Republic* [Online], April 28. Available: http://www.arizona republic.com

H. Con. Res. 4. 1997. English Plus Resolution, Jan. 7.

H.J. Res. 37. 1997. English Language Amendment. Feb. 4.

Hopwood, William. 1997. "Creating Our Own Quebec." *Washington Post*, Sept. 30. A20.

House Subcommittee on Early Childhood Youth and Families. 1995. *Hearings on the Language of Government Act*, Oct. 18 and Nov. 1.

H.R. 123. 1995. Language of Government Act of 1995. Jan. 4. Available: http://thomas.loc.gov/cgi-bin/bdquery/R?d104:FLD003:@1 (Rep+Emerson)

H.R. 123. 1996. Bill Emerson Language Empowerment Act of 1996. Aug. 1. Available: http://ourworld.compuserve.com/homepages/ jwcrawford/hr123d.htm

H.R. 856. 1997. "An Act to Provide a Process Leading to Full Self-Government for Puerto Rico." The United States/Puerto Rico Political Status Act, 105th Congress, 2nd session.

Lee, Chang-rae. 1996. "Mute in an English-Only World." *New York Times*, April 18. A17.

Lewin, Tamar. 1994. "Suit Says Disney's 'English Only' Policy Is Bias." *New York Times*, Oct. 13. A14.

Mears, Teresa. 1997. "Miami Hispanics Losing Their Spanish." *Boston Globe* [Online], Oct. 5. Available: http://www.boston.com/globe.

Oakland Unified School District. 1995. Resolution passed on Dec. 18; revised Jan. 15, 1996.

Perez-Pena, Richard. 1996. "English-Only Bill Is Vetoed." *New York Times*, Sept. 14.

Sanchez, Mary. 1998. "Backers of English as Missouri's Official Language Add Incentive to Plan." *Kansas City Star* [Online], Mar. 19. Available: http://www.kcstar.com

Senate Committee on Governmental Affairs. 1996. *Hearings on the Language of Government Act.* Mar. 7.

Sengupta, Somini. 1997. "Asian Students' Advances Often Obscure Their Poverty." *New York Times* [Online], Nov. 9. Available: http://www.nytimes.com

U.S. Department of Justice. 1996. Letter to the Honorable Ted Stevens, Chairman of the Committee on Governmental Affairs, U.S. Senate. May 14. Available: http://ourworld.compuserve.com/homepages/JWCRAWFORD/doj.htm. Accessed Oct. 16, 2000.

Verhovek, Sam Howe. 1995. "Mother Scolded by Judge for Speaking Spanish." 1995. *New York Times,* Aug. 30. A9.

———. 1997. "Clash of Cultures Tears Texas City." *New York Times,* Sept. 30. A10.

Waggoner, Dorothy. 1995. "U.S. Census Analysis." *Numbers and Needs* (Nov.): 1–2.

CHAPTER TWO

Statement on the Civil Liberties Implications of Official English Legislation before the United States Senate Committee on Governmental Affairs, December 6, 1995

EDWARD M. CHEN

American Civil Liberties Union of Northern California

Mr. Chairman and Members of the Committee:

Thank you for the opportunity to testify before you today on behalf of the American Civil Liberties Union (ACLU). The ACLU is a membership-based nonprofit organization representing more than 275,000 members dedicated to preserving civil rights and liberties protected under our Constitution. Since our founding seventy-five years ago, the ACLU has defended the rights of all, particularly unpopular and disenfranchised groups, against unconstitutional discrimination and restrictions on their liberties. Early in our history, the ACLU represented immigrant workers deported and imprisoned because of their political beliefs. We have long been active in protecting racial minorities from discrimination in connection with their right to vote, to participate in the political process, to obtain equal education and opportunity, and to obtain equal access to important governmental services and benefits.

The ACLU believes that English Only laws—laws such as S.356 that make English the "official" language of government— and particularly those which broadly restrict the government's ability to use languages other than English in communicating and delivering services to non-English-speaking Americans, violate civil rights and liberties. They do so in three ways.

First, by restricting the government's ability to communicate with and provide services to non-English-speaking Americans, many of whom are children and elderly citizens, English Only laws deny fair and equal access to government. These limits, especially as they apply to such rights and services as voting assistance, education in a comprehensible language, health services and information, financial assistance such as social security, and police protection, infringe upon important and fundamental rights.

Second, by prohibiting the government from communicating with its citizens in any language other than English, English Only laws violate the First Amendment rights of elected officials and public employees. They also impair the First Amendment rights of limited-English-proficient residents to receive vital information and to petition the government for redress of grievances.

Third, English Only laws are based on assumptions predicated on false and disparaging stereotypes about today's immigrants. Thus they foster anti-immigrant bigotry and intolerance and exacerbate ethnic tensions.

English Only laws are unnecessary, patronizing, and divisive. They run contrary to the spirit of tolerance and respect of diversity embodied in our Constitution.

Official English Laws Are Unnecessary

Laws declaring English the "official" language of government are entirely unnecessary. Since the founding of our nation, America has been linguistically diverse. There have been hundreds of Native American and African languages, and a substantial population of Spanish speakers in Florida, Texas, California, and the Southwest, French speakers in Louisiana and New England, German speakers in Pennsylvania, Dutch speakers in New York, and Swedish speakers in Delaware (Marshall 1986, 9). Yet the primacy of English as America's common language has never been in jeopardy.

Nor is it in jeopardy now. U.S. English, the largest organization dedicated to the establishment of English Only laws since 1983, concedes that 97 percent of Americans already speak English. According to the 1990 census, 13.5 percent of Americans over the age of five speak a language other than English at home. Of that 13.5 percent, 7.8 percent speak English "very well," and another 3.2 percent speak English "well." Only 2.9 percent reported that they spoke English either "not very well" or "not at all" (U.S. Bureau of Census 1989, 1990). Even within the largest single language minority, Spanish speakers, approximately 80 percent speak English (U.S. Bureau of the Census 1993). Just as significant, studies show that today's immigrants are learning English as fast as the immigrants of prior years. For instance, half of all recent Mexican immigrants in California already speak English. Among first-generation Mexican Americans, 95 percent are proficient in English; for second-generation Mexican Americans, the transformation is even more dramatic—more than 50 percent have lost their mother tongue (McCarthy and Valdez 1985). The rate of language assimilation among language minorities is just as rapid as in previous generations (Siobhan and Valdivieso 1988, i–x). A recent study examining English acquisition of immigrants found that, whereas approximately slightly more than 30 percent of five- to fourteen-year-old Latino immigrants spoke English very well in 1980, 70 percent spoke English very well ten years later in 1990. For Asian immigrants in the same group, the percentage went from a little over 40 percent to over 80 percent during that ten-year period (Myers 1995).

Official English laws are not needed to teach immigrants the importance of learning English. Immigrants more than any other Americans fully appreciate the importance of learning English. Each day they must negotiate the hardships of surviving in a society that is largely monolingual English, whether looking for a job; trying to get information about their children's school; communicating with health providers, law enforcement officers, or bus drivers; or even buying groceries or clothing. One need only look to the tens of thousands of immigrants waiting to get into adult English classes in Los Angeles and New York in order to understand their appreciation for the importance of learning English (Bliss 1988; New York Immigration Coalition 1994, 4; Woo 1986, 1). Indeed, in 1987 immigrants filed a lawsuit in Los Angeles Superior Court to force the county to expand English classes for non-English-speaking immigrants (*Perez et al. v. Los*

Angeles Unified School Dist. et al. 1987). And immigrant parents know very well that their children cannot fully participate in the economic mainstream of the United States without becoming proficient in English. That is why a survey taken in Florida in 1985 revealed that 98 percent of Latinos, as compared to 94 percent of White and Black parents, felt it was essential that their children read and write English "perfectly" ("New Miami Survey" 1985). Immigrants do not need a patronizing proclamation about English by Congress. What immigrants need are English classes. Ironically, "Official" English proposals do nothing to increase the resources needed to provide English instruction.

Nor are English Only laws needed to stem excessive bilingualism in government operations, as claimed by English Only proponents. In a study done by the Government Accounting Office (GAO) at the request of Senator Richard C. Shelby (R-AL) and Representatives William F. Clinger (R-PA) and Bill Emerson (R-MO), the GAO found that for the five-year period from 1990 through 1994, of the 400,000 documents printed by the federal government, only 265, or .065 percent, were printed in languages other than English (Bowling 1995).

If anything, despite forward-looking efforts to provide minimal language assistance to non-English-speakers through bilingual education and the Voting Rights Act, language minorities are vastly underserved. Even in California, which has the most comprehensive set of laws in the nation aimed at providing language assistance through governmental agencies (Crawford 1992a, 303–11), it is not uncommon for a Vietnamese cancer patient to wait for hours in a Bay Area county hospital waiting room until a translator is available (Chin 1991), for the five-year-old son of a Chinese-speaking couple to choke and lapse into a coma because emergency dispatchers could not understand their calls for help (Farrell 1987), for Latino earthquake victims to receive no assistance from relief workers who do not speak Spanish (Rojas and Asimov 1994), for a Cuban immigrant to be shot and killed by the police because no officer was available to command him to stop in Spanish (Coughalay 1989), for Spanish-speaking workers to be disproportionately injured by workplace toxic hazards because of the lack of Spanish-speaking OSHA inspectors and doctors, or warnings posted in Spanish (Freed

1993, 1), or for more than 50 percent of limited-English-proficient (LEP) students in California to receive no instruction in their native language (Macias 1995, 1). The harsh reality is that language minorities remain underserved, and the national resources devoted to foreign-language assistance, particularly outside of public education, are relatively minuscule.[1]

What few services and publications are provided in multiple languages make government more efficient, not less efficient as English Only proponents contend. Barring the government from choosing in specific circumstances to communicate with its non-English-speaking citizenry in languages comprehensible to these communities will result in miscommunications and hinder the implementation of governmental policies such as protecting public health (through multilingual notices, counseling, and so forth), enhancing water and resource conservation (through foreign-language bulletins and educational pamphlets), increasing tax collections (by use of bilingual service representatives and tax forms), and ensuring law compliance (by providing bilingual investigators; interpreters in administrative and criminal proceedings; translations of compliance bulletins issued by OSHA, EPA, Department of Commerce, etc.). For instance, the *Wall Street Journal* recently reported on the influx of immigrants to the prairie town of Worthington, Minnesota. Ethnic tensions over complaints that Vietnamese immigrant fishermen were overfishing the lake were diffused when local fishermen translated state fishing regulations into Vietnamese. The town then decided to prepare Laotian-, Vietnamese-, and Spanish-language videos on topics such as recycling that are foreign to newcomers (Kaufman 1995). It makes no sense to have a sweeping rule requiring English Only that straightjackets executive agencies and other governmental bodies from making particularized judgments about the need to use languages in addition to English under appropriate circumstances. Indeed, a recent decision by the Court of Appeals for the Ninth Circuit striking down Arizona's Official English law, the court found that the government's use of languages other than English in communicating with LEP residents increased rather than decreased efficiency, and that a law broadly prohibiting the use of different languages served no significant governmental interest (*Yñiguez v. Arizonans for Official-English* 1995).

Official English Laws Deny Important and Fundamental Services to Language Minorities

The actual effect of English Only laws on the provision of services depends on their text. Most of the laws which have been passed at the state and local levels, as well as the federal proposals pending in Congress such as S. 356, contain broad and ambiguous terms. For instance, what does it mean for the government to have "an affirmative obligation to preserve and enhance the role of English as the official language" of government (H.R. 123; S. 356.)? What is the scope of the injunction that "[t]he Government shall conduct its official business in English"? This wording is ambiguous even about whether the supplementary use of other languages in addition to English is permitted in official communications. For example, the California attorney general has interpreted California's 1986 Official English law as merely requiring that official governmental acts be conducted *at least* in English (Shimomura 1987). Do these provisions mean that a social security counselor cannot convey important information to a Chinese-speaking applicant or recipient otherwise entitled to benefits? Would they overturn existing requirements that federally funded migrant and community health centers and alcohol abuse and treatment programs provide language assistance where there are a substantial number of non-English-speakers (see H.R. 123, §175)? Do these provisions bar a member of congress from communicating with his or her constituents in Spanish, Russian, or Navajo? Do they prohibit the Immigration and Naturalization Service (INS) from employing interpreters to interview asylum applicants, speak with witnesses in an investigation, or translate in deportation proceedings? (Interpreters are used in the physical and mental examination of alien immigrants who want to enter the United States.) Would the Environmental Protection Agency (EPA) be barred from issuing or requiring the issuance of a Spanish-language summary of an environmental impact report on a proposed toxic waste site where the affected residents are primarily Spanish-speaking migrant workers? Will these laws affect the issuance of Federal Communications Commission (FCC) licenses to foreign-language television and radio broadcast stations? (It should be noted here that the largest organized proponent of English Only laws, U.S. English, has in the past opposed FCC licensing of Spanish-language stations [Crawford 1992b, 201–2].) Significantly, the definition of "official business" contained in S. 356 does not except "actions or documents that are primarily informational or educational," as had section 175. And the exception for "actions or documents that protect the public health" contained in S. 356 remains ill defined. Is providing individualized drug rehabilitation or rape counseling in Spanish or Chinese protective of "public" health? What is the line between public and private health?

Moreover, S. 356 does not appear to restrict only government conduct; it restricts "services, assistance, or facilities, *directly or indirectly* provided by the Government" (§ 163(b) [emphasis added]). Does this provision mean that services provided in Spanish or Russian by a private entity under a federal contract that receives federal monies would violate this provision? Would it mean that all state and local governments which receive federal money could not engage in foreign-language assistance to LEP residents? Would a city or county receiving federal funds be prevented from hiring bilingual police officers, social workers, or counselors? Would this law bar local school districts from providing bilingual education?

The potential mischief of Official English laws cannot be overestimated. At the very least, S. 356 would open up a Pandora's box of endless litigation on these and other issues, including the constitutionality of the law itself. More important, S. 356 and laws like it can cause substantial and concrete harm. Other English Only laws have been interpreted to impose severe restrictions on the use of languages other than English by government and its employees and officials. The first of such laws passed in recent times was enacted by Dade County, Florida, in 1980. Its effect was to bar distribution of bilingual materials on fire prevention; to stop the publication of Metrorail schedules in foreign languages; to ban Spanish-language consumer information and prenatal advice by the county hospital in Creole; and to discontinue funding for ethnic festivals (Castro, Haun, and Roca 1990, 156; Crawford 1992b, 108–9; also Dade County 1990). An Official English constitutional initiative passed by 51 percent of Arizona voters in 1988 has been held to bar legislatures from communicating with constituents in Spanish or Navajo, and bar public employees generally from communicating with the public in a language other than English (*Yñiguez v. Mofford* 1990).

Some current congressional proposals are explicit about the termination of specific language-assistance programs. H.R. 739, for instance, would expressly require that "[c]ommunications by officers and employees of the Government of the United States with United States citizens shall be in English" and repeal provisions of the Elementary and Secondary Education Act of 1965 and the Voting Rights Act of 1965, which provide for bilingual education and voting assistance. H.R. 1005 requires the federal government "to conduct its official business in English, including publications, income tax forms and informational materials." And as mentioned above, S. 356 contains no exception for informational or educational materials.

English Only laws which ban the provision of governmental services to non-English-speakers unjustly target and disenfranchise language minorities. Such deliberate withdrawal of and ban on services to this already disadvantaged and insular sector of the American public is callous and mean-spirited. It is also unconstitutional. Moreover, by discriminating against language minorities, English Only laws contravene international standards of human rights as well. The Universal Declaration of Human Rights, which interprets the United Nations Charter, specifically bans discrimination on the basis of language as well as race, sex, and religion (Charter of the United Nations 1948). The International Covenant on Civil and Political Rights, to which the United States is a signatory, also expressly bans language discrimination (see articles 26, 27).

The Right to Vote

The right to vote is a fundamental and inalienable constitutional right (*Reynolds v. Simms* 1964; *Dunn v. Blumstein* 1972. Laws and devices, such as literacy tests, that were designed to impose burdens on minority groups in the exercise of their franchise violate that right (*Louisiana v. United States* 1965; *United States v. Mississippi* 1965; *Alabama v. United States* 1962; *Schnell v. Davis* 1949; *South Carolina v. Katzenbach* 1966). A broad ban requiring the withdrawal of bilingual assistance to LEP citizens (many of whom are elderly and have limited English-*speaking* proficiency, but whose English-*reading* ability is insufficient to comprehend complex and lengthy ballots and voting materials) imposes such a burden (Loo 1985). That burden will fall most heavily on older Americans, who are the least likely to learn English as a second language, and who also have the greatest need for bilingual assistance (Veltman 1988).[2] The injurious impact of such a ban on ethnic minority bilingual voters cannot be overstated. A 1982 study for the Mexican American Legal Defense and Educational Fund found that 70 percent of monolingual Spanish-speaking citizens would be less likely to register to vote if bilingual assistance were eliminated. If bilingual ballots were unavailable, 72 percent of the monolingual Spanish speakers would be less likely to cast a vote (Brischetto 1982, 68, 100). S. 356 does not exempt voting assistance from its broad injunction that the government conduct its official business in English.

Education

Although not currently recognized as a "fundamental" constitutional right (*San Antonio Independent School District v. Rodriguez* 1973), education is nonetheless an important right affecting the futures and destinies of millions of schoolchildren (*Plyler v. Doe* 1982). As the Supreme Court stated in *Brown v. Board. of Education* (1954) forty years ago:

> Today, education is perhaps the most important function of state and local Governments. . . . In these days, it is doubtful that any child may reasonably be expected to succeed in life if he is denied the opportunity of an education. Such an opportunity, where the state has undertaken to provide it, is a right which must be made available to all on equal terms.

The purpose of bilingual education is to serve children who do not yet speak English in a language comprehensible to them during the period in which they are learning English. Denying these children this meaningful form of education amounts to denying them an equal educational opportunity (*Lau v. Nichols* 1974). In holding that the failure to provide language assistance to non-English-speaking immigrant students violates Title VI of the Civil Rights Act of 1964, the Supreme Court stated:

> [T]here is no equality of treatment merely by providing students with the same facilities, textbooks, teachers and curriculum; for students who do not understand English are effectively foreclosed from any meaningful education. (414 U.S. 566)

While there has been a longstanding debate about the effectiveness of different pedagogical techniques, it would be premature and inappropriate to permit a politically driven agenda to end bilingual education.[3] S. 356 would permit the use of non-English languages for the "teaching of foreign languages" (§165) but says nothing about the use of native-language instruction in teaching immigrant students.

Official English Laws Violate Equal Protection Principles

In addition to infringing on voting and educational rights, English Only laws which systematically limit the access of language minorities to governmental services are constitutionally suspect because (1) language discrimination is functionally equivalent to national origin discrimination, and (2) language minorities are a prime example of a "discrete and insular minority" (*United States v. Carolene Products Co* 1938) that deserves heightened judicial protection under the Equal Protection clause because language discrimination should be a quasi-suspect classification ("Quasi-Suspect Classes" 1981; *Olagues v. Russoniello* 1986/1987, in which bilingual voters requesting bilingual ballots have been held to be a suspect classification). Moreover, English Only laws which impose a sweeping ban on foreign-language assistance to language minorities constitute the *purposeful* disadvantaging of language minorities and are far more insidious than the mere failure to provide such assistance as a result of oversight or lack of funding. These laws disadvantage minorities "because of, not merely in spite of" their limited English proficiency (*Personnel Adminis-trator of Massachusetts v. Feeney* 1978).

Language Discrimination as an Aspect of National Origin Discrimination

There is an obvious correlation between a language and its cor-responding national origin group. The vast majority of non-En-glish-speakers are national origin minorities (Estrada 1984, 379–83). Ninety-seven percent of those who usually speak Span-ish are of Hispanic/Latino origin, and approximately 77 percent of Hispanic Americans speak Spanish. Similarly, a high correla-tion has been found between language and national origin among Asian Pacific Islanders (Gall and Gall 1993, 128). Moreover, lan-guage is the prime symbol of ethnicity and is a central aspect of the ethnic identity of national origin minorities (Fishman 1977, 23, 25–26). To many Americans, speech is a cultural indicator second in importance only to physical appearance (Conklin and Lourie 1983, 279). Language is often a proxy for race and ethnicity (*Gutierrez v. Municipal Court* 1988/1989; Califa 1989, 293). The Supreme Court recently observed: "It may well be, for certain ethnic groups and in some communities, that proficiency in a particular language, like skin color, should be treated as a surrogate for race under an equal protection analysis" (*Hernandez v. New York* 1991).[4] National origin discrimination, like race discrimination, is considered inherently suspect under Equal Pro-tection principles *(Hernandez v. Texas)*. Given the intimate and inextricable relationship between language and ethnicity, English Only laws which systematically and purposefully disenfranchise language minorities are therefore constitutionally suspect. This is particularly so given the fact that the negative images and ar-guments advanced by English Only supporters have at times been a thinly disguised attack on Hispanic/Latino immigrants in par-ticular (Califa 1989, 334). It is no coincidence that blatant anti-Hispanic/Latino statements have been attributed to the founder of U.S. English, Dr. John Tanton (Crawford 1992, 171–7), or that a former chair of the organization has argued that "we have Hispanic politicians who have an unstated or hidden agenda to turn California into a bilingual, bicultural state" (Lindsey 1986, 1).

Language Minorities Are a Discrete and Insular Minority

English Only laws are also constitutionally suspect because language minorities, as a class, are a discrete and insular minority "saddled with such disabilities, or subjected to such a history of purposeful unequal treatment, or relegated to such a position of political powerlessness as to command extraordinary protection from the majoritarian political process" (*San Antonio Independent School District v. Rodriguez* 1973).

Language minorities are also socioeconomically disadvantaged. Persons with limited English skills were more than two to three times more likely to have incomes below the poverty line, to have had far fewer years of formal education, and to be more unemployed than their fluent English-speaking counterparts (U.S. Bureau of the Census 1980, 623–26, 627). They suffer discrimination in practically all aspects of life, ranging from the justice system, to education, to social welfare, to employment (see U.S. Commission on Civil Rights 1970, 66–74, on discrimination against Spanish speakers in contacts with police and courts; U.S. Commission on Civil Rights 1972, 13–20, on discrimination against Spanish speakers in education). *Lau v. Nichols* (1974) stated that "the Chinese-speaking minority receive fewer benefits than the English-speaking majority from respondents' school system, which denies them a meaningful opportunity to participate in the [English Only] educational program—all earmarks of the discrimination banned by [federal Title VI] regulations."

In another case, concerning the refusal of the California Department of Social Services to provide bilingual welfare termination notices to those known unable to read and understand English, similar conclusions were reached (*Guerrero v. Carleson* 1973/1974). The implications of language discrimination in the workplace where "speak English Only" rules have been adopted, or where employers discriminate based on the employees' accent, have also been discussed ("English Only Rules" 1989, 387; Matsuda 1991, 1329).

As far as the language minorities' voting rights are concerned, Congress has expressly found that voting discrimination against citizens of language minorities is pervasive and national in scope. Such minority citizens are from environments in which the dominant language is other than English. In addition, they have been denied equal educational opportunities by State and local governments, resulting in severe disabilities and continuing illiteracy in the English language. The Congress further finds that, where State and local officials conduct elections only in English, language minority citizens are excluded from participating in the electoral process. In many areas of the country, this exclusion is aggravated by acts of physical, economic, and political intimidation. (42 U.S.C. § 1973b[f][1])[5]

In addition to voting discrimination, the political powerlessness of non-English-speakers is heightened by the simple fact that a disproportionate number of them are not citizens and cannot vote at all ("'Official English'" 1987, 1345, 1354).

Like other groups deemed to constitute a "suspect classification," language minorities have also been "subjected to a history of purposeful unequal treatment" (Rodriguez, supra, 411 U.S. at 28). Until the late 1800s, our nation had a tolerant policy toward linguistic diversity. Bilingualism in government and education was prevalent in many areas. The German language, for instance, was common in schools throughout the Midwest (Heath 1981, 12–14). But the influx of eastern and southern Europeans and Asians gave rise to nativist movements and restrictionist language laws in the late 1800s and early 1900s. The Federal Immigration Commission issued a report in 1911 contrasting the "old" and "new" immigrant. The report argued that the "old" immigrants had mingled quickly with native-born Americans and assimilated, while "new" immigrants from Italy, Russia, Hungary, and other countries were less intelligent, less willing to learn English, not assimilating, and criminally inclined (Leibowicz 1985, 519, 536–37).

In response, English-literacy requirements were erected as conditions for public employment, naturalization, immigration, and suffrage in order to "Americanize" these "new" immigrants and exclude those perceived to be lower class and "ignorant of our laws and language" (Leibowicz 1985, 533–39). The New York Constitution was amended to disenfranchise over one million Yiddish-speaking citizens by a Republican administration fearful of Jewish voters. The California Constitution was similarly amended to disenfranchise Chinese voters who were seen as a threat to the "purity of the ballot box" (*Castro v. California* 1970; Leibowitz 1969, 7, 34–35).

World War I gave rise to intense anti-German sentiment. A number of states, previously tolerant of bilingual schools, enacted extreme English Only laws. For instance, Nebraska and Ohio passed laws in 1919 and 1923 respectively prohibiting the teaching of German until the student passed the eighth grade. The Supreme Court in *Meyer v. Nebraska* (1923) ultimately held the Nebraska statute unconstitutional as a violation of due process.

Native Americans were also subject to federal English Only policies in the late 1800s and early 1900s. Native American children were separated from their families and forced to attend English-language boarding schools, where they were punished for speaking their native language[6] (Reyhner 1992, 41–47).

Thus English Only laws' discrimination and disenfranchisement of language minorities, a particularly vulnerable group, is profoundly unfair and constitutionally suspect. Moreover, to the extent that English Only laws restrict lower, more local levels of government from enacting laws, policies, and programs providing for bilingual services, these laws are unconstitutional for yet an additional reason. Such laws deny language minorities the ability to obtain favorable legislation from local political bodies and government agencies. For instance, under the Arizona Official English constitutional provision added by the voters in 1988, language minorities cannot obtain an ordinance written in their language from the local city council or a policy from the county department of social services, and this holds for bilingual forms, notices, and assistance as well. Indeed, language minorities cannot even seek from the Arizona legislature a statute requiring, funding, or even authorizing language assistance in matters such as voting, job training, or consumer fraud. In short, preemptive laws which disable state and local governments from deciding on their own to provide bilingual assistance (see, e.g., S. 356; H.R. 739, §167, which purports to preempt state and federal laws) exclude language minorities from equal participation in the normal political process and impose on them special burdens not placed on other groups (such as veterans and the disabled) that are free to seek favorable legislation at the local level. Barring such a discrete minority from equal access to the political process violates equal protection (*Washington v. Seattle School Dist. No. 1* 1982; *Hunter v. Erickson* 1969).

Official English Laws Violate the First Amendment

The prohibition in English Only proposals of the conduct of government business in any language other than English would bar communication between public employees and the public. The ban on informational materials in other languages significantly and affirmatively interferes with the ability of non-English-speaking Americans "to receive information and ideas," an interest protected by the First Amendment (*Virginia State v. of Pharmacy v. Virginia Citizens Consumer Council* 1976). It also interferes with public employees' First Amendment interest in communicating with language-minority citizenry (*Yñiguez v. Arizonans for Official-English* 1995). In the Yñiguez case, a state legislator and a public employee brought a lawsuit challenging an Arizona constitutional initiative which made English the "official" state language, and which required all public officials and employees to "act" only in English while performing government business. The legislator plaintiff was dismissed from the case on technical grounds. Before the passage of the law, the employee, a Latina employed by the Arizona Department of Administration who handled claims asserted against the state, had communicated in Spanish with monolingual Spanish-speaking claimants. The court found the provision facially invalid under the First Amendment, unconstitutionally restricting not only public employees' right to communicate with non-English-speaking members of the public, but also the right of elected officials to communicate with their constituents in Spanish, Navajo, or any other language.

Current congressional proposals make no exception for informational materials in languages other than English (e.g., S. 356; H.R. 123, 739, and 1005) and thus, like the Arizona initiative, could even prohibit elected officials from communicating with their non-English-speaking constituents. In the 1988 hearing before the House Committee on the Judiciary Subcommittee on Civil and Constitutional Rights on "Proposed Amendments to the Constitution to Establish English as the Official Language of the United States," Representative Stephen Solarz described the value of a Russian-language newsletter he sent out to the large community of émigrés from the Soviet Union in his district:

> My purpose in sending this newsletter was fourfold: I wanted to extend a personal welcome to these special individuals who had endured so much adversity in their lives in their successful quest to find freedom and democracy in this country. Secondly, I sought to explain my positions on issues that are very important to this community—Soviet Jewry and U.S.-Soviet relations. Third, I wanted to share with my constituents a heartwarming story of a family reunification that I was fortunate enough to help facilitate with the help of several hundred Brooklyn junior high school students. Finally, I urged my constituents to contact my office if they wanted me to intercede on behalf of relatives still awaiting permission to emigrate from the Soviet Union.
>
> Dozens of Soviet Jewish families responded to this newsletter. In their letters to me—most of them also written in Russian—I learned of many refusenik cases of which I was previously unaware. I was then able to contact Soviet officials in an effort to expedite their emigration requests. This was Congressman-constituent relations at its best. (Solarz 1988)

Enjoining elected government officials from communicating with their constituents in languages other than English would violate both the rights of elected officials under the First Amendment and the rights of constituents to receive important information, to communicate with elected officials, and to participate in the political process. In striking down a similar provision of the Arizona Constitution, Judge Brunetti stated:

> Article XXVIII offends the First Amendment not merely because it attempts to regulate ordinary political speech, but because it attempts to manipulate the political process by regulating the speech of elected officials. Freedom of speech is the foundation of our democratic process, and the language restrictions of Article XXVIII stifle informative inquiry and advocacy by elected officials. By restricting the free communication of ideas between elected officials and the people they serve, Article XXVIII threat-

ens the very survival of our democratic society. (*Yñiguez v. Arizonans for Official English* 1995, slip op. 12761–12762)

Official English Laws Foster Bigotry and Intolerance

The English language issue is one which concerns all of us but why is it necessary to adopt a measure declaring English as the official language? Is there a pending threat to the English language and our national unity, or have many Americans simply grown intolerant of our multilingual immigrant citizenry?
SENATOR JOHN MCCAIN, before the American
Bar Association, August 5, 1988

The answer, regrettably, is all too clear. Even if Official English laws did not ban the provision of particular services in languages other than English and were merely symbolic, the message underlying that symbolism is unmistakably pejorative of immigrants and a result of fear mongering. The critical question is why we now need a law declaring English the "official" language when we have lived without such a declaration for two hundred years. The answer invariably given by English Only proponents is that for the first time in U.S. history, the primacy of the English language—the purported common bond which holds this disparate society together—is being threatened by a new breed of immigrant, one who does not speak English, is not learning English the way previous immigrants did, and does not appreciate the importance of learning English. The following examples typify the rhetoric explaining the rationale for English Only laws:

1. I don't know about your forefathers, but when mine came to America, the first thing they did was learn English . . . .

2. Tragically, many immigrants these days refuse to learn English!

3. They never become productive members of the American society. They remain stuck in a linguistic and economic ghetto; many living off welfare and costing working Americans millions of tax dollars every year.

4. Incredibly, there is a radical movement in this country that not only promotes such irresponsible behavior, but actually wants to

give foreign languages the same status as English—the so-called "bilingual" movement . . . .

5. The leaders of the bilingual movement reject the "melting pot" concept that integrated the millions of immigrants who came to America and, working as one people, built the greatest nation on earth.

6. They don't want foreign language groups to learn English and assimilate into American culture—but they're funded by your tax dollars at the federal, state and local level to promote their divisive programs.

7. *As a result, they are slowly but surely driving a wedge between the English and non-English speaking members of our society.* (Solicitation letter from Jim Horn on behalf of English First, emphasis in original).

In a similar vein, Mauro Mujica, chairman of the board and CEO of U.S. English Inc. since 1993, stated in an interview on national television that Official English laws are needed "because unfortunately we have self-appointed leaders of minorities in this country that are telling these people that they do not need to learn the language" (Mujica 1995).

The equation of bilingualism with un-Americanism is a more vicious version of the nativist sentiment expressed in Theodore Roosevelt's oft-quoted diatribe at the turn of the century, "We have room for but one language here and that is the English language, for we intend to see that the crucible turns our people out as American, of American nationality, and not as dwellers in a polyglot boarding house." It is also a reiteration of the Americanization movement, which culminated in the Federal Immigration Commission's report in 1911 contrasting the "old" and "new" immigrants, and which led to restrictionist language policies. These arguments are predicated on false and negative stereotypes of today's immigrants and are informed by inaccurate assumptions about the language policy of our government. They portray today's immigrants, largely Latino and Asian, as being more resistant to assimilation, less willing and able to learn English, and more of a threat to the primacy of the English language and to Americanization than European immigrants of past generations. Nothing could be further from the truth. As discussed earlier, today's immigrants are no different from immigrants of the past in their desire to learn English and the speed at which they are learning English.

The episodes of the past should serve as reminders of the dangers of basing policy on false and negative stereotypes. To base legislation regulating language on false assertions not only makes for bad public policy, but by perpetuating false stereotypes, demonizing immigrants—an already unpopular segment of the public—and fostering the public perception that the English language and U.S. culture are being overrun by immigrants unwilling or unable to learn English, Official English laws also breed prejudice and bigotry. At best, regardless of its stated intent, such legislation is divisive and irresponsible, particularly in the current atmosphere of heightened racial tensions, economic insecurity, and anti-immigrant nativism. At worst, such legislation represents little more than hate mongering.

Immigrant bashing is as popular as ever. Although there are no official reporting mechanisms, the anecdotal evidence that does exist suggests that language discrimination, an aspect of the backlash against immigrants, is on the rise (Henry 1990,10; Nakao 1991, A1). For instance, after Californians passed Proposition 63 in 1986, making English the state's "official" language, a number of California cities enacted ordinances limiting the amount of foreign language that could appear on private business signs (*Asian American Business Group v. City of Pomona* 1989). In one case, Latino passengers on a Greyhound bus were threatened with expulsion for refusing to comply with the driver's demand that they stop speaking Spanish to each other (*Rodriguez et al. v. Greyhound Lines, Inc., et al.* 1987). In a much publicized decision, a Texas judge ordered a mother having custody over her five-year-old child to stop speaking Spanish to her at home, calling it "child abuse" ("Judge" 1995). Workplace complaints abound about discrimination against non-English-speakers and accented-English speakers, and about employees being disciplined for speaking to co-workers in their native tongue, and such complaints are particularly common in high immigration areas such as California. The Equal Employment Opportunity Commission (EEOC) reported approximately 120 active charges about speak-English-Only workplace rules in 1994 (*Garcia v. Spun Steak*

1993). Telephone complaint hotlines recently established by the Language Rights Project of the ACLU of Northern California, the Employment Law Center, and the Mexican American Legal Defense and Educational Fund (MALDEF) have received scores of complaints of language discrimination.

Legislation making English the "official" language implies that those who do not speak English are somehow less than "official," thus relegating them to second-class status in the eyes of the law. Because these laws are predicated on false and disparaging assumptions about today's immigrants, they can only fan the flames of prejudice, mistrust, and divisiveness. And because the disparaging arguments are directed against today's immigrants who are largely Hispanic/Latino and Asian, the racial undercurrents that lie beneath the surface of English Only efforts make these laws doubly dangerous and divisive. Rather than inspiring cohesion and unity, such legislation will, in the end, exacerbate societal discord and ethnic tension (Lindsey 1986, 1).

English Only Laws Undermine the Spirit of Tolerance and Pluralistic Ideals Embodied in Our Constitution

Undergirding the proponents' argument in favor of English Only laws is the assertion that the English language is the common bond or "social glue" that holds our diverse society together, and that multilingualism jeopardizes the social cohesion singularly owed to the English language. The proponents often cite the Quebec secessionist movement and even the conflict between Serbs and Croats as examples of societal discord and disintegration that occurs in the absence of a common tongue (H. Con. Res. 6, 5th "whereas" clause).

This assertion is wrong both empirically and as a matter of principle. Linguistic diversity need not lead to social conflicts. Switzerland, for instance, has four official languages. There is no single "official" language for the European Union. On the other hand, one need only look to deep conflicts in Northern Ireland and Bosnia to see that a common language does not ensure social tranquility. (Contrary to Mr. Emerson's assertion contained in H. Con. Res. 6, Serbs and Croats speak a common language.)

Indeed, America's own history dispels the notion that an "official" language is needed to preserve national unity. As noted previously, from the founding of this nation there have been substantial populations of speakers of languages other than English. Indeed, in the early 1800s a greater percentage of Americans spoke German than speak Spanish today (Castellanos 1992, 13, 17). Bilingual education in German and Yiddish was common throughout eastern cities and the Midwest. Official minutes of many town meetings in the Midwest were printed in German (Baron 1992, 40). The presence of language diversity and official bilingualism had no detrimental effect on the nation's social fabric.

A more recent example is New Mexico, with its historically large Spanish-speaking population and its proud history of tolerance and acceptance of Spanish heritage. New Mexico, which was officially bilingual, printed all government documents in English and Spanish. Far from ethnic balkanization, Hispanics/ Latinos in New Mexico enjoy one of the highest rates of political participation and hence integration in the nation. For example, U.S. census numbers reveal that the voter turnout in 1992 among Hispanics/Latinos was 60 percent in New Mexico, compared to less than 50 percent in California, Texas, and Arizona.

Where social tensions have arisen over language conflicts, such tensions are the *manifestation, not the cause,* of underlying social problems. Historically, language often has been used as a tool of social and political subjugation. It is the suppression of native and ethnic minority languages by a dominant group that most often gives rise to ethnic conflicts, be it the "Russification" of Soviet ethnic minorities, Franco's attempt to suppress the language rights of Basques and Catalans, or South Africa's attempt to impose the Afrikaner language as the language of instruction in the schools of Soweto. Racial and ethnic hostility are fostered not by language diversity, but by the attempts of certain language groups to suppress the use of other languages in political and social discourse. Leibowicz (1985) points out that social divisiveness has arisen and been exacerbated during the periods of intolerance and xenophobia that led to attempts to restrict the rights of language minorities. Karst (1986) describes Americanization and Know-Nothing movements, and enactment of restrictionist legislation, such as literacy laws, aimed at "new" immigrants during the nineteenth and early twentieth centuries. Beardsmore and Willemyns (1986) explain how tensions in bilingual nations such as Belgium are due not to bilingualism per se, but rather to historical factors and the lack of equality afforded people of subordinate language groups (117, 120–21).

Most scholars agree that the conflict between French and English speakers in Canada, often cited by English Only proponents as the prime example of the supposed threat posed by multilingualism, is the "result of the withdrawal of, or the failure to recognize, language rights rather than the result of linguistic tolerance and generosity" (Maldoff 1986, 105–6). According to commentators, the Quebec separatist movement is a reaction to perceived economic, political, and cultural subordination. If anything, Canada's tension was not caused but was in fact alleviated (at least temporarily) by the recognition of French as a co-official language (Woolard 1986, 191–92). There are vast differences in the roles of language, religion, political memory, geographic mobility, politics, and founding myths that make the Canadian/Quebec situation completely different from that of the United States (see Leibowicz 1985, 532–33). One of the most significant differences is the degree of language integration within the two societies. Twenty years ago, the rate of French speakers' acquisition of English was so slight that native-born Spanish speakers in the Southwest were *thirty times* more likely than French-speaking Québecois to adopt English as their dominant language (Crawford 1992b, 236). Even today only 32 percent of French speakers in Quebec are bilingual in English (compared to 80 percent of Hispanic Americans) (Swardson 1995). Most important, contrary to the inflammatory rhetoric of English Only proponents, there is no political movement in the United States to replace English with Spanish as our official language, or to effect the secession of the Southwest from the United States.

The ACLU does not question the importance of having a common language; obviously, a common language (or set of languages) is necessary as a practical matter for government and society to function efficiently. But the predicate assumption of English Only proponents—that English is the "social glue" that holds our society together—is facile. The common bond that unites Americans of all backgrounds, origins, and languages is our shared belief in and commitment to freedom, democracy, and liberty. That bond runs deeper than the English language.

Domestic tranquility is achieved not through coerced conformity but through tolerance and mutual respect. In this regard, Official English laws ignore the central teaching of the First Amendment. Many of the world's most virulent wars have been based on religious differences, yet, despite the diversity of religious faiths within the United States, our nation has avoided the intense heretical wars and violent theological conflicts experienced elsewhere. Why? Because the First Amendment guarantees tolerance and teaches mutual respect of different faiths rather than imposing an official orthodoxy. In contrast, Official English laws impose an official orthodoxy that breeds intolerance. It is intolerance, not diversity, which threatens our nation's unity.

Conclusion

Official English laws are unnecessary. If passed, they will impose material hardships, violate constitutional rights, and exacerbate ethnic tensions. We should celebrate, not fear, our diversity. The rich tapestry of ethnicities and languages that comprise the United States is one of our greatest strengths. Official English laws reflect our worst fears, not our highest ideals. The ACLU urges this committee to reject Official English proposals as unwise, unfair, and unconstitutional.

Notes

1. English Only proponents have contended that $8 to $10 billion is spent each year on bilingual education. That figure is unfounded, obtained by multiplying the number of LEP students by the total average spent on education per pupil. It ignores the fact that (a) only a small percentage of LEP students are in bilingual education programs, and (b) monies would have to be spent on these students even if there were no bilingual education. What is relevant is the *incremental* cost, if any, of bilingual education over and above the cost of alternative educational methods. At least one study by BW Associates in Berkeley, California, found no significant in-

cremental costs of bilingual education. In any event, the more relevant figure is $200 million, which is spent annually under Title VII of the Elementary and Secondary Education Act of 1965, 25 percent of which goes to non–bilingual education programs.

With respect to bilingual voting assistance, according to a 1984 GAO survey, 79 percent of 259 responding jurisdictions covered by the Voting Rights Act reported they incurred *no* costs in providing oral assistance; 101 of the responding jurisdictions that provided bilingual written assistance reported a cost totaling just $388,000 for such assistance (U.S. General Accounting Office 1986).

2. Sociologist Calvin Veltman (1988) found that approximately 80 percent of those aged fifteen to twenty-four at time of arrival will come to speak English on a regular basis. This figure declines inversely with the age of the immigrant at the time of arrival. Of those aged twenty-five to thirty-four at time of arrival, 70 percent will become regular English speakers. Twenty percent of those aged thirty-five to forty-four and 30 percent of those aged forty-five and over will come to speak English on a regular basis.

3. Most experts believe that bilingual education, properly administered, is an effective method of helping students make the transition to instruction in English (U.S. Government Accounting Office 1987; see also Crawford 1989). Indeed, the most comprehensive research on the subject indicates that the more extensive the instruction in the native language, the better the students perform in a variety of subjects, such as math and science, as well as English. The study indicates that students in longer-term bilingual education classes accelerate in their rate of educational growth faster than students in classes where no native-language instruction is used or where such instruction is ended quickly (Ramirez 1991; Asimov 1991).

Such a result should not be surprising. Native instruction allows students to keep up in math, science, and other courses while they learn English. Increasing proficiency in a child's native language increases his or her cognitive abilities and understanding of grammar and structure, thereby enhancing the ability to acquire a second language (English). Bilingual education also avoids the implied degradation of the child's native language and culture, which often accompanies traditional "sink or swim" methods; bilingual education thus fosters immigrant students' self-image and self-respect. As one federal court found:

> When Spanish-surname children come to school and find that their language and culture are totally rejected and only English is acceptable, feelings of inadequacy and lowered self-esteem develop. . . . If a child can be made to feel worthwhile in school then he will learn even with a poor English program. (*Serna v. Portales Municipal Schools* 1974)

The claim that experience proves that the traditional "sink or swim" method works best since prior immigrants "made it" without bilingual education is without foundation. Although some immigrants succeeded, many more sank than swam. In 1911 the U.S. Immigration Service found that 77 percent of Italian, 60 percent of Russian Jewish, and 51 percent of German children of immigrant parents were one or more grade levels behind in school (Cohen 1970).

4. See also *Hernandez v. Texas* 1954: Spanish surnames "provide ready identification of the members of this [Mexican American] class"; *Castenada v. Partida* 1977: Mexican American ethnicity is synonymous with "[p]ersons of Spanish language"; *Yu Cong Eng v. Trinidad* 1926: A Philippine ordinance requiring accounting records to be kept in only English, Spanish, or local dialects denied equal protection to Chinese merchants because it prohibited them from keeping records in their native language; *Lau v. Nichols* 1974: The failure of San Francisco public schools to provide educational services to non-English-speaking students constituted national origin discrimination, violating Title VI of the Civil Rights Act of 1964.

5. Voting discrimination against language minorities has injured Hispanics/Latinos in particular as well as other language minorities such as Asians and Native Americans. See, for instance, S. Rep. No. 295, 94th Cong., 1st Sess. 28–31, reprinted in 1975 U.S. Code Cong. & Admin. News 774, 794-97: Congressional finding that "language minority citizens [continue to be] excluded from the electoral process through the use of English Only elections," and that "[p]ersons of Spanish heritage was the group most severely affected by discriminatory [voting] practices, while the documentation concerning Asian Americans, American Indians and Alaskan Natives was substantial"); *Castro v. California* 1970: Concerned refusal to register as voters otherwise qualified Spanish speakers who could not prove and attest to literacy in English.

6. During slavery, African Americans were also subjected to restrictionist language policies. It was common practice for slave owners to mix up Africans of different tribes, limiting communication between slaves (Smitherman 1977, 7). Of course, it is well known that laws prohibited teaching slaves to read and write. Subsequent to emancipation, literacy laws were enacted to keep African Americans from voting (*Louisiana v. United States* 1965).

Works Cited

Asimov, Nanette. 1991. "Education Study Finds Flaw in English Only." *San Francisco Chronicle*, Feb. 12. B1.

Baron, Dennis. 1992. "Federal English." In James Crawford, ed., *Language Loyalties: A Source Book on the Official-English Controversy.* Chicago: University of Chicago Press. 36–40.

Beardsmore, Hugo Baetens, and Roland Willemyns. 1986. "Comment." *International Journal of the Sociology of Language* (60): 117–28.

Bliss, W. 1988. "Providing Adult Basic Education Services to Adults with Limited English Proficiency." Report prepared for Project on Adult Literacy of Southport Institute for Policy Analysis. © January 1989 by Southport Institute for Policy Analysis, Southport, CT.

Bowling, Timothy B. 1995. Letter to Hon. Shelby, Sept. 20.

Brischetto, Robert R. 1982. *Bilingual Elections at Work in the Southwest: A Mexican American Legal Defense and Education Report Fund.* San Antonio, TX: Mexican American Legal Defense and Education Fund.

Califa, Antonio. 1989. "Declaring English the Official Language: Prejudice Spoken Here." *Harvard Civil Rights-Civil Liberties Law Review* 24: 293–348.

Castellanos, Diego. 1992. "A Polyglot Nation." In James Crawford, ed., *Language Loyalties: A Source Book on the Official English Controversy.* Chicago: University of Chicago Press. 13–18.

Castro, Max J., Margaret Haun, and Ana Roca. 1990. "The Official-English Movement in Florida." In Karen L. Adams and Daniel T. Brink, eds., *Perspectives on Official English: The Campaign for English as the Official Language of the USA.* Berlin: Mouton de Gruyter. 151–60.

Charter of the United Nations. 1948. Chapter IX, Article 55. Dec. 10. Available : http://www.un.org/aboutun/charter/chapter9.htm

Chin, S. 1991. "Cultural Differences Hinder Asian Case." *San Francisco Examiner,* July 8. 1.

Civil Rights Act. 1964. Title VII of the Civil Rights Act of 1964. Available: http://www.eeoc.gov/laws/vii.html

Cohen, D. 1970. "Immigrants and the Schools." *Review of Educational Research* 40: 13–27.

Conklin, Nancy Faires, and Margaret A. Lourie. 1983. *A Host of Tongues: Language Communities in the United States.* New York: Free Press.

Coughalay, Dean. 1989. "Varied Languages a Hurdle for Police." *San Francisco Chronicle*, June 5. A7.

Crawford, James, ed. 1992a. *Language Loyalties: A Source Book on the Official English Controversy.* Chicago: University of Chicago Press.

―――. 1992b. *Hold Your Tongue. Bilingualism and the Politics of English Only.* Reading, MA: Addison-Wesley.

―――. 1989. *Bilingual Education: History, Politics, Theory, and Practice.* Trenton, NJ: Crane.

Dade County Attorney's Opinion. 1990. Nos. 81-29, 81-21, 80-37, 81-28. In Max Castro, Margaret Haun, and Ana Roca, eds., *Perspectives on Official English: The Campaign for English as the Official Language of the USA.* Berlin: Mouton de Gruyter. 126.

"English Only Rules and 'Innocent' Employers: Clarifying National Origin Discrimination and Disparate Impact Theory under Title VI." 1989. *Minnesota Law Review* 74: 387.

Estrada, Leobardo. 1984. "The Extent of Spanish/English Bilingualism in the United States." *Aztlan International Journal of Chicano Studies Research* 15. 379–83.

Farrell, Dave. 1987. "Major Says Computer Caused 911 Foul-Up." *San Francisco Chronicle*, Jan. 9. A3.

Fishman, Joshua. 1977. "Language and Ethnicity." In Howard Giles, ed., *Language, Ethnicity and Intergroup Relations.* London: Academic Press.

Freed, David. 1993. "Few Safeguards Protect Workers from Poisons; Labor: Some Latinos Toil Unaware of Dangers; Others Risk Their Health. Budget Woes Weaken Official Oversight." *Los Angeles Times*, Sept. 6. 1.

Gall, Susan, and Timothy Gall, eds. 1993. *Statistical Record of Asian Americans* 128.

Heath, Shirley B. 1981. "English in Our Language Heritage." In Charles A. Ferguson and Shirley B. Heath, eds., *Language in the USA.* Cambridge, U.K.: Cambridge University Press.

Henry, Sarah. 1990. "Fighting Words." *Los Angeles Times Magazine*, June 10. 10.

"Judge: Mom's Spanish Is Child Abuse." 1995. *Sacramento Bee.* Aug. 29.

Karst, Kenneth L. 1986. "Paths to Belonging: The Constitution and Cultural Identity." *North Carolina Law Review* 64: 303–81.

Kaufman, J. 1995. "Global Village, America's Heartland Turns to Hot Location for Melting Pot." *Wall Street Journal,* Oct. 31. A1, A15.

Leibowicz, Joseph. 1985. "The Proposed English Language Amendment: Shield or Sword?" *Yale Law and Policy Review* 3: 519–37.

Leibowitz, Arnold. 1969. "English Literacy: Legal Sanction for Discrimination" *Notre Dame Lawyer* 45(1): 7–67.

Lindsey. 1986. "Debates Growing on Use of English." *New York Times,* July 21. 1.

Loo, Chalsa. 1985. "The Biliterate Ballot Controversy: Language Acquisition and Cultural Shift among Immigrants." *International Migration Review* 19(3): 493–515.

Macias, Reynaldo. 1995. "CA LEP Enrollment Continues Slow Growth in 1995." *Newsletter of U.C. Linguistic Minority Research Institute* 5(1).

Maldoff, Eric. 1986. "Comment: A Canadian Perspective." *International Journal of the Sociology of Language* 60: 105–15.

Marshall, David. 1986. "The Question of an Official Language: Language Rights and the English Language Amendment." *International Journal of the Sociology of Language* 60: 7–77.

Matsuda, Mari J. 1991. "Voices of America: Accent, Antidiscrimination Law and a Jurisprudence of the Last Reconstruction." *Yale Law Journal* 100(5): 1329–1407.

McCarthy, Kevin F., and R. Burciaga Valdez. 1985. *Current and Future Effects of Mexican Immigration in California: Executive Summary.* Santa Monica, CA: The Rand Corp.

Mujica, Mauro. 1995. Interview. *Good Morning America.* ABC TV, Oct. 18.

Myers, Dowell. 1995. "The Changing Immigrants of Southern California." Exhibit 4.2. Lusk Center Research Institute, University of Southern California, October.

Nakao, Annie. 1991. "Workers Battle for Right to Speak Native Tongues." *San Francisco Examiner,* June 23. A1.

"New Miami Survey Finds 'Reverse Assimilation.'" 1985. *Hispanic Link Weekly Report* 3(20): 1, 3.

New York Immigration Coalition, The. 1994. "Position Paper Regarding New York State Funding of Newcomer Transition Assistance Services," October. Author.

"'Official English': Federal Limits on Efforts to Curtail Bilingual Services in the States." 1987. *Harvard Law Review* 100(6): 1345–62.

"Practically English Only." 1995. *Washington Post*, Sept. 27. A19.

"Quasi-Suspect Classes." 1981. *Yale Law Journal* 90: 912–31.

Ramirez, J. David. 1991. "Final Report: Longitudinal Study of Structured English Immersion Strategy, Early-Exit and Late-Exit Transitional Bilingual Education Programs for Language-Minority Children." Aguirre International, San Mateo, CA (Contract No. 300-87-0156).

Reyhner, Jon. 1992. "Policies toward American Indian Languages: A Historical Sketch." In James Crawford, ed., *Language Loyalties: A Source Book on the Official English Controversy*. Chicago: University of Chicago Press. 41–47.

Rojas, Aurelio, and Nanette Asimov. 1994. "Latinos Decry Lack of Relief Services." *San Francisco Chronicle*, Jan. 21. A20.

Shimomura, Floyd D. 1987. Letter to Stanley Diamond, May 20.

Siobhan, Nicolau, and Rafael Valdivieso. 1988. "The Veltman Report: What It Says, What It Means." Introduction to Calvin Veltman, ed., *The Future of the Spanish Language in the United States*. New York: Hispanic Policy Development Project.

Smitherman, Geneva. 1977. *Talkin' and Testifyin': The Language of Black America*. Boston: Houghton Mifflin.

Solarz, Stephen J. Hon. 1988. Statement before the Subcommittee on Civil and Constitutional Rights. May 11.

Swardson. 1995. "A Free Quebec: Prosperity or Ruin?" *Washington Post*, Oct. 30. A1, A13.

Universal Declaration of Human Rights. 1948. Article 2. Available: http://www.un.org/rights/50/decla.htm

U.S. Bureau of the Census. 1980. *Census of Population. Volume 1: Characteristics of the Population, Chapter D: Detailed Population Characteristics = Part 1: United States Summary, Section B: Regions*. Washington, D.C.: U.S. Department of Commerce, Bureau of the Census, 1984. Microfiche.

————. 1989. *200 Years of U.S. Census Taking: Population and Housing Questions, 1790–1990.* (Docs. Ref. C3.2: T93). Washington, DC: GPO.

————. 1990. *The Hispanic Population in the United States: March 1989* (Current Population Reports, Series P-20, No. 438). Washington, DC: GPO.

————. 1992. "Reported Voting and Registration by Race, Hispanic Origin, and Age for States: November 1992." Unpublished data.

————. 1993. Press release. CB93-78. April 28.

U.S. Commission on Civil Rights. 1970. *Mexican Americans and the Administration of Justice in the Southwest.*

U.S. Commission on Civil Rights. 1972. *Mexican American Educational Study, Report III: The Excluded Element.*

U.S. Government Accounting Office. 1986. "Bilingual Voting Assistance: Cost of and Use of During the November 1984 General Election." Briefing Report to the Honorable Quentin N. Burdick, U.S. Senate. 17, 20.

————. 1987. "Bilingual Education—A New Look at the Research Evidence." Briefing Report to the Chairman, Committee on Education and Labor, House of Representatives. GAO/DEMO-87-12 BR.

Veltman, Calvin. 1988. *The Future of the Spanish Language in the United States.* New York: Hispanic Policy Development Project.

Woo. 1986. "Immigrants—A Rush to the Classrooms." *Los Angeles Times,* Sept. 24. 1.

Woolard, Kathryn. 1986. "Comment." *International Journal of the Sociology of Language* (60): 191–97.

Court Cases Cited

Alabama v. United States, 371 U.S. 37, 1962.

Asian American Business Group v. City of Pomona, 716 F. Supp. 1328 C.D. Cal., 1989.

Brown v. Board of Education, 347 U.S. 483, 493, 1954.

Castaneda v. Partida, 430 U.S. 482, 486 n.5, 1977.

Castro v. California, 2 Cal.3d 223, 229-31, 1970.

Dunn v. Blumstein, 405 U.S. 330, 1972.

Garcia v. Spun Steak, Supreme Court No. 93-1222, 1993.

Guerrero v. Carleson, 9 Cal.3d 808, 1973; 414 U.S. 1137, 1974.

Gutierrez v. Municipal Court, 838 F.2d 1031, 1039 9th Cir., 1988; 490 U.S. 1016, 1989.

Hernandez v. Texas, 347 U.S. 475, 480 n. 12. 1954.

Hernandez v. New York, 500 U.S. 352, 412-13, 1991.

Hunter v. Erikson, 393 U.S. 385, 1969.

Lau v. Nichols, 414 U.S. 563, 1974.

Louisiana v. United States, 380 U.S. 145, 1965.

Meyer v. Nebraska, 262 U.S. 390, 1923.

Olagues v. Russoniello, 797 F.2d 1511 9th Cir., 1986; 484 U.S. 806, 1987.

Perez et al. v. Los Angeles Unified School District et al., Los Angeles Superior Court, October 14, 1987.

Personnel Administrator of Massachusetts v. Feeney, 442 U.S. 256, 279, 1978.

Plyler v. Doe, 457 U.S. 202, 1982.

Reynolds v. Simms, 377 U.S. 533, 1964.

Rodriguez et al. v. Greyhound Lines, Inc. et al., Sacramento Superior Court No. 95 A 501, 1987.

San Antonio Independent School District v. Rodriguez, 411 U.S. 1, 1973.

Schnell v. Davis, 336 U.S. 933, 1949.

Serna v. Portales Municipal Schools, 499 F.2d 2247,1150 10th Cir., 1974.

South Carolina v. Katzenbach, 383 U.S. 301, 1966.

United States v. Carolene Products Co., 304 U.S. 144, 152, n.4., 1938.

United States v. Mississippi, 380 U.S. 128, 1965.

Virginia State v. of Pharmacy v. Virginia Citizens Consumer Council, 475 U.S. 748, 757, 1976.

Washington v. Seattle School District No.1, 458 U.S. 457, 1982.

Yñiguez v. Mofford, 730 F.Supp. 309 D.Ariz, 1990.

Yñiguez v. Arizonans for Official-English, 9th Cir. Oct. 5, 1995.

Yu Cong Eng v. Trinidad, 271 U.S. 500, 528, 1926.

Official English Bills in Congress

105th Congress

- ◆ H.R. 123 (Cunningham)—"Bill Emerson English Language Empowerment Act"; the lead version of English Only legislation, 146 cosponsors; referred to Education and Workforce Committee.

- ◆ S. 323 (Shelby)—Similar to H.R. 123; 20 cosponsors; referred to Governmental Affairs Committee.

- ◆ H.R. 622 (Stump)—"Declaration of Official Language Act"; parallels H.R. 123 but with fewer exceptions to the English Only mandate; also would repeal the bilingual provisions of the Voting Rights Act; 36 cosponsors; referred to Education and Workforce and Judiciary committees.

- ◆ H.R. 1005 (King)—"National Language Act"; a more restrictive English Only measure that would repeal the Bilingual Education Act and make schools return unspent grant funds; 22 cosponsors; referred to Education and Workforce Committee.

- ◆ H.J. Res. 37 (Doolittle)—Constitutional English Language amendment; 3 cosponsors; referred to Judiciary Committee.

- ◆ H. Con. Res. 4 (Serrano)—English Plus resolution; a nonbinding policy statement in opposition to English Only measures; 37 cosponsors; referred to Education and Workforce Committee.

◆ H. Res. 28 (King)—Nonbinding resolution disapproving of the use of federal funds for school programs that recognize "Ebonics"; 7 cosponsors; referred to Education and Workforce Committee.

◆ H.R. 856 (Young)—Puerto Rico plebiscite bill includes Official-English provisions for statehood; 87 cosponsors; passed Resources Committee, 44-1, 5/21/97; discharged by Rules committee and placed on House calendar, 7/11/97.

◆ H.R. 1203 (Stump)—Prohibits the use of federal education funds to "promote the teaching or use of regional or group dialects"—e.g., African American Vernacular English; 128 cosponsors; referred to Education and Workforce Committee.

104th Congress

◆ H.R. 123 (Emerson)—Federal English Only bill, passed by the House of Representatives, August 1, 1996.

◆ H.R. 739 (Roth)—"Declaration of Official Language Act"; a more draconian version of the Emerson bill.

◆ H.R. 1005 (King)—An even more restrictive "National Language Act."

◆ S. 356 (Shelby)—Companion to the Emerson bill; text is identical to H.R. 123, as originally introduced.

102nd Congress

◆ H.R. 123 (Emerson)—First Version of "Language of Government" legislation, introduced January 3, 1991.

97th Congress

◆ S.J. Res. 72 (Hayakawa)—A constitutional English Language Amendment; the first Official-English bill ever introduced in Congress, April 27, 1981.

CHAPTER THREE

Acquiring a Slice of Anglo-American Pie: A Portrait of Language Shift in a Franco-American Family

ROBERT S. WILLIAMS
Saint Michael's College

KATHLEEN C. RILEY
CUNY Graduate Center

Processes of language shift within rural immigrant communities in the United States offer some instructive contrasts to those undergone by their urban counterparts, especially with respect to the impact of English Only ideology. To explore these processes, we conducted a study of language use and attitudes, both current and ethnohistorically reconstructed, within a Franco-American (FA) farming community in northeastern Vermont, referred to here pseudonymously as the town of Kingdom.

This essay presents the results of a case study in which shift from bilingualism and multidialectalism to monolingualism over the course of a single generation occurred within one FA Kingdom family, called here the Dumont family (again a pseudonym). Of thirteen siblings, now aged forty-five to sixty-nine, the eldest are fully bilingual (French-English with functional competence in two varieties of French); the youngest speak only English and comprehend very little French; and those in the middle represent a spectrum of competencies in between. The siblings' attitudes toward bilingualism/biculturalism among immigrant populations today, however, do not at all correlate with their own degrees of bilingual competence and identification with their French Canadian heritage. How and why did this happen?

Our study has been framed by an understanding that differences in the acquisition and use of, as well as attitudes toward, linguistic varieties within a community are influenced both by larger political, economic, and social forces (Fishman 1989; Gal 1979; Gumperz 1982; Hill and Hill 1986; Labov 1972; Milroy 1987) and by the particular communicative practices and beliefs influencing the socialization of individuals within their immediate social network (Kulick 1992; Ochs 1988; Schieffelin 1990; Zentella 1997). An ethnographic study of language socialization is specifically designed to explore this relationship between micro- and macroprocesses (Schieffelin and Ochs 1996). Unfortunately, the era for performing such a longitudinal study of natural discourse within a French-speaking community of FA children and their caregivers in northern Vermont is long gone. Nonetheless, by applying what Zentella (1997) refers to as an "anthropolitical linguistic" lens, we have found it possible to reconstruct the processes by which language shift was interactively accomplished within the FA farming community of Kingdom. Our methods include in-depth interviewing, archival research, and analogic interpolation using contextually similar situations. Additionally, attitudinal surveys and individual interviewing have shed light on the relationship between present-day ethnic identification, language use, and political ideology.

In the following sections, we first provide a brief ethnohistory of the emergence of the FA population in New England. We then present the case study of the Dumont family. Next, we discuss the results of an English Only poll which was administered to a sample of both Anglo-American and FA Vermonters in order to ascertain the relationship between ethnic identity and attitudes toward this ideologically loaded political linguistic issue in Vermont. The poll provides a backdrop for our analysis of the Dumont family's opinions on these subjects. In brief, the researchers conclude that while English Only legislation affects language-use patterns in clear if complex ways, FAs' opinions about such legislation cannot be so easily inferred from the history of impact.

To Melt or Not to Melt: An Ethnohistoric Survey of the Franco-American Population

Fifty years ago the French Canadians of New England were considered an unassimilable ethnic minority (Lemaire 1966), and yet the history of discrimination against them is now largely "forgotten" or "unknown" (Doty 1995, 86). In fact, FAs have engaged in several historic cycles of impact and reaction which date back to a time when (reminiscent of the situation at the Mexico-U.S. border) national boundaries were militarily under debate. But by far the largest waves of immigration occurred between 1840 and 1930, leading to a late-twentieth-century population of approximately 1,775,000 New Englanders of French/French Canadian ancestry (Guiguére 1996).

In this section we review several significant aspects of the ethnohistory of this group: (1) the early period of self-protective social organization, (2) subsequent struggles with discrimination and English Only policies, (3) socioeconomic pressures leading the majority into cultural and linguistic assimilation, and (4) present attempts to revive FA cultural identity.

"Les petits Canadas" and "la survivance"

The French Canadians left Quebec in the nineteenth century for economic reasons: the members of large farming families with diminishing amounts of depleted land to divvy up into smaller and smaller plots found little paid labor available in Quebec. They heard from family and friends who had already emigrated to the United States rumors of plentiful jobs in mills and on farms, and even of opportunities to rent or buy their own farms (Woolfson 1983b).

Once over the border, the immigrants tended to congregate in mill towns and farming communities throughout New England, but particularly in three regions which together came to be known as Franco-Américanie: (1) northern Maine, (2) western Vermont and upper New York state, and (3) Massachusetts, southern New

Hampshire, and southern Maine (Brault 1986, 2–3). They lived apart from mainstream society in ethnic enclaves characterized by dense and multiplex social relations; that is, one lived, worked, prayed, and played all with the same set of people. Although instigated early on by nineteenth-century factory employment practices (whole families—mother, father, and children—were employed by the same operation and housed with other, frequently related, families), this arrangement appealed also to newcomers' need to be ensconced in a familiar nexus of language, faith, and social intercourse (Lemaire 1966).

Additionally, this form of social organization was encouraged by an FA petit bourgeois and professional class whose interests were served by obscuring class differences through instilling a community consciousness of national identity (see Guiguére 1991). This elite leadership was instrumental in creating *les petits Canadas*, in which the parish institutions of Quebec were reproduced throughout New England: church, school, newspapers, and social and mutual aid associations. Many members of the elite had been educated in Quebec, where the parish-based system of schooling and social services overseen by the Catholic Church had been first instituted in the 1830s by clerics and educators brought from France (Brault 1986).

The network of extended families and social institutions spanning Quebec and *les petits Canadas* allowed for the dissemination and reproduction of the nationalistic ideology known as *la survivance*, much of it a distilled and romanticized version of traditional farming culture in Quebec (Brault 1986). This philosophy rested on the belief that it was Quebec's God-given mission to preserve and expand the dominion of Catholicism in the New World through the reproduction of French-language and agrarian parishes. *La survivance* promoted ideals of generosity and respect for authority within a large, extended, patriarchal family; a strong work ethic directed toward the self-sufficiency of the family; and a French Catholicism in which language and faith were inextricably intertwined: to lose one's language was to lose one's chance at eternity (Lemaire 1966).

Whether FA values and institutions are viewed as blinding opiates or as psychosocial support systems, they clearly bolstered FA social cohesion, sense of cultural identity, and linguistic maintenance for over a century. Within French Catholic parishes, the church provided a social hub where priests were respected as both social and spiritual leaders, and endogamous marriages and large families were the rule. Francophone or bilingual parochial schools ensured French literacy, Catholic training, a consciousness of French and French Canadian history, and the fusing of these together into a powerful sense of identity (Brault 1996; Chartier 1996). French newspapers provided the print media for the imagined community that combined Franco-Américanie with Quebec. This community was realized to some degree by extended family contact across the border (letters, visits, and new migrations) and was fed by not totally unrealistic dreams of return (debts paid off, ancestral farms reclaimed). Under these conditions, cultural assimilation was discouraged, and many first generation FAs never learned much English (Woolfson 1983a, 10).

The Imposition of English Only Ideology

Like many other immigrants to the United States, FAs have suffered discrimination against their religion, cultural organizations, and socioeconomic practices for as long as they have been here. Beginning in the mid-nineteenth century, the "nativist" Know-Nothing movement sparked anti-Catholic legislation and violence against Catholics, their homes, and churches (Woolfson 1983a). By the 1880s, FAs were officially dubbed "the Chinese of the Eastern States" because of their "passive, anti-union" stance (Doty 1995, 87). World War I saw the birth of patriotic associations such as the American Legion, Daughters of the American Revolution, and League of Women Voters, all of which put unprecedented pressure on immigrants to Americanize if they wanted to succeed (Brault 1986). For the purposes of this essay, however, we will focus on how FAs' home language has been both prejudicially targeted and otherwise influenced by Anglo-American ideology: the belief that America's integrity as a nation is somehow dependent on only English being learned and used within its boundaries.

The first strong English Only movements grew out of the patriotism and anti-immigrant sentiments of the early twentieth century. In 1919 the Americanization Department of the U.S.

Bureau of Education recommended that states legislate that only English be used in all public and private schools (Woolfson 1983a). In New England, English Only laws were aimed at curtailing the use of French in parochial schools. Proposed legislation in Vermont and Connecticut did not pass, but did in Rhode Island, New Hampshire, and Maine (Woolfson 1983a). Although in 1922 the Supreme Court ruled all such legislation unconstitutional (Brault 1986), it nonetheless supported the stipulation that private schools must cover all the state-mandated requirements for public school curriculum in addition to whatever was on their own agenda in teaching language, religion, culture, and history. Thus states could and did use an extended set of requirements for public education to make the parochial curriculum taught in French almost impossible to tack on (Lemaire 1966).

Additional problems for parochial schools using French as a medium of instruction were caused by French–Irish dissension within the Catholic Church (Roby 1996a). By the turn of the century, the Irish occupied the highest positions in the U.S. diocesan hierarchy and so had the power to block the institution of new French parishes and combine the "national" parishes which already existed (e.g., French, Polish, Italian) into "territorial" parishes (i.e., ethnically mixed, as the region the church served). Unlike in Quebec, local parish funds and properties were controlled in the United States by bishops and so could be siphoned off for larger diocesan projects such as the construction of high schools where only English would be used (Woolfson 1983a).

The FA elite was split by controversy about how best to promote *la survivance*—whether through cultural isolationism and a rigid adherence to the French language or through the adoption of a more moderate ideology of cultural pluralism and bilingualism (Brault 1986). In a schism referred to as the Sentinelle Affair (named after the Woonsocket, Rhode Island, newspaper which represented the more conservative faction's views), sixty-two Sentinellistes took an Irish bishop to court in a civil suit concerning parish funds. They not only lost the case but were also excommunicated. The movement died with the Sentinellistes' formal repentance the following year (Brault 1986).

This event also spelled the beginning of the end of the clerical elite's leadership of Franco-Américanie. For their religion, the

FA masses chose to stay on Rome's good side, even if this meant kneeling to the assimilationist and English-schooling moves of their Irish American bishopric. As a consequence, their priests too, in order to keep their flock, began to preach in the language that a growing number could best understand (Lemaire 1966).

Political and Economic Pressures
Contributing to Anglo-Americanism

With the stock market crash in 1929, immigration was halted both officially and unofficially (as the draw of economic prosperity was no longer apparent), ending the influx of new arrivals and the ethnolinguistic transfusion they offered (Lemaire 1966, 262). Additionally, massive layoffs of whole families and neighborhoods from shutdown factories meant that the old ideal of self-sufficiency and reliance on family was no longer possible. Mutual aid societies foundered, and many FAs sought welfare relief for the first time, which bred a new allegiance to their host country. Much restricted incomes made paying tuition for parochial schools difficult, while buying French-language newspapers became a luxury.

Then in the 1940s, the war-fed economy fueled a new wave of national pride over the role of the United States in liberating Europe: everyone listened to radio news and sang patriotic songs in English, and austerity measures and concern for family members fighting overseas brought people at home together across ethnic lines (see Doty 1997 for an interesting take on how the FA masses reacted against the fascist leanings of the French Catholic elite during World War II). Although many mills had closed down or moved south to find cheaper labor in the '30s, the defense industry provided new, relatively well-paid jobs which inspired suburban flight. Men back from the war no longer wanted to remain ensconced in little Canadas or on the farm. Thus the multiplex social networks based on work-play-worship all within *les petits Canadas* were broken up and new ties formed. A clear indication of this is that, while the majority of FAs still tended to find Catholic spouses, by the 1940s as many as half of all marriages were language exogamous; that is, FAs were marrying non-FAs.

In theory, the prosperity of the 1950s made the American dream seem accessible to all, on condition that one assimilate. And assimilation seemed inevitable as mass media spread, especially TV. The broadcasting of sports operated as a kind of ersatz war, with patriotism for one's team superceding any kind of ethnic pride. With the advent of busing, isolated farm kids were being transported to high school for the first time, the GI bill provided a college education to a much wider spectrum of the population, and jobs requiring higher education were opening up, particularly within education itself as the baby boomers needed educators. In reality, economic advancement came only to some, and the resulting class divisions have not been easily glossed over by a now failing call for ethnic solidarity.

The three bastions of linguistic *survivance*—religion, education, and print media—having begun their decline in the '30s, were in shreds by the '60s. With Vatican II in the early '60s, religious services in most parishes went from being conducted in some mixture of French, English, and Latin to all English. By the '70s, most FAs were in public school, and the parochial schools that remained were teaching French one hour a day as a foreign language (Brault 1986). Finally, the last major daily French-language newspaper in New England closed down in 1979 (Perreault 1996).

Since the '30s, there had been a growing comprehension among FAs that opportunities for employment and social advancement were based on literacy and competence in standard English. The '40s and '50s saw a resurgence at the federal level (taking the form of the National Defense Education Act [NDEA]) of the recognition that national security depended on strong educational standards, including competence in more than one world language. But this sense of symbolic capital attached to a second language did not trickle down to the FA masses. Having experienced discrimination against their accented English, Franco-American WWII veterans did not want their children to experience the same prejudice and began to send them to public rather than parochial schools. These children were then made to realize, somewhat painfully, that the variety of French they spoke at home was not the version being taught at school (Miller 1969). Finally, public schools transformed English into the language of solidarity/intimacy for younger FAs, becoming for them what French at home, church, and workplace had been for their parents.

FA Identity: Revived and Revised

Although the 1960s ushered in the era of civil rights, multiculturalism, and Title VII bilingual education programs, the brief flurry of federally funded activities supporting bilingualism among FAs came too little, too late. The earliest of these (1960–1964) included NDEA funding for several FA teacher training sessions (Brault 1986). A number of FA bilingual programs in elementary schools opened and closed again in northern Vermont, New Hampshire, and Maine between the late '60s and mid '80s. From 1978 to 1982, the University of Vermont housed a teacher training program for FA bilingual education (Jacobson 1984). In 1983 the Vermont Advisory Committee to the U.S. Commission on Civil Rights offered its assessment of the subordinated status of FAs in Vermont in order to substantiate the continued need for federally funded programs (Woolfson 1983a). These programs, however, were then on the verge of ending.

Nonetheless, by the 1970s FAs began to reorganize their rootedness along new and not necessarily Francophone lines (Roby 1996b). While language was still considered a loaded symbol of identity, it was now possible to be FA without speaking French. A number of bilingual conferences, publications, and institutes devoted to FA culture and language began to appear (for instance, the FA Center at the University of Maine, out of which comes *Le Forum* newspaper). Popular figures of FA descent such as Jack Kerouac were reclaimed, and more recently a general interest in genealogy, fed by the Internet, has proliferated. Old associations such as the Union Saint-Jean-Baptiste and the Fédération Féminine Franco-Américaine (LeBlanc 1996) are still in operation, and new ones (e.g., ActFANE—Action for FAs of the North East) are cropping up (see Quintal 1991 for a review of FA institutions' gains and losses in recent years). Finally, a number of FA heritage festivals are celebrated with considerable enthusiasm throughout New England each year, and a few FA individuals, mixing business and ethnic spirit, are able to garner federal and regional grants for taking their cultural education programs, involving music, dance, and storytelling, out on the road.

Language Shift within FA Farming Communities

The FA farming communities present a somewhat different pic-ture from that of the mill towns. While FA farmers encountered less of the obvious discrimination and exploitation experienced by laborers, they nonetheless benefited from fewer of the cul-tural support mechanisms operating within the larger popula-tion centers. Where the community was large enough, there might be a bilingual pastor who provided Mass in French, as well as, perhaps, some related church groups. But there rarely would be sufficient numbers to justify a parochial school that provided French or bilingual education, a local French-language newspa-per, or mutual-aid associations and professionals such as law-yers, bankers, and physicians.

Nonetheless, the farming lifestyle provided social and geo-graphic isolation from Anglo influences well into the twentieth century and in particular offered a buffer against the socioeco-nomic turmoil of the Depression that undermined the forces for cultural conservatism and social cohesion within *les petits Canadas*. Additionally, certain ideological and social structural supports were reproduced as if in miniature within the family and small farming communities. We now examine and illustrate in ethnographic detail these differences through reference to the reconstructed history of cultural assimilation and language shift within the Dumont family of Kingdom, Vermont.

The Dumont Family

Emile Dumont emigrated with his parents and siblings from an eastern Quebec township in 1915 and took up residence on a farm five miles outside of Kingdom at the age of eleven. There he attended no more than a couple of years of school and acquired limited but functional English, which served him well through-out his life. His wife, Rose Dumont, was born and raised within a large FA community in a Connecticut mill town and completed eighth grade at a bilingual parochial school, where she acquired bilingual and biliterate competence, which she retained throughout her life. All of their thirteen children were born in Vermont or Connecticut, and the ten eldest were mostly brought up on the farm, a stretch of years broken only by a four-year interlude spent in a Connecticut mill town and another half a year in a Westchester suburb. This period on the farm ended with the family's move to the village of Kingdom, where the three youngest siblings spent most of their growing up years. The eldest six living siblings exhibit variable degrees of performative competence in French, while the youngest six do not, retaining varying degrees of comprehension and at best a very limited speaking ability (see Table 3.1).

TABLE 3.1. Birth Sex, Birth Order, Birth Year, Subfamily, and Fluency of Dumont Siblings

Birth order of siblings	Year born	Subfamily	Self-reported French ability
F1	1929	1st	Fluent – 2 dialects
M2	1930 d. 1983	1st	Fluent
M3	1931	1st	Fluent – 2 dialects
M4	1935	1st	Fluent
M5	1936	1st	Fluent
M6	1937	1st	Fluent
F7	1940	1st/2nd	Fluent
F8	1943	2nd	Fluent
F9	1946	2nd	Uses some lexical items, but hasn't conversed in French since high school
F10	1947	2nd	Minimal production in the workplace
M11	1950	2nd	Uses some lexical items, low-level reading ability, some comprehension of spoken French
M12	1953	2nd	Uses some lexical items
M13	1953	2nd	Uses some lexical items
M = Male F = Female			

During interviews, the Dumont siblings spoke of the family as in reality two or three separate families. Predictably, they did not all concur on the composition or break-off points between families. What most of them spoke of was the sense that they had formed into cohorts based on age as well as something vaguely articulated having to do with their competencies in French. One version, which counts the older seven siblings in the first family and the last six in the second, is of particular interest for our analysis here because it happens in fact to mirror their French-language abilities. The siblings will hereafter be referred to as first-family and second-family siblings based on this division.

Pro-bilingual Influences

Acquisition of English is a certainty in the U.S. immigrant experience, and the process of language shift in general has been much documented, especially at the speech community level (e.g., Fishman et al. 1966). Of interest in the case of the Dumont family are the various processes and influences which allowed for the acquisition of English as well as the maintenance of the ancestral language for some siblings, while others lost French on their way to becoming monolingual English speakers. The major pro-bilingual influences can be found within the home and the wider Francophone farming community of Kingdom.

The home provided the overwhelming social, political, economic, and cultural forces which combine to work against a stable bilingualism in the United States; it is no small feat that the members of the Dumont first family retained some level of fluency in French. All Dumont children began life as monolingual speakers of French, primarily because the Dumont parents guided the family participation in each child's language acquisition in this direction. F1 recalls that she was explicitly instructed to speak French to her siblings. In other words, as was customary throughout Franco-Américanie at that time, the decision to speak to Dumont preschoolers only in French was a conscious effort on the part of the parents to maintain the French Canadian culture and dialect in the family. This decision indicates an early belief on the part of the parents that language and culture were inseparable, or that without knowing French, the children could not know and participate in the French Canadian culture. Moreover, speaking to children only in French was a necessity in some FA families, those in which parents did not have an adequate command of English, but this was not the case with the Dumont family, where the mother was fluent in both languages and the father had communicative ability in English, though his English was far from perfect.

While on the farm (1941–1954), all family members spoke French in the home. In addition to the parents and siblings, the paternal grandfather, a Francophone with limited English skills, also lived in the home. Neighboring children were more often than not present at the Dumont dinner table, but they were all Francophones, so dinner was also a French-language event. This rule was broken only after 1945, when M3 began to bring friends from high school into the home who could not speak French, and etiquette prevented the family from conversing only in French. Code-switching increased among the siblings as more and more of the younger ones entered school, but there was always a prohibition against family members speaking English to the preschoolers.

The family home was also a center for *soirées*, parties attended by family members and neighbors, which were held in the kitchen. The *soirée* included dancing and singing of French songs, often *chansons à répondre*, or call and response songs. These songs functioned to teach the language and culture to younger community members while still allowing those siblings who did not speak French to participate in the singing of French songs. The Dumont home was also the site of French-language storytelling, often by a beloved aunt. These stories would often stretch out over several evenings and were attended by neighboring children as well. In this way, the Dumont home functioned as a center for the preservation of French Canadian culture and for the socialization of children into that culture.

The farming community in which the Dumont farm was situated was located on several town roads within five miles of the village of Kingdom. This community consisted of some fifteen farms, all owned by Francophone families who had migrated from the Eastern Townships of Quebec during the first two decades of this century. Many of these families were neighbors before they emigrated and continued to follow the old patterns of social contact (daily visiting, *soirées*, shared child care and farm labor, etc.).

As a young man, Emile Dumont left the farm settled by his father in 1915 but came back with his young family for several stints during the Depression. Finally, after the four-year period spent in the Connecticut mill town, he returned to take over the farming operations from his father, and the family then occupied the farm continuously from 1941 to 1954. Thus the first-family siblings grew up for the most part within a Francophone community (especially if one considers the Francophone nature of the Connecticut mill town as well). The two eldest (F1 and M2) remained on the farm into their twenties, helping their parents run the farm; the next four (M3–M6) lived there until they left for college; and the youngest (M7) was entering high school by the time they moved to town. By contrast, most second-family siblings (F8–M13) spent a large part of their childhood and teenage years in the village, which was primarily a monolingual English community.

The first three children (F1–M3) attended four years of a bilingual parochial school in Connecticut during their early school years; thus it is no coincidence that they are (or were, in the case of the deceased brother) the most fluent speakers of both standard French and an FA variety of the language.

For the rest of their elementary schooling, the eldest and the rest of the first-family siblings attended Central School, a one-room, one-teacher school housing grades 1 through 8 located in the heart of the French farming community. Although Central was an English-medium school, all but one or two of its students were from surrounding Francophone farming families. Thus students could translate for one another when need arose (F1 remembers translating for fellow students and not getting in trouble for it) and were able to code-switch with one another when not in class.

Furthermore, over the years some Central teachers were bilingual Francophones themselves. Not only could they communicate in French with the Francophone parents of Central students and enjoy socializing with these families (some also boarded with them), but, as bilingual FAs in Anglophone society, they also served as important role models of successful integration. Thus, even though it was not a bilingual school, Central functioned for many years as a significant promoter of stable bilingualism in the predominantly Francophone farming community it served.

In addition, the community often had access to Francophone priests, and although Latin was the language of Mass, homilies were often given in both French and English, and confessions and last rites could also be made in French. According to F1, this arrangement had its drawbacks: "[The priest] would speak in both languages. He'd speak for ten or fifteen minutes in English and then he'd speak in French. If you understood both languages, it was pretty boring."

One other important community influence on the retention of a stable bilingualism was the French teacher at Kingdom High School, Mrs. C. Unlike most French teachers at the time, Mrs. C. recognized the validity of the Quebec dialect of French, as well as the value of the French Canadian culture. Mrs. C.'s attitude affected not only those Dumont siblings who were her students, but the younger ones as well. She encouraged and championed her Francophone students in what might have been a hostile Anglophone world and was largely responsible for encouraging the Francophone farm families to send their children to high school at a time when very few of them did. Mrs. C. became so involved in the FA community that she spent a summer with relatives of the FA students still residing in Quebec. In addition, Mrs. C. was also responsible for arranging scholarships which enabled M3, the first Dumont sibling to go to college, to attend a prestigious New England university.

Pro-language Shift Influences

Though many variables influenced language shift within the Dumont family, certain events were pivotal in the family's social and geographical integration into mainstream Anglophone culture. The most powerful of these variables were the school experiences of the children and the father's attendant change of attitude in favor of formal education; the United States' growing participation in world events, which pulled the Dumont boys away from the farm; and economic and social changes which eventually led to the family's move off the farm and into the village of Kingdom.

School was without question the most important influence on language shift for the Dumont siblings, as with most immigrant children. All of the first-family siblings (F1–F7) spent most or all of grades 1 through 8 at Central School, the one-room public school just outside of Kingdom. Although most of the students at this school began the first grade as either monolingual speakers of French or as bilingual French-English speakers, English was the language of instruction at the school, and the prohibition of the student's use of French in the classroom was strictly enforced. When recounting their school experiences, many of the siblings specifically mentioned this enforcement: "Mrs. P. [the teacher] . . . had to make a rule. . . . There would be no French spoken on the school grounds, because all of us would speak French. Occasionally, we would be scolded on the playground, because she would hear us" (M4). Thus, although students did use some French on the playground and occasionally in class when other students needed help understanding the lesson, many first-family siblings also recall that they were doing some involuntary code-switching into English on the walk home from school by the time they were in the second or third grade.

Unlike their first-family brothers and sisters, most second-family siblings (F8–M13) began school as bilingual French-English or monolingual English speakers. Although the two eldest second-family siblings (F8 and F9) attended Central School for four and two years respectively until its closing in 1953, second-family siblings spent most of grades 1 through 8 in the village schools with student populations which were mixed FA and non-FA. These schools were less a part of the FA farming community than was Central and thus were even more of a force for shift toward a more transitional and English-dominant bilingualism. Second-family siblings were also more likely to speak English to their peers, both on the playground and at other social gatherings, than were first-family siblings.

Another school-related event which had a significant impact on the family's language behavior was M3's insistence on attending high school, beginning in 1945. At the time, education in Vermont was compulsory only to age fourteen, so many farm families did not send their children to high school, which was located in the village of Kingdom. M3's subsequent success at high school, both as a scholar and an athlete, made attending high school the ambition of younger Dumont siblings and helped to change the Dumont father's attitude toward education. As the first Dumont sibling to attend high school, M3's English-speaking world was considerably broadened, and this world inevitably began to encroach on the farm, as non-Francophone school friends came to visit. During such visits, English was spoken in the house and at the dinner table, which heretofore had been strictly a French-language domain. As a result, important language domains, such as sports and popular culture, became English dominant. As more siblings entered high school, more non-French-speaking friends visited at the farm, with the result that younger siblings heard more and more English before they entered school and thus entered school as bilinguals. The language of high school for all Dumont siblings was primarily English, even when speaking to Francophone friends.

Though the speaking of French was still encouraged in the home, and especially with preschoolers, as time passed the Dumont children engaged in more and more code-switching, until they often were no longer cognizant of which language they were speaking. Because the use of French with preschoolers was still gently enforced at home, however, and because English was a language spoken by school-age siblings, English became an important marker of passage from early childhood to school age. Thus all second-family siblings were very motivated to speak English, and many were reported to ask F1, who functioned as a second mother to them, when they could begin speaking the language. Most younger siblings reported being able to speak English before they were allowed to.

> Yes, I could [speak English upon entering school]. Of course, we younger ones were learning English. We weren't supposed to be, but as preschoolers, we were learning English because the boys were in high school. And they brought friends. And when these English-speaking friends came to the house, well, of course they spoke English. So, we were learning the words. My recollection is that when I was five, I was allowed to start speaking [English], so I would know how to talk it for school. But, I knew it. I knew the words. It's just that now in the house, I was allowed to use the words. (F9)

No Dumont siblings, however, reported that they wished to speak only English and none seemed to feel stigmatized because of their French. As children, all except for the three youngest continued to speak French to family members who could not understand English, but they code-switched with family members and friends who commanded both languages.

World events such as the Second World War and the Korean War both greatly contributed to language shift among the Dumont siblings. All of the Dumont male siblings served in the armed forces, and this added important language domains which were dominated by English. In addition, all siblings sang patriotic English songs and listened to war news on English-language radio. Further, the GI bill helped put the male siblings through college (all but one earned at least a bachelor's degree) and moved them further away from the Francophone world of the family and farm. Finally, the burgeoning need for baby boomer educators sparked the careers in education of seven of the siblings, clearly an English-oriented occupation.

The family's move off of the farm into the town of Kingdom in 1955 seems to be a benchmark for the final shift from stable bilingualism to English predominance within the family. At this point, the Dumont father began working as a handyman and painter for summer residents at a nearby lake and interacted with his customers in English, though he still spoke French to his sons and their friends who worked for him. French was relegated to only one social domain, that of the home, and even there the remaining second-family children spoke mostly English to the Dumont father, who continued to speak French to them, and to the mother, who began now consistently to respond in English. According to M6, "before that, if we talked to her in English, she would say, you know, she'd stop, and you know, talk to me in French. But, then gradually, I don't know if we just wore her down at a certain age or she just said, they're getting older, just let it go."

By the mid-1950s, virtually all second-family siblings were speaking English to friends, even those who could speak French, and to one another. The last two siblings (twins M12 and M13) must have acquired some French as young children because they were spoken to by their parents in French until age three, the year the family moved to the village. But by the time they entered school, these two were almost completely monolingual English speakers. In fact, M12 has no memory of ever speaking French.

Finally, the passing of elders, many of whom were functionally monolingual Francophones, removed the need to speak French in order to communicate. After the Dumont paternal grandfather, who was the last of his generation in the nuclear family, died in 1950, it was possible for Dumont siblings to speak English to all nuclear family members. Since the father spoke to his children almost always in French, however, a passive knowledge of the language was still required for family communication.

Language Use and Attitudes

Although no English Only policies were in effect in Vermont during the Dumont siblings' school years, it is clear from our ethnohistoric survey that Anglo-American ideology was having a demonstrable impact on the wider FA community at this time in ways that eventually encroached on the bilingual/bicultural acquisition processes of the younger siblings. Whereas the first-family siblings benefited from institutions which nurtured their native language and culture while also enculturating them into the Anglophone world—bilingual parochial schools, a largely bilingual church, as well as a one-room schoolhouse in which their native language and culture were respected—second-family members were exposed to the deterioration of these institutions and thus had little opportunity to develop or maintain their bilingual capabilities. These are precisely the types of supportive institutions that, in the current political climate, would be eliminated or seriously undermined by the passage of restrictive English Only laws.

English Only Conditions in Vermont

Support for English Only has historically been considered to have variously anti-immigrant, anti-Hispanic/Latino, antibilingual education, classist, nativist, or conservative political roots. Vermont is an interesting venue for a study of language issues related to the English Only question because the state is not directly affected by most of these factors. Vermont is one of the most racially and linguistically homogenous states, with 98.7 percent of the population identifying themselves as white (U.S. Department of Commerce 1993) and 90.2 percent of Vermont households reported as speaking only English (U.S. Bureau of Census 1993). In addition, Vermont ranks relatively low (34th) among states in recent growth of its immigrant population, with only 0.3 percent immigrants admitted from 1987 to 1990 (Gale Research 1994). The state's small immigrant population is clustered around Burlington, Vermont's largest metropolitan area. Most recent immigrants, from Southeast Asia and Bosnia, have been generally well received by Vermonters. There is only a small Hispanic/Latino population (.07 percent), not all of whom are Spanish speakers. The population of LEP students is so small that there are currently no bilingual programs in Vermont public schools, though some schools do have ESL programs.

As to social class, as measured by income and education, the typical Vermonter is solidly middle class. Though the median family income for Vermonters ($34,780) falls slightly below the national average, Vermonters are relatively well educated. Vermont ranks ninth among states in persons twenty-five years or older who are high school graduates, twelfth for persons with bachelor's degrees, and eighth for persons with graduate or professional degrees.

Politically, Vermont is neither a Republican nor a conservative stronghold. Its present U.S. Senate delegation is made up of one Republican and one Democrat (James Jeffords and Patrick Leahy, respectively), both of whom are considered moderates. Vermont's lone member of the U.S. House of Representatives, Bernard Sanders, is the only independent member of Congress and is to the left of center politically. As to language politics, Vermont has no Official English law, nor is any such legislation pending at this time.

Attitudes toward English Only in Vermont

Despite the aforementioned political, social, and economic pressures on the Vermont FA population to assimilate, many second-generation FAs have managed to maintain a French Canadian identity and some degree of stable bilingualism. At the same time, Vermont's FA population has adapted very successfully to U.S. Anglophone society. This assimilation is reflected in recent attitudes about the official status of English in the United States. Although they are near victims of previous English Only policies regarding bilingual education, a majority (51.8 percent) of FAs surveyed support the passage of federal legislation which would make English the official language of the United States (Williams 1996).

Nonetheless, FA support for Official English is slightly less than that of the general population, their opposition is demonstrably greater, and their equivocation on the issue is less. The fact that FAs are more evenly split on this issue than the general population may be better explained through the following examination of more specific survey questions and an analysis of the Dumont siblings' attitudes (see Table 3.2).

Though there seems to be growing support in the United States for more restrictive language legislation, as evidenced by the passage in 1998 of an antibilingual initiative in California and the broad support for restrictive Official English legislation in the U.S. House of Representatives, this does not appear to be the

TABLE **3.2.** Support for Official English among FA and Non-FA Vermonters

Congress should pass a law making English the official language of the U.S.	Non-FA	FA
Agree	54.9%	51.8%
Undecided	17.6%	10.7%
Disagree	27.5%	37.5%

Source: Williams 1996

Note: The survey question asked respondents to agree or disagree, on a five-point scale, with the following question: *Congress should pass a law making English the official language of the United States.* Previous research has found that the more specific survey questions of support for English Only are, the less likely respondents are to favor such legislation (Crawford 1998; Zentella 1990).

case in Vermont. While most Vermonters support federal Official English legislation, this support is for mostly symbolic legislation, which would not prevent the government from providing services in languages other than English. Though both groups strongly support the acquisition of English as a prerequisite for U.S. citizenship, neither a majority of the FA nor the non-FA population supports the dismantling of current federal programs such as those which provide for bilingual education, multilingual voting materials, or court interpreters (see Table 3.3).

One apparent contradiction revealed by the poll is that, on the one hand, FAs favor suffrage for non-English-speaking immigrants at a dramatically higher rate than do non-FAs (item 5), while, on the other hand, FAs are much more likely than their non-FA counterparts to favor strict English requirements for prospective citizens (item 1). One possible explanation is that English as a marker of national identity takes on even more prominence for identifiable-but-assimilated ethnic groups, such as the FA, for whom the appearance of loyalty to the United States and to U.S. culture is of paramount importance. They also, however,

TABLE 3.3. Support for Official English and Restrictiveness of Legislation (Non-FA vs. FA)

Issues	Non-FA	FA
1. Immigrants should be required to read, write, and speak English before they are granted citizenship.	75.3%	86.2%
2. U.S. schools should not provide bilingual education for immigrant children.	34.4%	31.0%
3. Voting materials should not be translated into minority languages.	43.2%	41.4%
4. People accused of crimes who do not speak English should not be provided with an interpreter during court proceedings.	3.7%	0.0%
5. Citizens who do not speak English should still be able to vote.	58.4%	75.9%
6. People who work in stores and restaurants in Vermont should be able to speak some French.	40.5%	65.5%
7. All U.S. schoolchildren should be required to study a foreign language.	72.6%	75.9%

Source: Williams 1996

still fondly and clearly remember parents and/or grandparents who were intelligent, patriotic, and fully contributing members of the U.S. community who would have been excluded from voting privileges by such a linguistic restriction.

Another difference between non-FA and FA attitudes regarding language acquisition and usage is revealed through a comparison of items 6 and 7 in Table 3.3. FA responses to these questions show that, as a group, they see the value in bilingual competence more than do their non-FA counterparts. The greatest disparity between groups is seen in item 6, which asks whether Americans who interact with tourists should speak French. The FA response to this item shows perhaps some pride of linguistic heritage, but also a heightened sense that Vermont could be more accommodating to its Francophone neighbor to the north.

When asked to comment on their ethnic group identity, all Dumont family members emphasized that they were Americans first, even though some expressed strong FA identification as well. It is clear from the interviews that most consider speaking English an important marker of being American, view English as an essential tool for enculturation into mainstream U.S. society, and believe that such enculturation is essential to a successful life in the United States. In short, most agree with the majority of Vermonters that English is and ought to be supported by English Only legislation as a symbol of U.S. identity. Those who have retained some degree of bilingualism, however, are reluctant to abandon their French, while most who are no longer bilingual seem to feel some nostalgia for having lost what French-language competence they had. French, however, appears for many siblings to be less a symbol of their identification with French Canadian identity and more a useful tool in the world. This perspective is perhaps most true of M3, the best-educated member of the family and a high school teacher of French, who said simply: "[Knowing two] languages, you're going to be worth two men instead of one."

Clearly, support for Official English in Vermont, including the FA population and the Dumont family specifically, is due to causes other than those associated with nativist ideology. Both FA and non-FA responses to item 1, setting mastery of English as a threshold to citizenship, indicate shared normative views which hold English to be an important bond of common national identity. These findings are consistent with the results of previous research (Frendreis and Tatalovich 1997), which identified attitudinal variables regarding national identity and normative views concerning common identity as strong predictors of support for Official English legislation. Nonetheless, Vermonters in general tend not to support the more restrictive aspects of English Only legislation that are associated with anti-immigrant sentiments elsewhere in the country. Responses to items 5, 6, and 7, however, indicate possible group differences with regard to issues of cultural and linguistic diversity, with FAs being more tolerant of within-group cultural differences and more appreciative of multilingual ability.

Perhaps the most intriguing finding is that the Dumont siblings' attitudes toward restrictive legislation correlated much less to age (and therefore fluency in French as a result of early acculturation within a Francophone environment) than to present-day habitation and social patterns. That is, the least restrictive viewpoints are held by those who still live in Kingdom or in other nearby communities marked by FA culture and who thus retain some daily contact with an older generation of Francophones and with those of French Canadian heritage. On the other hand, those who have spent much of their adult lives in more urbanized and non-FA communities within or outside the state are the ones who are least sympathetic to the support of bilingual/bicultural institutions. It is beyond the scope of the present essay to discuss the intricacies of causality intimated by these correlations. For instance, did some imbibe the ideology of their new surroundings; did others move away in part because of already-held convictions? Nonetheless, it is an interesting fact that the two-family system of linguistic acquisition and retention is crosscut by family members' present day politico-linguistic beliefs.

Conclusion

In this chapter, we have set our study of language shift and cultural assimilation within one FA farming family in northeastern Vermont against the backdrop of social, political, and economic variables affecting FAs throughout New England over the past century and a half. We found that, as with influences elsewhere on FAs' maintenance of language and heritage, a number of key factors affected the Dumont family members' acquisition, use, and retention of French-speaking ability. The somewhat obvious bilingual/monolingual division according to the age of the siblings can be explained by two powerful variables: (1) differences in language socialization within the family and community and (2) access to bilingual/bicultural-"friendly" institutions: the Francophone farming community, the one-room schoolhouse, and the church.

In political climates hostile to multiculturalism and multilingualism, it becomes difficult for such institutions to function. The passage of restrictive Official English legislation would not only forbid schools from actively supporting the home cultures and languages of their students, but it would also foster beliefs among minority cultures that speaking English and only English is the best marker of a patriotic American.

While FA language-use patterns clearly have been affected by the kinds of social trends associated with Official English legislation, FAs' opinions about such legislation cannot be so easily inferred from the history of impact. Some of the contradictions indicated in the poll are borne out by family differences. Thus strong English Only proponents can be found among the most bilingual elder siblings of the Dumont family, whereas some of the younger and least bilingual siblings are opposed to restrictive legislation. The variables influencing these opinions are too complex to be fully addressed here. What is clear is that although all of the Dumont siblings evince a belief in an America symbolically united by a single language, they also all still express in a recognizably FA fashion a rich and nurturing sense of their family's linguistic strengths and unique heritage.

Works Cited

Brault, Gerard J. 1986. *The French-Canadian Heritage in New England.* Hanover: University Press of New England.

———. 1996. "The Achievement of the Teaching Orders in New England: The Franco-American Parochial Schools." In Claire Quintal, ed., *Steeples and Smokestacks: A Collection of Essays on the Franco-American Experience in New England*. Worcester, MA: Institut français, Assumption College. 267–91.

Chartier, Armand. 1996. "The Spiritual and Intellectual Foundations of the Schooling of Franco-Americans." In Claire Quintal, ed., *Steeples and Smokestacks: A Collection of Essays on the Franco-American Experience in New England*. Worcester, MA: Institut français, Assumption College. 233–66.

Crawford, James. 1998. "Opinion Polls on Official English." *James Crawford's Language Policy Emporium* [Online]: http://ourworld. compuserve.com/homepages/jwcrawford/home2.htm.

Doty, C. Stewart. 1995. "How Many Frenchmen Does It Take To?" *Thought and Action: The NEA Higher Education Journal* 11(2): 85–104.

———. 1997. "Monsieur Maurras est ici": French Fascism in Franco-American New England." *Journal of Contemporary History* 32(4): 527–38.

Fishman, Joshua A. 1989. *Language and Ethnicity in Minority Sociolinguistic Perspective*. Philadelphia: Multilingual Matters.

Fishman, Joshua A., ed. 1966. *Language Loyalty in the United States: The Maintenance and Perpetuation of Non-English Mother Tongues by American Ethnic and Religious Groups*. The Hague, Neth.: Mouton.

Frendreis, John, and Raymond Tatalovich. 1997. "Who Supports English-Only Language Laws? Evidence from the 1992 National Election Study." *Social Science Quarterly* 78(2): 354–68.

Gal, Susan. 1979. *Language Shift*. New York: Academic Press.

Gale Research, Inc. 1994. *Gale State Rankings Reporter*. Detroit, MI: Gale Research.

Guiguére, Madeleine. 1991. "Recent and Current Sociological and Anthropological Research on Franco-Americans." In Dean Louder, ed., *Le Québec et les francophones de la Nouvelle-Angleterre*. Sainte-Foy, Quebec: Les Presses de l'Université Laval. 85–106.

———. 1996. "New England's Francophone Population: Based upon the 1990 Census." In Claire Quintal, ed., *Steeples and Smokestacks: A Collection of Essays on the Franco-American Experience in New England*. Worcester, MA: Institut français, Assumption College. 567–94.

Gumperz, John J. 1982. *Discourse Strategies*. Cambridge, U.K.: Cambridge University Press.

Hill, Jane H., and Kenneth C. Hill. 1986. *Speaking Mexicano: Dynamics of Syncretic Language in Central Mexico*. Tucson: University of Arizona Press.

Jacobson, Phyllis L. 1984. "The Social Context of Franco-American Schooling in New England." *The French Review* 57(5): 641–56.

Kulick, Don. 1992. *Language Shift and Cultural Reproduction: Socialization, Self, and Syncretism in a Papua New Guinean Village*. Cambridge, U.K.: Cambridge University Press.

Labov, William. 1972. *Sociolinguistic Patterns*. Philadelphia: University of Pennsylvania Press.

LeBlanc, Charlotte Bordes. 1996. "History and Mission of the Fédération Féminine Franco-Américaine (1951–1991)." In Claire Quintal, ed., *Steeples and Smokestacks: A Collection of Essays on the Franco-American Experience in New England*. Worcester, MA: Institut français, Assumption College. 501–11.

Lemaire, Hervé B. 1966. "Franco-American Efforts on Behalf of the French Language in New England." In Joshua Fishman, ed., *Language Loyalty in the United States: The Maintenance and Perpetuation of Non-Engish Mother Tongues by American Ethnic and Religious Groups*. The Hague, Neth.: Mouton. 253–79.

Miller, Mary R. 1969. *Bilingualism in Northern New England*. Publication of the American Dialect Society, University of Alabama Press, No. 52.

Milroy, Lesley. 1987. *Language and Social Networks* (2nd ed.). Oxford, U.K.: Basil Blackwell.

Ochs, Elinor. 1988. *Culture and Language Development: Language Acquisition and Language Socialization in a Samoan Village*. Cambridge, U.K.: Cambridge University Press.

Perreault, Robert B. 1996. "The Franco-American Press: An Historical Overview." In Claire Quintal, ed., *Steeples and Smokestacks: A Collection of Essays on the Franco-American Experience in New England*. Worcester, MA: Institut français, Assumption College. 315–41.

Quintal, Claire. 1991. "Les institutions franco américaines: pertes et progrès." In Dean Lauder, ed., *Le Québec et les francophones de la Nouvelle Angleterre*. Sainte Foy, Québec: Les Presses de l'Université Laval. 61–84.

Roby, Yves. 1996a. "Franco-Americans and the Catholic Hierarchy." In Claire Quintal, ed., *Steeples and Smokestacks: A Collection of Essays on the Franco-American Experience in New England*. Worcester, MA: Institut français, Assumption College. 201–6.

————. 1996b. "From Franco-Americans to Americans of French-Canadian Origin or Franco-Americanism, Past and Present." In Claire Quintal, ed., *Steeples and Smokestacks: A Collection of Essays on the Franco-American Experience in New England*. Worcester, MA: Institut français, Assumption College. 609–25.

Schieffelin, Bambi B. 1990. *The Give and Take of Everyday Life: Language Socialization of Kaluli Children*. Cambridge, U.K.: Cambridge University Press.

Schieffelin, Bambi B., and Elinor Ochs. 1996. "The Microgenesis of Competence: Methodology in Language Socialization." In Dan Isaac Slobin, Julie Gerhardt, Amy Kyratzis, and Jiansheng Guo, eds., *Social Interaction, Social Context, and Language: Essays in Honor of Susan Ervin-Tripp*. Mahwah, NJ: Lawrence Erlbaum.

U.S. Bureau of the Census. 1993. "1990 Census Special Tabulation—Language Spoken at Home and Ability to Speak English for United States, Regions and States." Unpublished tabulation. CPHL 159.

U.S. Department of Commerce, Bureau of the Census. 1993. "Census of Population and Housing." Summary Tape File for the State of Vermont. Washington, D.C.

Williams, Robert. 1996. *Should English Be 'Official'? The 1996 Vermont Language Attitudes Survey*. Unpublished manuscript.

Woolfson, Peter. 1983a. *Franco-Americans in Vermont: A Civil Rights Perspective. Report of the Vermont Advisory Committee to the U.S. Commission on Civil Rights*. Washington, D.C.: Government Printing Office.

————. 1983b. "The Franco-Americans of Northern Vermont: Cultural Factors for Consideration by Health and Social Services Providers." In Peter Woolfson and André Senécal, eds., *The French in Vermont: Some Current Views*. The Center for Research on Vermont Occasional Papers Series, No. 6. Burlington: University of Vermont. 1–26.

Zentella, Ana Celia. 1990. "Who supports official English, and why? The influence of social variables and questionnaire methodology." In Karen Adams and David Brink, eds. *Perspectives on Official English*. New York: Mouton de Gruyter.

————. 1997. *Growing Up Bilingual: Puerto Rican Children in New York*. Malden, MA: Blackwell.

II

LANGUAGE, JUSTICE, AND LAW

E ach of the four chapters in this section approaches minority
  language and the position of bi- and multilingual individuals in predominantly monolingual societies from the perspectives
of social justice and law. David Corson's work represents the
most general theoretical perspective; that is, his inquiry is about
how minority-language speakers should be fairly treated in a just
society. Corson relies on a critical revision of John Rawls's theory
of justice and argues that a concept of social justice which is
based exclusively on individual rights cannot address the rights
of language minorities because language is communally owned
by individuals. With some modifications of the original liberal
theory, however, an emancipatory conception of social justice
can be developed that allows communities to examine the rights
and needs of language minorities through the lens of critical realism. Corson's chapter outlines three fundamental principles that
policymakers should follow in multilingual communities. These
principles can govern social action that fosters language awareness, a realistic and critical way of combining "respect for the
good of the individual with respect for the good of the social
group" (p. 118). One important feature of Corson's theorizing
about social justice as related to language minorities is that his
principles can be applied to "nonstandard language policy" in
general without distinguishing between minority-language and
"substandard" dialect or variety. Corson shares the view of those
linguists'who, following Labov, reject the stereotype that nonstandard varieties of language are incorrect. He maintains that
current practices of ostracizing nonstandard speakers in schools
are intolerant and discriminatory. These varieties deserve respect,
like any other language, and their speakers also have a right to
acquire the dominant-language variety in school.

Although both Juan F. Perea and Guadalupe Valdes examine similar, and even some identical court cases, these two chapters present the courtroom conflicts of bilingual individuals from two different perspectives. Perea, an expert of law, is frustrated with the court, state, and federal legislatures' failure to provide equal protection for language minorities simply because the exclusion of bilingual jurors from jury duty, or the prohibition against using a minority language in the workplace, does not seem to violate any basic rights and is not suspected of discrimination as the law is currently interpreted. The reason judges fail to recognize instances of discrimination in these language-related cases is that society in general is hostile toward immigrants and minorities. If legal procedures will not change until society changes, educators can make a vital contribution to changing the current social climate, which seems to be the only way society can move from the currently hostile position to appreciating the linguistic resources of the United States and using law to support this heritage rather than squelch it.

Valdes reaches similar conclusions and also stresses the need for social change. The popular support that English Only advocates get in many states demonstrates that many in the United States look on multilingualism as un-American and view the growing immigrant population as a threat. Basically, argues Valdes, English Only is a symptom of anti-immigrant sentiments, and as such cannot be challenged simply by reasonable arguments about rights, justice, or the nature of language acquisition. Valdes is also certain that the cited court cases violate multi- and bilingual individuals' civil rights, and society in general places a greater burden on bilingual individuals by forcing them not only to learn the dominant language, but also to eradicate or suppress their first language. This unfair practice is fostered by ignorance: monolingual individuals cannot understand the bi- or miltilingual perspective; they do not see why, for example, it would be reasonable and just to pay more for someone's bilingual services, or why it is odd to ask a bilingual individual to listen to what is said in one language only. Valdes also examines the potential benefits of making a case for linguistic human rights, as is done in international contexts, but concludes that language discrimination must take into account linguistic *civil* rights.

Finally, Randy H. Lee and David F. Marshall explore another aspect of English Only legislation, raising the question of when it is really worth going to law. As Molly Ivins pointed out, "the art of writing law so that it does precisely what it is supposed to do and does not do anything else has always been hard to come by" (qtd. on p. 172). Lee and Marshall cite many examples of ill-fated laws that actually created worse crises than those they were meant to remedy, and argue that making English the official language of the United States is a likely candidate for becoming such a counterproductive law. English is already the de facto official language in the United States, and the move to make it the de jure official language amounts to fixing a language policy that is not broken. After discussing what laws can and cannot do from a statutory perspective, Lee and Marshall enumerate seven unwanted and unanticipated consequences of English Only law that its proponents overlook.

CHAPTER FOUR

Social Justice, Language Policy, and English Only

DAVID CORSON
Ontario Institute for Studies in Education,
University of Toronto, Canada

In this essay, I try to offer a clear and accessible social justice framework for making language policy decisions in education and society, in particular for making key policy decisions related to the English Only debate in the United States. I begin with a critique of the rather individualist approach to justice offered by John Rawls that still dominates discussion about social justice in the United States. Then I contrast that approach with a "critically real" approach to judging social justice that is more respectful of minority-group interests and more closely linked to the way the world actually is. A critically real approach to social justice recognizes that diversity is part of the reality of the human condition. This is true for language diversity no less than other forms of diversity. Because human groups and individuals have distinctly different language interests, those differences often need to be addressed in different ways in public policy if social justice is to be served.

In the second and third sections of the chapter, I relate this approach to the English Only issue by dealing with two aspects of that issue:

◆ the importance, on social justice grounds, of providing bilingual education to minority-language students up to the middle years of childhood; or, at the very least, the importance of providing education that fully respects children's first languages

◆ the importance, on social justice grounds, of designing fairer language policies in education for the users of nonstandard varieties of English

Social Justice

Social justice has to do with ideas about legitimacy, about fairness and impartiality, about welfare and mutual advantage, and about political and social consensus. The fair treatment of speakers of language varieties that are not the dominant dialect is one key concern of social justice theorists. Justice itself relates to the way that benefits and burdens are distributed, and is usually said to exist when people receive that to which they are entitled (Barry 1989). The question of who is entitled to decide which language varieties should be used in public domains in the United States is at the heart of the English Only debate.

In discussions of ethics and political philosophy in the United States over recent generations, the social justice ideas of John Rawls have been dominant. Rawls (1973, 1980, 1993) sees the individual as the starting point for any discussion about the criteria for a just society. The following paragraphs summarize Rawls's theory, suggesting some of its weaknesses. Later I move to a more recent conception that modifies Rawls's stark individualism. This theory gives prominence to the justice needs of social groups, alongside and sometimes even ahead of the needs of individuals. This critically real approach recognizes that people are inevitably shaped by society and culture, and that a conception of individualism that ignores this fact is an impoverished one because it misses seeing the way people really are.

I argue that considerable room must be made for this critically real approach in any discussion of social justice and language if we are to give sufficient recognition to the most obvious feature of language itself: its essential role in allowing and promoting communicative interaction between social groups of two or more people. My general point, then, in opposition to a starkly individualist account of justice, is this: If our aim is to provide, in education and society, language arrangements that are just ones, while also considering the rightful needs of individuals, then we must inevitably consider the needs of the group at the same time as the individual, since language in its literal sense is a feature of human collectivities. A language is a set of social conventions having value and meaning only when it develops over time from the interactional and communicative needs of social groups. As a social institution itself, a language is not just an instrumental convenience made available by chance to the individuals who acquire it. Rather, it is the very means by which individual human beings are socialized and from which they develop a consciousness of themselves. This consciousness is a direct and unique reflection of the culture that comprises the many social, ethnic, class, and gender groups who share the language.

In promoting social justice in language policy matters, then, little can be done for the individual that does not begin with the group at the same time. And speakers of minority-language varieties are no less "language groups" than the different groups of majority-language speakers in a given setting.

The Rawls Account of Social Justice and Some Canadian Accounts

The basic idea to which Rawls is committed is also a cornerstone of ethics: no individual can be treated as a means to the ends of society. Working from this basic tenet, he sees social justice as the content of an agreement that rational people would reach under conditions that do not allow bargaining power to be translated into advantage. In other words, social justice decisions need to be made in an impartial way by decision makers who do not benefit unreasonably themselves by choosing as they do.

Under the terms of Rawls's theory, proponents of English Only policies would have to support those policies even if theywould be disadvantaged by them. These policymakers would try to work out what arrangements ought to exist and do this in a context free of self-interest and bias. They would decide what was just, after detaching themselves from their own interests and while adopting a standpoint of strict impartiality. Rawls calls this attempt at detachment a "veil of ignorance."

One of the earliest expressions of this impartial approach to justice is the New Testament's Golden Rule, which advises us to do unto others as we would have them do unto us. And most of the world's religions have a similar injunction. Yet even this cornerstone of beneficence from the world's scriptures has a dark underside, as George Bernard Shaw cautions: Don't do to others as you would have them do to you; their tastes might be different. This is a wry twist to the rule, but there is more than humor in Shaw's rider. He reminds us that we cannot easily see the world from the point of view of most other people because they are different from us, so we cannot easily make well-informed and fair decisions on behalf of those others in the neat way Rawls envisions.

In other words, it is usually difficult to determine in advance what fair treatment would be in any given context if one is not a participant in the discursive practices of that context and knowledgeable about all the cultural and historical influences that shape that context. This is especially true in matters of language policy, for which it is not easy to create a context free of self-interest and bias, because each of us is burdened with the bias of the language varieties we already possess, and few can be neutral in judging the interests of their own language variety's speakers against the speakers of language varieties that are not their own. We cannot step outside the interests that our socialization into a language variety creates for us, because it is these very interests, and the similar interests of those who share our language, that we feel ourselves obliged to defend, even through the use of the same language.

Indeed, Rawls's conception of the individual seems "unreal" because it sets the individual apart from the social being. Furby (1986) and Sandel (1982) argue that the individual in Rawls's account lacks human sociality. Even in his later modifications of the theory, it is hard to escape the conclusion that the individual agents in Rawls's account all display the attitudes and beliefs of men in modern market societies in a consistent and exclusive way. Moreover, he admits the practical limitations of his "well-ordered society"; it needs to be "a closed system" that has "no significant relations to other societies" (Rawls 1980, 526). This implies, of course, a society with no significant relations with other language speakers, where everyone has broadly the same goals, values, interests, and worldview.

For language policy issues, these are problematic aspects of a theory of justice because, as I have argued, language is a creation of social beings and has value for the individual largely in social interaction. Even the private language in which much of our thinking is conducted is fueled by social exchanges: To a real extent, our very capacity to think depends on the many previous dialogues in which we have engaged. So the sense of a collective being who is produced and produces him- or herself through interaction within and across groups in a society or culture is missing in Rawls's theory. Nor does his early work focus on the institutional relations that are part of the social being and which underlie economic classes (Nielsen 1978; Young 1981). Instead, he seems to see class inequality, and therefore cultural, gender, and linguistic inequality, as inevitable structures even in his ideal human social system.

In contrast, prominent liberal theories of social justice recently advanced in Canada have tried to incorporate aspects of a more collectivist ethic. Charles Taylor (1992) believes that a society with strong collectivist goals can still be liberal if it is capable of respecting diversity, especially diversity that includes those who might not share its common goals. For Taylor, the political search by Quebec for recognition of its distinctness as a society within Canada is a collective goal that can be allowed to override individual rights under certain circumstances. Taylor (1992) further suggests that the "rigidities of procedural liberalism may rapidly become impractical in tomorrow's world" (61).

As critics of liberalism often observe, "what defines liberalism is its disregard for the context of choice, for the way that choices are situated in cultural communities" (Kymlicka 1989, 206). This usually translates into an active hostility by proponents of liberalism to minority rights, so that "schemes which single out minority cultures for special measures," such as bilingual education programs, seem "irremediably unjust, a disguise for creating or maintaining racial or ethnic privilege" (4). As a liberal theorist himself, Will Kymlicka tries to rehabilitate liberalism as it is commonly interpreted, especially by addressing its failure to respond to people's strong intuitions about the importance of cultural membership. In doing so, he also reexamines and questions the moral ontology of liberalism itself—its individualism and its taken-for-granted, naive, and uncritical egalitarianism. He argues that membership in a cultural or linguistic community has to be a relevant criterion for distributing the benefits and burdens which are the concern of a liberal theory of justice.

Critical Realism: An Emancipatory Conception of Social Justice

The prominent British philosopher of science Roy Bhaskar calls his emancipatory conception of discovery "critical realism" (Bhaskar 1986; Corson 1997). Unlike Rawls's theory, this conception sees the needs of different groups as quite different needs that arise from different group interests, and which often require different forms of treatment. In other words, to treat people equally and fairly, we do not treat them as if they were all the same.

Critical realism is an ontology. It asks, what are the most basic things that exist in the social world; what are the things that need to be recognized in the search for justice, or in the search for knowledge about anything? Bhaskar shows that the most basic evidence we can have about the social world includes the reasons and accounts that relevant individuals offer to describe those things in the social world they value, or those things that oppress them.

Decision makers creating a policy need to consult the reasons and accounts of participants who have interests at stake in the decision. Policymakers do this early in the process, and they keep on doing it at every stage. In fact, the policymakers themselves change. They are different people as the policy comes closer to local settings because they need to be increasingly in touch with the reality of those settings. This implies an ordered, devolutionary approach to policymaking.

Briefly, this means devolving real decision-making power to those who are actually in touch with the things that oppress them or with the things that they value. For example, in multilingual settings, this decision making might include the following stages of increased devolution:

1. consulting at the wider system level (attending to the interests of those with a stake in the issue) to draw up any norms that could operate as principles across the system in an effort to increase the scope for optional use of any single minority language alongside English, and also alongside other minority languages

2. consulting in devolved local settings to establish more local norms for allotting status to minority languages, critically accepting the norms already identified at system level
as a necessary starting point, and making use of any grounds
for compatibility that follow from both sets of norms

3. consulting (as often as necessary) in decision making within
increasingly devolved local settings; establishing subnorms
where needed to determine compatibility; and eventually, if
necessary, compromising on incompatible issues

Throughout this process, compatible interests between language-
minority groups provide the material for constructing overriding
norms, while incompatible interests become the subject of compromise at more local levels (e.g., state, community, district,
school, grade-level, classroom, individual student).

The first norms, or principles, for policymakers to decide on
are those that apply at the whole-system level. Following are some
suggested principles for use in minority-language policymaking
in education at the state or national level (Corson and Lemay 1996).
To meet the type of diversity found in multilingual settings such as
the United States, three policy principles seem necessary:

1. This principle guarantees the right of children to be educated whenever possible in the same variety of language that
is learned at home or is valued most by the family. For instance, young speakers of Spanish or French as a first language would be taught through that first language as their
vehicle of instruction for most of the school day.

2. When the first policy principle cannot be met, the second
principle guarantees the right of children to attend a school
that shows full respect for the language variety learned at
home or valued most by the family, including respect for its
role in preserving important ethnic, traditional, social, gender, or religious values and interests. In other words, use of
the minority-language variety would be encouraged and valued in every school context, even while it is not used as the

vehicle of instruction. (For an extensive list of approaches to valuing minority languages in schools, see Corson 1999.)

3. This policy principle guarantees the right of children to learn, to the highest level of proficiency possible, the standard-language variety of wider communication used by the society as a whole. In other words, complete mastery of the local variety of English would be a key goal of children's education.

This third principle also meets the main concerns of English Only advocates in the United States, if I understand them correctly. Clearly it would be socially unjust if any student left school without sufficient mastery of the local variety of English to continue on to later stages of education and to live happily and autonomously in this country.

Later in this chapter I discuss further the first principle. The ethical justification for minority first-language maintenance comes from the reasons and accounts of relevant users of that language in the local context. If the local people value first-language maintenance in schools, then, following a critically real approach, policymakers are ethically obliged to support the first principle, or at least the second principle if local conditions of linguistic pluralism make it impossible to support the first.

On the other hand, if local people want nothing more than access to English-language instruction, policymakers are obliged to respect that view too, but only after they have engaged in community education to point out the likely negative consequences of following that policy. People need to be fairly informed of the academic advantages of bilingual education they would be denying their children (see the section "The Advantages of Being Bilingual"). And people need to be fairly informed of the intellectual advantages of being bilingual.

At the same time, in settings where many languages exist alongside one another, it might not be possible for more than a few schools to be organized to meet the first principle. In discussions of ethics, "ought" always implies "can": People are not obliged to do what they cannot reasonably do. Again, in these highly pluralist settings, the second principle becomes the second-best alternative for most schools.

Yet the second principle is hardly good enough for children from a broad range of backgrounds. Clearly, as I argue below, just valuing the minority language does not go far enough for many students, such as hearing-impaired children who sign, or users of Native American languages, or children in general for whom loss of their minority first language would create academic difficulties (Corson 1999). These children and many others will always need the support that the first policy principle offers.

The Choice: Socially Just Language Policies or English Only?

The demographic changes raise other questions about political and economic power. Will that power, now held disproportionately by whites, be shared in the new America? What will happen when Hispanics overtake blacks as the nation's single largest minority?

Fear of strangers, of course, is nothing new in American history. . . . [But] despite this strife, many historians argue that there was a greater consensus in the past on what it meant to be an American, a yearning for a common language and culture, and a desire to assimilate.

Today, they say, there is more emphasis on preserving one's ethnic identity, on finding ways to highlight and defend one's cultural roots. The question is whether, in the midst of such change, there is also enough glue to hold Americans together. (Booth 1998, 17)

Barely perceptible changes in status are occurring today in the United States perhaps more than at any other time in this country's recent past. And those who have a vested interest in the status quo are beginning to resent those changes. While there is nothing necessarily sinister about this resentment, it is dangerous if it encourages people to ignore the fact that diversity is part of the reality of the social world as a whole, not just part of the realities of dominant sectional groups in society. In democracies, dominant groups usually go to great lengths to permit diversity among their members: in religion, in social preferences, in lifestyle, and so forth. But nondominant groups often meet prejudice, which succeeds in ostracizing or oppressing because nondominant groups lack the voice to prevent it.

A critical realist perspective acknowledges the existence of diversity as something that can no longer be excluded from human affairs, or from deciding social policy. So for me, a major objection to the English Only movement is that it is sadly out of touch with the real world. And because it distorts this reality to serve the interests of sectional groups, the main idea behind English Only is a dangerous ideology, one that will have harmful results for those whose interests it does not serve, and eventually even for the sectional interests of those who promote it.

Status Planning and Social Justice

Changes in status, like those Booth mentions, affect languages and their speakers all the time in incidental ways. But the aim of the English Only movement is to advance planned language change to promote the status of English. Accordingly, the movement's activities fall firmly within the area of study known as status-language planning. In this approach to language planning, the way a language is used in society is changed in planned ways in order to affect its status (see Wodak and Corson 1997).

As an example: French and English in Canada have been made official languages of the country as a whole. A range of government programs and legislation now operate in Canada to help make this law work in practice. In contrast, in the United States there are some who would make English the sole official language. This would also require a range of government programs and legislation, so it would also be a form of status-language planning, albeit heading in a more narrow direction in justice terms. To change the status of English in this way would change the status of other languages in the United States, especially the widely spoken Spanish language. Also, when the status of a language changes, the status of its users is affected as well.

Canada's policy of bilingualism deliberately raised the status of speakers of French across the country, and it did so in ways that are more consistent with a critically real approach to social justice because the policy responded directly to the reasons and experiences of French speakers. I should add that the policy has caused some petty inconveniences in some places for speakers of

English. On a more serious level, it has left speakers of Native and immigrant languages in an undefined policy position. But overall the inconveniences have been minor, especially when balanced against the greater good that has resulted for French speakers and the markedly better climate for diversity in general that Canada has begun to enjoy as a result of this expression of tolerance (Corson and Lemay 1996).

In contrast, an English Only policy in the United States would deliberately reduce the status of many Spanish and other minority-language speakers in the country and privilege speakers of English in almost every public context. And in this case, the inconveniences inflicted on the minority-language speakers would go well beyond the petty. By restricting the use of minority languages, this policy would impose severe constraints on freedom of movement, freedom of action, and freedom of speech for the speakers of those languages. Indeed, I doubt that the U.S. Constitution could tolerate the resulting long-term inconsistencies. But my concern here is with the pursuit of social justice, which always runs well ahead of archaic constitutional details, or at least should do so.

An English Only policy is the result of the kind of decision that Rawls's approach to social justice should be able to discourage. Yet in practice, the Rawls approach would actually sanction English Only policies in many contexts. As mentioned, Rawls works from a first principle rather like the Golden Rule, but his first principle avoids the rider that George Bernard Shaw adds to that rule. It avoids the fact that decision makers cannot see the world from the point of view of those who are different from themselves and who do not enjoy the same privileged language position.

The work of language planners now attracts more critical attention because so much language planning directly or indirectly bolsters the language varieties of speakers who are already privileged in many ways. Often it does so at the expense of the majority of people in a given language community whose language varieties are marginalized as a result of their speakers' lowly sociocultural status and near powerlessness. Bilingual education is even stigmatized by many as being a part of the problem, rather than a major part of the solution (Fillmore 1998).

DAVID CORSON

Bilingual Education, Social Justice, and English Only

A helpful definition of bilingual education contrasts it clearly with English as a second language (ESL) education. Bilingual education differs from ESL in using a nondominant language as the medium of instruction during some substantial part of the school day (Cummins and Corson 1997). Regrettably, this distinction seems to escape the notice of many educational policymakers in the United States and elsewhere.

The United States' Bilingual Education Act legislation seems to respond directly to the fact that the premature loss of minority students' first languages tends to inhibit their transition to learning the majority tongue. But in practice, the response of most schools and school districts has been to treat language-minority students solely as English deficient. These students lack English, so the typical policy response in schools is to give them extra teaching in English and to expect a rapid transition to the use of English across the curriculum. This is close to the zero level of first-language support sanctioned by the Unz initiative in California.

Indeed, given the fact that speaking only English has been repeatedly upheld as essential to a truly American ethnicity, there seem to be major obstacles to moving beyond this attitude in the discourses of power in the United States. And today, these "English first" policies get far wider political support in the United States than in other countries (Ricento 1997; Cummins and Corson 1997). The clear trend in the United States seems to be away from bilingual education (Fillmore 1998), away from the realities of the world, and away from social justice.

For most of the history of schooling in English-speaking countries, minority-language children have not had the valuable start that bilingual education offers. Almost everywhere in the English-speaking world the standard practice, after enrolling minority-language students, is to ignore their first languages and give them as much ESL as possible as soon as possible. Teachers and administrators often do more than ignore the minority language, forbidding its use in the school environment and mocking its users, arguing wrongly that to allow its use in any way would interfere with the learning of English and prevent students from becoming fully involved in the majority culture.

Recently, much more thought has been given to the fairness and the educational effectiveness of this policy. Educators are more aware these days of what happens when schools do not build on children's first languages in the early to middle school years. They realize the importance for brain development of the signs and symbols that children experience in learning their first language. These signs, especially first-language words and other expressions, shape the early brain development of the young long before they arrive in school (Corson 1995). Although this is not a shaping in any final sense, it is incorrect to think that the different encounters with cultural signs that minority-language children have had are irrelevant to their learning in the new setting. Acting on this false belief is likely to disadvantage many minority-language children academically. It also prevents them from making use of the best vehicle available to them for engaging with their new culture: their first language.

Indeed, there are powerful intellectual and cultural advantages to maintaining young children's first languages in school. By giving young minority-language students carefully designed bilingual education, schools provide benefits that go well beyond those offered by ESL education.

The Advantages of Being Bilingual

Until the 1950s, most research on bilingualism viewed it as a rather unhelpful possession, useful mainly for professional interpreters. Bilingualism was seen as a problem for education to remove, mainly through intensive teaching in the majority language aimed at bringing students quickly into the majority culture. But highly successful programs in the 1960s, especially those provided for Anglophones in French-immersion programs in Montreal, helped bring about change. New theories developed that took account of sociocultural factors in the development of bilingualism. This work added weight to the growing body of evidence suggesting that there are real intellectual and sociocultural advantages to having a bilingual education.

The bilingual education issue is complicated by sharp differences in the value placed on minority languages in schools in different places and at different times. The early bilingual research studies, from 1910 to 1960, were themselves affected by bias and distortion (Corson 1998, 1999). Widespread racism in the early twentieth century helped make minority languages unpopular, and the users of these languages often became ashamed of them. So in most countries, including the United States and Canada, whole generations of people refused to use their minority first languages in public. These language varieties were also thought to pose a threat to social cohesion and national solidarity. As a result, in formal education efforts were made almost everywhere to replace minority languages with the dominant language. Additionally, policymakers selectively preferred research evidence showing the negative effects of bilingualism, while other positive research was ignored. Although recent research confirms the great benefits of bilingual education (Collier 1992; Cummins and Corson 1997), the effects of the earlier distortions continue in some places, and they certainly continue to influence public policy.

Since the 1960s, evidence has been growing to confirm a point that might seem obvious with the benefit of hindsight: bilingual children have much more experience in using language, which should translate into improved performance in most of the areas of activity where language and thought converge (Collier 1992; Cummins and Corson 1997). Research in the physical sciences has long supported this claim; bilinguals are said to mature earlier than monolinguals, both in the development of cerebral lateralization for language use and in acquiring skills for linguistic abstraction. But there are other advantages too. For example, maintaining the minority language is said by many to develop a desirable form of cultural diversity in societies; it promotes ethnic identity, leads to social adaptability, adds to the psychological security of the child, and develops linguistic awareness (Crystal 1987).

Research on bilingualism also shows that becoming bilingual has cognitive advantages for the learner (Cummins 1996). There is growing evidence for the following claims:

◆ bilinguals are superior to monolinguals on divergent thinking tests

- bilinguals have some advantage in their analytical orientation to language

- bilinguals show some increased social sensitivity in situations requiring verbal communication

- bilinguals have some advantages in clear thinking and analytical functioning

These advantages prompted further questions about the value of offering bilingual education more widely. An important question to answer is whether schools for language minorities are better at doing what they do if they offer quality bilingual programs. The evidence suggests that they are.

The Advantages of Bilingual Education for Young Children

Quality bilingual education is a recent development in its early stages of evolution. But these programs are developing rapidly in some places to serve very different national needs: as a step in moving toward recognizing a single or several national languages; as a way of making national contact with a world language; as a way of putting to use the multilingual resources that immigrants bring to a country; and as a way of extending language rights and social justice to linguistic minorities. As mentioned, this kind of bilingual education is still not widely available in the United States, for reasons that are partly historical and partly ideological.

Cummins and Corson (1997) provide a guide to the international research in bilingual education. The consistently positive reviews from the forty countries surveyed overturn some earlier views about bilingualism and education:

- They offer strong evidence that quality bilingual programs have been influential in developing language skills and building academic achievement generally.

- They prove the common view—that immersion programs are only effective with the very young—to be mistaken.

♦ They suggest that in some respects older learners have advantages over younger ones.

♦ They report evidence that lower-ability children also benefit from immersion programs.

♦ They conclude that a quality bilingual program will support and aid development in the first language.

Two theories developed by Cummins provide a backdrop to much of the recent research.

CUMMINS'S TWO HYPOTHESES

In 1976 Cummins published his "threshold hypothesis," which has become influential in explaining differences in the achievement of students in second-language programs, and its conclusion is widely supported by research studies in many places, notably Australia, Italy, and India (Cummins 1996). According to this theory, there may be minimum or threshold levels of competence that bilingual children must attain in their first languages to avoid cognitive disadvantages and to allow the potentially beneficial aspects of becoming bilingual to influence cognitive functioning.

This first hypothesis helps explain many different things about the educational success and failure of minority-language groups. As a basis for educational policy, it suggests that minority-language maintenance should be available to minority-language children until the years of middle childhood if their academic achievement is not to suffer. In other words, on social justice grounds, language policies should sanction bilingual education whenever possible as an alternative form of education that language-minority communities can avail themselves of.

A second hypothesis from Cummins (1996) is also relevant. The "interdependence hypothesis" looks at the relationship between the learner's first and second languages. Certain aspects of language proficiency are common to both first and second languages—aspects that are interdependent. As a result, less instruction in the second language often results in higher second-language proficiency scores for students who are young users of a minority language. But more instruction in their second language results in higher second-language proficiency scores for majority-language students.

Three key points about minority bilingual education follow from these two theories:

◆ A high level of proficiency in both languages is likely to provide an intellectual advantage to children in all subjects over their monolingual classmates.

◆ In social situations where there is likely to be serious erosion of the immigrant language, that language needs maintaining until the years of middle childhood to support the learning of English and to support academic learning.

◆ High-level second-language proficiency depends on well-developed first-language proficiency (i.e., like the proficiency in their first language that older ESL students have).

Arguing from these three points, Cummins (1996) concludes that young children from language-minority groups profit from bilingual programs if their minority first language plays the major role because this lays a language foundation that cannot otherwise be guaranteed. This contrasts with the findings for children from majority-language backgrounds, who benefit from bilingual programs in which the second language is used more frequently. In this second case, a firm foundation in the majority first language develops quite naturally because it is the language of wider communication in society. Similarly, older immigrant students whose first languages are already well developed benefit most from English Only programs in which their first language is not supported as a vehicle of instruction (Corson 1999).

Maintenance Bilingual Education Programs at Work

Increasingly, maintenance bilingual education programs—programs with the objective of maintaining minority languages and literacy—are living up to the research on bilingualism. Bilingual programs for minority-language children are the subject of extensive study and development in many places (see Cummins and Corson 1997; Corson 1999). In the United States, Lily Wong

Fillmore conducted research into the effectiveness of different instructional practices in developing the academic English-language skills of Hispanic/Latino and Chinese minority-language students (Chamot 1988). She reports four major instructional factors as significant:

◆ high-quality teaching, including clear lesson organization, directions and explanations, appropriate aids, attention to higher-level skills, and opportunities for oral activities

◆ high-quality instructional language, including clarity, coherence, use of contexts, paraphrasing, responding to student feedback, and discussion of grammar and vocabulary

◆ effective classroom management with stress on academic rather than nonacademic activities

◆ provision for equal opportunities for the practice of English

In these studies, effective classrooms displayed a balance of teacher-directed and individualized activities. In bilingual classrooms, students did best when the languages were presented separately without translations. But there were differences in the learning styles of the Chinese and the Hispanic/Latino students. The Hispanic/Latino students gained most from interaction with their peers; the Chinese students gained most in structured and fairly quiet classrooms. Here we see clear differences in instructional needs that would be missed by policymakers who are not from the relevant language-minority community.

A long-term comparison study in the United States (Chamot 1988) examined three approaches to bilingual schooling for Hispanic/Latino children:

◆ immersion, in which content subjects are taught through simplified English

◆ early-exit or short-term transitional bilingual programs of two to three years

◆ late-exit or long-term transitional bilingual programs of five to six years

Researchers report that long-term bilingual programs are most effective in promoting progress in both Spanish and English, and that immersion programs lead to a greater use of English in school by students. Elsewhere in the United States, Spanish-language-dominant children benefit academically and in their English-language acquisition when their mother tongue is used as the language of instruction in the early school years (Gándara 1994). A synthesis of research undertaken in the United States finds that bilingual education is much more effective than monolingual approaches to language acquisition. Bilingual education promotes long-term academic gains and also leads to improvements that continue to grow in consistent ways (Collier 1992).

In majority-Anglophone parts of Canada, the more long-standing attention given to the needs of Francophone minorities has also led to research and changes in policy and practice for immigrant children. Clearly, subtractive bilingual education is unsuitable for Francophone Canadians who live in Anglophone areas. Although these students certainly need English to live in that environment, the evidence confirms that strong French-maintenance approaches are the best way to ensure their English-speaking abilities. For example, Francophone minority children in Ontario schools who get most of their education in French, tend to have higher academic achievement and to succeed better in the work world than those taught in English or in only nominally bilingual schools. Although this finding is relevant to immigrant Canadian children as well as Canadian-born language-minority children, maintenance forms of bilingual education for immigrant Canadians are still rare, as they are for U.S. immigrants.

Clearly, the provision of bilingual education under conditions like those just described is consistent with a critically real approach to social justice. On the evidence provided, the first policy principle, outlined in the first half of this chapter, deserves support whenever possible; the ideal way to do this is to provide bilingual immersion programs for young children who need them and whose parents are convinced of the value of bilingual education.

This sort of provision, however, is beyond the reach of many schools and school systems where many different language varieties are in use. In these settings, the second policy principle comes into play. Schools provide second-best arrangement by valuing student minority languages in other ways. Practical methods for implementing this move away from my theme of a critically real approach, but there are many different ways to support minority first-language development even when the school does all its teaching in English. For now, I turn to the different varieties of English itself that schools use as vehicles of instruction.

Standard and Nonstandard Varieties: Ebonics and Critical Language Awareness

This second, rather intractable issue asks about fairer policies for the users of nonstandard varieties of English. Much of what follows is drawn from Corson (1998; 1999), where I set out policies and school practices in more detail. A myriad language varieties exist in all communities, but people have little awareness of them. In the United States, for example, the debate over the use of Ebonics in the 1990s suggests that considerable public confusion exists about language varieties and what they are. While the intensity of that debate confirms that bias against nonstandard varieties of English is still rampant (Baugh 1997), I believe that the English Only movement will only confuse things further by lowering the status of any and every language variety that is not the variety of standard English that English Only policymakers believe they favor.

Ebonics is a name given to the many varieties of African American English which retain traces of African languages in their form and structure. There are many rival views on the place these varieties should have in formal education, as revealed by the contributors to a prominent publication on the topic ("Ebonics" 1997). In that delicately balanced essay, each contrasting view is supported by different authorities who are respected for their links with the community of nonstandard variety users. But the use of the single name—Ebonics—is probably not very helpful to the debate, because this label wrongly suggests that these many varieties of language are a single variety of English. This misperception compounds a related difficulty people have when thinking about so-called "standard English," because this is also not one but many varieties, probably best represented only by written English. In fact, the most "standard" variety of English (or any language) seems to be little more than its written version. And even this variety will vary orthographically, semantically, and even syntactically.

Toward a Just Nonstandard Language Policy

In language there is a constant dynamism at work, and this is true even in the more standard varieties of English, although few of us notice it much. Because infants arrive in the midst of a language system that is already fully developed and functioning, there is a tendency for us to see language as stable and natural. People often view language as unaffected by social forces, struggles, and historical events.

The history of prejudice against nonstandard language varieties is probably as long as the history of language itself. Even the ancient Greeks used different dialects as a way of stereotyping other Greeks. Most of their wars with one another tended to be fought by armies allied by dialect, despite the fact that all of the Greek city-states spoke different varieties of "Greek." But linguists today are more cautious about using the word *dialect* because of the negative associations it tends to have. They find it more logical to use *variety* because every type of language is a variety. Even a standard language is no more than a variety with a polished reputation.

Different language varieties exist *because* of historical events. They grow out of different patterns of behavior, especially differences in power and language experience. Typically, nonstandard varieties are associated with the powerless rather than the powerful, but even affluent people can face discrimination if they use a geographical variety that differs from a dominant local one.

The nonstandard language varieties of socially marginalized people are often used unfairly as a guide to their potential and their worth as human beings. Many children arrive in schools with only irregular contact with the more standard variety used at their school. Formerly, these children were heavily penalized for having and using a language variety different from the one awarded high status by the school. Even today, children who use a nonstandard variety tend to consider the variety used in schools as the model of excellence against which their own is measured. They often see the school's variety as "correct," while their own varieties are "less correct." People still condemn themselves to silence in public settings because of feelings of shame created during their school years.

But all this began to change in the 1960s when research by William Labov and others confirmed that people from different backgrounds speak different kinds of English that vary systematically and regularly from each other. These and other studies have gradually overturned the common stereotype that nonstandard varieties are incorrect forms of a language. Instead, these varieties have their own norms and rules of use. And they deserve respect, like any variety.

So what can be done in schools? Would the first policy principle apply in this case, or the second? In the 1996 Ebonics debate in California, policymakers tried to apply the first policy principle. They wanted to use the nonstandard varieties as a vehicle of instruction in schools to supplement the local standard variety. But in most contexts of great diversity, the second policy principle seems more relevant. Nonstandard varieties need to be valued in schools, just as languages other than English should be valued in highly pluralist contexts, but they can rarely be used as the vehicle of instruction when many different varieties exist alongside one another.

Again, some version of the same devolved process of consultation seems appropriate here, because the variety of a language given status in a given situation needs to be decided by the actual participants in that context or situation. That is to say, which nonstandard varieties are valued in a school will be decided by locals, not by a remote agency unconnected with the context and the values of the people who inhabit it.

And it is essential to put an end to the long-running tragedy once common in all schools, when teachers believed their job was "to stamp out error." Not long ago, because nonstandard varieties were mistakenly perceived as incorrect and slovenly speech, children were punished for using them. Usually these children were from immigrant, low-income, or Native American communities, at the margins of society. And their speech helped mark them as candidates for educational failure. They were stereotyped.

We know that language helps confirm stereotypes and activate prejudices. We know that negative teacher attitudes toward children's speech affect teachers' expectations, which affect pupil performance. And even today, the more standard varieties tend to be more respected in schools than nonstandard varieties. Most teachers still consider a standard variety as more than just the variety used by the privileged individuals of society. They see it as the standard language of education, the complete mastery of which is the mark of school success.

While people disagree about how to pass on mastery of the standard variety, it gets preference these days not so much because of its "correctness" but more often because of what is considered its general "appropriateness." If a standard variety is linked historically with the written language and with literacy, it will always seem a more appropriate vehicle for education. If it is the variety used in higher and technical education, familiarity with it provides easier access to scientific and academic discourse. And if some version of a standard variety is used nationally and internationally, ability in it offers a medium of communication across national boundaries.

Yet different international varieties of English are appearing all the time, bringing variants on "the standard." In North America, even written English is veering increasingly away from the norms for written English used elsewhere, especially at the source of English—England. So whatever "the standard" might be, it is forever beyond our grasp. And what can teachers do about nonstandard varieties in schools when even the "standard variety" is really nothing of the kind? In most places, and in line with the second principle, the main thing teachers are trying to do is give more respect to nonstandard varieties, especially by not penalizing their use or mocking their users.

Just as important, though, is helping all students understand why political and historical events have made one local variety of the language seem more "appropriate" in contexts of power such as schools, and why nonstandard varieties are still unfairly kept on the margins. In their own interests, students need to be aware that less prestigious varieties are still judged unfavorably in many settings, which might disadvantage them in those settings. But at the same time, children need to know that nonstandard language is not incorrect or even inappropriate except in the stern eyes of the disapproving. Indeed, this kind of critical language awareness is a necessary prerequisite for children to have if they are to help change unjust social and linguistic arrangements.

Passing on critical language awareness is never easy, even for skilled teachers. At least today teachers are better equipped for the job as they begin to shed some of the prejudices of the past. Seeing the world stripped free of the distorting ideologies that human beings have imposed on it is what critical realism is all about. Its aim is to reclaim reality.

Conclusion

Schools can take several complementary lines of action in treating language and social justice issues in education (Corson 1999). Each of these forms of social action can foster the language awareness that people need in order to see through and past distorting ideologies like the English Only policy and to approach the world in a more critically real way. Each of these forms of social action combines respect for the good of the individual with respect for the good of the social group.

First, we need to create better patterns of communication within school organizations, in classrooms, and in staff rooms, patterns which free participants to consider planned, rational, just, and consensual action in pursuit of their educational aims. Second, schools in many places are finding they need commonly agreed on local policies for meeting the kinds of complex problems considered in this chapter: language policies on race and minority cultures, bilingualism, poverty, and disadvantage. Third, many suggest that children in schools need to acquire "critical language awareness" (see van Lier and Corson 1997) through a language curriculum that promotes social awareness of discourse, critical awareness of variety, and consciousness of and practice for change.

Works Cited

Barry, Brian. 1989. *A Treatise on Social Justice: Volume 1—Theories of Justice.* Berkeley: University of California Press.

Baugh, John. 1997. "Research on Race and Social Class in Language Acquisition and Use." In Nancy Hornberger and David Corson, eds., *Research Methods in Language and Education.* Boston: Kluwer. 111–21.

Bhaskar, Roy. 1986. Scientific Realism and Human Emancipation. London: Verso.

Booth, William. 1998. "The Washington Post Pages." *Guardian Weekly,* April 12. 17.

Chamot, Anna U. 1988. "Bilingualism in Education and Bilingual Education: The State of the Art in the United States." *Journal of Multilingual and Multicultural Development* 9(1-2): 11–35.

Collier, Virginia P. 1992. "A Synthesis of Studies Examining Long-Term Language-Minority Student Data on Academic Achievement." *Bilingual Research Journal* 16(1-2): 187–212.

Corson, David. 1995. *Using English Words.* Boston: Kluwer.

———. 1997. "Critical Realism: An Emancipatory Philosophy for Applied Linguistics?" *Applied Linguistics* 18(2): 166–88.

———. 1998. *Changing Education for Diversity.* Philadelphia: Open University Press.

———. 1999. *Language Policy in Schools: A Resource for Teachers and Administrators.* Mahwah, NJ: Lawrence Erlbaum.

Corson, David, and Sylvie Lemay. 1996. *Social Justice and Language Policy in Education: The Canadian Research.* Toronto: OISE Press.

Crystal, David. 1987. *The Cambridge Encyclopedia of Language.* Cambridge, U.K.: Cambridge University Press.

Cummins, Jim. 1996. *Negotiating Identities: Education for Empowerment in a Diverse Society.* Ontario, CA: California Association for Bilingual Education.

Cummins, Jim, and David Corson, eds. 1997. *Bilingual Education.* Boston: Kluwer.

"Ebonics." 1997. *The Black Scholar: Journal of Black Studies and Research* 27(1).

Fillmore, Lily Wong. 1998. "At the Crossroads: Can Bilingual Education Survive California politics?" Unpublished paper, Toronto.

Furby, Lita. 1986. "Psychology and Justice." In Ronald L. Cohen, ed., *Justice: Views from the Social Sciences.* New York: Plenum. 153–204.

Gándara, Patricia C. 1994. "The Impact of the Education Reform Movement on Limited English Proficient Students." In Beverly McLeod, ed., *Language and Learning: Educating Linguistically Diverse Students.* Albany: State University of New York Press. 45–71.

Kymlicka, Will. 1989. *Liberalism, Community and Culture.* Oxford, U.K.: Clarendon Press.

Nielsen, Kai. 1978. "Class and Justice." In John Arthur and William H. Shaw, eds., *Justice and Economic Distribution.* Englewood Cliffs, NJ: Prentice-Hall.

Rawls, John. 1973. *A Theory of Justice.* London: Oxford University Press.

———. 1980. "Kantian Constructivism in Moral Theory: The Dewey Lectures." *Journal of Philosophy* 77: 515–72.

———. 1993. *Political Liberalism: The John Dewey Essays in Philosophy No. 4.* New York: Columbia University Press.

Ricento, Tom. 1997. "Language Policy and Education in the United States." In Ruth Wodak and David Corson, eds., *Language Policy and Political Issues in Education.* Boston: Kluwer. 139–49.

Sandel, Michael. 1982. *Liberalism and the Limits of Justice.* Cambridge, U.K.: Cambridge University Press.

Taylor, Charles. 1992. *Multiculturalism and "The Politics of Recognition."* Princeton, NJ: Princeton University Press.

van Lier, Leo, and David Corson, eds. 1997. *Knowledge about Language.* Boston: Kluwer.

Wodak, Ruth, and David Corson, eds. 1997. *Language Policy and Political Issues in Education.* Boston: Kluwer.

Young, Iris. 1981. "Towards a Critical Theory of Justice." *Social Theory and Practice* 7: 279–302.

CHAPTER FIVE

The New American Spanish War: How the Courts and the Legislatures Are Aiding the Suppression of Languages Other Than English

JUAN F. PEREA
University of Florida

The Spanish language and persons who speak it are currently under attack in legislatures and in the federal courts. It is a relatively silent attack, apparent only to those who study carefully these major U.S. policymaking institutions. Yet the relatively low public profile of attacks on the Spanish language does not make these attacks less effective, nor less devastating, for many of us who observe tolerance for linguistic differences fading.

The courts and state and federal legislatures are major battlegrounds where rights affecting the recognition of language differences are currently being debated and decided. In the courts, two kinds of cases are determining the scope of language rights. One series of court cases has decided that employers can legally implement English Only rules that effectively prohibit the use of languages other than English in workplaces under most circumstances. Another series of cases has successfully challenged the constitutionality of Official English laws that restrict the speech of bilingual state employees. I discuss each of these lines of cases in greater detail below.

In the state legislatures and in Congress, the Official English movement continues to campaign with success to formalize the legal status of English as the official language of the United States. Increasing numbers of states have, either by referendum or legislative action, adopted English as the official language of their jurisdictions. Congress has also considered legislation making English the official language of the federal government. Furthermore, in California popular referendums have curtailed the availability of bilingual education, prohibited affirmative action, and restricted the access of undocumented immigrants to public services and education. Such initiatives have in the past been harbingers of similar legislation likely to be enacted in other states and perhaps by Congress.

Finally, recent recommendations for reform of our immigration and naturalization laws pose another potential threat to linguistic and cultural diversity. The federal Commission on Immigration Reform recently issued its final report and recommendations. Among these recommendations was a renewed program of "Americanization" and more difficult English-language and knowledge tests prior to the granting of naturalized citizenship. The net effect of these proposals, if implemented, will likely be that more aspiring citizens will be denied citizenship, and, as occurred during earlier eras of Americanization, greater governmental and societal coercion toward conformity in language and values will be exerted.

Educators may ask why these legal developments should be of concern to them. What do court decisions, Official English laws, and immigration policy have to do with educating and understanding students who speak a language other than English? To paraphrase Dr. Martin Luther King Jr.'s (1967) warning during a different era of civil rights struggle, don't fall asleep during the revolution. Educators who care about preserving the varied linguistic heritage of the United States must pay attention to important developments in the legislatures and in the courts, for it is in these forums that major limitations on the ability to teach, to learn, and to express oneself in Spanish and other languages will be (and are) imposed. Indeed, every person who cares about preserving the rich variety of American identities, as expressed through language, race, culture, and religion, must pay careful attention to the increasing suppression of language differences through law.

And while all of these developments also affect speakers of Asian, Native American, and other languages, there can be little doubt that their principal target is the growing population of

Spanish speakers, which constitutes by far the largest linguistic group in the United States after English speakers. According to the 1990 census, approximately 31.8 million persons spoke languages other than English in their homes. Of these 31.8 million, 17.3 million—over half—spoke Spanish at home.

So what explains the apparent increase in the desire to regulate the use of languages other than English and to enhance the relative stature of English through the creation of official status by law? Advocates of Official English stress the importance of a common language to create and preserve national unity. They also argue that knowledge of English is essential for academic achievement, economic success, and mobility. With respect to the national unity argument, with or without Official English laws and legal support, English is obviously the dominant and common language of the United States. Recent census figures show that approximately 97 percent of Americans rated themselves as speaking English well or very well. To the extent that language is a proxy for national unity, we currently have just about as much national unity as the English language can provide. History suggests, however, that language is a poor proxy for national unity. Our most significant national struggles, such as the Revolutionary War, the Civil War, and the civil rights movement, have all been fought by people speaking the same language and sharing much of the same culture.

Alternatively, the country has never been threatened in any significant way by the presence of other languages within our national borders. For example, during the nineteenth century several states, including Pennsylvania, Louisiana, California, and New Mexico, were officially bilingual in English and German, French, or Spanish. By "officially bilingual," I mean that as a matter of their state constitutions and statutes these states required that their laws and other official proceedings be published in more than one language. If, as argued by advocates of Official English, linguistic uniformity is necessary for national unity, the country should have fallen apart due to the manifest linguistic diversity apparent during the nineteenth century. While the country did fall apart during the Civil War, this was a war made and fought by English speakers. Language is, therefore, a poor proxy for national unity (Perea 1992a; Baron 1990).

Advocates for Official English argue that mastery of English is necessary for academic achievement and success. This merely restates the obvious—we live in an English-dominant society. And while Official English advocacy organizations can always parade a recent immigrant of color providing a testimonial about the importance of English for achieving success (a point no one disputes), everyone—immigrants included—knows that mastery of English is important. I would note, however, that the mastery of English promoted so heavily by U.S. English poster-people has so far been achieved without Official English. Which makes one wonder just how necessary the official status for English is in the face of overwhelming economic and social incentives to know the language. Advocates of Official English should spend their ample funds subsidizing scarce English-language instruction if their aim is truly to enhance the English-language skill of immigrants.

The more likely reason for the war on Spanish and Spanish speakers lies in recent demographic trends. Our current demographics show an increasing Latino population within the United States, currently numbering approximately 11 percent of the population. Future projections of the Latino population estimate that early in the twenty-first century, Latinos will become the largest minority in the United States (U.S. Census Bureau 1998). Other demographic projections indicate that by the year 2050, people of color, counted together, will outnumber white Americans for the first time (Anderson 1998).

These projections have caused great concern among those who conceive of the United States as a static, white country, speaking English Only for all time. For example, Peter Brimelow's *Alien Nation* (1995) argues for immigration restriction based explicitly on the notion that the United States must preserve what he takes to be the country's white ethnic core. Brimelow, however, is hardly the first to make such an argument. Indeed, it was this concern about demographics that gave birth to U.S. English, a principal proponent of the Official English movement, and to the Federation for American Immigration Reform, a leading proponent of immigration restriction. In 1986, Dr. John Tanton, founder of both organizations, wrote:

How will we make the transition from a dominant non-Hispanic society with a Spanish influence to a dominant Spanish society with non-Hispanic influence? . . . As Whites see their power and control over their lives declining, will they simply go quietly into the night? Or will there be an explosion? . . . *Gobernar es poblar* translates "to govern is to populate." In this society where the majority rules, does this hold? Will the present majority peaceably hand over its political power to a group that is simply more fertile? . . . Will Latin American migrants bring with them the tradition of the *mordida* (bribe), the lack of involvement in public affairs, etc.? . . . In the California of 2030, the non-Hispanic Whites and Asians, will own the property, have the good jobs and education, speak one language and be mostly Protestant and "other." The Blacks and Hispanics will have the poor jobs, will lack education, own little property, speak another language and will be mainly Catholic. (qtd. in Califa 1998; Stefancic 1997, 122–23)

Tanton's memo was deemed so anti-Latino that Linda Chavez, then president of U.S. English, felt compelled to resign (Arocha 1988). With Tanton's memo, we begin to see the demographic roots of the war against Spanish and Latinos, which has proceeded unabated ever since.

English Only in the Workplace

U.S. workplaces have become one of the main arenas within which battles over English and Spanish are fought. Title VII of the Civil Rights Act of 1964 prohibits discrimination in employment on the basis of race, color, religion, sex, and national origin. The language issue has emerged in litigation over the legitimacy of English Only rules imposed by private and state employers seeking to restrict the use of Spanish and other languages in their workplaces.

In the early and still leading case of *Garcia v. Gloor* in 1980, the court upheld an employer's English Only rule with reasoning that continues to be applied today. In that case, Hector Garcia, a young Mexican American, was employed as a salesperson for Gloor Lumber and Supply, Inc. Gloor Lumber had an English Only rule prohibiting employees from speaking Spanish on the sales floor unless they were communicating with Spanish-speaking customers. One day Garcia was asked by a fellow Mexican American employee whether an item requested by a customer was available. Garcia responded in Spanish that the item was not available. Garcia's response was overheard by Alton Gloor, an officer and stockholder of the company. Subsequently, Garcia was fired for having spoken Spanish in violation of the rule.

Garcia sued his employer, claiming that the English Only rule discriminated against him on the basis of his Mexican American national origin. The court rejected Garcia's arguments and decided that Gloor Lumber's English Only rule did not violate the prohibition against national origin discrimination enacted by Title VII. There were several important facets to the court's reasoning. The court wrote that "[t]he statute forbids discrimination in employment on the basis of national origin. Neither the statute nor common understanding equates national origin with the language that one chooses to speak." The court also reasoned that there was no discriminatory impact "if the rule is one that the affected employee can readily observe and nonobservance is a matter of individual preference. [As a bilingual,] Mr. Garcia could readily comply with the speak-English Only rule; as to him nonobservance was a matter of choice." The court continued, observing that "the language a person who is multi-lingual elects to speak at a particular time is by definition a matter of choice." Accordingly, the court ruled that Gloor Lumber had not violated Title VII with its English Only rule.

The court's reasoning depends on several unwarranted conclusions that have made it practically impossible for plaintiffs to prevail in lawsuits challenging English Only rules. First, the court interprets the "national origin" term in Title VII very narrowly to mean one's country of origin or the countries of origin of one's ancestors, but not any of the racial and cultural traits associated with one's birthplace or ancestry. While the court's interpretation of national origin conforms to the literal meaning of the words, it is so narrow as to be useless in combating the kinds of discrimination faced by persons whose national origin or ancestry is deemed "foreign" or outside the United States. Most prejudice results not from the fact of one's birthplace or national origin, but rather because of the attributed "foreignness" of one's characteristics such as non-English or non-mainstream language, accent, appearance, name, or culture (Perea 1994; Allport 1979). An interpretation of national origin that precludes recognition of discrimination on the basis of traits closely associated with different national origin makes Title VII's prohibition against national origin discrimination illusory.

The court also misunderstands the nature of the "choice" bilinguals make when they speak one or another language. It is a much more complex choice than, say, what to wear for work on a given day. A bilingual person's choice of which language to speak is dependent on many factors including "the participants, setting, topic of discourse, the form of communication, and the function or norm of the interaction" (Fantini 1982). The choice of language is thus a complex choice dependent on many social factors, most of which are not taken into account in this court's, or most employers', notion of choice. Hector Garcia's choice of Spanish to communicate with a fellow Mexican American employee, who presumably understood Garcia, was thus entirely appropriate based on an understanding of linguistics, even if in violation of the employer's rule.

Even the employer had some sense of the propriety of communication in the language with which customers felt most comfortable. Gloor Lumber encouraged Spanish-language conversations with Spanish-speaking customers and English-language conversations with customers who spoke English. The employer's intuitive understanding of what works best for customers is right. Part of the injustice of English Only rules is that the same intuitive understanding that concedes employer accommodation and use of Spanish for its profit maximization does not extend to employees' natural use of Spanish among themselves. Sadly, profit maximization may indeed be at work in decisions to limit Spanish, since restrictions on Spanish cater to the prejudices and discomfort of monolingual English-speaking customers. Gloor Lumber defended its rule in part because English-speaking customers objected to employee conversations in Spanish. But imagine if "customer preference" or "customer discomfort" could have been asserted successfully as a defense with respect to the hiring of African American employees in the South during the 1960s. Wouldn't such a customer or co-worker preference defense entirely defeat the equality goals of the Civil Rights Act of 1964? And if we recognize this proposition with respect to race, why do courts fail to recognize it with respect to the regulation of language differences?

Furthermore, as Garcia unsuccessfully attempted to argue in court, language is inextricably tied to one's sense of identity, as much for English speakers as for Spanish speakers. An important way to understand such battles over English and Spanish in the workplace is to understand them as struggles for identity: mainstream-owned or controlled workplaces will try to maximize their mainstream identity by emphasizing English and suppressing Spanish; Latino/Latina employees will try to hang on to their identities by using Spanish when possible.

Interestingly, it is this conflict over the management of identity in the workplace that underlies the decision in *Garcia v. Gloor*. The court decision from which I quote above was the court's second opinion in the case. The court withdrew its first opinion and omitted some crucial sentences that had appeared in the first version. I reproduce a paragraph from the first, withdrawn opinion, with the subsequently omitted sentences italicized:

> *An employer does not accord his employees a privilege of conversing in English. English, spoken well or badly, is the language of our Constitution, statutes, Congress, courts and the vast majority of our nation's people.* Likewise, an employer's failure to forbid employees to speak English does not grant them a privilege. . . . If the employer engages a bilingual person, that person is granted neither right nor privilege by the statute to use the language of his personal preference.

The court is saying that English is the dominant language of the country and that English goes to the core of our national identity. But the Spanish language is likewise an important aspect of racial and ethnic identity for the people most affected by English Only rules, and not a simple "choice." The court thus reinforces mainstream norms of language and identity in the workplace, which would seem to contradict the command of nondiscrimination present in Title VII. In its *Garcia v. Gloor* decision, the court delegates the management of national linguistic identity, at least in workplaces, to predominantly English-speaking employers, who will act to reinforce their preferences for identity and profit maximization.

In response to the *Garcia v. Gloor* decision, the Equal Employment Opportunity Commission (EEOC), the expert agency that enforces the Civil Rights Act, has issued detailed guidelines making clear that language discrimination is prohibited under Title VII and that in many cases English Only rules will violate the statute. These are the EEOC guidelines:

> Speak English Only rules.
> (A) When applied at all times. A rule requiring employees to speak only English at all times in the workplace is a burdensome term and condition of employment. The primary language of an individual is often an essential national origin characteristic. Prohibiting employees at all times, in the workplace, from speaking their primary language or the language they speak most comfortably, disadvantages an individual's employment opportunities on the basis of national origin. It may also create an atmosphere of inferiority, isolation and intimidation based on national origin which could result in a discriminatory working environment. Therefore, the Commission will presume that such a rule violates title VII and will closely scrutinize it.
> (B) When applied only at certain times. An employer may have a rule requiring that employees speak only in English at certain times where the employer can show that the rule is justified by business necessity.
> (C) Notice of the rule. It is common for individuals whose primary language is not English to inadvertently change from speaking English to speaking their primary language. Therefore, if an employer believes it has a business necessity for a speak-English Only rule at certain times, the employer should inform its employees of the general circumstances when speaking only in English is required and of the consequences of violating the rule. If an employer fails to effectively notify its employees of the rule and makes an adverse employment decision against an individual based on a violation of the rule, the Commission will consider the employer's application of the rule as evidence of discrimination on the basis of national origin. (EEOC 1998)

There is much to commend in the EEOC's regulations. The EEOC has recognized the important link between speaking a non-English language and racial identity for many persons. The regulations also recognize the discriminatory effects of English Only restrictions. Businesses may be able to justify English Only rules, however, if they prove to the satisfaction of the court that such rules constitute a "business necessity." Unfortunately, there are no clear guidelines on what constitutes business necessity, so it will come down to a judge's or a court's opinion on what constitutes business necessity for a language restriction. Again unfortunately, many justifications for language restrictions that may seem superficially plausible and acceptable to a court, such as the need for safety and efficiency or the need for effective supervision, on closer scrutiny turn out not to be particularly persuasive (Perea 1990). Even more unfortunately, some courts have ignored the EEOC's guidelines altogether.

While courts generally enforce expert agency interpretations of the law, some courts that have considered the validity of English Only rules have generally ignored the EEOC's interpretation of the Civil Rights Act. How do courts ignore the EEOC? Following the lead of the *Garcia v. Gloor* opinion, some courts reason that the meaning of the term "national origin" cannot be extended to include the foreign languages of bilinguals. Furthermore, some courts reason, the EEOC has only limited power to issue guidelines that are not legally binding, so the courts need not pay attention to the expert agency's interpretation of its own statute. A good example is the fairly recent decision in *Garcia v. Spun Steak Co.* (1993), wherein the court, applying the reasoning from *Garcia v. Gloor*, decided that an English Only restriction during work did not violate Title VII's prohibition on national origin discrimination.

It is worth pointing out that, despite multiple opportunities, the Supreme Court has consistently refused to either ratify or reverse these rulings of the lower courts (Perea 1994). A Supreme Court decision, either way, would be helpful because it would point advocates for language rights in the most productive direction. If the Supreme Court affirms current lower court decisions, then advocates for the protection of language rights can direct their efforts toward the amendment of Title VII. If the Supreme Court reverses current lower court rulings, then advocates can use the courts with greater success.

The Supreme Court and Language Discrimination

The Supreme Court, however, is also quite confused about the meaning of language equality, so there is little reason to think that it will make a favorable decision without changing its conception of race discrimination to include language discrimination. In its only recent decision addressing language differences, *Hernandez v. New York* (1991), the Supreme Court decided that jurors who are bilingual in Spanish and English may be dismissed from juries that will consider Spanish-language testimony. In this case, a prosecutor had used peremptory challenges to remove two bilingual, Spanish-speaking jurors from a jury. Peremptory challenges are used to remove jurors thought to be undesirable for virtually any reason by either side in a court case. The Supreme Court has ruled, however, that peremptory challenges may not be used to remove jurors because of their race. In *Hernandez,* the Court had to decide whether the peremptory exclusion of two Latino jurors was tantamount to exclusion because of race and whether this violated the equal protection clause of the United States Constitution.

The Court concluded that the peremptory exclusion of bilingual jurors in this case did not violate the equal protection clause. Because the *Hernandez* case required testimony in Spanish by some witnesses, the prosecutor was uncertain whether the bilingual jurors would adhere to the official English-language interpretation of the testimony. Despite the jurors' assurance that they would adhere to the official interpretation, the prosecutor "felt from the hesitancy in their answers and their lack of eye contact that they would not be able to do it." The Court decided this was a race-neutral reason for the prosecutor's exclusion of the bilingual jurors, and concluded that there was no violation of the equal protection clause. While allowing the prosecutor to exclude the bilingual jurors, a plurality of the Court (meaning an opinion on behalf of four justices) also suggested, paradoxically, that a prosecutor's use of peremptory challenges to exclude Latinos/Latinas because of their ethnicity would violate the equal protection clause. Just as paradoxically, the plurality suggested that the prosecutor's actions would have violated the Constitution if his reason had been that he "did not want Spanish-speaking jurors."

I cannot perceive any meaningful difference between a prosecutor's discomfort with bilingual jurors hearing translated testimony and an exclusion of these same Latino jurors "by reason of their ethnicity" or because the prosecutor "did not want Spanish-speaking jurors." Each of these statements amounts to the same thing, the exclusion of bilingual jurors. Therefore it is difficult to understand why the Court did not conclude in this case that the prosecutor had discriminated unconstitutionally. One could argue that perhaps this prosecutor was justified because of these jurors' demeanor—their hesitation and their lack of eye contact. But consider what these jurors were asked to do: they were asked to ignore what they heard and understood (the Spanish-language version of the testimony) and to pay attention only to the official, translated version in English. How can one ignore what one has already heard and understood? And what if the interpreter makes a mistake? Should a bilingual juror adhere to a mistaken interpretation of testimony? These are inevitable questions for a bilingual juror and would explain the jurors' hesitation in answering the prosecutor. A more troubling question is why the prosecutor and the Court are more concerned with blind adherence to the official interpretation, which may easily be wrong, than with preserving the ability of bilingual jurors to act as a check on the interpreter and so contribute to the accuracy of the truth-finding function of the jury (Perea 1992b). The Supreme Court misunderstood the nature and implications of bilingualism, as well as the truth-finding function of juries, when it allowed a prosecutor's concerns over whether the bilingual jurors would follow the official interpretation of testimony (regardless of whether the interpretation was right or wrong) to outweigh the presence of Latino/Latina jurors on a jury. Since prosecutors can always raise such a concern, it seems quite unlikely that bilingual jurors will be allowed to sit on cases involving Spanish-speaking victims or defendants, when any testimony will be in Spanish and subject to interpretation.

One of the major failures of the courts, then, is their failure to recognize that discrimination against the language of Spanish speakers and speakers of other languages is a form of race discrimination. This failure has rendered our most important equality laws virtually useless in redressing language discrimination. Courts must interpret Title VII of the Civil Rights Act of 1964 in such a way that language discrimination is prohibited as either a form of race discrimination or national origin discrimination. A plurality of the Supreme Court in *Hernandez* wrote that "[i]t may well be, for certain ethnic groups and in some communities, that proficiency in a particular language, like skin color, should be treated as a surrogate for race under an equal protection analysis." Having made this connection, the Supreme Court must begin to interpret the equal protection clause so that language discrimination violates equal protection principles in the same way that race discrimination does. One should not infer from these statements that I believe our equality laws protect adequately against race discrimination. In fact, I do not think that current interpretations of the civil rights laws and the Constitution protect adequately against race discrimination. But these laws seem to protect better against race discrimination than they do against language discrimination simply because courts recognize at least some forms of race discrimination. Language discrimination must be understood as part of the race discrimination against Latinos.

Official English Laws and the First Amendment

On the legislative front, the Official English movement has made steady gains, particularly in state governments, approximately half of which currently have legislation or constitutional amendments making English their official language (Perea 1992a). Even states with virtually no Latinos have adopted such laws, perhaps on the theory that a preemptive strike will discourage Latinos from coming. Proposed federal legislation that would make English the official language of the federal government (and would repeal sections of the Voting Rights Act that require bilingual ballots), however, appears to have stalled (Perea 1996).

Legal challenges to restrictive Official English laws that have been based on the First Amendment have enjoyed more success recently than challenges attempted under Title VII of the Civil

Rights Act. In *Yñiguez v. Mofford* (1995) and *Ruiz v. Hull* (1998), advocates for Spanish-speaking plaintiffs argued successfully that Official English laws that prohibit Spanish-language speech violate the First Amendment, which protects speech from excessive government interference. The *Yñiguez* case, though the first to invalidate an Official English enactment under the First Amendment, was ultimately invalidated by the Supreme Court (at 520 U.S. 43, 1997) because one of the parties to the case on appeal lacked a sufficient stake in the litigation to have legal standing.

The recent *Ruiz* decision by the Arizona Supreme Court invalidated the Official English provisions of the Arizona Constitution that were enacted by popular referendum in 1988. This lawsuit challenging the constitutionality of the Official English provisions was brought by several bilingual persons, including state employees, elected officials, and one public school teacher. Among other regulations, Arizona's Official English provisions required that state employees and officials "act in English and in no other language," with certain limited exceptions. The Arizona Supreme Court concluded that this law violated the First Amendment in several ways. First, the Official English law restricted Spanish-language speech through its overly broad and extensive prohibition on the use of other languages. Second, the law inhibited the free discussion of governmental affairs both by depriving some Arizona citizens of access to governmental information in the languages best understood by them, and by interfering with the rights of citizens to effectively receive redress from their government. In short, the law interfered with speech and with effective communication between citizens and their government for no compelling reason.

The success of the plaintiffs in the *Ruiz* case is encouraging because it sets an important precedent. It remains to be seen, however, whether other state supreme courts will interpret the First Amendment in the same way and how the U.S. Supreme Court will decide the issue. Despite the emerging success of the theory that Spanish speech is protected from governmental interference under freedom of speech principles, this represents only a partial legal victory. The First Amendment and the federal Constitution only limit governmental action. There is no First Amendment right to freedom of speech with respect to private employers, so the situation in private workplaces will not necessarily change. In other words, even though the *Ruiz* case has been decided favorably, recognizing that Spanish speakers enjoy certain First Amendment freedoms from *governmental* restriction, First Amendment cases do not necessarily make any difference with respect to English Only restrictions in *private* workplaces.

Conclusion

To make this survey of legal developments affecting language rights more complete, consider also the legislative changes enacted recently by popular referendum in California, which should be cause for concern for Spanish speakers, Latinos, and people of color in general. California's attack on affirmative action, coupled with recent Supreme Court decisions cutting back on affirmative action mandates, guarantee that in that heavily Latino state, Latino students will have fewer opportunities to obtain a college education. Although two Supreme Court decisions have limited affirmative action considerably, the Court has not yet ruled on the applicability of these cases in the field of education, which may be considered significantly different from situations in which affirmative action is considered in the awarding of government contracts. (See *City of Richmond v. J. A. Croson Co.* 1989; *Adarand Constructors, Inc. v. Peña* 1995; *Regents of Univ. of Cal. v. Bakke* 1978). California's Proposition 227 (1998) seeks the elimination of bilingual education with its mandatory, one-size-fits-all approach. These referenda demonstrate, if any of us needed further demonstration, that we live in a time of backlash against people of color and Spanish speakers.

Unfortunately, in racial policy, where California leads, the rest of the nation often follows. This was the case with California's move in the 1870s and 1880s to exclude the Chinese from active civil participation, and the effort in the early twentieth century to exclude the Japanese. This was the case with Proposition 187, which inspired the enactment of federal legislation limiting the access of undocumented immigrants to welfare benefits. We should expect attacks on affirmative action and bilingual education to continue and to enlarge in scope. We should not be surprised if federal legislation seeking the same objectives is introduced and perhaps enacted.

These are some of the important challenges that Latinos and advocates of language rights face today and will continue to face in the near future. What can and should Latinos and sympathetic advocates and educators do in response to a discriminatory and hostile status quo? As Frederick Douglass stated on August 4, 1857, during a speech on West India emancipation, "This struggle [against slavery] may be a moral one, or it may be a physical one, and it may be both moral and physical, but it must be a struggle. Power concedes nothing without a demand. It never did and it never will" (Foner 1950, 437). So we cannot simply wait to be acted upon. We must struggle and we must demand equality in the particular ways that equality has meaning for us.

One of Derrick Bell's crucial insights into modern critical theory is his conception of interest convergence. Simply stated, this theory argues that minorities will gain civil rights and make progress toward equality only when it is in the interest of the dominant majority to concede civil rights and equality (Bell 1980). This makes perfect sense. Majorities act in their self-interest; and it has always been self-interest, in one form or another, and not altruism that has accounted for progress in civil rights. To give just one major example, the organized protest and resistance of the civil rights movement, coupled with the internationally televised violent white resistance to the movement, cast a negative image of race relations in the United States to the world during the cold war competition with the Soviet Union for influence with nonaligned countries. One of the principal arguments made on behalf of the Civil Rights Act by President Kennedy when he introduced the legislation was that because of our poor race relations, we were losing political ground in the international cold war competition (Perea 1994).

The current question for Latinos and sympathetic readers, then, is what, if anything, will make the English-speaking majority care about the presently unrecognized equality needs of Latinos? This, I believe, is the crucial question. I recently participated in a conference during which one of the speakers, a prominent professor of languages and linguistics, lamented the fact that California's truncation of bilingual education directly contradicted the accumulated wisdom of at least twenty years of research on bilingual education. This speaker wondered aloud why it was that all of this research and knowledge was simply being ignored. The answer, I suggest, is that advocates for bilingual education (and for language rights generally) have not made a persuasive case for why a majority of English-speaking Americans should care about bilingual education and other language rights.

It is not sufficient to rely on the dramatic demographic changes we are currently witnessing. Increased numbers of Latinos, alone, will not ensure political success and greater equality and respect for language differences and pluralism. The more likely outcome is that the increasing numbers of Latinos will generate more of the political and cultural backlash we have already experienced. Latinos must find productive ways of joining together with other oppressed groups for the mutual benefit of all.

This will entail a program of education and self-education, and it is here that educators can make a vital contribution. Educators who care about linguistic and cultural diversity must educate the public about why languages other than English matter, and why it is foolish to squelch, rather than nurture, the linguistic resources extant in the various heritages of Americans. The suppression of languages other than English has an old and ignoble history. Unfortunately, this tradition of suppression is being replayed through the Official English movement and English Only in the workplace. Most Americans do not celebrate the tradition of suppression of linguistic and cultural diversity associated with the Americanization movement of the early twentieth century. The current movements for Official English and English Only, however, advocating and implementing linguistic uniformity and conformity, parallel the Americanization movement to an uncomfortable degree. Today's linguistic and cultural McCarthyism contradicts core American values such as respect for equality, individual identity, and religious and cultural diversity.

Educators can help students learn about the multilingual, multiracial history of the United States and begin to shape an American self-image that is multilingual rather than monolingual and English speaking. Through the process of education, more Americans may come to recognize that the United States is a multilingual nation in which languages spoken include English, Spanish, Chinese, Japanese, German, French, and a plethora of Native American languages. English is clearly the dominant and primary language of the country, but it is not at all inconsistent to recognize that other languages are, have been, and will be spoken here.

Works Cited

Adarand Constructors, Inc. v. Peña, 115 S.Ct. 2097. 1995.

Allport, Gordon. 1979. *The Nature of Prejudice.* Reading, MA: Addison-Wesley.

Anderson, Craig. 1998. "Hispanic Population Climbing; Latinos in Arizona to Outnumber Anglos by 2040, Figures Hint." *Arizona Republic,* Aug. 7. A1.

Arocha, Zita. 1988. "Chavez Quits U.S. English Organization: Ex-Reagan Aide Objected to Memo." *Washington Post,* Oct. 20. A18.

Baron, Dennis. 1990. *The English-Only Question: An Official Language for Americans?* New Haven, CT: Yale University Press.

Bell, Derrick. 1980. *Race, Racism and American Law* (2nd ed.). Boston: Little, Brown.

Brimelow, Peter. 1995. *Alien Nation: Common Sense about America's Immigration Disaster.* New York: Random House.

Califa, Antonio J. 1998. "Declaring English the Official Language: Prejudice Spoken Here." *Harvard Civil Rights-Civil Liberties Law Review* 24: 293–326.

City of Richmond v. J. A. Croson Co., 488 U.S. 469, 1989.

Equal Employment Opportunity Commission. 1998. "Guidelines on Discrimination Because of National Origin." *Code of Federal Regulations.* Vol 29, Section 1606.

Fantini, Alvino E. 1982. "Social Cues and Language Choice: Case Study of a Bilingual Child." In Paul R. Turner, ed., *Bilingualism in the Southwest* (2nd ed.). Tucson: University of Arizona.

Foner, Philip S., ed. 1950. *The Life and Writings of Frederick Douglass: Vol. 2, Pre-Civil War Decade.* New York: International Publishers.

Garcia v. Gloor, 609 F.2d 156. 5th Cir., 1980 (opinion withdrawn).

Garcia v. Gloor, 618 F.2d 264.5th Cir., 1980.

Garcia v. Spun Steak Co., 998 F.2d 1480. 9th Cir., 1993.

Hernandez v. New York, 500 U.S. 352., 1991.

King, Martin Luther, Jr. 1967. *Where Do We Go from Here: Chaos or Community?* New York: Harper and Row.

Perea, Juan F. 1990. "English Only Rules and the Right to Speak One's Primary Language in the Workplace." *University of Michigan Journal of Law Reform* 23: 265.

————. 1992a. "Demography and Distrust: An Essay on American Languages, Cultural Pluralism, and Official English." *Minnesota Law Review* 77: 269–373.

————. 1992b. "*Hernandez v. New York*: Courts, Prosecutors, and the Fear of Spanish." *Hofstra Law Review* 21(1): 1–61.

————. 1994. "Ethnicity and Prejudice: Reevaluating 'National Origin' Discrimination under Title VII." *William and Mary Law Review* 35(3): 805.

————. 1996. "The Language of Government Act of 1995: Hearings on S.356 Before the United States Senate Committee on Governmental Affairs." Statement.

Proposition 227. 1998. Available: http://ourworld.compuserve.com/homepages/jwcrawford/unztext.htm. Sept. 28.

Regents of Univ. of Cal. v. Bakke, 438 U.S. 265, 1978.

Ruiz v. Hull, 957 P.2d 984, 1998.

Stefancic, Jean. 1997. "Funding the Nativist Agenda." In Juan F. Perea, ed., *Immigrants Out! The New Nativism and the Anti-Immigrant Impulse in the United States.* New York: New York University Press. 119–35.

U.S. Bureau of the Census. 1998. "U.S. Metropolitan Area Population Estimates." United States Department of Commerce.

Yñiguez v. Mofford, 69 F.3d 920.9th Cir., 1995.

CHAPTER SIX

Bilingual Individuals and Language-Based Discrimination: Advancing the State of the Law on Language Rights

GUADALUPE VALDÉS
Stanford University

The Case of *Garcia v. Spun Steak*

In 1990 the Spun Steak Company of south San Francisco passed an English Only rule for all of its thirty-three employees, twenty-four of whom were bilingual speakers of English and Spanish and two of whom were Spanish monolinguals. In letters announcing the new rules, managers claimed that the rule was necessary because Hispanic/Latino employees had made insulting remarks in Spanish about their African American and Asian American co-workers. The English Only rule was limited to working hours. Marcela Buitraga and Priscilla Garcia, two bilingual employees, were reprimanded for speaking Spanish and were not permitted to work next to each other. Buitraga and Garcia filed charges of discrimination with the Equal Employment Opportunity Commission (EEOC). The case went to trial and the district court granted the Spanish-speaking employees' motion for summary judgment, concluding that the English Only rule disparately impacted Hispanic/Latino workers without sufficient justification. Unfortunately, the Court of Appeals for the Ninth Circuit did not agree with the position of the lower court. Reversing the decision, the appeals court held that the employer's English Only rules did not constitute national origin discrimination, because bilingual workers could readily comply with the rule and thus suffered, at best, a mere inconvenience in having to speak to each other exclusively in English. The Ninth Circuit thus invalidated EEOC guidelines, which state that "a worker may make out a prima facie case of Title VII national origin discrimination under an adverse impact theory by merely establishing the existence of an English Only rule" (Tamayo 1996, 1). The Supreme Court did not agree to hear the case.

The *Spun Steak* case is important because it involves issues of bilingualism and public policy. It addresses a particular problem that affects individuals who are speakers of both the societal language and their own ethnic or heritage language. Moreover, it demonstrates that the problems facing bilingual populations in nation-states in which policies are set primarily by monolingual individuals are serious and far-reaching. These policies are often based on misunderstandings about the nature of bilingualism in general, fear and suspicion about the consequences of bilingualism, and expectations that monolingualism is the norm to which all individuals should aspire.

Contrary to what is generally believed by monolingual individuals, however, most of the world's population is bilingual. Monolingualism is characteristic of a *minority* of the world's peoples. From figures reflecting the number of languages spoken in the world today, the number of ethnic groups in the world, and the number of currently recognized nation-states, it is evident that few nations are either monolingual or monoethnic. Each of the world's nations has groups of individuals living within its borders who do not speak the societal language or who may speak it with limitations, and who use other languages in addition to or instead of the national language to function in their everyday lives. As Stavenhagen (1990) points out:

> In general, however, most nations are monolingual in an official sense. What this means is that, although they are generally polyethnic and often multilingual, their governmental institutions employ only the dominant or designated national language in all interactions with its citizenry. Ordinarily such monolingual nations tend to ignore the special needs and circumstances of its immigrant and indigenous linguistic minorities who for numerous reasons carry out their lives using two languages. (30)

Numerous policies made by "monolingual" states, then, seriously affect the rights and privileges of those citizens who have not had the same access to the national language nor had the same opportunities as the majority or dominant group within the nation, and who are identifiably different from the majority in power. The situation becomes more complex at those moments in history when strong antiminority sentiments are present in the dominant population. At those times, religion and language in particular become especially symbolic.

By examining the situation in the United States, I describe in this chapter a number of instances of language-based discrimination as it primarily affects *bilingual groups* that are citizens or residents of a monolingual nation. In reviewing a number of cases involving language discrimination, it is my purpose to describe the process of language policy making in the United States—not at the level of legislation, national resolution, or even national report, but rather in what I call "the trenches." As I hope I make evident, much of the work in advancing the law on language rights in this country has been carried out by civil rights attorneys using civil rights tools.

I first outline five major cases of language discrimination, describe the key language problems raised by each, and discuss the relationship between these problems and research on bilingualism and second-language acquisition. I then present a brief agenda of language issues that are of greatest concern to civil rights attorneys as they work to expand the legal protection against language bias. Finally, based on my discussion of the civil rights paradigm within which a great deal of language policy activity has been carried out in the United States, I conclude with a discussion focusing on the degree to which the language rights of bilingual individuals can be accommodated within the recently articulated scope of the concept of linguistic human rights.

Language Discrimination in the United States

Currently, in the United States language discrimination against bilingual individuals is not subtle. The following five examples illustrate the dimensions of the problem:

Example 1: The Hernandez *Case*

In 1991 the Supreme Court of the United States rendered a decision in the case of *Hernandez v. New York* (1991), which involved the exclusion of bilingual Latinos from jury service. The decision in the *Hernandez* case held that the use of peremptory challenges by a prosecutor to exclude prospective jurors who were bilingual in English and in Spanish did not violate the equal protection clause of the U.S. Constitution. The Court accepted as race neutral the prosecutor's explanation that he had excluded potential Latino jurors because, when they were asked if they would be able to abide by the interpreter's English-language version of the testimony to be heard and to disregard the original Spanish-language version, these individuals hesitated. In the prosecutor's words:

> We talked to them for a long time; the Court talked to them, I talked to them. I believe that in their heart they will try to follow it, but I felt there was a great deal of uncertainty as to whether they could accept the interpreter as the final arbiter of what was said by each of the witnesses, especially where there were going to be Spanish-speaking witnesses, and I didn't feel, when I asked them whether or not they could accept the interpreter's translation of it, I didn't feel that they could. They each looked away from me and said with some hesitancy that they would try, not that they could but that they would try to follow the interpreter, and I feel that in a case where the interpreter will be for the main witnesses, they would have an undue impact upon the jury. (*Hernandez v. New York* 1991, 1864–65)

The Court did not accept the petitioner's claim that Spanish-speaking ability is, in the case of Latinos, closely related to ethnicity. Nor was the Court swayed by the argument that a high percentage of bilingual jurors might hesitate before answering questions such as those asked by the prosecutor. The Court granted that the exclusion of bilinguals from jury services was not wise and that it might not be constitutional in all cases. It agreed that language proficiency might serve as a surrogate for race, but it also emphasized that, in the particular case in question, no discriminatory intent was inherent in the prosecutor's explanation.

The legal implications of this decision are many, and several scholars have already attempted to analyze them in some detail. Mendez (1993), for example, argues in his critique of the *Hernandez* decision that the Court's holding is erroneous for several reasons: (1) it prescribes the wrong remedy for correcting inaccuracies by court interpreters, (2) "the Court's decision reinforces a deeply embedded fear that retaining a language in addition to English might undo the fragile bond of our society," and (3) "the Court's standard guarantees that most defendants will be unsuccessful in challenging the State's use of peremptories to exclude bilingual venirepersons who happen to know the language spoken by non-English speaking witnesses" (Mendez 1993, 193–202).

The case was complex, and a total of four opinions were filed. Justice Kennedy announced the judgment of the Court and delivered an opinion in which Chief Justice Rehnquist, Justice White, and Justice Souter joined. Justice O'Connor filed an opinion concurring with the judgment, in which Justice Scalia joined. Justice Blackmun filed a dissenting opinion; and Justice Stevens also filed a dissenting opinion, in which Justice Marshall joined. It is important to note that all nine justices were monolingual speakers of English.

At its most fundamental level, *Hernandez v. New York* is important because, as Piatt (1993) has pointed out, it raises the question of the unresolved legal status of language itself. Is language, for example, a national origin characteristic? Is it an immutable characteristic such as skin color? Is language always a suspect category because it can be used as a surrogate for race? And finally, are all language-based exclusions discriminatory?

In addition to raising fundamental questions about the legal status of language, the *Hernandez* case makes evident the difficulties experienced by monolinguals in making sense of bilingualism and bilingual abilities. In this particular case, the research on bilingualism was actually brought to the attention of the Court. The opinion written by Justice Kennedy makes reference to this scholarship and seems to reflect at least some awareness of the issues raised here:

Indeed some scholarly comment suggests that people proficient in two languages may not at times think in one language to the exclusion of the other. The analogy is that of a high-hurdler, who combines the ability to sprint and to jump to accomplish a third feat with characteristics of its own, rather than two separate functions (Grosjean 1985). This is not to say that the cognitive processes and reactions of those who speak two languages are susceptible of easy generalization, for even the term "bilingual" does not describe a uniform category. It is a simple word for a more complex phenomenon with many distinct categories and subdivisions (Sánchez, Our Linguistic and Social Context, in Spanish in the United States 9,12 [J. Amastae and Elias-Olivares 1982; Dodson 1985])

Our decision today does not imply that exclusion of bilinguals from jury service is wise, or even that it is constitutional in all cases. It is a harsh paradox that one may become proficient enough in English to participate in trial, see, e.g., 28 U.S.C. §§ 1865(b)(2), (3) (English-language ability required for federal jury service), only to encounter disqualification because he knows a second language as well. As the Court observed in a somewhat related context: "Mere knowledge of [a foreign] language cannot reasonably be regarded as harmful. Heretofore it has been commonly looked upon as helpful and desirable. *Meyer v. Nebraska* 262 U.S. 390,400, 43 S.Ct. 625,627, 67 L.Ed. 1042, 1923. (*Hernandez v. New York* 1991, 1872)

It is evident that the justices endeavored to make sense of the research on a population about which they knew little. While the opinion made reference to the work on bilingualism and to the particular characteristics of bilingualism within the Spanish-English bilingual population in this country, the Court failed to make important connections. It did not at any point reflect a true awareness of the fact that *bilinguals are different from monolinguals* and that a greater burden may be placed on these individuals than would ever be placed on monolinguals.

For example, from a monolingual perspective, the expectation that bilinguals can "turn off" one of their language channels and act as though they can hear only the English version of testimony being given appears harmless enough. It seems to be merely a request to disregard evidence heard in another language. Superficially, this request seems no different than the frequent request made of English-monolingual jurors to disregard particular information that the judge has ruled to be inadmissible. From the perspective of bilingual individuals, however, the request itself is absurd if it is understood to mean that they must block or shut down one of their language-processing channels. Research on bilingualism carried out from the psycholinguistic perspective has determined that this is an impossible task (Albert and Obler 1978; Hamers and Lambert 1974; Mack 1986; Magiste 1986; Moore, MacNamara, and Tucker 1970; Obler and Albert 1978; Triesman 1964, 1969). Expecting bilinguals to attempt to carry out such a feat—to do the impossible—is placing on them a very great burden indeed.

On the other hand, if the request is understood as a directive to disregard not a particular small amount of information but all testimony presented during an entire trial, one must conclude that again a much more difficult burden is being placed on bilingual individuals than is normally placed on monolinguals. Indeed, during "normal" trials, whenever extensive testimony is expected—the admissibility of which is in question—the jury is removed from the courtroom. Jurors are not expected to be able to sit through such testimony and yet disregard all they heard. But this is exactly what the prosecutor in the *Hernandez* case was demanding of bilingual jurors.

A different kind of burden is being placed on bilingual jurors if the request to abide by the interpreter's translation is understood as a directive to set aside their own understanding of the testimony presented and to replace it with that of the interpreter. In this case, the assumption is that during the trial both language channels remain functional and that the testimony heard in the original is not disregarded. But here the instructions to bilingual jurors require that, if and when they identify discrepancies between their understanding of the testimony given in the non-English language and the interpreter's rendition of the same testimony, they are to accept the interpreter's version of the facts as the true and correct interpretation. What this means is that bilinguals—as opposed to monolinguals—may not use their own judgment about a portion of the testimony presented. They must abide by the "official interpreted version," and they must not be concerned about truth or accuracy.

Again, monolingual jurors are not placed in the ethical position of having to disregard their own understanding of testimony for the sake of expediency. And, as Perea (1993) has argued, exclusion based on the possibility of undue influence on other members of the jury is *not* routinely carried out. Monolinguals who have special knowledge of a field or area (e.g., medicine or engineering) that is of central importance to a particular case are not automatically excluded because their understanding of the testimony of expert witnesses may be greater or different from that of the average juror.

What the *Hernandez* case raises, then, are a series of questions about whether and how bilingual individuals can be treated fairly by policies that are made—perhaps innocently enough— without taking into account the possibility that a greater burden may be placed on such individuals.

Examples 2 and 3: The Perez v. FBI Case and the Cota Case

In 1988, Hispanic American FBI agent Bernardo M. Perez brought suit on behalf of himself and a class of 310 persons who were or had been special agents of the FBI. The case involved, among a number of other issues, the FBI's practice of requiring Hispanic American special agents to use their Spanish-language abilities. The court found that Hispanic American FBI agents, whether native or non-native speakers of Spanish, were "assigned to Spanish language wiretaps in proportion significantly greater than Anglo Spanish-speaking counterparts" (*Perez v. FBI* 1988, 906). It also determined that Hispanic American individuals who entered the bureau under a category other than language (such as accounting or law) were assumed to speak Spanish and were forced to take Spanish-language examinations. Once tested, these agents were routinely and consistently required to carry out translations, wiretaps, and other special assignments. As a result of being assigned disproportionately to such tasks, Hispanic American agents had few opportunities to take on the kinds of assignments that normally led to promotion and advancement within the FBI.

The case of *Perez v. FBI*, among a number of similar cases

(e.g., *Buelna v. Chandler* and *Equal Employment Opportunity Commission and Communications Workers of America v. Contel of California, Inc.*), brings up the question of whether and to what degree an employer has the right to require an employee to use his or her two languages on the job. If monolinguals and bilinguals are paid at the same rate, does the employer have a right to insist that employees who speak two languages use them? Should the employer provide extra compensation? Are greater burdens being placed on bilingual individuals? Does this unequal treatment have important consequences?

In the case of *Perez v. FBI*, which involved the mandatory testing of all Hispanic American FBI agents, bilingualism was considered desirable and essential for the work of the bureau; at the same time, the presence and use of bilingual skills was not compensated. Rejecting the statistical summaries presented by the FBI, the court ruled that:

> The statistical summaries presented at trial are not relevant to this Court's findings relating to the utilization of Spanish language skills by the Bureau: that is, the disparities between policy and practice; distinctions between duty assignments for Hispanic linguists and non-Hispanic Spanish language specialists; presumption that all Hispanics are bilingual; significant differences in the conditions of employment where burdens fall disproportionately on Hispanic agents; unjustified accelerated promotion program for some skills to the exclusion of Spanish language skill; or the informal practice of requiring exceptional duty by Hispanic agents without reward in terms of benefits or promotion. Nor do the statistical models address the deficiencies this Court found in the Bureau EEO program. (*Perez v. FBI* 1988, 916)

In this particular instance, the court reviewed the evidence before it and concluded that Hispanic Americans were indeed being penalized for their bilingualism. It determined, moreover, that the expectation of Spanish-language use for Hispanic American or Latino agents was significantly different from the expectation for non-Hispanic American Spanish-speaking individuals. For example, non-Hispanic American (elective) bilinguals were not expected to use their Spanish in job assignments, nor were they required to perform wiretap duties. More important, however, the court determined that *because of their knowledge of*

Spanish, Latinos had been discriminated against in terms of benefits and promotions.

The *Cota v. Tucson Police Department* (1992) case, on the other hand, presented a very different result. In this case, although the department required that its police officers speak Spanish when necessary, the court found that these police officers (as opposed to the FBI agents) had not been denied promotions or opportunities for promotion, had not been given involuntary assignments, had not been denied pay increases, and so forth. Indeed, the court found that Spanish-speaking (bilingual) police officers were treated exactly like their monolingual counterparts. It found no evidence that Hispanic Americans performed extra work, only that

> Plaintiffs sometimes perform work that differs from that performed by non-Hispanic employees. But the fact that it differs, of course, does not mean that it's more difficult or that there is more of it. Moreover, although the work performed by Hispanic employees is different, it does not follow that the performance thereof results in an adverse effect. (*Cota v. Tucson Police Department* 1992, 473)

In the *Cota* case, the court was not convinced that the requirement that bilingual police officers speak Spanish on the job, help with translations, and help other officers when the need arose resulted in placing a greater burden on these officers than on the monolingual members of the force. In the *Perez v. FBI* case, the outcome centered not on the language demands made on a particular group of agents, but rather on the effect of those demands on promotions and advancements. Indeed, it was implied by *Perez v. FBI* that, as long as there were no discriminatory consequences in terms of pay, advancement, and promotion, requiring bilingual agents to speak Spanish was not problematic in and of itself. The court never addressed the question of whether speaking Spanish on the job might be particularly stressful for a bilingual whose language experiences have not included ease in the required forms and registers of that particular language domain. It simply assumed that an employee's bilingual ability was at the service of his or her employer whether or not the employee felt stressed or ill at ease about using Spanish to carry out job responsibilities. The issue of additional pay for additional or special competencies was not addressed in either case.

A 1996 article in the *Wall Street Journal* titled "Tongue Twister: Bilingual Employees Are Seeking More Pay, and Many Now Get It" suggests that the question of compensation for bilingual skills is a subject of importance in the United States (Fritsch 1996). The article pointed out that extra compensation among the "rank and file" in blue collar jobs was becoming increasingly more controversial because many workers found it unfair to pay someone for a skill that "may come as naturally as talking" (Fritsch 1996, A1). For the rank and file, extra compensation seems to break an important human services rule of "pay the job, not the person." The article went on to point out, however, that at the threat of strike by bilingual U.S. Customs Service inspectors, the Treasury Department agreed to pay them more. It emphasized the fact that the debate is complex and that companies such as Southwestern Bell, Delta Airlines, Charles Schwab, and MCI have instituted and sometimes revoked extra compensation policies. These employers are concerned about accusations that certain minorities (who also happen to be bilingual) are somehow being given special treatment compared to other ethnic groups that are not bilingual.

The issues surrounding the ownership of employees' language abilities are many, and attempts to treat employees fairly will often involve making difficult determinations about the ways in which language proficiency can be assessed by employers, about the burdens placed on bilingual personnel who must deal with clients or customers in *two* languages rather than one, and about the rights of bilingual personnel to refuse to use the minority language in the workplace.

Example 4: The Case of the Service Station Franchise

A successful businessman and his wife, both of immigrant background, were denied the right to sell their service station franchise to two gentlemen also of immigrant background. The oil company with which the service station was affiliated required that all day-to-day managers of service stations be able to communicate with customers in English. Before permitting the sale of the franchise, the company administered the TOEIC (The Test of English for International Communication) to the two prospective buyers. A passing score of 750 was established based on the performance of nine individuals who were franchise candidates. A score of 740 obtained by one of the prospective buyers was considered unacceptable. The company did not take into account the fact that the prospective buyers had lived in the United States for many years, were graduates of U.S. high schools, and at the time were managing another service station in a nearby, predominantly white, community. For the moment, the sale of the service station franchise has been blocked entirely, and attorneys representing the couple are considering whether to bring suit against the oil company.

This particular dispute raises the general issue of the validity of English-fluency requirements. More specifically, however, it raises questions about the standards of English fluency that can be applied to bilinguals who are members of large minority communities in this country and who speak varieties of English that are influenced by their immigrant language. This case, more than any other, speaks directly to questions of language assessment. The prospective buyers were required to take a test which, as Lowenberg (1992) pointed out, is based on norms from native-speaker varieties, norms which exclude non-native varieties. Oil company personnel, however—with general guidance from the Educational Testing Service (ETS)— established proficiency levels using the TOEIC so that they could require that this test be used with all "non-native" speakers of English both within the United States and in foreign countries.

Needless to say, there are serious questions about the appropriateness of administering the TOEIC to bilingual U.S. residents who have attended public schools in this country and who have acquired English in natural, as opposed to exclusively instructed, settings. The validation studies of the TOEIC were carried out in Japan, a context in which English is *not* a societal language. In that context, a "non-native speaker" of English is a speaker whose first language is Japanese and who spends a lifetime in a setting in which Japanese is used for all or most communicative purposes. The TOEIC was designed for such persons.

It is not clear exactly what the term "non-native speaker of

English" means within the U.S. context. All the examples given by ETS in its publicity materials for the TOEIC mention foreign contexts (e.g., Korea, Indonesia, Pakistan) and not the United States. This suggests that for the purposes of the TOEIC, a non-native speaker of English is a foreigner who resides in a foreign country and who has studied the language primarily in a formal classroom context.

The United States contains large numbers of individuals who could technically be classified as non-native by a variety of different criteria (e.g., place of birth, first language, citizenship, immigration status). The definition of *non-native*, however, is slippery. It is not enough to say, for example, that a non-native is a person who acquired a non-English language as a mother tongue. As the U.S. Bureau of the Census has found over the years in trying to design questions that will identify the percentage of speakers of other languages, the fact that a person has a non-English mother tongue says very little about the language use and language abilities of that individual in either English or the non-English language. For example, a person whose first language is Gujerati might come to the United States at the age of three and be educated exclusively in English, use English as a dominant language both socially and professionally, and—at the age of forty—still speak English with a trace of an Asian Indian accent. Is this person non-native? Does the fact that she spoke another language as a child and learned English among people who spoke slightly accented English make her use of English suspect? Would she in any way fit the profile of the individuals with whom the TOEIC was validated?

Persons who have lived in this country, attended school in this country, and acquired English by interacting with other Americans in real-life settings are unlike foreigners who study language in foreign classroom settings and who spend perhaps short periods of time studying in this country. There are many different types of U.S. minority bilinguals, and it is difficult to generalize about their abilities and proficiencies. What is important is that neither the TOEIC nor the Oral Proficiency Interview (OPI), with which it is said to be correlated, has been validated with bilingual populations in this country. Indeed, a number of individuals, myself among them (Valdes and Figueroa 1994), have argued strongly that the OPI (a derivative set of rubrics based on the Government Rating Scale [DLI] and used in language teaching in this country) is invalid for use with bilingual speakers. Research carried out among French Canadian speakers (Marisi 1994), for example, suggests that the accuracy construct undergirding the language descriptions used in such rating scales unfairly disadvantages speakers who use a perfectly legitimate variety of a given language.

No matter how this case is resolved, it raises many questions: Are all bilingual speakers part of a suspect category no matter how fluent in English they may be and regardless of other evidence of their ability to function professionally in English in this country? Can English-language proficiency be assessed for such individuals using existing assessment instruments? And how much English is *enough* English for different occupations?

Example 5: The Fragante v. City and County of Honolulu Case

In 1981, at the age of sixty-one, Manuel Fragante, emigrated from the Philippines to Hawaii. Having received all of his education in English-medium schools in the Philippines, Fragante was a fluent English speaker. In Hawaii, Fragante applied for an entry-level civil service clerk position in Honolulu's Department of Motor Vehicles. Among the 721 individuals who took the written civil service examination required for the job, Fragante received the highest score. He was then interviewed by two individuals familiar with the demands of the position. Both individuals agreed that he had a pronounced Filipino accent that would make him difficult to understand, and ranked him lowest of three finalists. Fragante filed a claim against the city and county of Honolulu claiming that his nonselection for the position was based on national origin discrimination. The court dismissed the suit, stating that the job in question required talking extensively with the public. The judge noted that Fragante had a "difficult manner of pronunciation" and that he did not respond directly to questions asked him. He noted further that Fragante maintained much of his military bearing. Fragante's appeal to the Court of Appeals for the Ninth Circuit was not successful. The court

once again determined that his nonselection for the position resulted not from discrimination but from his inability to communicate successfully as required by the demands of the position in
question.

The accent discrimination case against Manuel Fragante, like
the case against the prospective buyers of the service station franchise, is directly related to issues of standardness, of native-speaker
norms, and of the use of linguistic characteristics to mask national origin discrimination.

In the United States, Title VII of the Civil Rights Act of 1964
prohibits employment discrimination on the basis of race, color,
religion, sex, or national origin. According to Piatt (1993), the
act was intended to ensure equality of employment, eradicate
discrimination, and provide remedies for victims of discrimination. Title VII is concerned not only with discriminatory firing
and hiring, but also with discriminatory terms and conditions of
employment. It prohibits intentional discrimination as well as
apparently neutral rules that result in "a disparate impact on
protected groups of workers" (Piatt 1993, 36).

As Piatt further points out, Title VII does not define the term
"national origin." The Supreme Court, however, in *Espinoza v.
Farah Mfg. Co.* (1973) stated that national origin "on its face
refers to the country where a person was born, or more broadly,
the country from which his or her ancestors came." Moreover, in
1970 the Equal Employment Opportunity Commission (EEOC)
(the administrative body created by the Equal Employment Opportunity Act) issued a set of guidelines that provided numerous
examples of practices that could involve impermissible national
origin discrimination on the basis of language. In the revised guidelines issued in 1987, the commission emphasized that primary
language is to be considered an essential characteristic of national
origin.

As Tamayo (1996) and Matsuda (1991) have pointed out,
however, the tendency has been for courts to rule that employers
may legitimately take into account job candidates' language difficulties that interfere with job performance. According to
Matsuda (1991), bilingual speakers who have accents in English
(*accent* defined as characteristics of speech that are *unlike* those
found in monolingual native speakers of English) are frequently

subjected to accent discrimination, but plaintiffs who bring suits arguing employment discrimination because of their accents almost never win. Courts have considered that "difficult manners of pronunciation" are a justifiable reason for not hiring persons otherwise judged to be outstanding. Matsuda argues that courts have never required employers to demonstrate that the speech of bilinguals was fairly evaluated by a set of unprejudiced individuals who might normally interact in the community with such accented speakers. Employers have simply claimed that a certain style or type of English was or would be "incomprehensible" to their customers.

Tamayo (1996), in his review of accent discrimination cases, concluded that the courts have in general considered accent discrimination to be permissible if communication is an "essential job element" (9). Thus, for example, the nonselection of Fragante by the Honolulu Department of Motor Vehicles was justified because of the clerk's need to communicate with the public. Similarly, in *Gideon v. Riverside Community College District* (1985), rejection of an applicant of Indian origin as a full-time instructor of nursing was also justified because—although she had served as an instructor for two years—the evaluation committee had a hard time understanding her. In a case involving a Palestinian instructor who had been teaching for thirteen years (*Salem v. La Salle High School* 1983), the court ruled that the plaintiff's language problem "was not an immutable characteristic of his national origin, but rather was a correctable condition which the plaintiff had chosen not to remedy despite suggestions from his superiors to do so." The question of to what degree accents are correctable was also raised in *Kahakua v. Hallgrem* (1987), in which the judge ruled (as cited in Matsuda 1991, 1345) that "there is no race or physiological reason why Kahakua [a native speaker of Hawaiian English] could not have used standard English pronunciations." In this particular case, the judge—a visitor from Fresno—rejected the expert testimony of a linguist specializing in Hawai'i Creole English and instead accepted the testimony of a "speech consultant" who had rated Kahakua's native Hawaiian speech as unacceptable for weather broadcasts.

The results of accent discrimination cases, however, as Lippi-Green (1994) has pointed out, are more complex than they first appear. It is important to point out that, in contrast to *Fragante* and *Kahakua*, in those cases where it was established that communication was not an essential job element, accent discrimination has been considered impermissible. According to Tamayo (1996), plaintiffs have prevailed in cases filed by a librarian, a loan officer, a laboratory supervisor, and a welfare analyst because courts ruled that in these particular occupations their accents had not directly interfered with job performance.

The possible impact of "justifiable" accent discrimination is clearly far reaching in this country and in every other country in which the monolingual prestige language variety is accepted as the norm. Most speakers of world Englishes and most immigrant origin or indigenous origin bilinguals who grow up in communities where they learn the societal language from other bilinguals— who themselves have accents—do not and may not ever speak the prestige variety of English like mainstream monolinguals.

Implications of the Spun Steak Case

The case of *Garcia v. Spun Steak Co.* (1993/1994) involved the establishment of English Only rules in the workplace. Increasingly more popular, English Only rules have been implemented by employers in a variety of work settings for a number of different reasons. According to EEOC guidelines (*Federal Register* 1980, 85634-5), however,

> [a]n employer's rule which requires employees to speak English at all times, including during their work breaks and lunch time, is one example of an employment practice which discriminates against persons whose primary language is not English. Under § 1606.7 (a) the Commission presumes that totally prohibiting employees from speaking their primary language violates Title VII because it is a burdensome term and condition of employment which discriminates on the basis of national origin by disadvantaging an individual's employment opportunities and by creating a discriminatory working environment. Therefore, where such a rule exists, the Commission will closely scrutinize it.

The guidelines go on to point out that employers may require employees to speak English at certain times if employers can show that it is justified by business necessity and they have clearly informed employees of the circumstances in which they must speak English, as well as the consequences of not doing so. Both the EEOC compliance manual (1986) and the EEOC revised guidelines issued in 1987 set out the commission's policy and interpretation of Title VII with regard to language. Employers claiming business necessity must show that for safety and efficiency, communications among co-workers must be conducted in a language understandable to all workers. Business necessity defenses claiming productivity needs and needs of supervisory personnel must be supported by clear evidence that other measures—that is, measures other than an English Only rule—could not be used. Defenses claiming customer preference or the desire to improve employee English-language skills as reasons for the establishment of an English Only workplace rule are considered almost impossible to sustain.

To date, the results of challenges to English Only workplace rules have been mixed. In one case (*Garcia v. Gloor* 1980/1981), for example, the Fifth Circuit found that an English Only rule did not discriminate on the basis of national origin because Mr. Garcia was bilingual and could readily choose to comply with the English Only rule. When this case was decided, however, the EEOC guidelines cited above had not been issued; moreover, as Piatt (1993) points out, the court made reference to the fact that it would have deferred to such guidelines had they been in effect.

A far different conclusion was reached by the Ninth Circuit in the case of *Guiterrez v. Municipal Court* (1988). Here, bilingual court employees had been required to speak English except on lunch breaks or when serving as interpreters. The court held that the defendants (three municipal court judges) failed to demonstrate a business necessity for an English Only rule. Citing a number of law review articles focusing on language discrimination, the court pointed out that:

> [t]he cultural identity of certain minority groups is tied to the use of their primary tongue. . . . The mere fact that an employee is bilingual does not eliminate the relationship between his primary language and the culture that is derived from his national origin . . . . Because language and accents are identifying characteristics,

rules which have a negative effect on bilinguals, individuals with accents, or non-English-speakers may be mere pretexts for intentional national origin discrimination. (1039)

Unfortunately, in the *Spun Steak* case—which also involved bilingual employees protesting an English Only workplace rule—the judges of the Ninth Circuit took the opposite position from that of the *Guiterrez* decision. The court specifically stated that it was not bound by the EEOC guidelines and that it had been impressed by Judge Rubin's analysis for the Fifth Circuit in *Garcia v. Gloor.* They concluded that

> (5) Title VII does not protect the expression of cultural heritage on the job. (6) Bilingual employees were not denied a privilege of employment by an English Only policy. . . . (8) In light of the facts of this case, the effect of the policy on bilingual employees was not so pronounced as to amount to a hostile environment. (7527)

The court simply did not agree that the plaintiffs had been subjected to harsher working conditions than the general employee population, or that the denial of the privilege limited, segregated, or classified employees in a way that would deprive them of opportunities. It further stated that

> [t]he Spanish-speaking employees argue that fully bilingual employees are hampered in the enjoyment of the privilege because for them, switching from one language to another is not fully volitional. Whether a bilingual speaker can control which language is used in a given circumstance is a factual issue that cannot be resolved at the summary judgment stage. However, we fail to see the relevance of the assertion, even assuming that it can be proved. Title VII is not meant to protect against rules that merely inconvenience some employees, even if the inconvenience falls regularly on a protected class. Rather, Title VII protects against only those policies that have a significant impact. The fact that an employee may have to catch himself or herself from occasionally slipping into Spanish does not impose a burden significant enough to amount to the denial of equal opportunity. (7538)

For the study of both individual and societal bilingualism, the question highlighted by the *Spun Steak* case is a particularly interesting one. What needs to be determined is how uncomfortable the sustained exclusive use of one language is for bilinguals who normally use a code-switching style in all or most of their communicative interactions. Does the insistence on the use of one language result in seriously adverse effects? Do rules insisting on the exclusive use of the societal language for all worker-to-worker communication during working hours create an atmosphere of both isolation and intimidation? Myers-Scotton's (1993) work provides evidence that for many bi- or multilinguals, code-switching is the unmarked style. The overall pattern of switching itself is significant in that it signals dual membership in the groups associated with the two languages.

The court, however, in analyzing the arguments presented by the plaintiffs, appeared to imagine that code-switching involves a momentary use of a word or two of Spanish. They did not have at their disposal samples of transcripts of actual interaction among English-Spanish bilinguals in which speakers code-switch constantly at sentence, clause, and phrase boundaries.[1] As Muysken (1995) points out, identifying the base language of a speech segment in which two languages alternate often presents a number of difficulties even for experienced language specialists. It is possible that when accused of speaking Spanish in the workplace, bilingual individuals were actually using a code-switching style, the base language of which was, in fact, English.

Bilinguals and Language Discrimination: A Summary

Language discrimination against bilingual individuals in the United States has involved violations of *civil rights* (that is, of rights guaranteed citizens and residents under a constitution) rather than *human rights* (those rights that accrue to individuals simply because they are human). More important, perhaps, attorneys in defense of language rights have marshaled arguments that link language to national origin discrimination.

Advancing the State of the Law on Language Rights for Bilingual Minorities

In a number of English-speaking countries around the world such as New Zealand and Australia, discussions about language policy (e.g., Benton 1996; Herriman 1996) include details about the work of national commissions, the drafting of national reports on language use (e.g., Australia's Lo Bianco Report, Green Paper, and White Paper), and the effect of these reports on language policies. In other English-speaking countries (such as Great Britain), discussions of language policies (e.g., Thompson, Fleming, and Bryam 1996) emphasize the absence of stated policies and focus on the implicit language policies embedded in reports and curricula that deal primarily with the teaching of English as a school subject. By comparison, in the United States language policy activities are often described (e.g., Ricento 1996) as involving a composite of legislative, governmental, and judicial instruments.

While this composite perspective is indeed accurate, it is important to recall that except for recent English Only legislation, only a few laws have been passed that are directly concerned with language. These include, for example, the Bilingual Services Act of 1973, the Court Interpreters Act of 1978, the Voting Rights Language Assistance Law of 1992, and the Native American Language Act of 1990/1992. The Voting Rights Language Assistance Law was concerned with language only to the degree that it allowed certain language-minority groups (American Indians, Asian Americans, Alaskan natives, and persons of Spanish heritage) to participate effectively in the electoral process. Moreover, the Bilingual Education Act of 1968, as Martha Jiménez (1992) reminds us, did not mandate bilingual education.

The cases discussed in this chapter—as well as the many precedent-setting cases in bilingual education—reflect deliberate and systematic attempts by civil rights attorneys to expand legal protection to language discrimination. Compared to contexts such as Canada and France, where, according to Turi (1994), litigation has focused on clarifying language legislation, in the United States the real work in language policy has taken place in the courts based on civil rights legislation and on guidelines (e.g., EEOC guidelines) and regulations (e.g., Lau Remedies) set up by the administrative bodies created by such legislation.

More important, perhaps, for the future of language rights in the United States, civil rights efforts continue. For example, the Language Rights Project of the American Civil Liberties Union (ACLU) Foundation of Northern California is an advocacy project established in 1994 to provide "legal assistance to those who have been unfairly targeted in the workplace, in the marketplace, or in other important arenas because (a) they choose to communicate in their native, non-English language, or (b) they are unable to speak standard English" (ACLU 1996, 2). The project currently runs a language rights hotline that provides legal advice and referrals to individuals who have been victims of language discrimination; it also identifies cases that can potentially expand legal protections against language bias. The message communicated by the Language Rights Project is

- ◆ that language rights are a matter of civil rights;
- ◆ that governmental or institutional mandates for everyone to speak standard English often deprive deserving people of jobs, advancement, and vital services;
- ◆ that forcing someone to communicate in personal and social discourse in a language not his or her own inflicts a discriminatory injury just as serious as overt racial or ethnic bias;
- ◆ that our society suffers irreparable harm when it suppresses this critical cultural attribute of much of its minority population. (ACLU 1996, 1)

Attorneys working with the ACLU, EEOC, Asian Law Center, MALDEF (Mexican American Legal Defense Fund), PRLDF (Puerto Rican Legal Defense Fund), and META (Multicultural Education Training and Advocacy Project) are currently engaged in litigating a wide variety of language-related cases. A recent victory by Chris Ho of the Asian Law Center, in *Kim v. Northwestern Mutual Life Insurance*, involved a settlement by the insurance company in which it agreed not to deny life insurance policies to people who are not proficient in English. Besides closely following the *Yñiguez* case (involving Arizona's English Only legislation), the ACLU Language Rights Project is specifically targeting cases in the areas of (1) English Only workplace rules, (2) unreasonable English-fluency requirements and accent discrimination, (3) Official English laws, and (4) language discrimination in provision of services and benefits.

A commitment to realizing linguistic human rights in the United States, then, involves what Dasgupta (1990) refers to as a series of policy episodes, a wider field of activities, and a complex process of bargained actions. Language policy efforts, to the degree that they involve the application of the "wisdom of experts," require that this application happen not in the orderly process of planning but in the often hectic give and take of plotting strategy in the trenches.

The most important aspect of current efforts to define language rights is the desire to support efforts to promote linguistic justice. Clearly, efforts to combat language discrimination in the case of bilingual populations will involve expanding the discussion of language rights to encompass the experiences of bilingual indigenous and immigrant populations around the world. It is also exceedingly clear from examining language discrimination cases in the United States that discussions of language policies and language rights that focus primarily on *monolingual* immigrant and/or *monolingual* indigenous populations are incomplete because they fail to take into account the struggles experienced by individuals who may already be dominant in the societal language. By outlining types of language discrimination against bilinguals, I have suggested the enormous complexity of policy issues that interconnect definitions of individual language competence, the acceptance and usage of language in the larger community, and the allocation of opportunities on the basis of perceived language competencies and perceived language usage. Taken individually, each one of these issues defies simple understanding or easy simplification, as evidenced by the fractured vote in the *Hernandez* case. In fact, it can be argued that these issues are so entangled and complex that scholars and policy analysts currently do not have the tools and methodologies to speak to them in terms that consistently make good policy sense—even in a climate in which xenophobia might not be present.

The question for scholars concerned with language minorities in general and with policies affecting these populations is: to what degree do the individual rights of *bilingual persons* or the collective rights of *bilingual populations* fall within the recently articulated scope of the concept of linguistic human rights? In the case of bilingual individuals, policies enacted *for* monolinguals *by* monolinguals inevitably deprive members of bilingual populations—even those who may be quite fluent in the societal language—of important rights. It is my position that we must vigorously focus on violations of the rights of bilingual individuals and bilingual populations as we move forward to map out the area which Phillipson, Rannut, and Skutnabb-Kangas (1994) have so ably described as "uncharted." In defining the contours and scope of language rights, it is important that these definitions take into account the particular violations of these rights encountered by minority populations even after they have become bilingual.

Recent elaborations of a theory of linguistic human rights argue that all human beings have a fundamental right to learn their mother tongue, the right to receive at least a basic education in that tongue, and the right to learn at least one of the official languages of one's country of residence. According to Phillipson, Rannat, and Skutnabb-Kangas (1994), individuals who are deprived of linguistic rights may be simultaneously deprived of other basic human rights such as the right to a fair trial, the right to access to education, the right to freedom of speech, and the right to maintenance of cultural heritage. I have attempted to demonstrate that bilingual minorities, although they have already learned their mother tongue and the official language of the country in which they reside, are routinely subjected to linguistic injustice. I have also suggested that for bilingual individuals as well as for monolingual non-English-speaking minorities, language rights in the United States are a matter of *civil rights*, involving the deprivation of the fundamental rights of citizens or residents of this country. Therefore I would argue that discussions focusing on language discrimination in a worldwide context must take into account not only linguistic *human* rights but also linguistic *civil* rights.

Language, whether viewed on a broad international canvas

or in a single country, continues to be "one of the least visible, least measurable, and least understood aspects of discrimination" (Roberts, Davies, and Jupp 1992). Scholars and activists concerned about language rights and about mapping out areas that can bring conceptual clarity to this important area face many issues. As Grabe (1993/94) points out, however, language planning and policy efforts involve a "complex interplay of multiple relationships and factors" (viii).

Conclusion

In their everyday lives, members of the English language arts teaching profession come into contact with immigrant students in their classrooms. They may have little awareness, however, of how language discrimination operates in the lives of these young people and in the lives of their parents. My hope is that, through the examination of the five cases presented here and the issues that undergird each of them, instructors will gain an understanding of the dilemmas that surround a truly multicultural society, especially when this multiculturalism brings with it multilingualism as well. As I have pointed out the problems and challenges continue—especially in an anti-immigrant age—even after individuals acquire English.

The question for those of us concerned about whether a greater burden is being placed on bilinguals than on monolinguals by existing policies and by the interpretation of these policies is how to inform monolingual policymakers, policy interpreters, and members of the legal profession about the nature of these burdens on a growing segment of the U.S. population without simultaneously provoking the wrath of those who view concessions to linguistic diversity as fundamentally un-American. In a moment in which certain ethnic groups such as Latinos are suspect, language issues become symbolic. Rational discussion becomes difficult, and even issues of truth and justice fade in importance behind the waving flag of national unity.

Currently, as Fishman (1992) has argued, facts appear not to matter. In the face of change and economic difficulties, the United States is in the process of what Nunberg (1992) has termed "reimagining" its national identity. Whereas in the past what was thought to hold the United States together were the democratic principles under which it was founded, now the country is moving into a period in which cultural bonds are more important. Fear of what the presence of large numbers of immigrants from economically developing nations will mean to the U.S. context has led to the use of language as a symbolic rallying point. The United States is undergoing a transformation in which members of the majority or dominant group have deliberately chosen to use language as a strategy of exclusion. Unlike the course of events in some other multilingual nations, ethnic groups, in their competition for goods and services, are not using language as a symbol; instead, the dominant, monolingual population has chosen to mobilize around English and to once again revive the one-nation-one-language principle.[2]

In light of such thinking, it matters little that bilingual populations have already learned English. It matters even less that, by definition, bilingual individuals are not identical to monolinguals. Given such an atmosphere, it is unlikely that language issues involving bilingual persons can be viewed by the dominant population as anything other than divisive and problematic. The choice is, again, a double bind. Persons advocating equitable language policies will inevitably be accused of promoting dissension. In order to address common concerns about language inequality, worries about divisiveness must be set aside, considered situational and temporary and as part of an era in U.S. history that will at some point—hopefully—be left behind.

For those of us concerned about the lives of our students outside of school and about the challenges faced by their parents even when they are succeeding by mainstream standards, my hope is that an understanding of these challenges will help us relate to these parents and their children in ways that clearly acknowledge that their lives are unlike those of mainstream monolingual individuals. We must acknowledge that the mere learning of English is not a magic potion that will solve all of the problems new immigrants will encounter. Many immigrant students in our classrooms will never be indistinguishable from native English speakers, no matter how hard they try. We must honestly acknowledge the challenges they face and work with them to build a truly just society.

Notes

1. I served as an expert witness for the plaintiffs in *Garcia v. Spun Steak Co.* and provided a declaration in which I reviewed the research on language use in Chicano communities and the research on language choice and interaction among bilinguals. I also discussed the importance of language to ethnic and cultural identity. It did not occur to me, however, to provide transcripts of actual interaction among bilinguals who use codeswitching as the unmarked style.

2. For an excellent discussion of ethnicity and nationalism that brings into focus how groups use resources such as language, religion, and territory as strategies for mobilization, see Paulston (1986).

Works Cited

Albert, Martin, and Loraine K. Obler. 1978. *The Bilingual Brain: Neuropsychological and Neurolinguistic Aspects of Bilingualism.* New York: Academic Press.

Amastae, Jon, and Lucía Elias-Olivares. 1982. *Spanish in the United States: Sociolinguistic Aspects.* Cambridge, U.K.: Cambridge University Press.

American Civil Liberties Union. 1996. *Proposal to the San Francisco Foundation on the Language Rights Project.* San Francisco, CA.

Benton, Richard A. 1996. "Language Policy in New Zealand: Defining the Ineffable." In Michael Herriman and Barbara Burnaby, eds., *Language Policies in English-Dominant Countries.* Clevedon: Multilingual Matters. 62–98.

Dasgupta, Jyotirindra. 1990. "Language Planning and Democratic Becoming." In Brian Weinstein, ed., *Language Policy and Political Development.* Norwood, NJ: Ablex. 222–40.

Dodson, C. J. 1985. "Second Language Acquisition and Bilingual Development: A Theoretical Framework." *Journal of Multilingual and Multicultural Development* 5(6): 325–46.

Federal Register. 1980. 45(250).

Fishman, Joshua. 1992. "The Displaced Anxieties of Anglo-Americans." In James Crawford, ed. *Language Loyalties: A Source Book on the Official English Controversy.* Chicago: University of Chicago Press. 165–70.

Fritsch, Peter. 1996. "Tongue Twister: Bilingual Employees Are Seeking More Pay, and Many Now Get It." *Wall Street Journal,* Nov. 13. A1, A6.

Grabe, William. 1993/94. "Foreword." *Annual Review of Applied Linguistics* 14: vii–xii.

Grosjean, Francois. 1985. "The Bilingual as a Competent but Specific Speaker-Hearer." *Journal of Multilingual and Multicultural Development* 6(6): 467–77.

Hamers, Josiane F., and Wallace E. Lambert. 1974. "Bilingual Reactions to Cross-Language Semantic Ambiguity." In Stephen T. Carey, ed., *Bilingualism, Biculturalism and Education.* Edmonton: University of Alberta Printing Department. 101–14.

Herriman, Michael. 1996. "Language Policy in Australia." In Michael Herriman and Barbara Burnaby, eds., *Language Policies in English-Dominant Countries.* Clevedon: Multilingual Matters. 35–61.

Jiménez, Martha. 1992. "The Educational Rights of Language-Minority Children." In James Crawford, ed., *Language Loyalties: A Source Book on the Official English Controversy.* Chicago: University of Chicago Press. 243–57.

Lippi-Green, Rosina. 1994. "Accent, Standard Language Ideology, and Discriminatory Pretext in the Courts." *Language in Society* 23(2): 163–98.

Lowenberg, Peter H. 1992. "Testing English as a World Language: Issues in Assessing Non-Native Proficiency." In Braj B. Kachru, ed., *The Other Tongue: English Across Cultures.* Urbana: University of Illinois Press. 108–21.

Mack, Molly. 1986. "A Study of Semantic and Syntactic Processing in Monolinguals and Fluent Early Bilinguals." *Journal of Psycholinguistic Research* 15: 463–88.

Magiste, Edith. 1986. "Selected Issues in Second and Third Language Learning." In Jyotsna Vaid, ed., *Language Processing in Bilinguals: Psycholinguistic and Neuropsychological Perspectives.* Hillsdale, NJ: Lawrence Erlbaum. 97–122.

Marisi, Paulette M. 1994. "Questions of Regionalism in Native Speaker OPI Performance: The French-Canadian Experience." *Foreign Language Annals* 27(4): 505–21.

Matsuda, Mari. J. 1991. "Voices of America: Accent, Antidiscrimination

Law, and a Jurisprudence for the Last Reconstruction." *Yale Law Journal* 100: 1329–1407.

Mendez, Miguel A. 1993. "Hernandez: The Wrong Message at the Wrong Time." *Stanford Law and Policy Review* 4: 193–202.

Moore, G. A., J. MacNamara, and R. Tucker. 1970. *Interlingual Dichotic Interference*. Unpublished research report. McGill University.

Muysken, Pieter. 1995. Code-Switching and Grammatical Theory. In Lester Milroy and Pieter Muysken, eds., *One Speaker, Two Languages: Cross-Disciplinary Perspectives on Code-Switching*. Cambridge, U.K.: Cambridge University Press. 177–98.

Myers-Scotton, Carol. 1993. *Social Motivations for Codeswitching: Evidence from Africa*. Oxford, U.K.: Clarendon Press.

Nunberg, Geoffrey. 1992. "Afterword: The Official English Movement: Reimagining America." In James Crawford, ed., *Language Loyalties: A Source Book on the Official English Controversy*. Chicago: University of Chicago Press. 479–94.

Obler, Lorraine, and Martin Albert. 1978. "A Monitor System for Bilingual Language Processing." In M. Paradis, ed., *Aspects of Bilingualism*. Columbia, SC: Hornbeam Press. 156–64.

Paulston, Christina. B. 1986. "Linguistic Consequences of Ethnicity and Nationalism in Multilingual Settings." In Bernard Spolsky, ed., *Language and Education in Multilingual Settings*. San Diego, CA: College Hill Press. 117–52.

Perea, Juan. F. 1993. *Hernandez v. New York: Courts, Prosecutors, and the Fear of Spanish*. Unpublished research report. University of Florida, College of Law.

Phillipson, Robert, Mart Rannut, and Tove Skutnabb-Kangas. 1994. "Introduction." In Tove Skutnabb-Kangas and Robert Phillipson, eds., *Linguistic Human Rights: Overcoming Linguistic Discrimination*. Berlin: Mouton de Gruyter.

Piatt, Bill. 1993. *Language on the Job: Balancing Business Needs and Employee Rights*. Albuquerque: University of New Mexico Press.

Ricento, Thomas. 1996. "Language Policy in the United States." In Michael Herriman and Barbara Burnaby, eds., *Language Policies in English-Dominant Countries*. Clevedon: Multilingual Matters. 122–58.

Roberts, Celia, Evelyn Davies, and Tom Jupp. 1992. *Language and Dis-*

crimination: A Study of Communication in Multi-ethnic Workplaces. London: Longman.

Roos, P. D. 1986. "Implementation of the Federal Bilingual Education Mandate: The Keyes Case as a Paradigm." *La Raza Law Journal* 1(3): 257–76.

Stavenhagen, Rodolfo. 1990. *The Ethnic Question: Conflicts, Development, and Human Rights.* Tokyo: United Nations University Press.

Tamayo, William. 1996. "National Origin Discrimination in Violation of Title VII of the Civil Rights Act of 1964: "English Only" and Accent Discrimination Cases." In *English Only? Language Rights in the 90's: A Seminar Discussing Constitutional Issues, Voting Rights, Access to Public Services, Bilingual Education and Employment.* San Francisco: California Chapter, ACLU; Employment Law Center of the Legal Aid Society of San Francisco; Human Rights Committee, State Bar of California, Legal Services Section; Multicultural Education, Training and Advocacy, Inc.

Thompson, Linda, Michael Fleming, and Michael Byram. 1996. "Languages and Language Policy in Britain." In Michael Herriman and Barbara Burnaby, eds., *Language Policies in English-Dominant Countries.* Clevedon: Multilingual Matters. 99–121.

Triesman, Anne M. 1964. "Verbal Cues, Language and Meaning in Selective Attention." *American Journal of Psychology* 77: 210–19.

———. 1969. "Strategies and Models of Selective Attention." *Psychological Review* 76: 282–99.

Turi, Joseph G. 1994. "Typology of Language Legislation." In Tove Skutnabb-Kangas and Robert Phillipson, eds., *Linguistic Human Rights: Overcoming Linguistic Discrimination.* Berlin: Mouton de Gruyter. 111–19.

Valdés, Guadalupe, and Richard A. Figueroa. 1994. *Bilingualism and Testing: A Special Case of Bias.* Norwood, NJ: Ablex.

Court Cases

Castañeda v. Pickard, 648 F.2d 989 (5th Cir.), 1981.

Cota v. Tucson Police Department, 783 F.Supp. 458 (D.Ariz.), 1992.

Equal Employment Opportunity Commission and Communications Workers of America v. Contel of California, Inc., SACV89-506-AHS (RWRX) (C.D. Cal.), 1989.

Espinoza v. Farah Mfg. Co., 414 US 86, 1973.

Fragante v. City and County of Honolulu, 888 F.2d 591 (9th Cir. 1989), amended, 51 FEP Cases 190, cert. denied, 494 U.S. 1081, 1990.

Garcia v. Gloor, 618 F.2d 264 (5th Circ. 1980), reh'g denied, 625 F.2d 1016, cert. denied, 449 U.S. 1113, 1981.

Garcia v. Spun Steak Co., 998F.2d 1480 (9th Cir.1993), reh'g en banc denied, 13 F.3d 296 (9th Cir.1993), cert. denied, __US__, 114 S. Ct. 2726, 1994.

Gideon v. Riverside Community College Dist. l, 43 FEP Case 910, 916 (C.D. Cal.), 1985.

Gutierrez v. Municipal Court, 838 F.29 1031 (9thCir.1988), reh'g en banc denied, 861 F.2d 1187 (9th Cir. 1988), vacated as moot, 490 U.S. 1016, 1989.

Hernandez v. New York, 111 S. Ct. 1859, 1991.

Kahakua v. Hallgrem, No. 86-0434 (D. Hawaii 1987), aff'd sub nom, *Kahakua v. Friday*, 876 F.2d 896 (9th Cir.), 1989.

Keyes v. School Dist. No.1, 576 F. Supp. 1503, 1516-18 (D. Colo.), 1983.

Lau v. Nichols, 414 U.S. 563, 1974.

Perez v. F.B.I., 707 F.Supp. 891 (W.D. Tex.), 1988.

Salem v. La Salle High School (March 29, 1983, C.D. Cal.) No. CV 82-0131-ER, 1983.

Yñiguez v. Arizonans for Official English, 41 F. 3d 1217 (9th Cir. 1994), reh'g en banc granted, (9th Circ. 1995), *cert. granted*, March 25, 1996 (U.S. Supreme Court No. 95-974).

CHAPTER SEVEN

"Shooting Themselves in the Foot": Consequences of English Only Supporters "Going to Law"

RANDY H. LEE, J.D.
University of North Dakota

DAVID F. MARSHALL
University of North Dakota

The supporters of English Only amendments and laws in the United States have overlooked some unwanted and unanticipated consequences of their position. We are not talking here about the hyperbolic claims that the English language is under attack in the United States, the major argument furthered by these groups clamoring for protective legislation. The ongoing hegemony of English around the world demonstrates that such arguments for English being imperiled, here or elsewhere, are ludicrous (see Fishman 1989, 233–63, 638–54; Nunberg 1997). Even more ludicrous is the fact that supporters of English Only do not recognize the imminent dangers of "going to law" to accomplish their goals.

The doctrine of unintended consequences often accompanies the act of "going to law," meaning that legislation per se sometimes generates rulings that rebound on its advocates, creating just those situations the legislation was supposedly written to overcome. The history of U.S. attempts to prohibit the sale and consumption of liquor demonstrate that the only thing worse than a crisis that prompts legislation to solve it is legislation that creates a crisis worse than the crisis that existed prior to its adoption.

Molly Ivins (1998) explained the problem of unintended consequences when she wrote:

RANDY H. LEE, J.D., AND DAVID F. MARSHALL

Bad governance is, in its own way, an interesting study—not un-like those monsters in sci-fi films that start as small blobs and then turn into something that eats Chicago. You start with just a li'l ol' bill to deregulate the savings and loans, and before you know it, it's a screaming horror that costs the taxpayers $500 billion.

The art of writing law so that it does precisely what it is supposed to do, and does not do anything else, has always been hard to come by. The careful, painstaking, legislative craftsman-ship . . . is starting to look like a lost skill.

The law of unintended consequences may be unavoidable, but when you see legislation deliberately deformed for some cheap political purpose—not just the OPO (obvious payoff) to big cam-paign contributors but some evanescent partisan advantage—it is . . . discouraging. (2C)

With this doctrine of unintended consequences in mind, it is possible to anticipate at least seven reasons why making English official would be harmful:

1. The passing of legislation to make English the official lan-guage of the United States would create a situation worse than the one it was supposed to prevent. As Geoffrey Nunberg (1997) suggests:

At the local level, the public discussion of English-only has en-couraged numerous private acts of discrimination. In recent years, for example, dozens of firms and institutions have adopted En-glish-only workplace rules that bar employees from using for-eign languages even when speaking among themselves or when on breaks. More generally, the mere fact that politicians and the press are willing to take the proposals of English-only seriously tends to establish the basic premise of the movement: that there is a question about the continued status of English as the com-mon language of American public discourse. (41–42)

Nunberg continues by demonstrating that English is not endan-gered or even remotely challenged in the United States or in other countries. The argument presented metaphorically in a U.S. En-glish advertisement showing a knife labeled "official bilingual-ism" slashing through a map of the United States is absolutely unfounded, a case of "nonsense from beginning to end" (Nunberg

1997, 42). But while the arguments are specious, when they are raised in the public mind, they create a climate of hostility to other languages, which in turn creates the potential for the loss of free speech. How much more endangered—or certainly chilled—would free speech in another language be if the U.S. government instituted linguistic legislation demanding that only English be spoken in all public places?

When in 1988 Arizona narrowly passed a constitutional amendment (Article XXVIII), which provided that English was the official language of the state of Arizona, and that the state and its political subdivisions—including all government officials and employees performing government business—must "act" only in English, action was brought to challenge the constitutionality of the amendment. In 1998 the Arizona Supreme Court (No. CV-96-0493-PR) found:

> The Amendment violates the First Amendment to the United States Constitution because it adversely impacts the constitutional rights of non-English-speaking persons with regard to their obtaining access to their government and limits the political speech of elected officials and public employees. We also hold that the Amendment violates the Equal Protection Clause of the Fourteenth Amendment to the United States Constitution because it unduly burdens core First Amendment rights of a specific class without materially advancing a legitimate state interest. (957 P.2d 984)

Obviously, the English Only amendment in Arizona created a situation in which basic freedoms under the U.S. Constitution were imperiled; thus the amendment created a situation worse than that which existed prior to its passage.

Cultural behavior remains extremely difficult to legislate, and few elements of culture become more difficult to control, much less legislate, than the daily language use of individuals in a democracy that specifically guarantees freedom of speech. Attempting to legislate human behavior is the legal equivalent of trying to herd cats. (For the problems in attempting to word the first several English Only federal amendments, see Marshall 1986; for similar problems at the level of state constitutions, see Tatalovich 1995.)

If phrased as a meaningless designation such as the state flower or the state insect or the state quadruped, legislation establishing the state language is innocuous, but if proponents attempt to give such legislation "legal teeth" by demanding compliance, the law quickly becomes a magnet for arguments of unconstitutionality. Thus we arrive at the second reason why English Only supporters face failure.

2. The doctrine of unintended consequences guarantees that any law attempting to control human linguistic behavior either becomes innocuous or develops the potential to imperil constitutional freedoms.

The consequences resulting from hasty "going to law" litter the history of U.S. jurisprudence. In late nineteenth-century America, the campaign waged against the codification of common law witnessed many debates in which arguments proliferated against enacting a law that could have unforeseen consequences. One major leader of the anticodification movement was James C. Carter, who argued that "codes impaired the orderly development of the law; they froze it into a form which prevented evolution" (qtd. in Friedman 1973, 87). Carter argued: "The social standard of justice grows and develops with the moral and intellectual growth of society. . . . Hence a gradual change unperceived and unfelt in its advance is continually going on in the jurisprudence of every progressive State" (qtd. in Friedman 1973, 87). The proof of Carter's and others' arguments in just the past three decades is in the courts' efforts to interpret new applications of statutes unforeseen by their original drafters.

The ability of judges to interpret legislation is a necessity occasioned by societal as well as legislative change. As Guido Calabresi, former dean of Yale Law School, states:

> Continuity and change are essential attributes of a legal system. Although abrupt and frequent changes are often not desirable, laws must change to meet the needs of changing times and, in democratic systems, the demands of changing majorities or, perhaps more accurately, of changing coalitions of minorities. If legal-political institutions are too responsive to change, however, temporary and unstable majorities are apt quickly to impose their will. New laws are passed only to be followed by quick reversal

at the next election, leading to uncertainty and to the defeat of legitimate expectations. Abrupt changes, moreover, can create deep ruptures in society, ruptures that slower, more organic change would avoid. (Calabresi 1982, 3)

The current debate over moving from a de facto to a de jure official status for English in the United States is a clear example of what Calabresi would term potential "deep ruptures in society" caused, in part, by a too quick response to changing U.S. demographics.

There can be no doubt whatsoever that English is the de facto official language of the United States (see Kloss 1986 for a distinction between "explicit" and "implicit" status). Two "sense of Congress" declarations have been passed—one in the Senate (*Congressional Record* 1983e, s. 12642) and another, similar "sense of the Senate" in the Simpson-Mazzoli bill (*Up.date* 1984, 6)—that declare "the English language is the official language of the United States." A sense of Congress declaration, in the House and/or the Senate, however, is not sufficient to override existing law ("English as the Official Language" 1982, 9).

The problem of moving from de facto to de jure status continues to present problems for federal and state constitutional amendment drafters seeking to make English the official language of the United States. When attempting to write legislation that does not endanger itself as unconstitutional, drafters of English Only legislation have had to resort to pious gestures, such as stating that English is official in much the same way that the state flower, bird, insect, mineral, song, and so forth are official. Whenever any statutory teeth have been included in the bill, it has run into problems. (For more on state efforts, see Tatalovich 1995; for earlier national efforts, see Marshall 1986, and for later developments, Marshall 1996; see also Baron 1990; Piatt 1990; Schmidt 1993, 1998.) It is no accident that supporters of English Only have turned from national to state legislation, and, after finding limited success there, to individual programs they object to, developing campaigns such as those against bilingual education and multilingual voting.

"Going to law" is not an easy process, nor should it be, for the body of law has built-in safeguards that reject incompatible legislation. In the nineteenth century, the prevailing notion of the role of courts was that they would *not* change laws through interpretation; "legislatures, in a sense, had the final say," and the "constitutional weapon . . . was sparingly used because, unlike the others, it denied to the legislatures, to the government's most direct representatives of the people, their last say" (Calabresi 1982, 4):

> Yet once the legislature did act in a constitutional fashion, with sufficient clarity to overcome strict interpretation, its actions were final and virtually untouchable by later courts. Nor was there a pressing need for judicial interference. Statutes were rare enough so that, even when they became middle-aged and no longer desirable, they would not greatly inconvenience the polity. In time they would become completely obsolete, and ignored. Even before then they could, unless revised by the legislature, continue to govern as minor anachronisms or small inconveniences—the price paid for the maintenance of a democratic system that gave both change and continuity and that, to do so, seemed to require that legislative actions be taken as final. (5)

It became necessary, however, to combat the doctrine of unintended consequences through means other than simply ignoring the obsolete law.

> In the Progressive Era and especially during the New Deal, a change took place in the judicial-legislative balance. First, laws were drafted differently, more specifically and with greater detail; unlike the codes, which were compilations of the common law, the new statutes were frequently meant to be the primary source of law. Courts, limited to honest interpretations of these statutes and committed to legislative supremacy, soon began to give them the authority they claimed for themselves. (5)

Gilmore accurately details the problems that resulted:

> [W]ith the New Deal, a style of drafting which aimed at an unearthly and superhuman precision came into vogue, on the state as well as the federal level. Eventually the problem of obsolescent statutes solves itself. No statutory craftsman has a crystal ball in which he can read the future. The best he can do is to make some kind of sense out of the recent past. A well-drafted statute will deal sensibly with the issues which have come into litigation during the twenty or twenty-five years which preceded

the drafting. However, the focus of litigation has a way of shifting unexpectedly and unpredictably. New issues, which no one ever dreamed of, present themselves for decision. With luck, the statute will turn out to have nothing to say that is relevant to the new issues, which can then be decided on their own merits. In this way any statute gradually becomes irrelevant and will finally be reabsorbed within the mainstream of the common law. But that takes a long time. The most difficult period in the life of a statute—as in the life of a human being—is middle age. Admittedly the statute is no longer what it once was but there is life in the old dog yet. An occasional subsection still has its teeth and subparagraph (3)(b) may burn with a gem-like flame. We are now passing through our statutory middle age. Statutory language—like any other kind of language—almost always presents alternative possibilities of construction. There will, however, be cases in which even the most disingenuous construction will not save the day. In such a case, it has always been assumed, a court must bow to the legislative command, however absurd, however unjust, however wicked. Once the legislature has taken over a field, only the legislature can effect any further change. So far as my own knowledge takes me, it is only within the past ten or fifteen years [dated from 1977] that there have been suggestions in some judicial opinions to the effect that courts, faced with an obsolete statute and a history of legislative inaction, may take matters into their own hands and do whatever justice and good sense may seem to require. These suggestions have, for the most part, been put forward with an understandable degree of hesitant reluctance. As the idea becomes more familiar to us, I dare say that we will live to see that the reformulation of an obsolete statutory provision is quite as legitimately within judicial competence as the reformulation of an obsolete common law rule. Indeed, if we do not, we will presently find ourselves lost in a legal jungle with no hope of finding a way out. (Gilmore 1977, 96–97)

Calabresi (1982) also describes the problems that arose from this new type of legislative drafting:

When these laws were new and functional, so that they represented in a sense the majority and its needs, the change presented few fundamental problems. Soon, however, these laws, like all laws, became middle-aged. They no longer served current needs or represented current majorities. Changed circumstances, or newer statutory and common law developments, rendered some statutes inconsistent with a new social or legal topography. Others were oddities when passed (in the throes of a crisis or, perhaps, in an experimental spirit that started no new trend in the law). Still others became increasingly inconsistent with new constitutional developments without, for all that, actually becoming unconstitutional. Despite this inconsistency with the legal landscape, however, such statutes remained effective and continued to govern important areas of social concern, because getting a statute enacted is much easier than getting it revised. They remained effective, even though some of them at least could not have been reenacted and thus could be said to lack current majoritarian support; checks and balances still worked, and interests served by these outdated laws could successfully block their amendment or repeal. (6)

Calabresi refers to this dilemma as "statutorification," wherein judges were sometimes obligated "with open aversion" to make such laws constitutionally functional through ever broadening interpretation, or else admit failure of justice. Calabresi carefully notes, almost two decades ago, "I would argue that much of the current criticism of judicial activism, and of our judicial system generally, can be traced to the rather desperate responses of our courts to a multitude of obsolete statutes in the face of the manifest incapacity of legislatures to keep those statutes up to date" (1982, 6–7). Calabresi distinguishes two responses to the problem of "statutorification": the New Deal solution, in which administrative agencies are delegated the authority to update law, and legislative solutions such as sunset clauses, by which statutes containing them, unless reenacted, expire. He proposes a third solution, which involves "a new relationship between courts and statutes, a relationship that would enable us to retain legislative initiative . . . while restoring to courts their common law function of seeing . . . that the law is kept up to date" (7)—a solution, unfortunately, still awaiting enactment. This discussion provides a third reason why the English Only lobby is wrong in advocating a legislative solution to its nonproblem.

3. Once enacted, statutory solutions are difficult to change, and they face the threat of becoming quickly obsolete.

To see how a law can raise unexpected havoc, one has only to look to the recent case of *United States v. Singleton* (1998), in which the United States Court of Appeals first found that the law against bribing a witness applied to prosecutors who offered witnesses leniency for testifying against others. The bribery statute (18 U.S.C. 201[c][2]) "outlaws promising or paying anything of value to a witness who gives sworn testimony at a trial or other proceeding" (Heller 1998). Prosecutor bargains with defendants to reduce the charge or recommend a lower sentence in exchange for testimony against others thus became a federal crime under 18 U.S. 201 (c)(2). The practice is widely used; according to Steven Zeidman, a professor of criminal law at New York University Law School, "In the culture of this country, nobody likes a snitch, yet that has become the crux of the criminal justice system. But nobody likes to think about it, and now we're being forced to think about it" (qtd. in Glaberson 1998). Judge Federico A. Moreno of the federal district court in Florida stated: "The holding of the Singleton panel would dangerously disable the Government's investigatory and prosecutorial powers"; however, Judge Ginger Berrigan of the federal district court in Louisiana noted that "any inducement is as much if not more a temptation to fabricate than it is to tell the truth" (Glaberson 1998). Notwithstanding the National Association of Criminal Defense Lawyers' filing a "friend of the court" brief in the case, in the 10th Circuit rehearing en banc the mischief of the panel decision was "corrected" on January 8, 1999, it being determined that the "whoever" in 18 U.S.C. 201(c)(2) does not include the United States government (1999 WL 6469).

From the legal fireworks surrounding *United States v. Singleton* (1998), the doctrine of unintended consequences is obviously alive and well, creating havoc and reminding us that law is not to be approached lightly, especially by those who have a hidden agenda such as U.S. English and other English Only advocates.

It is difficult to understand how the English Only lobby does not see the contradiction in trying to repeal the bilingual education and the multilingual ballot statutes, which it claims are obsolete (although the need still exists for both programs, perhaps more than when they were originally enacted), or understand that the legislation it proposes would ultimately create conditions that would exacerbate the original problems.

Another difficulty with the doctrine of unintended consequences is that the definition of what is and is not constitutional continues to change. Bruce Ackerman (1998) argues in *We the People: Transformations* that the people understand what is constitutional far better than was previously thought and that their understanding can and has changed, often with noticeable effect. Ackerman postulates that U.S. history is marked by "transformative moments" when succeeding generations have, in their concensus, inexplicitly rewritten what the Constitution means for them. He believes that this inexplicit shift in public understanding is precisely what the framers of the Constitution had in mind when making their document elastic enough to develop and meet new thoughts and theories.

Ackerman argues that the 1787 Constitutional Convention in Philadelphia acted illegally; instead of revising the Articles of Confederation as promised, the convention threw the articles out and instituted a totally different form of government, based not on confederation but on federalism. In defiance of the articles, the convention announced that the new Constitution would be adopted if only nine of the thirteen states approved—an action impossible, definitely unforeseen, and unthinkable under the provisions and understanding underlying the Articles of Confederation.

Since its adoption, there have been "illegalities" (the word explicitly used by Ackerman) connected with the Constitution. For example, Ackerman notes that Article 5 provides for the orderly enactment of amendments; not following this methodology would be, prima facie, unconstitutional. If after the Civil War, however, the Republican Congress had faithfully followed the procedures in Article 5, the Thirteenth and Fourteenth Amendments would have been blocked. The Reconstruction Congress made adoption of the amendments mandatory for readmission to the United States by the former Confederate states. Such a requirement could be construed as distinctly unconstitutional, but again the people, acting through Congress, allowed a new interpretation of the Constitution so that readmission would not nullify the larger meaning of the outcome of the Civil War.

According to Ackerman, another reinterpretation took place during the New Deal when Roosevelt attempted to pack the Supreme Court. After his second election, with his overwhelming popular support in Congress generated by a landslide victory,

Roosevelt (and indirectly the people) was able to persuade the Supreme Court to interpret the Constitution differently, upholding the New Deal program statutes previously held unconstitutional. The people's changed concept of what was constitutional was belatedly recognized by the Supreme Court (Ackerman 1998). Our understanding of the Constitution, the bedrock of U.S. law, has changed decidedly over the years, not only in its interpretation by the courts and Congress, but also by what the people allow. The supreme law of the land changes to meet new challenges and new societal and governmental needs, and underlying that change is the voters' altered perception of what is and is not constitutional. The people seem to have decided that the courts should not be challenged if they play the constitutionality card when laws become obsolete or farcical.

For another example of how a law can turn on its advocates, consider *Chung Fook v. White* (1924). A statute provided that "the wife of a 'naturalized' citizen, married to him after naturalization, may be admitted with a contagious disorder" (§ 22 of the Immigration Act of 1917). Chung Fook, a native-born U.S. citizen whose wife suffered a contagious disorder, was denied benefit of the Congress's wisdom, and could not bring his wife into the country, although he could have were he merely "naturalized." The Ninth Circuit Court noted: "The words of the statute being clear, if it unjustly discriminates against the native-born citizen, or is cruel and inhuman in its results, as forcefully contended, the remedy lies with Congress and not with the courts. Their duty is simply to enforce the law as it is written, unless clearly unconstitutional" (*Chung Fook* 1924). The Immigration Act of 1917 had been written to stem the influx of immigrants and to move the nation toward "Americanization." The irony was that in this instance the law, intended to severely limit immigration, allowed naturalized citizens rights that a native-born citizen could not enjoy. The intention of the legislation backfired by creating problems for native-born U.S. citizens, problems not faced by naturalized immigrants.

How laws can change to the extent that they become farcical is also illustrated by three cases prosecuted under the Mann Act, also called the White Slave Traffic Act of 1910, which makes it illegal to transport a woman in interstate commerce for the purpose of prostitution or concubinage. In *Caminetti v. United States* (1917), a man who took his mistress from Sacramento to Reno was charged; the case was heard with *Diggs v. United States,* in which another man had done the same from the same cities, and *Hays v. United States,* in which the woman was transported from Oklahoma City to Wichita. Because these men were not married to the women, they were, under the law, found guilty. How many times a day would this law be broken today? The enormity of enforcement boggles a sane mind.

In *United States v. Beach* (1945), the Mann Act was found to operate where no white slave traffic was involved, even when state lines were not crossed. The law was also found to be applicable to any transportation taking place wholly within the District of Columbia. The ability of Congress to control interstate commerce was interpreted as being extended to the capital district, even when state lines were not crossed. This interpretation means that "hanky-panky" is a federal offense in Washington even when it serves no purpose at which the statute was clearly aimed. How many government leaders—executive, congressional, or judicial—have broken this law?

In *Mortensen et ux. v. United States* (1944), a man and wife who operated "a house of ill repute" in Nebraska were convicted under the Mann Act when they took their two employees to Wyoming and Utah, solely for purposes of vacation. It was not the trip *from* Nebraska that violated the law, but the journey from Utah *back to* Nebraska, and the couple became federal criminals because they had taken their employees on an innocent vacation crossing state lines. The dissenting opinion noted, wryly, that for a prostitute, it is necessary to vacation in-state.

These are only a few of numerous examples of one law that had reached middle age, creating ridiculous consequences; there are multitudes of other outdated laws, still current but, happily, simply ignored. For a long time, it was illegal to carry a concealed pair of pliers in Texas, a statute dating back to barbed wire cutting. Other examples of outdated laws could fill volumes, and have. As Calabresi (1982) notes, it is far easier to pass a statute than to revise it, and the current race "to go to law" regarding human behavior—specifically how we speak and in what language—presents an open invitation to predictable if not immediate obsolescence.

4. The English Only advocates are foolish because human behavior, specifically one's conversation, is not only difficult but also unnecessary, useless, and harmful to control by law.

Part of the rationale behind the English Only law attempts is the nature of the United States' rapidly changing demographics; the hidden agenda is an attempt to preserve middle-class White political power. But that power, at least in terms of population, is rapidly eroding. According to Bureau of the Census figures, from 1980 to 1990 Asian and Pacific Islanders experienced the highest growth of any U.S. component group—108 percent—and their numbers had already doubled once before in the previous decade. The Black or African American population increased 13 percent; the Native American or American Indian, Inuit, and Aleut population gained 38 percent; while the White population increased only 6 percent. The Hispanic/Latino component, listed under the White category, grew by 53 percent. Census Bureau projections indicate that White non-Hispanics/Latinos will become a minority of U.S. citizens by 2050; from 1990 to 2015, the American Indian, Alaska Native, and Black populations will almost double; the Hispanic/Latino population will triple; and the Asian/Pacific Islander population will quadruple, while the White non-Hispanic population will increase only 5 percent. Presently, only three of the ten largest cities in the United States have non-Hispanic White majorities—Philadelphia, Phoenix, and San Diego (*Review of Federal Measurements of Race and Ethnicity* 1993, 3–4, 39; for the implications of this demographic change on English Only legislation, see Marshall 1996).

The changing demographics of the United States, which probably triggered the English Only efforts in the first place (see Marshall 1996), have now begun to affect the political arena with a startling force. In the 1998 California election, it was obvious that "Hispanics [were] still furious at GOP support for anti-immigrant and English-only measures, and they delivered 78 percent of their votes to Democratic Gray Davis for governor and 70 percent to Democrat Barbara Boxer for Senate, based on exit polls conducted for the Associated Press by Voter News Service" (Meckler 1998, 5A). Seeing the political light, Governor George W. Bush of Texas campaigned in Spanish and was able to get half of his state's Hispanic/Latino vote, usually Democrat, by making "it clear that he had no interest in the sort of anti-immigrant policies backed by California Republicans" (Meckler 1998, 5A). As Cecilia Muñoz of the National Council of La Raza noted, "If they [politicians] expect to get elected, they better start learning. The bottom line is, as voters, we expect to be respected. We expect to be treated like Americans, which is what we are" (Meckler 1998, 5A). Politicians are now paying an expensive price for supporting an anti-Hispanic/Latino agenda, according to former Housing Secretary Henry Cisneros, now president of Univision Television in Los Angeles: "Frankly, the effectiveness of those [anti-Hispanic/Latino] tools has come to an end. The numbers are now too large to do it and get away with it" (Meckler 1998, 5A).

Insight into changing demography and voting and campaigning patterns shows another failing that the English Only advocates invite when they go to law.

5. A knee-jerk reaction to the increased focus in U.S. life on minorities is now recognized by more and more in the electorate as an attempt to preserve White, non-Hispanic/Latino, middle- and upper-class privilege.

Today, any English Only law would be a too-quick reaction to changing demographics, doomed by these same demographics to failure over time. In fact, given the present circumstances as outlined by Cisneros, it may already be too late to pass an English Only bill in many states. The continued failure to do so in Texas may provide a template for the future (for discussion of this issue, see Tatalovich 1995).

"Going to law," moving from a de facto to a de jure status for an official language, does not always result in problems, although there will always be the usual quirks in new-law application. Switzerland functions well on three official languages (French, German, and Italian) and four national languages (the official languages plus Romansch). The territoriality of each language is protected by the individual cantons. Because of Switzerland's excellent educational system, there is widespread multilingualism and even diglossia between Swiss German and standard German (Fasold 1984, 41). Tanzania has solved several of its nation-building problems through the adoption of Swahili as the official language, although English still functions as the major instrument for higher education (Fasold 1984, 266–77). Ireland has had problems attempting to resuscitate Irish, but no serious social division has resulted from its language-planning efforts (Fasold 1984, 278–85). Paraguay continues to serve as an example of a nation successfully functioning with two major languages—Spanish and Guarani—held in a diglossic partnership (Fasold 1984, 13–20). Some nations, however, have suffered social disruption when language has been utilized as a symbol for identification in the process of political and ethnic bifurcation.

Horowitz (1985) discovered that ethnic conflict arises when one of two groups considers both groups equal while the other group does not. In some cases, language planning has resulted in the passage of legislation to overcome this situation, but the act of "going to law" has created conflict without solving the ethnolinguistic imbalance in opportunity (for a discussion of how perception of unequal opportunity reinforces ethnic conflict, see Beer and Jacob 1985).

In the United States, the declining White, non-Hispanic/Latino majority perceives the rapidly growing minority populations as having equality (one half of Horowitz's equation), but these minorities do not see themselves as having equal access to economic and political power, although they are beginning increasingly to exercise that power (see Meckler 1998). To pass an English Only law at this time would sharply focus the nation's minorities' attention on an apparent inequality—freedom of speech for monolingual English speakers but not for non-English or bilingual speakers. This focus would increase the sense of inequality among minorities, thus providing the potential for ethnic conflict (since Horowitz's other half of the equation would be realized). This perspective provides our next reason why English Only advocates should not go to law.

6. "Going to law" by English Only advocates does not create calm within the body politic, as they claim; on the contrary, their actions exacerbate tensions already present and result in more, not less, ethnic conflict.

It is interesting to note that in the Arizona Supreme Court opinion on Amendment XXVIII's unconstitutionality (Proposition 106 1988), the court stated that this amendment "unduly burdens core First Amendment rights of a specific class without materially advancing a legitimate state interest" (957 P.2d 984). It is necessary for legislation to advance "a legitimate state interest" to avoid the charge of unconstitutionality; interestingly, another recent instance of state policy regarding language not fulfilling a legitimate state interest is found in Alabama, where in Judge Ira De Ment's opinion in *Sandoval v. Hagan* (1998), it was found that Alabama's policy of administering driver's license examinations in English only was a facially neutral practice (i.e., not invidiously discriminating on its face) that, on the basis of national origin, had a disproportionately adverse effect. This policy violated the regulations promulgated under Title VI of the 1964 Civil Rights Act, which prohibits such disparate impact. The court found no substantial legitimate justification for the policy; concerns for highway safety, examination integrity, and limiting government expense were not legal justifications for the program.

The *Sandoval* case erodes the arguments made by the English Only lobby that its legislation will provide advantages, especially that of limiting government expense through the use of only one language. As did Arizona in the same year, the federal court stressed that no legitimate state interests override "the disparate impact" of the policy. One is prompted to wonder: Exactly what state interest would be served by enacting an English Only law? This observation leads to the last reason why the English Only law would be harmful.

7. No explicit state interest is sufficiently advanced by an English Only law to outweigh its impact on free speech or other rights enjoyed under the Constitution.

Advocates of English Only have not thought through the legal implications of moving from de facto to de jure status for

English as the official language of the United States. Far from solving the current problems they perceive in the American body politic, such a move could cause the equivalent of a contagion that moves from a minor sniffle to a potentially terminal disease. The act of "going to law" dares not be undertaken lightly or without careful study. English Only advocates have no clue where their efforts may lead, but if the experiences of the past, both remote and recent, are any indication, "going to law" is capable of creating legislation that rears up and bites its supporters. The best solution for the United States would be to stick to the already-worked-out compromise of having English official only de facto. Such a solution has served Great Britain quite as well as the United States so far; to attempt to "fix" our current language policy that is not broken seems, at best, idiotic and self-destructive.

The English language is not the glue that holds the United States together; the glue is the body of law founded on the Constitution, a document that we dare not amend without adequate cause and most careful study. The rush to law by the English Only advocates will probably prove to be a case of their shooting themselves in the foot; but for the unknowable consequences, one might be tempted to load the weapon for them.

Works Cited

Ackerman, Bruce. 1998. *We the People: Transformations.* Cambridge, MA.: Belknap Press of Harvard University Press.

Baron, Dennis. 1990. *The English-Only Question: An Official Language for Americans?* New Haven: Yale University Press.

Beer, William R., and James E. Jacob. 1985. *Language Policy and National Unity.* Totowa, NJ: Rowman and Allanheld.

Calabresi, Guido. 1982. *A Common Law for the Age of Statutes.* Cambridge, MA: Harvard University Press.

Congressional Record. 1983e. S.12642.

"English as the Official Language." 1982. *New York Times,* Aug. 8. 9.

Fasold, Ralph. 1984. *The Sociolinguistics of Society.* Oxford, U.K.: Basil Blackwell.

Fishman, Joshua A. 1989. *Language and Ethnicity in Minority Sociolinguistic Perspective.* Clevedon: Multilingual Matters.

Friedman, Lawrence M. 1973. *A History of American Law.* New York: Simon and Schuster.

Gilmore, Grant. 1977. *The Ages of American Law.* New Haven, CT: Yale University Press.

Glaberson, William. 1998. "Ruling Puts Leniency, a Top Tool for Prosecutors, Under Scrutiny." *New York Times,* Oct. 27. A1.

Heller, Emily. 1998. "Defenders Saw Snitch Ruling as Too Good to Be True—and It Was." *Fulton County Daily Report,* July 15. 1.

Horowitz, Donald. 1985. *Ethnic Groups in Conflict.* Berkeley: University of California Press.

Ivins, Molly. 1998. "Putting the Law into Words No Easy Task." *Grand Forks Herald,* June 15. 2C.

Kloss, Heinz. 1986. "Comment." *International Journal of the Sociology of Language* 60: 169–76.

Marshall, David F. 1986. "The Question of an Official Language: Language Rights and the English Language Amendment" and "Rebuttal." *International Journal of the Sociology of Language* 60: 7–75; 201–11.

———. 1996. "The Politics of Language in America: Attempts to Prevent an Emerging Renationalization in the United States." In Winfried Herget, ed., *What Became of the Great Society? Comparative Perspectives on the U.S.A. in the 1960s and 1990s.* Trier: Wissenschaftlicher Verlag. 67–80.

Meckler, Laura. 1998. "A Stronger Voice." *Grand Forks Herald,* Nov. 10. 5A.

Nunberg, Geoffrey. 1997. "Lingo Jingo: English-Only and the New Nativism." *The American Prospect* 33 (July-August): 40–47.

Piatt, Bill. 1990. *Only English? Law and Language Policy in the United States.* Albuquerque: University of New Mexico Press.

Proposition 106. 1988. Invalid Amendment to the Arizona Constitution, Article XXVIII. Available: http://ourworld.compuserve.com/

homepages/JWCRAWFORD/art28.htm. See also *Ruiz v. Hull* (No. CV-96-0493-PR). Available: http://www.supreme.state.a2.us.opin/pdf98/cv960493.pdf

Review of Federal Measurements of Race and Ethnicity: Hearings before the Subcommittee on Census, Statistics and Postal Personnel of the Committee on Post Office and Civil Service, House of Representatives [April 14, 1993], serial no. 103-7. Washington: U.S. Government Printing Office, 1994.

Schmidt, Ronald J. 1993. "Language Policy Conflict in the United States." In Crawford Young, ed., *The Rising Tide of Cultural Pluralism: The Nation-State at Bay?* Madison: University of Wisconsin Press. 73–92.

———. 1998. "The Politics of Language in Canada and the United States: Explaining the Differences." In Thomas Ricento and Barbara Burnaby, eds., *Language and Politics in the United States and Canada: Myths and Realities.* Mahwah, NJ: Lawrence Erlbaum. 37–70.

Tatalovich, Raymond. 1995. *Nativism Reborn? The Official English Language Movement and the American States.* Lexington: University of Kentucky Press.

Up.date. 1984. "English Requirements for Amnesty in New Immigration Law." 2(3)(June-July). 6.

Court Cases Cited

Caminetti v. United States, 242 U.S. 470, 1917.

Chung Fook v. White, 264 U.S. 443, 1924.

Mortensen et ux. v. United States, 322 U.S. 369, 1944.

Sandoval v. Hagan, 7F. Supp. 2d. M.D. Ala., 1998.

United States v. Beach, 324 U.S. 193, 1945.

United States v. Singleton, 97-3178 10th Cir. July 1, 1998.

III

LANGUAGE AND IDEOLOGY

As Terry Eagleton (1991) observes, coming up with a single and adequate definition of *ideology* is nearly impossible because the term has a wide range of meanings currently in use, many of which are incompatible. Eagleton sifts through sixteen commonly used and popular definitions to describe ideology as "peculiarly 'action-oriented' discourse, in which contemplative cognition is generally subordinated to the furtherance of 'arational' interests and desires" (1991, 29). In this sense, ideologies that relate to language include all public and disciplinary discourses that have some agenda to change the world around us in which mono-, bi-, and multilingual individuals coexist. These discourses are often "arational"; that is, they are not exclusively governed by reason, but as Eagleton also remarked, ideologies are not completely "immune to rational considerations" either (1991, 31).

Alastair Pennycook's chapter examines English language policies as components of the ideology of colonialism. His examples from the history of British colonialism in India demonstrate how beliefs about language, modernization, and progress were intermingled to produce language policy that made English a world language, one not only promoted by the dominant British groups, but willingly adopted by the indigenous populations as well. In fact, as Pennycook's archival research illustrates, the dividing lines between colonizers and colonized did not coincide with the dividing lines between "English only" and "orientalism," or between the promotion of English and the protection of local languages. Therefore, Pennycook argues, language policy needs to be examined as a complex phenomenon that is embedded in an intricate social, economic, and political context, its meaning complemented by the influence of broader social ideologies and rule. The parallels with current English Only ideologies in the

United States should encourage us to step out of the dichotomies between forces of good and bad as they have been replayed in history in order to fight for "the greater human possibilities opened up by bilingual education and multilingual language policy" (p. 218). These greater human possibilities cannot be achieved simply by accepting liberal claims that more diversity in languages, like more diversity in nature, is inherently good, unless this belief is supported, confirmed, and rewarded by the broader social practices of employment, education, and social life in general.

Lynn M. Goldstein's paper examines the almost anecdotal contrast between popular beliefs about language and knowledge accumulated by linguistic studies. Since everybody uses language, and speaking seems to be a natural human faculty, everybody has some knowledge about how language works, is learned, or needs to be regulated by policy. Goldstein analyzed newspaper articles about language and language policy matters and found a collection of popular beliefs such as "language is the glue that holds us together," "lack of Official English impedes immigrants from learning English," and "the government already spends millions of taxpayer dollars on bilingual education and other inefficient programs." Not all of these popular beliefs support English Only, and not all of them are completely unfounded. Goldstein also cites press sources that express concern about a restrictive English Only policy undermining U.S. economic prestige. Some publications comment that it is cruel to deny life-saving services to immigrants who do not speak English, or that multilingualism should be viewed as an asset. Goldstein, therefore, concludes that linguists should be interested in bridging the gulf between popular and expert knowledge, and should study the role that popular knowledge or beliefs about language play in people's reactions to English Only proposals. On the other hand, linguists should be equally interested in examining their own ideologies of language instead of simply assuming that their view of language as a neutral and rule-governed system of structures is based on nothing but factual knowledge and has no ideological implications.

Ideology, according to Eagleton, has the capacity to discriminate between power struggles that are central to a whole form of social life and those that are not. Jane H. Hill's essay illustrates this thesis by pointing out that U.S. society has a racist culture in which most processes of cultural expression, both material and symbolic, are "racialized," i.e., expressed in terms of whiteness and color. Linguists, claims Hill, will fail to understand the language debate as long as they do not realize that most of these debates are not about bilingualism, second-language acquisition, or dialect variation, but in fact are expressions of racism in the form of language panic. Therefore recurrent flare-ups of the English Only debate successfully draw public attention to the power struggle between the dominant white culture and marginalized minorities, and are instrumental in the reproduction of racism in the United States.

Ideologies often present themselves as if they were describing the way things actually are, but in fact they express certain fears, hopes, and nostalgias and belong to the realm of "rhetorical act[s] of defiance and self-affirmation" (Eagleton 1991, 19). Amanda Espinosa-Aguilar's chapter approaches English Only as rhetoric and performs a rhetorical analysis on this movement's most widely circulated texts and proposals. The result of her analysis reveals both masked and unmasked hostility toward minorities and immigrants and an appeal to the cooperation of these powerless groups that hope to secure their fragile socioeconomic position by supporting English Only. This is a rhetoric, points out Espinosa-Aguilar, that works best at times when socioeconomic success is hard to achieve and when the loss of relative social prestige creates anxiety in many societal groups.

Work Cited

Eagleton, Terry. 1991. *Ideology: An Introduction.* New York: Verso.

CHAPTER EIGHT

Lessons from Colonial Language Policies

ALASTAIR PENNYCOOK
University of Technology, Sydney, Australia

Colonialism and Language Policy

By drawing on an understanding of colonial language policy within the British Empire—particularly in India, Singapore, Malaya, and Hong Kong—I hope to shed light on current language policy debates in the United States and elsewhere. I want to draw attention to a number of specific concerns. First, we need to be cautious in discussions of language policy that we do not fall into the trap of discussing languages as if they were nothing but media for the neutral conveyance of ideas. Such an approach to language policy has been dominant in contexts such as Hong Kong, where the question of which language (English or Chinese) should predominate in schools has been debated almost entirely in terms of the "medium of instruction" rather than in terms of the social, cultural, political, or colonial implications of using one language or the other. Thus, while the choice of one language or another in educational contexts has immense political implications, there has often been a tendency to view such questions simply in terms of the educational efficiency of one code over another.

A similar concern needs to be addressed in debates over language in the United States: it is not enough to contrast an English Only policy with bilingualism or multiculturalism solely in terms of the medium of instruction or the educational efficiency of one code over another; far broader cultural and political issues are at stake here. This links to the second, and closely related, concern, namely that there has often been a tendency to deal with languages as if they were discrete objects that can be given to some people and withheld from others. My argument is that we need to understand how language policy and use are embedded in a range of different material and ideological concerns, and that therefore we need to understand the contextual and ideological underpinnings and implications of language policies.

Finally, the connection of current language policy debate to colonialism is not merely one of learning lessons from a distant past; rather, the discourses produced in the contexts of colonial language policy are constantly being reproduced in the contexts of current debates. In order to remove ourselves from this replay of colonialism, we need to step outside the framework of many of these discussions to ask different questions that are informed by a postcolonial politics of difference.

Colonial language policies can be viewed as constructed between four poles (for a detailed analysis, see Pennycook 1998a): first, the position of colonies within a capitalist empire and the need to produce docile and compliant workers and consumers to fuel capitalist expansion; second, local contingencies of class, ethnicity, race, and economic conditions that dictated the distinctive development of each colony; third, the discourses of Anglicism and liberalism with their insistence on the European need to bring "civilization" to the world; and fourth, the discourses of Orientalism with their insistence on exotic histories, traditions, and nations in decline. From amid these often competing demands emerged colonial language policies of many different hues that worked generally to bolster the economic and political position of Great Britain, but which also operated along particular ideological positions that gained sway in particular contexts.

This chapter, then, explores ways in which colonial ideologies were reflected in language education policies; I am interested in showing how different policies on the medium of education were constructed as part of colonial governance. We therefore need to understand education policy within the larger material and discursive positions that surround it, including broad background ideological positions as well as particular material (economic, political, social) conditions of education. We need to understand not only this embeddedness—how education discourses reflected wider social and ideological conditions—but also how the educational context was *productive* of colonial discourse. Therefore I want to show how such policies both reflected colonial ideology and produced it; that is to say, I argue that language policy and language education were—and are—crucial sites of colonial cultural production. Education and education policy were significant domains of colonial encounter and of the production of colonial discourse. As a result, they helped produce colonialism more generally and also have had lasting effects into the present. And it is this continuation of colonial discourse that still has an effect on current language policy far beyond the former colonial contexts.

The fact that colonial language policy became another site of colonial knowledge production is particularly important to understand since I argue that this knowledge was produced in India as a form of "trial run" for the liberal state of the nineteenth and twentieth centuries. Such knowledge, suggests Metcalf (1997), "could effectively subordinate and contain the Company's Indian underlings" (23). But the effects of such knowledge went beyond their role in the control of the Indian populace. India, as Viswanathan (1990) argues with respect to the development of the English canon of literature, was a key site for the development of policies that then flowed back to England. One crucial way to view the notion of empire is as a system that allowed the flow of knowledge and culture produced in the colonial encounter to flow back to the imperial center. Similarly, in terms of general administrative and educational policies, India became a laboratory for liberal reforms, "a laboratory for the creation of the liberal administrative state, and from there its elements—whether a state sponsored education, the codification of law, or a competitively chosen bureaucracy—could make their way back to England itself" (Metcalf 1997, 29).

This argument touches on two other points: First, we need to avoid overmaterialistic views of the production of ideology and discourse; these are produced not so much as justifications or as superstructural correlates of economic endeavors (in the Marxist view) but instead have their provenance in a much more complex series of social, cultural, and ideological relationships. And second, colonial discourses emerged from the contexts of colonialism and passed back through the empire's web to the colonial nations rather than being produced in the center—Great Britain—and then diffused. Both of these points will be crucial to my larger argument. We need to understand discourse and ideology as more than reflections or justifications of prior economic or political goals so that when looking at language policy in the United States or elsewhere today, we can avoid reducing arguments about language policies to questions of basic economic or other interests and see them as located amid complex discursive constellations. Likewise, when we understand that colonial language policies were produced in the context of colonialism rather than being exported from the colonial center, we can see how broader ideologies and local contingencies of control intertwined to produce particular policies. And from this position, the significance of the empire can be understood not as primarily commercial or political control but rather as a discursive web, a mechanism for the global movement of colonial language policy. Such discourses are still embedded in many domains of current thought and action, and still have significant effects on how the English language and the Others of current language policy are constructed.

The Poles of Colonial Language Policy

British colonial language policy was expressed in four different but interrelated contingencies. The following section examines each and explores the closer ties between the global functioning of the empire and the Anglicist vision, and between local rule and British interests in Asian culture. But these contingencies were related in other complex ways as well.

Imperial Capitalism

Despite the obvious importance of the very real economic drive behind colonialism, imperial capitalism was not the governing factor in the production of colonial language policy. Nevertheless, it is worth briefly noting the commercial significance of educating a population to be both producers and consumers of the goods of empire. According to the 1854 *Despatch* from the East India Company—the commercial body which was to set the educational policy for the rest of the century and beyond, put firmly in place the principal of the Englishman's moral duty to educate, and establish a policy of vernacular education—there were material reasons for providing education to the Indian population, since such an education

> will teach the natives of India the marvellous results of the employment of labor and capital, rouse them to emulate us in the development of the vast resources of their country, guide them in their efforts and gradually, but certainly, confer upon them all the advantages which accompany the healthy increase of wealth and commerce; and, at the same time, secure to us a larger and more certain supply of many articles necessary for our manufactures and extensively consumed by all classes of our population, as well as an almost inexhaustible demand for the produce of British labor. (From *Despatch from the Court of Directors of the East India Company, to the Governor General of India* in Bureau of Education 1922, 365)

Alongside its moral duties and benefits, education was conceived in this document as a crucial component in the construction of a global capital empire.

Anglicism

Anglicism, including the vehement support for educational intervention through the medium of English, is often assumed to be the dominant mode of colonial language ideology, but it was actually far less common. Nevertheless, it was voiced by a number of influential figures, including Thomas Babington Macaulay in his famous Minute of 1835 (1972). Charles Grant (1746–1823), a member of the Clapham Sect (an evangelical group which included William Wilberforce, Zacharay Macaulay, and others) and one of the early and vociferous advocates of strong educational intervention in India, made his position clear toward the end of the eighteenth century in a paper titled "Observations on the State of Society among the Asiatic Subjects of Great Britain, Particularly with Respect to Morals, and on the Means of Improving It," written chiefly in 1792 and dated August 16, 1797:

> The true cure of darkness is the introduction of light. The Hindoos err, because they are ignorant, and their errors have never fairly been laid before them. The communication of our light and knowledge to them, would prove the best remedy for their disorders, and this remedy is proposed, from a full conviction that if judiciously and patiently applied, it would have great and happy effects upon them, effects honourable and advantageous for us. (Bureau of Education, 1920, 81)

And the language in which this light should be brought to the people of India was English: "Thus superior, in point of ultimate advantage does the employment of the English language appear; and upon this ground, we give a preference to that mode, proposing here that the communication of our knowledge shall be made by the medium of our own language" (82). Thus Grant argued fervently for the importance of English as the language through which benefits would reach the Indian populace: "The first communication, and the instrument of introducing the rest, must be the English language; this is a key which will open to them a world of new ideas, and policy alone might have impelled us, long since, to put it into their hands" (83). English, he suggested, would open up a new world of literature, reason, history, virtue, and morality, by which "the general mass of their opinions would be rectified; and above all, they would see a better system of principles and morals. New views of duty as rational creatures would open upon them; and that mental bondage in which they have long been holden would gradually dissolve" (84).

Other examples of such Anglicist rhetoric are not hard to find. Apart from Macaulay's famous Minute of 1835, in which he argued for the worthlessness of Indian language, culture, and knowledge and for the importance of English as the language of education, there were other significant Anglicists, such as Frederick Lugard, who was instrumental in setting up Hong Kong University before he went on to become governor of Nigeria. Lugard was known not only for his work as a colonial administrator but also for his development of the colonial theories of indirect rule and the dual mandate. In his most important work,

The Dual Mandate in British Tropical Africa (1926), Lugard emphasized the importance of understanding "that Europe is in Africa for the mutual benefit of her own industrial classes, and of the native races in their progress to a higher plane; that the benefit can be made reciprocal, and that it is the aim and desire of civilized administration to fulfill this dual mandate" (617).

Lugard remained steadfastly convinced of the idea that while Britain could gain materially from its colonies, the trusteeship of the world had been left to Britain so that it could spread the benefits of British civilization: "I am profoundly convinced that there can be no question but that British rule has promoted the happiness and welfare of the primitive races. We hold these countries because it is the genius of our race to colonize, to trade, and to govern" (618–19). In his work on the use of English at Hong Kong University, Lugard expressed a similar view of Britain's imperializing mission:

> In conclusion I would emphasize the value of English as the medium of instruction. If we believe that British interests will be thus promoted, we believe equally firmly that graduates, by the mastery of English, will acquire the key to a great literature and the passport to a great trade. On the one hand we desire to secure the English language in the high position it has acquired in the Far East; on the other hand since the populations of the various provinces in China speak no common language, and the Chinese vocabulary has not yet adapted itself to express the terms and conceptions of modern science, we believe that should China find it necessary for a time to adopt an alien tongue as a common medium for new thoughts and expressions—as the nations of the West did when Latin was the language of the savants and of scientific literature—none would be more suitable than English. (1910, 4)

Grant's arguments that Indian beliefs and customs would be not only changed but also corrected by Western knowledge, and Lugard's insistence that the Chinese would be better off speaking English, are splendid examples of the arrogance of Anglicist thinking. But it is important to observe that, as suggested earlier, the views of such colonial administrators went much further than financial benefit: they saw themselves as fulfilling a moral duty to the world. These thinkers were at the forefront of the "frenzy of liberal reform known as the 'civilizing mission'" (Singh 1996, 89). This liberalism, as Metcalf (1997) points out, was informed by a "radical universalism": "Contemporary European, especially British, culture alone represented civilization. No other cultures had any intrinsic validity. There was no such thing as 'Western' civilization; there existed only 'civilization.' Hence the liberal set out, on the basis of this shared humanity, to turn the Indian into an Englishman" (34). And this liberal interventionist view of civilization was to form one of the central discourses that continued through the colonial period: "Macaulay and Mountbatten, the last viceroy, were . . . linked indissolubly together as the beginning and the end of a chain forged of liberal idealism" (Metcalf 1997, 233). This chain of liberal idealism, however, did not end with Mountbatten in India, but needs to be seen in its new guise at the beginning of the twenty-first century.

This Anglicist vision also forged an indelible link between a civilizing mission and the promotion of the English language. In such discourse, particular constructions of English and its benefits were produced and solidified. And it is against such constructions that we must wage war today. Finally, although such Anglicist rhetoric is common in colonial documents, it is by no means the dominant discourse. As we shall see, while such Anglicist rhetoric probably best matches common stereotypes of colonial discourse, it was in fact both matched by Orientalist discourse and tempered by local contexts. This raises further significant issues to which I shall return.

Local Governance

While the broader economic dictates of empire and the imperializing ideologies of Anglicism were highly influential, policies were often far more influenced by local conditions and concerns. Education was seen as a crucial means for more effective governance of the people. As W. Fraser wrote in a letter to the Chief Secretary, W. B. Bayley, in 1823:

> It would be extremely ridiculous in me to sit down to write to the Government or to you a sentence even upon the benefit of teaching the children of the Peasantry of this country to read and write.

> I shall merely observe that the greatest difficulty this Government suffers, in its endeavours to govern well, springs from the immorality and ignorance of the mass of the people, their disregard of knowledge not connected with agriculture and cattle and particularly their ignorance of the spirit, principles and system of the British Government. (Bureau of Education, 1920, 13)

While such a statement might appear to lead yet again to the Anglicist position—suggesting that the ignorance of the people could be alleviated if they were taught English—this argument is significantly different, for it is concerned first with the problems for governance caused (supposedly) by lack of knowledge, and second, with the need for a pragmatic solution by way of education in local languages.

The development of language policies in Malaya followed a similar tendency to "play safe" and promote local languages rather than English. In the 1884 Straits Settlements report on education, E. C. Hill, the inspector of schools for the colony, explained his reasons against increasing the provision of education in English: Apart from the costs and the difficulties in finding qualified teachers to teach English was the further problem that "as pupils who acquire a knowledge of English are invariably unwilling to earn their livelihood by manual labour, the immediate result of affording an English education to any large number of Malays would be the creation of a discontented class who might become a source of anxiety to the community" (171). This position was extremely common and is echoed, for example, by Frank Swettenham's argument in the *Perak Government Gazette* (July 6, 1894): "I am not in favour of extending the number of 'English' schools except where there is some palpable desire that English should be taught. Whilst we teach children to read and write and count in their own languages, or in Malay. . . . we are *safe*" (emphasis in original). Thus, as Loh Fook Seng (1970) comments, "Modern English education for the Malay then is ruled out right from the beginning as an unsafe thing" (114).

The other side of this policy—the promotion of vernacular education for the Malay population—although frequently couched in terms of a "moral duty," was closely linked to questions of social control and local economic development. As George Maxwell, chief secretary to the government of the Federated

Malaya States, 1920–1926, said in a 1927 speech, the main aims of education in Malaya were "to improve the bulk of the people and to make the son of the fisherman or peasant a more intelligent fisherman or peasant than his father had been" (Maxwell 1983, 406). In an article on vernacular education in the state of Perak, Inspector of Schools H. B. Collinge explained the benefits of education in Malay as taking "thousands of our boys . . . away from idleness," helping them at the same time to "acquire habits of industry, obedience, punctuality, order, neatness, cleanliness and general good behaviour" (qtd. in Straits Settlements 1894, 177). Thus, after a boy had attended school for a year or so, he was "found to be less lazy at home, less given to evil habits and mischievous adventure, more respectful and dutiful, much more willing to help his parents, and with sense enough not to entertain any ambition beyond following the humble home occupations he has been taught to respect." Not only does the school inculcate such habits of dutiful labor, but it also helps colonial rule more generally since "if there is any lingering feeling of dislike of the 'white man,' the school tends greatly to remove it, for the people see that the Government has really their welfare at heart in providing them with this education, free, without compulsion, and with the greatest consideration for their mohammedan sympathies" (qtd. in Straits Settlements 1894, 177).

This policy of favoring vernacular education for colonial governance developed in interesting ways in Hong Kong. E. J. Eitel, inspector of schools from 1879 to 1897, a former German missionary and "sound orientalist and sinologist" (Lethbridge 1983, vii) who had written a Cantonese dictionary and books on Buddhism and Feng Shui, was most concerned that education should give students sufficient grounding in morality. Indeed, although he clearly supported the teaching of English, he also argued that students in the village schools were getting a better education than those receiving a secular education in English. By studying Chinese classics, students learned "a system of morality, not merely a doctrine, but a living system of ethics." Thus they learned "filial piety, respect for the aged, respect for authority, respect for the moral law." In the government schools, by contrast, where English books were taught and from which religious education was excluded, "no morality is implanted in the boys" (Hong Kong 1883, 70). Thus the teaching of Chinese was "of higher advantage to the Government" and "boys strongly imbued with European civilization whilst cut away from the restraining influence of Confucian ethics lose the benefits of education, and the practical experience of Hongkong is that those who are thoroughly imbued with the foreign spirit, are bad in morals" (70).

What also becomes increasingly clear in the case of colonialism in Hong Kong is the way in which educational policy reacted to local conditions of unrest. Following the massive 1925 strike and boycott of goods in Hong Kong, R. H. Kotewall (1926) pointed directly to the schools as the source of problems, and recommended increased supervision: "Obviously the first remedy is an increased watchfulness in the schools. Special care should be exercised in the supervision of the vernacular schools in particular, for these can the more easily become breeding grounds for sedition" (455). His recommendations reach further, however, for he goes on to suggest particular orientations for Chinese school curricula:

> The Chinese education in Hong Kong does not seem to be all that it should be. The teaching of Confucian ethics is more and more neglected, while too much attention is being paid to the materialistic side of life. . . . In such a system great stress should be laid on the ethics of Confucianism which is, in China, probably the best antidote to the pernicious doctrines of Bolshevism, and is certainly the most powerful conservative course, and the greatest influence for good. (455–456)

Thus "money spent on the development of the conservative ideas of the Chinese race in the minds of the young will be money well spent, and also constitutes social insurance of the best kind" (456). This idea was supported most actively by Governor Sir Cecil Clementi, a long-term colonial administrator in Hong Kong and a scholar of Chinese folk songs. Inviting senior Chinese literati to Government House in 1927, Clementi addressed them in Cantonese and asked for their help in developing a curriculum that would promote traditional morality and scholarship, a curriculum based on orthodox Confucianism emphasizing social hierarchy and subservience to patriarchal authority (Luk 1991).

Clementi's goal was to counter the rising tide of Chinese nationalism by emphasizing traditional Chinese notions of hierarchy and loyalty. "Appeal was made to the cultural tradition of the native people to help safeguard foreign rule against the growth of nationalistic feelings among the younger generation" (Luk 1991, 660). Often far more important than the civilizing zeal of English teaching, therefore, was the conservative use of vernacular education. And crucially, as can be seen from the examples provided, such policies were implemented by Orientalist scholars.

Orientalism

Clearly, one aspect of vernacular education was its ability to promote loyalty, obedience, and acceptance of colonial rule. Another dimension of the colonialist promotion of vernacular education was tied to the Orientalist interests of many of the scholar-administrators who were closely connected to educational policies. It was the long-term colonial administrators and Orientalists such as Eitel and Clementi who saw the strongest possibilities of using vernacular language policies for colonial ends. Meanwhile, in Malaya, Swettenham—who warned against the teaching of English in Malaya—"earned his Knighthood on the strength of his ability to understand the ignorant unspoilt Malays," while another Orientalist administrator, R. J. Wilkinson, "believed as many an Englishman has believed before him and since that the native must not be taken away, must not be uprooted from his fascinating environment, fascinating to a brilliant Malay scholar" (Loh Fook Seng 1970, 114). Thus, as Loh Fook Seng goes on to suggest, "Much of the primitive Malay education that continued to be supplied by the British Government was in no small degree due to this attempt to preserve the Malay as a Malay, a son of the soil in the most literal sense possible" (114).

Orientalism has, of course, become a widely studied aspect of colonialism since Edward Said's (1978) classic study. Singh describes the apparent paradox at the heart of this colonial study of other languages and cultures: "on the one hand, the Orientalists as civil servants shared the standard colonial belief in the superiority of Western knowledge and institutions. On the other hand, these Indologists 're-discovered' a glorious India by identifying a certain resemblance between East and West in a shared ancient past" (Singh 1996, 71). It was from amid these paradoxical studies of Indian, Malay, and Chinese culture that conservative policies for the preservation of culture and knowledge—as defined by these colonial scholars—emerged, and, most important, from which policies to promote conservative forms of education were developed.

What emerges from many colonial documents is an apparently balanced educational policy promoting the spread of European knowledge by means of English in higher education and vernacular languages in primary education: "We have declared that our object is to extend European knowledge throughout all classes of the people. We have shown that this object must be effected by means of the English language in the higher branches of instruction, and by that of the vernacular languages of India to the great mass of the people" (Bureau of Education 1922, 392). Revealed here, then, is the complicity between Anglicism and Orientalism. Although Anglicism is often considered the stereotypical colonialist position, it is worth noting that the Anglicist position shared many similarities with the various Orientalist positions: the main point of disagreement was the medium through which colonial populations should be civilized. Thus, although the patronizing colonialism of Macaulay, Grant, or Lugard may seem particularly obnoxious, it is not much worse than the view held by many Orientalists of Asian despotism and static history. In this view, India, Malaya, China, and other colonial populations were stuck in an immutable past and were irredeemably corrupt, despotic, and diseased. Macaulay's patronizing colonialism was more liberal and optimistic, even if it implied a cultural imperialism more threatening than the cultural imprisonment implied by the Orientalists.

In terms of practical policies, it would be misguided to endorse the prominence historically given to the view that the Anglicist position represented colonial discourse. But just as I have suggested that Anglicism by no means won out over Orientalism, it is important to clarify that neither was this a victory for Orientalism. Rather, the two positions continued to play out alongside each other, and it becomes clear that Anglicism and Orientalism were complementary rather than antagonistic aspects of colonial discourse. Loh Fook Seng (1970) argues that Macaulay's dismissal of Indian culture and scholarship should not be seen as oppositional to the Orientalist position: "They are but two sides of the same colonial coin sharing the same rationale, to bring light into the native darkness as well as facilitate the exigencies of trade and government" (108). Similarly, Viswanathan (1990) argues that the two positions should be seen "not as polar opposites but as points along a continuum of attitudes toward the manner and form of colonial governance" (30). Ultimately, she suggests, "both the Anglicist and the Orientalist factions were equally complicit with the project of domination" (167). With these two discourses in a complementary relationship with each other and deeply complicit with colonial rule, colonial language policy can be understood to both reflect colonial ideologies and be a crucial site of their production.

Complexity, Contextuality, and Complementarity

Where does this quick look at colonial language policy leave us? Let me summarize briefly: colonial discourses on language education are interwoven both with broader colonial discourses and with modes of colonial governance. The need to provide education for Indian people became framed among sometimes competing and sometimes complementary discourses: the liberal discourse of the civilizing mission and the moral obligation to bring enlightenment to backward peoples; the need to provide a productive and docile workforce that would also become consumers within colonial capitalism; the various Orientalist positions, including an exoticization and glorification of a distant Indian past and a belief that vernacular languages were the most efficient way to spread European knowledge in India; and the Anglicist insistence that English should be the language of education. This understanding of language policy suggests several important concerns for current language policy debates, issues of complexity, contextuality, and complementarity.

Complexity

First, we need to understand the complexity of both colonial and contemporary language policies. I have tried here to contradict those overly simplistic accounts of the triumph of Anglicism and the rabid rhetoric of Macaulay. Too often (see, for example, Kachru 1986; Phillipson 1992) the history of colonial language policy has been cast as a victory for the English language, which explains the current role of English (generally a good thing, in Kachru's view) or the need to develop policies to oppose its spread (in Phillipson's view). Thus Kachru sees the resolution passed as a result of the Minute as "epoch-making" and resulting in the "diffusion of bilingualism in English on the subcontinent" (1986, 35). Phillipson argues that "Macaulay's formulation of the goals of British educational policy ended a protracted controversy which had exercised planners both in India and in the East India Company in London" (1992, 110). Yet, without understanding the relationships between support for English or vernacular languages and other material and discursive forces of colonialism, we will not have an adequate appreciation either of colonialism or of current language policies.

My attempt to move beyond the simplistic portrayal of Anglicism as the archetypal version of colonialism has significant implications. First, it helps us readdress relations between simple pasts and complex presents. By focusing on Anglicism, labeling Macaulay the designer of educational policy and exposing his bigotry, modern-day liberals, leftists, and conservatives alike are able to distance themselves from colonial complicity. Second, it enables us to see the complicity of various forms of Orientalism in colonial governance. Understanding how support for vernacular languages was integral to the colonial project has significance for contemporary language policy.

Thus, just as Thomas (1994) argues for "a pluralization and historicization of 'colonial discourse,' and a shift from the logic of signification to the narration of colonialism—or rather, to a contest of colonial narratives" (37), so an understanding of current language policies needs to look beyond the apparently transparent arguments for one language or for many, and to try to understand the complex interconnections between language policies, different ideological positions, and forms of governance. As became clear from the discussion of the ways in which colonial language policies operated, they were never simply about the "medium of instruction," but rather part of an educational policy aimed at "enlightening" the Indian population and making them aware of the system and benefits of colonial rule; producing a well-ordered, docile, and cooperative population that could be both producers and consumers of goods within the system of colonial capitalism; fulfilling a moral and imperial duty to bring to the Indian population the benefits of European knowledge; and using indigenous forms of culture and knowledge to ensure social stability.

Contextuality

Second, we need to understand language policies contextually. Although on one level this may seem obvious, the point I wish to draw attention to here is that we need to be suspicious of arguments that do not account for the complexities of local contingencies. This is not to say that all policy is either contextually determined or contextually bound: I am not arguing for either a materialist stance that suggests language policy is merely a reflection of local material conditions, nor for a relativist position that suggests nothing is understandable outside its context. Rather, just as I tried to show that colonial language policies were deeply embedded in their colonial contexts but were not reducible to them, so I want to suggest that language policy generally is locally embedded but also traverses local contexts.

An important implication of this position is that we cannot assume that a policy is inherently good because it appeals to some moral position on "pluralism" or "language rights"; instead, we must understand its significance in context. This historical perspective questions the common claim that the bestowal of education or access to literacy and languages is in some way inherently beneficial (see Pennycook 1996; 1998b). The easy assumptions often made about a "language of power," or of dominant and dominated languages, become more suspect in light of this historical analysis, which reveals that both English and vernacular languages were used to promote particular forms of colonial governance. As we have seen, language education policies were consistently designed to maintain the inequitable social conditions of India, Malaya, and Hong Kong.

One of the lessons we need to learn from this account of colonial language policy is that in order to make sense of language policies, we need to understand their location both historically and contextually. We cannot assume that promotion of local languages instead of a dominant language, or promotion of a dominant language at the expense of local languages, is in itself good or bad. Too often we view such strategies through the lenses of liberalism, pluralism, or anti-imperialism, without understanding the actual location of such policies. Crowley (1996), for example, compares Gramsci and Bakhtin, who developed very different orientations toward language based in part on the different political contexts in which they worked. For Bakhtin, working in the Stalinist Soviet Union with its massive projects of centralization, including the standardization and spread of the Russian language throughout the empire, the necessary emphasis was on heteroglossia, on the diversity and differences within language being understood and promoted as a reaction against monoglossic centralization. For Gramsci, by contrast, working (and being imprisoned) in Mussolini's Italy, in which the emphasis was on the promotion of local Italian dialects as an expression of Italian identity (and a means to rule the country by maintaining diversity), the emphasis was on the need for a unified language to unite the peasantry.

According to Crowley (1996),

> Gramsci's contention is that in the historical and political conjuncture in which he was located, rather than arguing for heteroglossia, what was required was precisely the organising force of a form of monoglossia. In particular what Gramsci argued for was the teaching of prescriptive grammar to the children of the working class and peasantry in order to empower them with literacy as part of a larger radical project. (43)

Thus, in the historical situation in which Gramsci was located, "a preference for heteroglossia over monoglossia would be a reactionary stance" (45). If, then, an argument for monoglossia or heteroglossia is made in the abstract, without reference to the actual historical location of the languages and political struggles involved, the political outcomes of such an argument will be unclear. Therefore, we need clear, contextualized understandings of the political contexts of language policies, for while it is important to understand, say, the significance of promoting plurality in the face of standardization in Britain or the Soviet Union, "the diffuse and politically disorganized situation of early twentieth century Italy, in which lack of common literacy amongst the national-popular mass served the interests of the governing class, requires a quite different analysis" (Crowley 1996, 46).

Indeed, the way in which both Anglicist and Orientalist discourses, or the support for both English and local languages, can be seen to have been complicit with the whole colonial project raises some fundamental questions about current language policies. The promotion of both English and vernacular education policies in Malaya and Hong Kong was clearly in general in line with broader colonial policies of social stability and exploitation. This suggests that we need to investigate very carefully whose interests are served by different language policies. Therefore it is not enough to juxtapose a liberal multiculturalism (possibly the descendant of Orientalism) with a rapacious, conservative, pro-English stance (more obviously a descendant of Anglicism) in terms of the language ideologies that each seems to espouse. Rather, we must look at what such policies promote or deny within the broader social, political, and economic structures and ideologies they support.

Complementarity

Third, and most important, I want to point to the complementarity of pro-English and pro-pluralist discourses. Just as I argue that Anglicism and Orientalism, while apparently two competing camps of colonial ideology, were actually complementary aspects of colonial rule, so I want to argue that the complementarity of an English Only versus a multiculturalist position continues to support a broader framework that too often remains unexplored. And this is where the notion of the colonial context as a site of cultural production is crucial, for I want to suggest that the colonial context of language relations produced images of English and of other languages that are replayed in these debates even today (Pennycook 1998a).

Returning for a moment to the debates over Anglicism in India, the effects of the Minute in India were limited, as Frykenberg (1988) argues, but as Macaulay's fame grew in England in subsequent years, "the influence of this Minute was probably cumulative, so that it became more pervasive with each successive generation" (315). That is to say, the significance of Anglicism was not in determining educational policy in Britain's colonies, but rather in developing a discourse about English as the crucial medium for the purveyance of knowledge. Therefore the effects of Macaulay's Minute and colonial Anglicist discourse were far less significant within colonial language policy than they are today within global institutions of support for English Only. Anglicism has been able to reemerge in a new world order in which promotion of English has become a far more viable option. It is, it would seem, easier to promote English within the global capitalist empire of the late twentieth century than it was in the colonial contexts that formed part of the expanding capitalist empire in the late nineteenth century.

But what the complementarity of Anglicist and Orientalist views on language also produced were images of English that suggested it was the language of progress, development, improvement, modernity, and so on, while local languages were the guardians of culture, tradition, and all that was static. This complementarity between languages has now found its way into the standard liberal position on language as expressed, for example, by Crystal (1997), who argues that the global spread of English is a good thing as long as we also support local languages. This dichotomy between "international intelligibility" and "historical identity" leaves other languages as static markers of identity. Hogben's (1963) proposal for Essential World English, for example, develops a formulation similar to Crystal's in which English serves people around the world as a "medium of communication about what will matter to most of us in what we hope will be the One World of Tomorrow" (7), a universal second language "for informative communication across their own frontiers about issues of common interest to themselves and others" (20), while other languages are supported as "a home tongue for love-making, religion, verse-craft, back chat and inexact topics in general" (20). Hogben claims that all language planners agree that we need a bilingual world "in which one language has priority by common consent as the sole medium of informative communication between speech communities which properly prefer to retain their native habits of discourse for reasons which have little or no relevance to the exacting semantic demands of science" (28–29).

As Dua (1994) points out, in the context of India, such a view is inadequate: "the complementarity of English with indigenous languages tends to go up in favour of English partly because it is dynamic and cumulative in nature and scope, partly because it is sustained by socioeconomic and market forces and partly because the educational system reproduced and legitimizes the relations of power and knowledge implicated with English" (132). Here, the view that English and other languages should live in a complementary relationship is a refusal to acknowledge the power of English as well as a construction of languages as unchanging markers of tradition and identity. Such discourses, I suggest, are also products of Anglicist/Orientalist complementarity and complicity. Risky though it may be, it is worth considering Coulmas's (1998) claim that the notion that language shift is necessarily a catastrophe, based as it is on a "nineteenth-century romantic idea that pegs human dignity as well as individual and collective identity to individual languages" (71), may be a passing ideological fashion.

To escape the replaying of this dichotomy and the colonial and neocolonial relationships that it supports, we need to step outside arguments that suggest that English can be maintained as a language of wider communication while local languages can be supported for cultural maintenance. Instead, we need to look for an alternative space, a place from which it is possible to see that, while the arguments remain stuck between these poles, we are replaying colonial constructions of language. We need to rethink how English can be appropriated to serve different ends, how English needs to be reclaimed to become a language of cultural support for other language groups, and how other languages need to move away from reproducing traditional relations, and instead acknowledge that languages and cultures can never be static, or they are lost.

Implications

Such a place and way of thinking have a number of significant pedagogical and political implications For many of us, setting language policy seems to be something that other people do, and while we may get a chance now and then to vote on a policy initiative, it is difficult to see how we can do more than suffer the policies of others. But language policies and language politics are actually part of what each of us does every day. When we fight in support of a community-based language program, when we allow or disallow the use of one language or another in our classrooms, when we choose which language to use in Congress, conversations, conferences, or curricula, we are making language policy.

There are two important aspects to these political choices: on the one hand, the choices we make about which language to use in which context are choices that reflect broader cultural and political views; on the other hand, such instances of language use also *produce* cultural and political views. So to use or to promote the use of one language or another in different contexts does not merely convey a political decision on language, but it also potentially changes others' views on language, or at least forces others to engage with the politics of language. Thus language politics becomes what we do every day in our interactions, our classrooms, and our curricula. And because, as I have suggested, languages are bound up with a broad array of cultural, economic, social, and political concerns, while it might not at first seem that a microdecision about language will shake the world, it is nevertheless worth considering that just as the decision whether or not to stoop to pick up a piece of litter does make a difference, so our decisions on language are part of a much bigger picture.

How, then, can we address language policy in terms of the need to step outside the replaying of the colonial dichotomy of Anglicism versus Orientalism? My argument is this: It is important to consider when we speak in and about languages that they are not so much neutral media of communication as tools of cultural expression. Languages should not be seen as transmitting static cultural forms but rather as tools for changing the world. If we allow English to continue to be viewed as the language of modernity, development, and progress, while other languages are viewed as the purveyors of tradition, history, and culture, we will fail to grasp the opportunity to shift the cultural politics of languages. Unless we can find ways to step outside the English-versus-other-languages dichotomy to appropriate English to serve different ends, to reclaim English to become a language through which other cultures can find expression, and to appropriate other languages for nontraditional purposes, we will have failed to learn the lessons of postcolonial politics, the lessons of all those thinkers and writers from many regions of Africa, India, Hong Kong, or Malaysia who have emerged from colonial contexts and are now using English for postcolonial ends. Such an argument is not meant in any way to suggest that the fight against English Only should not continue, or that there is no point in fighting for bilingual schools and classrooms. The lesson postcolonial contexts teach is that only through a long history of struggle have such postcolonial possibilities emerged. This has been a struggle not just to resist English but also to use it, not just to maintain local languages but also to change them. It has been a struggle fought in classrooms, in conversations, and in curricula, as well as in Congress, but it is also a struggle that is different in each context. So how such an engagement with the cultural politics of language may work is a question of local contexts and complexities.

Conclusion

In discussions of language policy, we are often confronted with various "good guy/bad guy" positions: The conservative Right argues that multiculturalism, bilingual education, and so on are inefficient, un-American, and lead to "ghettoization," and that making English the national and the only language of the United States will return the United States to American ideals (see Wiley and Lukes 1996). Meanwhile, the liberal position argues for pluralism and tolerance and for various positions ranging from the pragmatic argument that to overlook diversity is to ignore language resources, to the more idealistic argument that diversity in languages, like diversity in nature, is inherently good. From a more leftist position comes the argument that English Only is yet another manifestation of linguistic imperialism, and that people have a basic linguistic right to education and use of their first language (see, for example, Phillipson and Skutnabb-Kangas 1996). The benefit of hindsight, however, has clarified the need to understand the complexity, contextuality, and complementarity of discourses on language policy. Language policies promoting both English and vernacular languages were part of larger aspects of colonial governance having to do with the attempt to bring particular versions of civilization, knowledge, and culture to the colonies and to produce a compliant and docile workforce. These historical hindsights demand that we ask ourselves harder questions about the ideological assumptions we make about the rightness of our conservative, liberal, or leftist positions on rights, plurality, and monolingualism. What kind of post-Orientalist essentialisms and exoticisms may guide a pluralist stance? How do such policies fit into both global and local modes of governance? How do we understand ways in which language policy and education are tied to forms of culture and knowledge? To what extent might we see the "two sides" of current arguments—diversity or English Only—as complicit with each other and with a broader politics? Is a view of complementarity between English and other languages a dream, and if so, what needs to be done? Unless we constantly ask ourselves such questions, we run the danger of remaining stuck in a static politics whose agenda has in a sense already been set by the monolingual myopia of the Right.

Languages are not mere media but instead stand at the very core of major cultural and political questions. We must seek to understand the complex totalities of these relations. And we need to find alternative spaces and strategies for dealing with language possibilities, a so-called third space (see Kramsch 1993), an attempt to step out of the dichotomies that are constantly being replayed, and a way of engaging with difference through both

English and other languages. Language maintenance in a postcolonial context must be understood as an issue of change and hybridity; there is no going back. So, yes, of course we need to fight the colonial echoes of English Only and the crass bigotries, monolingual myopia, and racism that are so tightly bound up with this position. And, yes, of course we need to fight for the greater human possibilities opened up by bilingual education and multilingual language policy. But a longer historical perspective suggests we need to go further, that we also need to question the construction of a battle between two poles: English Only versus multiculturalism. We need to take on English and change it, and we need to take on other languages and make sure they change, too.

Works Cited

Bureau of Education (Henry Sharp, ed.). 1920. *Selections from Educational Records, Part I: 1781–1839*. Calcutta: Superintendent of Government Printing.

Bureau of Education (J. A. Ritchie, ed.). 1922. *Selections from Educational Records, Part II: 1840–1859*. Calcutta: Superintendent of Government Printing.

Coulmas, Florian. 1998. "Language Rights—Interests of State, Language Groups and the Individual." *Language Sciences* 20(1): 63–72.

Crowley, Tony. 1996. *Language in History: Theories and Texts*. London: Routledge.

Crystal, David. 1997. *English as a Global Language*. Cambridge, U.K.: Cambridge University Press.

Dua, Hans. 1994. *Hegemony of English: Future of Developing Languages in the Third World*. Mysore: Yashoda.

Frykenburg, Robert. 1988. "The Myth of English as a 'Colonialist' Imposition upon India: A Reappraisal with Special Reference to South India." *Journal of the Royal Asiatic Society* 2: 305–15.

Hogben, Lancelot. 1963. *Essential World English*. London: Michael Joseph.

Hong Kong, Government of. 1883. *Report of the Education Commission Appointed by His Excellency Sir John Pope Hennessy, K.C.M.G . . . to Consider Certain Questions Connected with Education in Hong Kong, 1882.* Hong Kong: Hong Kong Government.

India, Government of. 1960. *Selections from Educational Records of the Government of India: Volume 1, Educational Reports, 1859–1871.* Delhi: National Archives of India.

Kachru, Braj J. 1986. *The Alchemy of English: The Spread, Functions and Models of Non-Native Englishes.* Oxford, U.K.: Pergamon Institute of English.

Kotewall, R. H. 1926. Colonial Office Documents 129/489. Unpublished documents, British Colonial Office, Hong Kong.

Kramsch, Claire. 1993. *Context and Culture in Language Teaching.* Oxford, U.K.: Oxford University Press.

Lethbridge. H. J. 1983. "Introduction." In E. J. Eitel, *Europe in China.* Hong Kong: Oxford University Press. (Original work published 1895)

Loh Fook Seng. 1970. "The Nineteenth Century British Approach to Malay Education." *Journal Pendidekan* 1(1): 105–15.

Lugard, Frederick. 1910. *Hong Kong University: Objects, History, Present Position and Prospects.* Hong Kong: Noronha.

———. 1926. *The Dual Mandate in British Tropical Africa* (3rd ed.). Edinburgh: William Blackwood.

Luk Hung-Kay, B. 1991. "Chinese Culture in the Hong Kong Curriculum: Heritage and Colonialism." *Comparative Education Review* (35(4): 650–68.

Macaulay, Thomas Babington. 1972. "Minute on Indian Education." In J. Clive and T. Pinney, eds., *Thomas Babington Macaulay: Selected Writings.* Chicago: University of Chicago Press. (Original work published 1835)

Maxwell, George. 1983. "Some Problems of Education and Public Health in Malaya." In Paul H. Kratoska, ed., *Honourable Intentions: Talks on the British Empire in South-East Asia Delivered at the Royal Colonial Institute 1874–1928.* Singapore: Oxford University Press. (Original work published 1927)

Metcalf, Thomas. 1997. *Ideologies of the Raj.* Cambridge: Cambridge University Press.

Pennycook, Alastair. 1996. "Language Policy as Cultural Politics: The Double-Edged Sword of Language Education in Colonial Malaya and Hong Kong." *Discourse: Studies in the Cultural Politics of Education* 17(2): 133–52.

———. 1998a. *English and the Discourses of Colonialism.* London: Routledge.

———. 1998b. "The Right to Language: Towards a Situated Ethics of Language Possibilities." *Language Sciences* 20(1): 73–87.

Phillipson, Robert. 1992. *Linguistic Imperialism.* Oxford, U.K.: Oxford University Press.

Phillipson, Robert, and Tove Skutnabb-Kangas. 1996. "English Only Worldwide or Language Ecology?" *TESOL Quarterly* 30(3): 429–52.

Said, Edward W. 1978. *Orientalism.* New York: Vintage.

Singh, Jyotsna. 1996. *Colonial Narratives/Cultural Dialogues: Discoveries of India in the Language of Colonialism.* London: Routledge.

Straits Settlements. Various years. *Straits Settlements Annual Departmental Reports.* Singapore: Government Printing Office.

Swettenham, Frank. 1894. *Perak Government Gazette.* July 6.

Thomas, Nicholas. 1994. *Colonialism's Culture: Anthropology, Travel and Government.* Oxford, U.K.: Polity Press.

Viswanathan, Gauri. 1990. *Masks of Conquest: Literary Study and British Rule in India.* London: Faber and Faber.

Wiley, Terrence, and Marguerite Lukes. 1996. "English-Only and Standard English Ideologies in the U.S." *TESOL Quarterly* 30(3): 511–35.

CHAPTER NINE

Three Newspapers and a Linguist: A Folk Linguistic Journey into the Land of English as the Official Language

LYNN M. GOLDSTEIN
Monterey Institute of International Studies

Imagine yourself at a party, the only sociolinguist there. The discussion in your corner turns to language. Someone makes a comment—it doesn't matter about what. It could be bilingual education, the Official English amendment, correct usage. What matters is that what is said contradicts what you as a sociolinguist believe to be true. As you have done before, you enter the fray, giving your point of view, but you are told that you are wrong. No, you may protest, these are linguistic matters, and as a sociolinguist *you know* about such things. Nonetheless, the conversation continues amongst several people, all of whom share a view different from yours, and they proceed to leave you out of the conversation. Like every other time this has happened, you are frustrated, not only by your perceptions of the nonlinguists' lack of knowledge, but also by their refusal to accede to your expertise and by your inability to persuade them to accept your point of view.

As Cameron (1995) aptly states, "there is clearly a vast gulf between what interests linguists about language and what seems to interest everyone else about it. . . . The incomprehension is mutual. Linguists not only disapprove of the forms that popular interest in language take; they find the whole phenomenon somewhat bewildering" (x). It is this frustration and this conflict between the views of sociolinguists and those of nonlinguists (e.g., people who have not been informed about sociolinguistic issues through linguistics courses or the reading of the literature in linguistics) that prompted the study discussed in this chapter.

The research reported here began with the belief that if I am to overcome this frustration and find a way to enter into the discourse of nonlinguists, I have to know what they believe. In addition, as a teacher of sociolinguistics and an educator of teachers of English as a second language (ESL), I have long felt the need to inform my students about how nonlinguists view language and to give them tools to discover these views on their own. ESL teachers need to know about the nature of language and the relationships between language and society in order to develop "sensitivity to and conscious awareness of the nature of language and its role in human life" (Donmall 1985, 7). Traditionally, teachers learn such information through pre- and inservice courses. What teachers learn in these courses, however, is "received" information—that is, information handed down and handed out by linguists. It is not my contention to question the validity of such information. It is my argument, however, that what teachers get from these courses is only part of the picture, and as such it is a distortion of the reality they will encounter when they leave our classes to teach, live, and work in communities that are comprised largely of nonlinguists. Such circumstances lead to the necessity for ESL teachers to understand the views of language held by the lay community. As Preston (1996a) states:

> Many linguists (applied and even theoretical) have done a great deal to promote "language awareness" in the sense of understanding scientifically discovered aspects of language structure and use, and there is no doubt that such understandings are important for many in public life (e.g., teachers, lawyers, health professionals). I believe this program should be coupled with one which asserts that the discovery of what non-linguists believe about and do with language ("folk linguistics" in general) is equally important not only for its independent scientific value but also for the undeniable importance it has in the language professional's interaction with the public in the most human of concerns. (72)

But few sociolinguistic studies have been dedicated to exploring the views of nonlinguists, or what Preston terms "folk linguistics." There are, of course, the many attitude studies that span the current history of sociolinguistics. These are designed, however, to tap into the unconscious attitudes people hold, and in some cases to determine how these attitudes influence behavior. Notwithstanding their importance, these studies do not tell us what nonlinguists are *aware* of—what attitudes they would openly profess to, or what behaviors they believe are influenced by such attitudes.

Some research does shed light on the beliefs of nonlinguists, although this function of the studies was not necessarily the authors' intent. For example, Sato (1991) and Lippi-Green (1994) examine how the views of nonlinguists prevail over the views of linguists in critical moments such as educational, legal, and employment decisions which involve linguistic issues. In a different avenue of research, Goldstein (1987) examined the target language varieties of Hispanic boys learning English, and in doing so, directly elicited who they felt they talked like, who they wanted to speak like and why, as well as their direct characterizations of varieties in their speech community. Although these three studies had different research aims and did not position themselves as folk linguistic in nature, they do provide some insight into nonlinguists' beliefs about varieties, "good" usage, and language learning.

Studies that have, at least in part, a direct folk linguistic aim are rare, however. One area of research is the ethnography of speaking, which "has legitimized the study of the awareness of and regard for the shape and uses of language in standardized speech communities" (Preston 1993a, 334). Work such as Heath's (1983) study of the language use of different communities, for example, enables ordinary people—nonlinguists—to understand their discourse practices through self-examination of such practices. Other sociolinguistic research includes folk linguistic studies on bilingual education, dialectology, English as the official language, and prescription versus description. For example, Hakuta (1986) examines letters to the editor and data collected from telephone surveys to understand nonlinguists' beliefs about bilingual education, while Dyste (1989) uses questionnaire surveys to determine nonlinguists' views about Proposition 63, California's Official English proposition. Preston (1993a, 1993b,

1993c, 1996a, 1996b) has closely examined folk dialectology—looking at, for example, where people believe the boundaries of varieties are and their attitudes toward different varieties. Another area of study is that of Cameron (1995), who explores what nonlinguists believe about "good" language and "bad" language as well as what she terms the "gulf" between linguists and nonlinguists. Second-language acquisition researchers have also seen the value of exploring nonlinguists' views, advocating the use of first-person narratives as a primary source of data, which provide "the richness of insight available on aspects of second language learning from the data which have not been part of the mainstream literature in our field" (Pavlenko and Lantolf 1997, 21).

Examining Three Newspapers

More research is needed which systematically and directly uncovers what nonlinguists believe and say about language, including what they believe about critical issues such as bilingual education, the Official English movement, and Ebonics. The purpose of the research reported here was to discover how one particular "type" of nonlinguist—newspapers—approaches one topic of concern to sociolinguists: English as the official language. As Cameron (1995) points out, "The press is an important forum for language mavenry in general: it is striking how many newspapers run regular language columns and how much feature space they devote to linguistic topics" (viii). Newspapers are a particularly helpful avenue into the views held by nonlinguists since they often contain articles, editorials, and letters to the editor about sociolinguistic matters. Goldstein (1996) found, for example, that sociolinguistic issues were frequently discussed in three newspapers over a six-month period. In addition, while some may argue that journalists research articles before writing, Goldstein (1998) found in a study on the Oakland School District Ebonics resolution that journalists neither researched the issues through the sociolinguistic literature nor discussed the issues with sociolinguists, or if they did so they failed to report on either the literature or such discussions. Thus they remained "nonlinguists" because they overwhelmingly used sources other than linguists in their reporting. Additionally, newspapers may contain letters to the editor on a sociolinguistic topic that are written by nonlinguists. For example, in Goldstein's Oakland study, not one published letter to the editor about Ebonics was written by a linguist. Newspapers are therefore a rich source of information about the beliefs of nonlinguists on topics that concern sociolinguists, and they are a rich source of information regarding the views to which nonlinguists who read them are exposed.

The data examined here are part of a larger study (Goldstein 1996) that looked at which sections of the newspaper and in what types of discourse language topics were discussed, what language topics were discussed and which were discussed most frequently, and what folk views of language were revealed in the topics most frequently discussed. This chapter focuses on nonlinguists' views of language on one of the most frequently discussed topics, the movement to make English the official language of the United States.

Three daily newspapers were examined: one national newspaper (*The New York Times*), one paper local to the general area in which my students (language teachers in training) and I reside (*The San Francisco Chronicle*), and one local to the city in which the educational institution where I teach is located (*The Monterey County Herald*). The rationale for examining these three papers was to have both a local view of how language is discussed in newspapers with which my students, and the communities in which they and their students reside, might come into contact, and a national view of how language might be discussed.

All issues of the three newspapers were collected over a six-month period (September 1995 to March 1996), and every piece of writing in which language was mentioned was extracted from every issue, regardless of where and how language was discussed or how much space was devoted to this discussion. Subsequently, the content of articles mentioning English as the official language was examined for the actual folk linguistic views embedded in the discussions.

Newspapers and English as the Official Language

Wherever appropriate, the results discussed in the following paragraphs are illustrated with quotes from the writer. It is important that readers not just understand the views espoused in the newspapers on English as the official language, but that they "hear" the authentic voices behind these views.

The Monterey County Herald

The *Monterey County Herald*'s two mentions of English as the official language appear in a commentary and in a letter to the editor. The commentary, which occurs on the editorial page, is by a columnist, Henrietta Hay, who writes for the Grand Junction, Colorado, *Daily Sentinel*. In this article, Hay addresses both the English as official language movement and bilingualism. She believes that English is the de facto official language, that it is not threatened by a diversity of languages, and that prejudice drives the Official English language movement. Her position is summed up thus:

> The recent election in Quebec made very clear the importance of language in the diversity versus multiculturalism debate. The issue is heating up now that there is a prejudice-driven effort to have a constitutional amendment saying that we must speak English only. . . . What's the big deal? The whole issue hardly seems to pose a danger to the nation. . . . Of course, English is and should continue to be our common language. But it does not need to be encased in the concrete of a constitutional amendment." (Hay 1995, 9A)

In contrast, the writer of the letter to the editor is the chair of the Official English Committee and a member of the American Ethnic Coalition and supports making English the official language. He argues that it will not prohibit immigrants from using their native languages in their everyday lives but that we should not be spending tax dollars on translating government documents, and that "[a] common language is the unifying force of a people" (Robbins 1995, 8A).

The New York Times

Those who wrote about English as the official language in the *New York Times* represent a diversity of writers as well as positions, with all discussions appearing on the editorial page. The six who are against English as the official language include Thomas Freidman, who writes a regular Foreign Affairs column for the *New York Times,* two who wrote editorials, and three who wrote letters to the editor, including a writer-in-residence working with bilingual children in the Houston public schools and a New York City congresswoman with a Hispanic surname. The three who wrote in favor of English as the official language included a naturalized citizen born in Estonia who has lived in the United States since childhood, a German editor of the editorial page of a German daily, and a New York City congressman.

Those against English as the official language provide a number of different reasons to support their position. Four of the six make it clear that English should be the common language of the United States but then go on to argue that requiring immigrants to deny their linguistic and cultural heritages has negative consequences for all. As Thomas Freidman (1995) states,

> I think in America English should be the primary language . . . [but t]he objective we should be working towards is community. But how? Well, unless we give people of diverse ethnic backgrounds a sense of belonging, unless we give them a sense that their identity and heritage are valued threads in the tapestry of American society, real community is impossible. That is why it is important to bridge people into the community, if necessary with languages other than English and to encourage people of different backgrounds to express their cultural identities as a way of enriching the community as a whole. (17E)

Some of these writers feel that denying immigrants' native languages and cultures will send the message that they are not welcome and will restrict their self-expression: "But requiring it by law is a sign that the society is not so open after all, that people who speak foreign languages are not so welcome" and that "the issue is divisive and reeks of xenophobia" ("Campaign English" 1995, E16).

Several writers also see this as a political and divisive issue, one raised by Bob Dole during a campaign year to serve his political interests rather than to unite the country. According to Freidman, "Senator Dole has suddenly raised them not to unite the country but to divide it—to play on the patriotism of the American Legion and the fear of new immigrants. . . . [I]f Mr. Dole really wanted to wrestle with this issue he would have begun his speech to the American legion . . . 'My fellow immigrants'" (1995, E17). Furthermore, some feel that it is freedom, including linguistic freedom, that binds the United States rather than a common language; one person also states that requiring immigrants to speak English offends freedom. In an editorial arguing against Bob Dole's position and his exploitation of the issue to further his political goals, the *New York Times* contends that "[o]thers would say the glue that truly binds this nation is a common belief in freedom, including the freedom to speak any language you please" ("America Needs" 1995, A22).

Writers also cite the practical benefits of not having an amendment making English the official language:

1. Different cultures and languages enrich our communities: "multilingualism is a tremendous resource to the United States because it permits improved communications and cross cultural understanding" (Velazquez 1995, A14).

2. Official English "measures undermine the economic competitiveness of the United States" (Velazquez 1995, A14).

3. In certain situations, it would be ludicrous not to use a language other than English: "How about foreigners seeking help, even seeking asylum? It is obviously more efficient for a government clerk to speak Spanish with a Hispanic American who is uncomfortable in English. Moreover, what would all those Congressional sponsors say if the language police told them they could not communicate with constituents who have not mastered the official tongue?" ("America Needs" 1995, A22).

4. Needed bilingual services including emergency services would be denied, with negative consequences for all: "Moreover, people unable to obtain bilingual services may fail to get immunizations against contagious diseases or to seek essential medical attention, further endangering public health" (Velazquez 1995, A14).

The two remaining justifications against English as the official language include one writer of a letter to the editor who gives Switzerland as a counterexample against the fear that more than one official language would be divisive:

> I am also astonished at Representative King's naive idea that countries cannot function effectively with more than one official language. Poor Switzerland! If only the Swiss would come to their senses and speak just English. Maybe their trains would run on time and maybe we could finally count on their banks. (Storrow 1995, A20)

The other writer of a letter to the editor makes an appeal to fairness and justice. He argues that an Official English policy in the United States would be contradictory since it has allowed Puerto Ricans to serve in the United States armed services and die in such service without knowing English: "If knowing English has not been required to die for our country, it should not be required to benefit from the products of those sacrifices" (Pagan 1995, A10).

Two of those in favor of English as the official language produce arguments in part as rebuttal to some of the writers above. One letter to the editor argues against the notion that immigrants would be prevented from using their native languages, or that anyone would be prevented from learning foreign languages: "I am an Estonian-born, naturalized citizen, and during my years I have never been prohibited from expressing myself in a language other than English, nor prevented from learning additional languages. I do not have fears that this freedom will be curbed by a language law" (Cannon 1995, A22). This writer, as well as another writer of a letter to the editor, also argues that, along with a belief in freedom or freedom of speech, language is the glue that holds the United States together. As the second writer, a German man who is the editor of the editorial page of a German weekly, states, "Freedom of speech, the most precious of rights, presupposes a common language. If I get up on a soapbox and harangue the crowd in the Urdu language, I am not exercising freedom of speech but freedom of babble" (Joffe 1995, A22).

Political arguments about power are also raised: "The free-speech argument is used by some ethnic political leaders to preserve their positions of power . . . and to obtain from legislators public funding for certain projects." This writer then identifies one specific group: "In Connecticut, for example, English as a second language in the public schools has a large Spanish speaking lobby," and she questions "the motives of those who are against English as our common language. . . . Why is the Spanish minority cited as the interested population in these debates? Why are Cambodians, Bosnians, Chinese, Poles, Koreans and myriad other groups not pushing the issue?" (Cannon 1995, A22).

Practical issues, including economic and language-learning concerns, are mentioned as well. A congressman, in his letter to the editor, argues about the economic effect on taxpayers: "This debate is about more than just declaring English 'official.' It is about spending billions of taxpayer dollars on printing government documents in several languages and on failed bilingual education programs" (King 1995, A18). This writer, along with the Estonian, also believes that the lack of an official language law impedes immigrants from learning English. The Estonian writer implies this when she states,

> My legislator, a member of the committee, asked me how long it took me to learn English after arriving as a child in this country. I replied, 'Three months.' The gasp in the packed room was such that I thought I would be crucified on the spot. That experience, as well as other observations over the years, has led me to question the motives of the people who are against English as our common language. Do they want a segment of our population to remain second-class citizens? (Cannon 1995, A22)

The congressman states this view quite explicitly: "Nearly three decades of linguistic welfare have discouraged new Americans from learning English and barred their access to the American dream" (King 1995, A18).

The San Francisco Chronicle

English as the official language was discussed six times in the *San Francisco Chronicle*, twice in letters to the editor, twice in feature articles, once in an extended opinion piece, and once in a short report. Writers include staff writers (articles and report), two writers of letters to the editor, and one syndicated columnist from New Mexico. Of these six discussions, three are against English as the official language, one is in favor, and two present arguments both for and against English as the official language. In addition, two short wire pieces describe instances in which a judge and a police officer respectively tried to enforce the use of English as opposed to Spanish and enforce the use of "better" English by a speaker of Spanish.

Several writers question whether making English the official language would have any practical effect. One bill, sponsored by Representative Bill Emerson and Senator Richard Shelby, proposed eliminating forms and documents printed in languages other than English. Yet, as those against this bill point out, an examination of 400,000 such documents produced over five years found only 265 printed in languages other than English. Furthermore, most of these 265 concerned health or emergency issues and would therefore, under the terms of the bill, be exempt from a ban on printing in other languages. One writer takes this issue further, in effect questioning the motives of the supporters of the Emerson/Shelby bill: "Where is the so-called bilingual threat? A General Accounting Office study reports that 99.94 percent of federal documents are printed in English. . . . But, not content with the English dominance, Senator Richard Shelby, R-Ala., said the numbers (265) were 'overwhelming'" (Armas 1996, A15). This lack of practical effect is also reported in Allentown, Pennsylvania, where the passing of an English ordinance permitting government documents only in English resulted in a net savings of $36.00 ("Town's English Law" 1995, A12).

Given the negligible economic effect, several of those against English as the official language, like some writers in the *New*

York Times, feel that politics motivate its supporters, mentioning in particular that Dole is using English Only rhetoric to his political advantage. As one writer of a letter to the editor says, "However, a love of English has nothing to do with Dole's stance. Instead, his is a Wilsonesque ploy to sail into office on the wave of jingoism currently washing over the land, a transparent political contrivance to buttress his sagging presidential campaign" (Cochran 1995, 8). One writer even claims that Dole's support of making English the official language is a deliberate distraction from pressing problems of the day. He quotes Liz Balmased, another columnist, who says,

> It never fails. The political embrace of English is the preferred tool of distraction of the new American demagogues. People all over the country are getting laid off, health care is in crisis. Social Security is teetering. AIDS is devouring entire villages and what does a serious presidential candidate wrap around himself like lamé in a drag show? English. (Armas 1996, A15)

Some also feel, again like some writers in the *New York Times* and the *Monterey County Herald,* that an underlying discrimination against immigrants and certain ethnic groups fuels sentiments for English as the official language, or that English as the official language will result in discrimination. The mayor of Allentown, Pennsylvania, is reported as "struggling with bigger challenges from the migrant wave . . . the discord made worse by the bigotry he believes has underpinned some of the backlash" ("Town's English Law" 1995, A12). In addition, two lawsuits are described in which the plaintiffs felt that English as the official language laws and policies were discriminatory. Both suits were filed in states (California and Arizona) where these laws were in effect. In the Arizona case, the plaintiff claimed that she was unable to do her job because the law would not allow her to use Spanish with her Spanish-speaking clients (Armas 1996, A15). In the California suit, employees at a nursing home filed charges of discrimination with the United States Equal Employment Opportunity Commission and the California Department of Fair Employment and Housing alleging that they suffered discrimination because they were disciplined for using languages other than

English at work ("Hillhaven Employees" 1995, A23). In another case, "a judge ignited a storm of controversy by ordering a Mexican American woman to speak English to her child" instead of Spanish ("Judge Backs Off" 1995, A13).

Some writers also feel that immigrants are well aware that they need to learn English, and that largely they do. One article reports that "Representative Ed Pastor . . . said that generations of immigrants have understood that learning English is vital to succeed. Pastor noted that more than 95% of Americans speak English" ("Designating English" 1995, A6). In addition, two of those against English as the official language contend that the law would only create greater dissension among those it targets, a view also found in the *New York Times*. One immigrant from Allentown says the law exists "because they want people who don't speak English to leave," and her sentiment is echoed by the mayor, who feels that "a national language law would merely create hard feelings" ("Town's English Law" 1995, A12). Another writer against English as the official language makes the case that "it's forced monolingualism that breeds revolt" and gives the example of Franco forbidding Catalan and Basque in Spain, which "provoked armed insurrection, secession attempts, and created bitter divisions that linger today. Franco was forced to back down, and today, in addition to Spanish, Catalan and Basque, other foreign languages (such as English) are spoken in Spain. Who's the poorer?" (Armas 1996, A15).

Those who favor English as the official language cite the positive practical effects of enacting such a law. First, to assuage the concerns of those who fear the negative consequences, they claim that the Emerson/Shelby bill would not affect bilingual education and would exempt essential services. Like one writer to the *New York Times*, they believe that no one would be prohibited from using his or her native language because, as Senator Shelby claims, "the bill would have no impact on a person's right to speak any language at home, at work, or elsewhere" ("Designating English" 1995, A6). The positive practical effects they foresee include the fact that the law would encourage immigrants to learn English since "government should lead by example in encouraging people to learn English," and success would follow learning English since "English is the language of opportunity" ("Designating English" 1995, A6). Furthermore, immigrant children would learn English because English as the official language would result in "upending the 'linguistic ghettos' that keep foreign school children in their native tongue," and the law would also speed assimilation ("Town's English Law" 1995, A12). Finally, some also hope immigration would lessen: "the push has wider goals: . . . in some cases discouraging immigration itself" ("Town's English Law" 1995, A12).

Supporters of English as the official language also report feeling frustrated or even angered by the use of languages other than English. In Allentown, where eighteen different languages are spoken, "the ordinance was prompted by city council members who found it galling to see Spanish signs like one saying 'Piso Mojado,' warning of a wet floor in a public bathroom" ("Town's English Law" 1995, A12). Or as one who wrote a letter to the editor reports:

> More and more frequently when I call any kind of office or store, the person who answers the phone can't understand me enough even to refer me to someone who can communicate in English with basic fluency. America needs one language that all permanent residents, citizens or not, can speak and understand. . . . [They need to] learn the majority language at least well enough for everyday transactions." (Chirich 1996, A16)

Finally, as in the *New York Times* discussion, what it means to be an American also plays a role in the support of English as the official language. To some, to be American is to speak English. In referring to the 265 government documents in languages other than English, one writer argues, "But even that scant multilingualism is much too much for some as it trickles into areas that, while home to periodic waves of immigration, have thought of themselves as American to the core." Bob Dole, in a speech supporting Official English, echoes a similar sentiment: "Language, history, and values—these are the strings that bind our hearts to America" ("Town's English Law" 1995, A12).

Comparing the Views of Those for and against English as the Official Language

At the time of this study, English as the official language was very much in the public view, particularly within the legal and political arenas. With the presidential election looming, candidates such as Bob Dole looked for topics to galvanize voters and win their support. Given the political, economic, and social climate of the time, including a backlash against immigration, Dole could safely surmise that English as the official language could be one such topic. Additionally, two bills to make English the official language of the United States were being debated: the King bill and the Emerson/Shelby bill. The *New York Times* and the *San Francisco Chronicle*, in covering the presidential election and the reemergence of English as the official language legislation, would have to focus on the issue of English as the official language. Additionally, once they did so, through editorials or feature articles, the debate became "public." And, given the climate of the times, where immigration policies as well as policies regarding the education of immigrants are hotly debated, it is not surprising that much of this public debate occurred on the editorial pages.

In the newspapers examined, the different sides present a diversity of beliefs about English as the official language. Since the people we work with, have contact with, or teach are more likely to be exposed to these beliefs through the media than through conversations with us or through the classes such as sociolinguistics that we might teach, it is important for educators of English as a second language to understand what these beliefs are. First, the two sides are ideologically opposed about the role of language in unifying the United States. Those against English as the official language state that language does not necessarily define or unite the United States; instead, it is a belief in freedom, including linguistic freedom, that binds the United States. In contrast, supporters of Official English firmly believe that the English language does indeed hold the United States together. Second, those against English as the official language believe that multi-lingualism should be viewed in the United States as an asset, a resource rather than a problem, while supporters point to the divisiveness of multilingualism in other countries. Those against English as the official language counter the divisiveness claim with arguments about the divisiveness that they believe ensues when people are denied their linguistic rights, asked to deny their heritage, or made to feel unwelcome. In addition, those against English as the official language believe that language learning cannot necessarily be forced and that attempts to do so can back-fire, causing some immigrants not to want to learn English be-cause they feel coerced. Meanwhile, supporters argue that not having an official language law impedes English learning.

Both sides believe that the issue is exploited for political gain, but those against English as the official language comment on exploitation by politicians during an election year, while those for English as the official language comment on the apparent political self-interest of groups such as Hispanic Americans. The two sides also disagree about the economic and the practical implications of English as an official language. Those against English as the official language foresee no economic benefit from abolishing bilingual services; they also fear that denying immi-grants emergency services in their native language would be di-sastrous. On the other hand, supporters believe that English as the official language would save taxpayers money, and yet they also believe that the amendment would not cut essential bilin-gual services.

Only a few points have been raised by one side but not the other. Those against English as the official language note the ab-surdity of trying to force people who share a common lan-guage to not use that language in activities such as conducting business. They also question the underlying motives of support-ers as racist and/or anti-immigration. And they believe that with-out English as the official language, immigrants actually do feel the need to learn English and are doing so. Those who support English as the official language address none of these issues.

Likewise, some supporters feel that promoting English would ensure immigrants' employment, an issue not addressed by those against English as the official language. They also express anger at the use of languages other than English in public encounters, an anger that is not dealt with by those against English as the official language.

What can we learn from these stated differences and beliefs? Underlying them are contradictory ideologies and emotions: a celebration of diversity versus a fear of diversity; a belief that a nation can thrive as a linguistically heterogeneous entity versus a belief that a nation may not even be able to survive in such a state; a view of the fundamental nature and strength of this country as one of immigration versus a view of immigration as a fundamental drain on limited resources; an embracing of the unknown versus a fear of the unknown; a belief in accommodation versus a belief in assimilation; a fascination with language for its own sake versus feelings of being threatened by public use of a language one cannot understand; a belief that language learning is affected by more than motivation versus the belief that with the will to learn anyone can learn a second language.

Some may argue that the arguments on both sides come as no surprise and have been written about in the TESOL and sociolinguistic literature. What is different is that the views discussed here are the views as they are expressed directly by nonlinguists, unedited by linguists or language educators, voices seldom heard in any direct way in our literature. In addition, these are points of view that nonlinguists are exposed to through the everyday act of reading newspapers. Without examining commonplace sources of information such as newspapers, we have little information about what people learn about issues such as English as the official language.

It is also important to note that while language professionals have access to the same sources of information, most nonlinguists do not have access to our sources of information. As a case in point, no writers on either side of this issue appealed to the knowledge or the literature of sociolinguistics or TESOL in making their arguments. In fact, what stands out in this study is that readers of these newspapers were not exposed to the views of linguists or educators of English as a second language at all. No linguist or language educator is mentioned, no linguistic research is cited or described, and no linguist or language educator is quoted about English as the official language. Linguists and language educators appear therefore to be effectively marginalized by nonlinguists in discussions of what we would claim as our rightful territory. Other linguists have remarked on this marginalization. Lippi-Green (1994) writes about what happens in some court cases, in which "the judges who wrote these opinions are willing to depend on their own expertise in matters of language in a way they would never presume to in matters of genetics or mechanical engineering or psychology" (177). Later, in discussing language policy issues and the knowledge of linguists, she says, "That knowledge is often not sought; and if sought, it may be summarily rejected, but in either case, it is often hotly resented" (188). Cameron (1995), writing about linguistic prescription and the chasm between linguists and nonlinguists, echoes that sentiment: "It produces discourse . . . in which it seems that what linguists know about language can simply be dismissed, because linguists do not care about language" (xii).

Conclusion

This study has reconfirmed for me what I have often felt: language fascinates us all and is owned by all, linguist and nonlinguist alike. This seems an immutable and positive fact. Nevertheless, for a number of reasons I am concerned by the gulf between linguist and nonlinguist, a gulf that has everyday implications for how people see language and the role it plays in their lives, as well as for how they react to issues such as English as the official language. On the one hand, the results of this study take me back to those dinners and the frustration of not being heard. On the other hand, they have opened my eyes to the ways in which nonlinguists talk about issues I hold so important in my professional and personal life. The question is how to show respect for the validity of nonlinguists' opinions at the same time that I try to share and have heard other ways of seeing. The answer, I believe, lies in a number of positive actions.

The first is that sociolinguists and language educators, myself included, need to give voice to nonlinguists' views by carrying out more folk linguistic research. This serves several purposes.

Sociolinguistics is incomplete if it does not acknowledge, learn about, and include as part of the discipline an essential relationship between language and society—that is, the views that nonlinguists hold and express directly about all facets of language. As Cameron argues, "the beliefs about language that inform people's use of it arguably fall within the scope of what descriptive linguistics ought to be able to give an account of" (1995, xi). In addition, and returning to my original premise, my own language awareness as a sociolinguist and as an educator of language teachers, as well as that of my students, is inadequate if I am not aware of the views of the people I work with. In discussing the views of nonlinguists, Cameron says, "this requires some understanding of and perhaps some sympathy with the concerns that lie behind [these views]" (1995, xiii).

This leads to a second activity. While the intent of this essay was to examine the beliefs of nonlinguists only, having done so has made me acutely aware of the need to examine my own beliefs. As one who is against English as the official language, I can cite many justifications from the sociolinguistics literature to support my arguments. Nonetheless, I am also aware that I hold to certain ideological precepts, such as a belief in the fundamental benefits and "rightness" of diversity, that also influence my stance on English as the official language. I extend therefore the call to all of us in the discipline to examine our beliefs. If we are to enter into a productive dialogue with nonlinguists and each other, we need to admit to whatever beliefs we support. We must recognize how these shape our lives as sociolinguists and language educators whether these ideologies coincide with the views of Fishman (1989), who believes that "most sociolinguists favor, and seek to foster, a linguistically heterogeneous world" (3), or with the views of Edwards (1993), who has "problems with the extreme advocacy position of the Fishmans of this world" (31), or with views that lie somewhere in between. My intention here is not to justify either Fishman's or Edwards's stance. My contention is that when faced with issues such as English as the official language, sociolinguists and language educators need to closely examine the degree to which their views are formed by knowledge of sociolinguistic principles, by their own political and social ideologies, or by the combination of both. Armed with such self-knowledge, we would be better equipped to discuss topics such as English as the official language with nonlinguists. In fact, my discussions with nonlinguists have led me to believe that they see right through us—they know that we do not react to sociolinguistic issues strictly through a sociolinguistic lens but rather as they do, through a personal lens. Conversations with nonlinguists might be far more productive if we acknowledged this.

The final activity is to share our linguistic knowledge with nonlinguists. I do hold certain positions and I would like to convince others who may not agree with me that I have views worth considering. I cannot do this if I do not know what the views of nonlinguists are, where they come from, or what emotions they raise or reflect. I cannot do this if I disdain these views as invalid. Cameron (1995) advocates much the same position in her discussion of prescription and the difference in views between linguists and nonlinguists: "If this is to change, and if linguistics is to make any contribution to changing it, we must acknowledge people's genuine concerns about language, understand the fears and desires that lie behind these concerns, and try to work with them, not against them" (236).

Sociolinguists have a wealth of knowledge to offer nonlinguists about topics such as English as the official language. For example, our research has helped us understand how social, political, and economic forces act together in language-contact situations and influence the language-learning and language-use strategies of a group. Armed with such knowledge, I have had productive conversations with nonlinguists about how the United States differs from countries such as Canada, and thus have been able to explain why multilingualism may not be as divisive in the United States as it has been in Quebec. To do so, I readily acknowledge that I understand why people are afraid of the seeming divisiveness of multilingualism. I can then help nonlinguists to see why legislating a shift to English would not ensure such a shift and might in fact lead to the very divisiveness and lack of English learning that people fear.

We are remiss if we do not find a way to get our views across to nonlinguists. At the 1997 Association of Applied Linguistics conference, I listened to a paper about the myth of appropriacy.

I shared many of the speaker's concerns and ideologies. I asked her the question that has been so much on my mind: How do we share these views with nonlinguistics? Her reply was that we do so when we teach our sociolinguistics classes. I disagree. We do so only in part, because we are talking to those who are largely inclined to agree with us. It is those outside our professional walls we need to reach. When the debate over Ebonics came to the forefront, for example, how many of us sat down with the nonlinguists we know and talked about the issues involved? For that matter, while the newspapers examined in this study marginalized us, how many of us contributed to this marginalization by not writing editorials to these newspapers? How many classes in our public schools have students, as van Lier (1998) advocates, "examine the role of language in social life from the immediate environment of the learners to global considerations of language use" (91)? How many of us have advocated for such classes? If we want to share our views on English as the official language, for example, we need to actively seek avenues for sharing our knowledge with those who are not linguists. In sum, the approach I am advocating here is three pronged: it must include learning about the views of nonlinguists from folk linguistic research, examining closely our own beliefs and the roles they play in the formation of our sociolinguistic views, and the sharing of our views with nonlinguists. I believe that such an approach might lead to a more productive exchange about such crucial issues as Official English.

Works Cited

"America Needs No Language Law." 1995. *New York Times*. Nov. 25. A22.

Armas, Jose. 1996. "Heading Off a Bilingual Threat?" *San Francisco Chronicle*. Jan. 2. A15.

Cameron, Deborah. 1995. *Verbal Hygiene*. London: Routledge.

"Campaign English from Senator Dole." 1995. *New York Times*. Sept. 10. E16.

Cannon, Ilvi. 1995. "An English-Only Law Makes Common Sense." *New York Times.* Nov. 30. A22.

Chirich, Nancy. 1996. "A Common Language." *San Francisco Chronicle.* Jan. 8. A16.

Cochran, Tom. 1995. "Linguistic Chauvinism." *San Francisco Chronicle.* Sept. 24. 8.

"Designating English Hearings in House." 1995. *San Francisco Chronicle.* Oct. 19. A6.

Donmall, Gillian, ed. 1985. *Language Awareness: NCLE Papers and Reports 6.* London: CILTR.

Dyste, Connie. 1989. "Proposition 63: The California English Language Amendment." *Applied Linguistics* 10(3): 313–30.

Edwards, John. 1993. "What Can (or Should) Linguists Do in the Face of Language Decline?" In Margaret Harry, ed., *Papers from the Seventeenth Annual Meeting of the Atlantic Provinces Linguistic Association.* Halifax, Can.: Saint Mary's University: 25–32.

Fishman, Joshua. 1989. *Language and Ethnicity in Minority Sociolinguistic Perspective.* Clevedon: Multilingual Matters.

Freidman, Thomas. 1995. "My Fellow Immigrants." *New York Times.* Sept. 10. E17.

Goldstein, Lynn. 1987. "Standard English: The Only Target for Nonnative Speakers of English?" *TESOL Quarterly* 21(3): 417–36.

———.1996. *What Do People Really Think: Language Attitudes in the Media.* Paper presented at the American Association for Applied Linguistics Conference, The Intercontinental Hotel, Chicago. March 24.

———.1998. *Ebonics and the Media: Folk Views versus Sociolinguistic Expertise.* Paper presented at the American Association for Applied Linguistics Conference, Madison Hotel, Seattle. March 15.

Hakuta, Kenji. 1986. *Mirror of Language: The Debate on Bilingualism.* New York: Basic Books.

Hay, Henrietta. 1995. "Bilingualism No Threat to America." *Monterey County Herald.* Dec. 5. 9A.

Heath, Shirley Brice. 1983. *Ways with Words: Language, Life, and Work in Communities and Classrooms.* Cambridge: Cambridge University Press.

"Hillhaven Employees Fight Company's Language Policy." 1995. *San Francisco Chronicle*. Nov. 17. A23.

Joffe, Josef. 1995. "Freedom of Babble." *New York Times*. Nov. 30. A22.

"Judge Backs Off English Order." 1995. *San Francisco Chronicle/Examiner*. Sept. 17. A13.

King, Peter. 1995. "Bilingual Education Is Linguistic Welfare." *New York Times*. Dec. 5. A18.

Lippi-Green, Rosina. 1994. "Accent, Standard Language Ideology, and Discriminatory Pretext in the Courts." *Language in Society* 23(3): 163–97.

Pagan, Gilberto. 1995. "English-Only Plan Slights Puerto Ricans." *New York Times*. Sept. 18. A10.

Pavlenko, Anna, and James Lantolf. 1997. *Voices from the Margins: SLA as (Re)construction of Self*. Paper presented at the American Association of Applied Linguistics Conference, Holiday Inn, Orlando. March 9.

Preston, Dennis. 1993a. "Folk Dialectology." In Dennis Preston, ed., *American Dialect Research*. Amsterdam: John Benjamins. 333–77.

———. 1993b. "Two Heartland Perceptions of Language Variety." In Timothy Frazer, ed., *Heartland English: Variation and Transition in the American Midwest*. Tuscaloosa: University of Alabama Press. 23–47.

———. 1993c. "The Uses of Folk Linguistics." *International Journal of Applied Linguistics* 3(2): 181–259.

———.1996a. "Whaddayaknow? The Modes of Folk Linguistic Awareness." *Language Awareness* 5(1): 40–74.

———. 1996b. "Where the Worst English Is Spoken." In Edgar Schneider, ed., *Focus on the USA: Varieties of English around the World*. Amsterdam: John Benjamins. 297–360.

Robbins, Terry. 1995. "Official English Not English Only." *Monterey County Herald*. Nov. 9. 8A.

Sato, Charlene. 1991. "Sociolinguistic Variation and Language Attitudes in Hawaii." In Jenny Cheshire, ed., *English around the World: Sociolinguistic Perspectives*. Cambridge: Cambridge University Press. 647–63.

Storrow, Amy. 1995. "Bilingual Education Should Be Goal for All." *New York Times*. Dec. 7. A20.

"Town's English Law Has Little Effect." 1995. *San Francisco Chronicle*. Oct. 20. A12.

van Lier, Leo. 1998. "Critical Language Awareness and Language Use in Multilingual Classrooms: A Social-Interactionist Perspective." *Plurilinguisme* 14: 69–100.

Velazquez, Nydia. 1995. "Bilingualism Enhances Our Competitiveness." *New York Times*. Dec. 11. A14.

CHAPTER TEN

The Racializing Function of Language Panics

JANE H. HILL
University of Arizona

In recent years, Americans have lived through several episodes of intense public attention to "language problems." Especially notable for the intensity of media coverage and citizen involvement at all levels were the Ebonics controversy of 1996–97 and the controversy around bilingual education in the 1997–98 campaign for California's Proposition 227, an initiative to eliminate bilingual education in that state. On June 2, 1998, after a bitter battle that drew national and international attention, the initiative passed overwhelmingly, with exit polls showing Whites and Latinos sharply polarized.[1] In this chapter, I analyze some of the written public discourse that formed these "language panics." My texts include newspaper articles, many posted on Web sites, and Internet postings by major organizations and individuals involved in these controversies. They do not include recordings of talk radio shows (which were intensely involved in both panics) or of materials that appeared on television. I argue that analysis of this discourse suggests that language panics are not really about language. Instead, they are about race, the single most important category of social organization in the United States. Language panics are one of the characteristic discourses of racist culture as it has developed in the United States. They comprise one small part of a struggle over who will be "racialized," and how the nature of racialized people is to be understood.

I take the concept of "racist culture" from Goldberg (1993), who uses this term to refer to an enduring yet dynamic cultural formation that is by no means an archaism but instead strongly shapes our lives today. Racist culture and its discourses exhibit two major components. First are the processes of expression, including the ongoing classifying projects, both material and symbolic, of racialization: the creation of a division between "whiteness" and "color."[2] Second are the processes of exclusion. These elevate and privilege "whiteness," reserving resources to Whites while simultaneously lowering, oppressing, or excluding from these resources those assigned to the zone of color. With Goldberg (1993), Feagin and Vera (1995), Omi and Winant (1994), Winant (1994), and many other contemporary theorists of racist culture, I find that the discourses that comprise it include far more than such prototypical expressions as a conscious belief in the biological inferiority of people who have been racialized as "colored," and include many forms of exclusion beyond the use of physical violence. Certainly, people who believe in the biological inferiority of the "colored" races continue to be taken as serious interlocutors at the highest levels of public debate. Indeed, to take such people seriously is regarded by many Americans as simply "fair," as part of the American way of letting all sides of an issue be heard.[3] Thus this utterly discredited body of ideas continues, zombielike, to stalk the terrain of debate about race, distracting antiracists by exhausting their resources and permitting people who hold milder forms of racist views to remain complacent about their own ideas. Furthermore, physical violence against members of racialized groups both by law enforcement agents and private citizens continues to be an important feature of life in the United States, functioning to instill fear and caution (and consequent self-exclusion from valued resources) among potential victims and providing pleasures and satisfactions to many Whites. Contemporary racist culture, however, is reproduced especially through practices which are never condemned as racist—practices which appear (at least to many Whites) to constitute mere common sense. An example is the belief—contrary to findings of biological anthropology and human genetics that have been the stuff of introductory college courses for forty years—in the existence of races as a meaningful dimension of the structure of human populations, and the belief that it is possible to assign individuals to races. Not only are such beliefs not disappearing, but, as Goldberg (1993) observes, "we have come, if often only silently, to conceive of social subjects foremost in racial terms" (3).[4] Finally, I emphasize that I am not concerned here with individual intentions or the diagnosis of individuals as racist. We are all a part of racist culture, and no American, regardless of his or her racial identity, can get through a day without participating in commonplace examples of what Winant (1994) has called "racial practices"—of noticing and of sensing racialized closeness or racialized distance in relation to those we encounter. I am, however, particularly interested in the discourses of the dominant White population, which is the beneficiary, witting and unwitting, of racist culture, and the most important practitioner of its various forms of structural violence. I examine some of the ways in which these discourses accomplish the elevation of whiteness and the exclusion of color through the production of texts about language in the course of language panics.

This perspective on language panics is not widely shared by linguists and language educators. For instance, in a survey of thirty-four entries, encompassing about one hundred messages, found under the heading Ebonics in the archives of Linguist, the Internet list that probably reaches the largest number of people in the linguistics profession, I found only one explicit mention of racism, an early posting by a contributor who used the expression "institutional racism." One contributor euphemistically mentioned the need to recognize the "special" situation of African Americans in the United States. Even linguists who have concluded that racism is involved in these issues do not position this perspective at the center of their thinking. An excellent example is found in a valuable essay on the Ebonics panic by Rickford (1988/1999), who raises the issue of racism only in the face of the most egregious provocation. Speaking of the shocking proliferation of racist jokes about Ebonics on the Internet during the panic (see also Ronkin and Karn 1998), Rickford (1998/1999) observes:

> In cases like these, language was no longer at issue; "Ebonics" had become a proxy for African Americans, and the most racist stereotypes were being promulgated. This cruel humor might remind us . . . that behind people's expressed attitudes to vernacular varieties, there are often deep-seated social and political fears

and prejudices about their speakers. If we don't take the "socio" part of sociolinguistics seriously, we won't be prepared to understand or respond to such attitudes effectively.

With few exceptions, linguists and language educators presuppose that language panics are really about language.

In the case of the Ebonics and the bilingual education panics, linguists took the impoverished and retrograde content of public debate as evidence of our failure to "get the facts out" about scholarly understandings of these phenomena. Among the "facts" that scholars want known are the following: Regarding bilingual education, sociolinguists universally agree that bilingualism is in no way an intrinsic source of social division or a barrier to educational success or social mobility. Instead, they argue that bilingualism can be an important national resource in a globalizing economy. They are in general agreement that in nearly all contexts, early primary education is best conducted in the child's home language.[5] Regarding Ebonics or African American English (AAE), for forty years all linguists have agreed that the forms of speech used by African Americans are fully grammatical. Scholars recognize the rich linguistic traditions of the African diaspora not only for their social functions of the construction of solidarity and the resistance to oppression in African American and Afro-Caribbean communities, but also as the vehicle of a tradition of verbal art that ranges from the composition of folk forms such as toasts and raps to the Nobel Prize–winning literary achievements of Derek Walcott and Toni Morrison. While the precise details of the contribution of African languages to African American English are a matter of ongoing scholarly debate, scholars agree that there is much evidence for such a substratum.

Both the Ebonics and the bilingual education panics revealed a widespread lack of acceptance of these positions among the general public. In reaction to this revelation, scholarly and professional societies such as the Linguistic Society of America, the American Anthropological Association, the National Association for Bilingual Education, and the American Association for Educational Research issued resolutions reaffirming the scholarly synthesis. Individual linguists rededicated themselves to the clarification of this synthesis in the classroom and in public. These exercises duplicated earlier efforts dating back at least to the 1960s. Yet in spite of the long history of scholarly effort to get the word out, even highly educated people, including Latinos and African Americans, spoke up on the "wrong side" (from the linguist's point of view) during these episodes.

I believe the reason that the educational efforts of scholars to get the facts out about the nature of bilingualism, second-language education, and dialect variation have failed is that language panics are, as noted previously, not about language. Therefore scholars must reshape their messages so as to directly engage racist culture and show how thinking about language within that system is inevitably as damaging and distorting as racism itself.

The Discourse of Language Panics

What lines of evidence suggest that language panics are not really about language but about race—that is to say, that they are part of the discourse system of racist culture, with a principal function to produce "racial subjects" (Goldberg 1993)? The first kind of evidence is the sheer intensity of these episodes: it is the extraordinary excess of discourse, and its hyperbolic quality, that leads me to adopt the term "language panics."[6] Language panics seem to be about relatively obscure technical matters: Should we understand African American English as a dialect of English or, because of its African substratum, as a distinct language? Precisely what mix of mother tongue and target language in the primary school classroom makes for the most effective student achievement? Anyone who has ever struggled to build enrollments or to hold student interest in linguistics or sociolinguists classes should find it astonishing that such matters can attract massive public attention. The very fact of such intense attention suggests that technical linguistic matters are not what is at stake here. Instead, language panics must somehow engage deeper cultural principles.

The Ebonics panic is a paradigm case. It started in Oakland, California, perhaps best known for native daughter Gertrude Stein's remark that "there is no there there." Oakland made the national news in the 1980s and 1990s when spectacular fires destroyed its wealthiest neighborhoods and when an earthquake pancaked its double-deck expressway. But Oakland, featuring a large African American population and gritty industrial zones lining the mud flats of the East Bay, is in no way part of the imagined California that normally obsesses the national media. Therefore it was remarkable that a moderately worded resolution passed by this obscure city's school board on December 18, 1996, created a media firestorm that continued for months. The resolution (its text can be found on a number of Internet sites)[7] opened with a summary in layperson terms of some scholarly reflections on the origins of African American vernacular language (which the resolution called Ebonics).[8] The resolution continued by noting that the use of contrastive analysis, which would include classroom presentation of Ebonics and standard English structures and even instruction in Ebonics in accordance with the principles of bilingual education, should be useful in the education of African American students. Federal funds designated for bilingual education should be sought for this purpose.

Suddenly, the Oakland school board found itself at the epicenter of a national language panic. Front page stories, op-ed pieces by leading pundits both Black and White, background feature pieces, and a rich harvest of cartoons appeared in all the California newspapers, the *New York Times,* the *Chicago Tribune,* and the *Washington Post.* Many of these items were nationally syndicated. Celebrities Black and White weighed in on the pros and cons of the resolution (mostly the cons). The Internet positively roiled with comment and debate, and repulsive new "Mock Ebonics" (Ronkin and Karn 1998) Web sites, rich with the obscene and scatological racist humor that the relative anonymity of cyberspace apparently invites, sprouted like mushrooms after a good rain. Radio talk show hosts and television public affairs pundits made Ebonics a featured topic of discussion. Legislators at all levels took up the issue. The superintendent of the Oakland public schools and leading linguists were summoned to Washington, D.C., to testify before a U.S. Senate hearing convened by the Senate Subcommittee on Labor, Health and Human Services, and Education Appropriations, led by Arlen Specter, a prominent Pennsylvania Republican.[9] In another legislative move,

California State Senator Raymond Hayes introduced a bill that forbade any use of state funds, or any application for federal funds, "for the purpose of so-called Ebonics instruction." Any funds currently being used for such instruction should be immediately shifted to the teaching of "the English language."

The campaign for Proposition 227, the "Unz initiative" to eliminate bilingual education (the formal title is English Language Education for Children in Public Schools), elicited a similarly intense reaction. National media attention was partly driven by political reporters who saw Proposition 227 as the continuation of a California trend that included 1995's Proposition 187, which eliminated all social services for undocumented immigrants including public education for children, and 1997's Proposition 209, which eliminated affirmative action programs.[10] Analysts saw the success of these propositions as harbingers of a national shift of mood against generosity to the unfortunate. Yet, even given this interesting political trend, media attention and the intense level of public debate on Proposition 227 nationwide seemed disproportionate. Indeed, as I was completing the final draft of this essay, my Sunday *New York Times* arrived with a front-page feature, two columns wide above the fold, on Ronald K. Unz, a hitherto obscure California Republican who authored Proposition 227 (Bruni 1998). In summary, it is precisely the media-firestorm, panicky quality of language panics that suggests their discourse touches deeper cultural concerns than technical issues about language.

A second piece of evidence that language panics are not about language is that the level of technical linguistic and policy discourse in language panics is extremely low. Notable in the discourse of language panics is the almost universal neglect of—indeed, disdain for—the views of language professionals in favor of anecdotes and "stories" from ordinary people who are taken as a reservoir of "common sense."[11] While this is to some degree a problem for any technical or scientific policy debate in the United States, it would be interesting to compare the frequency with which recognized scholars (as opposed to otherwise unemployed ideologues supported by deep-pocketed conservative think tanks) are cited in reference to language issues with the frequency of such citations in discussions of, say, global warming or other issues that are difficult to link to the discourses of racist culture. Rickford (1998/1999) discusses this problem. Although he was a visitor on several local California radio talk shows during the Ebonics panic, and contributed an invited essay to the Discover channel, he notes that the elite media generally ignored linguists. The *New York Times* published several uninformed op-ed pieces on Ebonics but, according to Rickford, rejected submissions by himself, Salikoko Mufwene, Geoffrey Pullum, and Gene Searchinger (1998/1999, 3). Nonetheless, mere neglect may be preferable to vicious attacks, including hate mail. In searching the published texts on the Unz initiative, I encountered extremely scurrilous verbal assaults on Steve Krashen, Lily Wong Fillmore, and James Crawford. The assault on Krashen in the *Los Angeles New Times* (Stewart 1998) accused him of cynically profiting by advocating bilingual education that destroys the hopes of poor Latino children,[12] and of being the "movement guru" of hordes of mindless true believers in the California public schools. The attack on Fillmore was authored by Gloria Matta Tuchman, who became the cosponsor of the Unz initiative, in the *San Diego Union-Tribune* in 1992.[13] Fillmore is accused of wanting to "segregate" language-minority children and, through "getting political," of protecting "the failed bilingual education system and the jobs that go with it." In an e-mail exchange between Ronald Unz and James Crawford (ourworld.compuserve.com/homepages/jwcrawford/unzmail. html), Unz called Crawford an "academic loony" and a "kook," and refused to debate him (Crawford, a journalist, rejected "academic" but otherwise kept his temper largely in check).

In addition to disdain for scholarly expertise and the utter neglect of published research findings (except for reports put out by conservative foundations), the lack of serious attention to language policy scholarship is visible in the texts produced by the attacking side in both panics. For instance, the language of Proposition 227 does not specify any level of funding for the "sheltered immersion" programs that it prescribes as a replacement for bilingual classrooms. An independent legislative analysis estimated that the Unz initiative will cost public education in California approximately fifty million dollars in federal funding (National Association for Bilingual Education). Furthermore, the initiative directs that fifty million dollars be put into English-language programs for adults who pledge to help children learn English. Funds for this adult program will presumably have to come from the K–12 education budget. The National Association for Bilingual Education's analysis pointed out many other problems with the language of the Unz initiative, including the failure to provide for evaluation or accountability[14] of the programs it prescribes, the failure to require any special training for teachers of "sheltered immersion" (in contrast to the endorsement requirements for bilingual educators), and peculiar innovations such as the grading of sheltered immersion classes by level of English competence rather than by age or school grade. Therefore it is not surprising to find the childless Unz, whose degrees are in physics, admitting to the *New York Times* that he had "never set foot in a bilingual classroom" (Bruni 1998, 24).

Moves that masqueraded as "policy initiatives" in opposition to the Oakland school board's Ebonics resolution were equally opaque. For instance, the Haynes bill, California SB 205: "Equality in English Instruction Act," characterized Ebonics completely within the framework of a deficit theory—outdated thirty years ago in the scholarly world—as "poor linguistic skills [and] . . . poor communication patterns." Like the Unz initiative, the Haynes bill prescribed vague new forms of funding in the form of financial incentive to school districts "that improve linguistic or communication skills of students in low-income areas of the state," as well as "financial penalties for school districts where these skills have deteriorated, as measured by objective testing data." The bill, which stated that no state agency should use any funds for Ebonics instruction, if passed would have probably rendered illegal substantial portions of the content in sociolinguistics courses in the California university system.

A third line of evidence that leads me to characterize the discourse of language panics as framed within racist culture is its specifically racist content. Many elements of this discourse fall clearly within the system of exclusions: the denial of resources to racialized persons and the constant attack on their full humanity. Examples of this type are so numerous that I can mention only a very small sample. For instance, critics of bilingual education often expressed their horror at the fact that certified bilingual teachers were paid a $5,000 bonus for their skills (e.g., Stewart 1998). This is a classic example of the attempt to deny resources to a racialized population for a skill that is valued and recompensed among the dominant White population. The battle to move bilingual skills out of the realm of what Ivan Illich (1981) called "shadow work" and into the realm of remunerated qualification is one of the most important economic struggles for Latinos, and has been fought on a variety of fronts including in health care facilities and police departments (cf. González 1989; for a discussion of the same issue for French Canadians, see Levine 1990).

Latino supporters of bilingual education are constantly stereotyped in the pro-227 discourse as bureaucrats at best, and at worst as corrupt. For instance, Linda Chavez (1998) argued that A. Jerrold Perenchio, head of Univision Communications, contributed funds to the anti-227 campaign only to preserve a monolingual audience for his Spanish-language television stations. This is an interesting example of a rhetorical move that Woolard (1989) called "Bossism": the accusation that minority political leaders are corrupt. Woolard identified this move in her analysis of texts in support of Proposition O, an early Official English initiative passed in San Francisco in 1983. Another example attests to the hardball use of the "corrupt Hispanic leader" theme. Nativo Lopez, president of the Santa Ana public schools board of education, gave an anti-227 interview to the California Latino daily *La Opinion* that was published on May 21, 1997 (www. onenation.org/lopez.html). On May 22 the *Los Angeles Times* reported that Mr. Lopez's employer, Hermandad Mexicana, a fifty-year-old Latino service agency dedicated to providing services to immigrants and the elderly, had encountered problems in accounting for federal funds (Wilson 1997); the *Times* article (but not Lopez's original interview) is featured on Unz's Web site (www.onenation.org/lopez.html). The fact that the audit had been commissioned by the agency itself, and the auditor's statement that "they are trying very hard to correct these things," were buried late in the article; the lead paragraphs implied that the problems were due to corruption (Wilson 1997).

Of special interest are texts produced by Ronald K. Unz himself. The mainstream press is fond of pointing out that Unz is "not a bigot" because he had opposed Proposition 187, the initiative to deny social services to undocumented immigrants (Unz's actual position was that it would be "right and proper" to deny social services to undocumented immigrants as long as welfare was denied to everybody, a move that he advocates [Unz 1994]). Seldom did articles on Unz, which often included slavish paeans to his "genius,"[15] point out that he was a strong supporter of Proposition 209, the initiative to end affirmative action. But I would concur that reasonable people can differ on affirmative action, so this is not evidence that Unz is a bigot. That, however, is not the issue here. One of the difficulties with getting reasonable debates about racism underway is the use of terms like "bigot," which imply personal malice. Unz may not be bigoted, but on the evidence of his own writing he is profoundly embedded in the racist cultural system I have been sketching. Unz's publications as represented on his Web site are filled with superb examples of what van Dijk (1993) has called "elite racist discourse." Like most educated White Americans, Unz refutes accusations that his motives are racist as a "vile charge" (Unz 1997b). His texts in support of his initiative express compassion for "powerless Latino immigrants and their children" (Unz 1997a, M6). Other texts, however, undercut this compassionate purpose. For instance, for Unz the primary sources of racial divisiveness in the United States are those that trouble Whites: that is, any claim of minority privilege, such as affirmative action or minority preferences in government contracting. Unz seems to see the salaries paid to bilingual teachers and "bureaucrats" as examples of unwarranted minority privilege and as incitements to corruption rather than a reward for skills. Theoreticians of racism in the social sciences are almost universally agreed that systems of White domination and minority exclusion are the main reason for racial polarization in the United States. A revealing essay Unz published in *Policy Review* (Unz 1994) as part of his campaign against Proposition 187 includes a fevered passage on Black violence as a force that Republicans can exploit to attract immigrants to the party (since Blacks are Democrats): "the death rate of Korean shopkeepers in black neighborhoods was as high as that of American soldiers in the Vietnam war. . . . Hispanic families with small children were attacked and brutalized by black mobs." Unz, as is typical of elite Whites, sees the prototypical example of ethnic violence not in the actions of White police officers or in the hideous conditions faced by migrant farmworkers or inhabitants of inner-city ghettos, but in rioting by Blacks.

Unz's opponents often cite a letter he wrote to the *Los Angeles Times* in March 1997 characterizing his own Jewish immigrant ancestors as people who "came to work and be successful, . . . not to sit back and be a burden on those who were already here." (This text is posted at http://ourworld.compuserve.com/homepages/jwcrawford and was once posted at http://www.nabe.org/unz, but the letter cannot be found on Unz's own Web site.) James Crawford (1998) comments that since the only ethnic group mentioned in the letter is Latinos and the only language mentioned is Spanish, one can only take this remark as anti-Latino.

Discourses surrounding the Ebonics panic included not only relatively subtle racist discourse similar to the examples above, but also many examples of more obvious racism. In addition to the Internet sites discussed by Rickford (1998/1999) and Ronkin and Karn (1998), and political cartoons featuring images of thick-lipped louts that appeared even in mainstream newspapers, media mavens and language policy arrivistes of all stripes repeatedly quoted characterizations of African American speech patterns as "lazy" and "ungrammatical."

Both the Ebonics panic and the bilingual education panic featured many texts that reviewed with loving attention statistics on the failures and inadequacies of African American and Latino schoolchildren that were often selected to present the most exaggeratedly negative picture. The overtly stated purpose of citing such statistics is to demonstrate the failures of bilingual education or to show why the Oakland school board might consider including attention to Ebonics in the curriculum. But the statistical reviews also presented the children's language as a "problem."[16] The effect—especially in the absence of constructive policy proposals—is almost certainly to renew in the public mind ideas about the inadequacies of these racialized populations (in spite of pious references to "innocent children" who "only want to learn"). A genuinely critical analysis would consider the likelihood that the differential school achievement of African American and Latino children is not an indicator of the children's' problems, but is instead a powerful sign of the continuing importance of structural racism in the schools. Indeed, in California, where the public schools have been devastated in the long dreary aftermath of the Proposition 13 taxpayers' revolt of 1978, what Jonathan Kozol (1991) called "savage inequalities" are particularly exacerbated. To blame this differential achievement on bilingual education programs that serve only 30 percent of children diagnosed in California as "limited English proficient" is misleading and cynical. It seems highly likely that the presentation of such statistics in the sound-bite contexts characteristic of media treatment of the bilingual education issue invites their interpretation as evidence of the biological (or, in the more recent kind of elite racist discourse, "cultural") inferiority of racialized populations. There is much evidence that the college placement test scores of minority children presented in the 1996–97 campaign for Proposition 209 were widely interpreted this way.

One striking fact is that the dialects of Whites (with the possible exception of Whites in Appalachia) are never identified as a language problem. Unquestionably, much of African American English, especially the vernacular varieties, includes substantial departures in phonology, syntax, and pragmatic and discourse patterns from varieties of English used by most Whites. But varieties of White English have been identified that are equally distant from the mainstream "standard" on technical linguistic grounds. Ironically, one of the most innovative and deviant regional and sociolectal varieties of English found in the United States today is the Valley Girl English (for lack of a better term, I use this well-known designation, although of course VGE is also spoken by males) spoken by middle-class White and Asian young people in California (Hinton et al. 1987; Luthin 1989; Moonwomon 1989). A conversation among White teens in full VGE can be as difficult to understand for anyone over the age of about thirty-five as the most avant-garde African American hip-hop performance. Yet no scholar has ever suggested that VGE might constitute a language problem requiring special education for students and teachers. Instead, teachers simply adapt by assigning VGE to the domain of the unnoticeable and unremarked behaviors that define whiteness (cf. Frankenberg 1993).

It is important to point out that this analysis requires a certain amount of reading between the lines. If we take the discourse of language panics at face value, we find that its most prominent themes promise not exclusion but inclusion. Thus we hear language such as the following from the Haynes bill against the teaching of Ebonics:

> The justification for "Ebonics" instruction is the same as that used to justify prohibiting language instruction to slaves, and to justify separate educational institutions for African-Americans [as] prior to the case of Brown v. Board of Education. It is the perpetuation of the "separate but equal" philosophy that has harmed race relations in this country for far too many years.

Advocates for Proposition 227 argue that to teach children whose home language is Spanish in that language in the primary grades is to deny them the hope of opportunity through English that every American child deserves. Woolard (1989) has brilliantly analyzed this rhetoric of inclusion in the early campaigns for Official English. All of the major themes she identified are found in the language panics analyzed here. These include Waste (programs to teach students about Ebonics or for bilingual education are a waste of taxpayer money); Unfairness (past immigrants learned English without this kind of support); National Unity (such programs promote racial divisiveness); Hinder English Acquisition (such programs deny students the opportunity to learn good English); Full Life (with opportunity so denied, the child is condemned to life as a second-class citizen); and Bossism (the theme of corrupt minority leaders who hope to imprison their followers by denying them access to English) (Woolard 1989, 272).[17] Woolard's analysis reveals the hidden assumptions and contradictions of these themes (as pointed out earlier in the discussion of the theme of Bossism articulated by supporters of Proposition 227, the hidden assumptions of this theme include racist stereotypes), but she argues that they are extremely attractive to voters, including people who are quite liberal politically. It is these themes that attracted a number of prominent Latinos to the campaign for Proposition 227 in spite of its obvious problems. Opponents tried to develop the theme of choice by parents and local school systems as a strongly held value that would be denied by 227's rigid prescriptions, but this theme made little headway against the pro-227 rhetoric of inclusion. Similarly, African American leaders were attracted by the rhetoric of inclusion to the anti-Ebonics position.

Conclusion

An analysis of discourse produced by anti-Ebonics sources in the 1996–97 Ebonics panic and of discourse produced by opponents of bilingual education in the Proposition 227 campaign suggests that the principal function of such discourses is not to stimulate rethinking and reform of inadequate educational policies, but to reproduce racist culture and to produce what Goldberg (1993) has called racial subjects. The main lines of evidence I have advanced for this position are the panicky and intense production of discourse within language panics, the profoundly uninformed and counterproductive nature of policy recommendations that are put forward in the context of language panics, and the racist and racializing language that is easily found in a review of language panic discourse. In functioning to reinforce the dominance of whiteness and the subordination of color, and to reproduce the racialization of "colored" populations, language panic discourses are part of a larger discursive complex that includes similar moral panics over teenage pregnancy (where the prototypical pregnant teenager is African American), school drop out rates (where the prototypical school dropout is Hispanic/Latino), youth crime (where the prototypical youth criminal is either African American or Hispanic/Latino, depending on the region of the country), illegal immigration (somehow the Irish are almost never mentioned in this connection), women who give birth to cocaine-addicted infants (here again the image is African American), and so on. These moral panics elevate "whiteness" by the public display of concern for the civic and economic success of minority populations, usually accompanied by the strong denial of racism. Their covert function, however, is to subordinate color by representing members of racialized populations as problems. While I refer to this function as covert, it is quite obvious to many minorities, who report fear and confusion in the face of such debates, and who may begin to modify their behavior even when a panic results in no enforceable legislation. Speakers may, for instance, refrain from speaking their languages in public places for fear of censure, or become hypersensitive and self-conscious about their accents (see Urciuoli 1996). No similar discipline exists for "white" populations, who can use a full range of expressions originating in foreign languages, as well as slangy or dialectically innovative speech, without concern that they will be noticed or censured.

At the same time that language panics represent racialized populations as a problem, they fail to produce truly meaningful policy initiatives. Instead, language panic policy typically takes the form of a superficially attractive quick fix that tends to cause more problems than it solves. This point of view on language panics suggests that the traditional forms of "education" about language that we scholars have practiced are inadequate. Our presentation of scientific findings must be integrated into a critical analysis of the workings of racist culture and the way erroneous beliefs about language fit into its system. From this perspective, we might present an analysis along the following lines. Whites, often quite unconsciously, find in their dominant position in the racial hierarchy the foundations of a morally meaningful universe. Even quite small threats to this domination provoke great anxiety, as we would expect in any case where the fundamental presuppositions of a cultural system are questioned. A paradigm example of this type is the well-known problem of maintaining racially balanced urban neighborhoods, where White flight occurs, often at considerable economic and social sacrifice for those who may sell homes at fire-sale prices and abandon contacts with nearby family and friends, as soon as African Americans constitute more than a very small percentage of residents. Bilingual education and instruction about Ebonics may present a similar deep challenge to the White comfort zone, for these are fields where Latinos and African Americans respectively control the most expertise and can rise to high positions within educational institutions. "Bilingual education" and "Ebonics" are thus useful metonyms that provide ways to talk about White anxiety—and, in a state like California, where the percentage of people of color is beginning to precipitate White flight into rural areas of the Mountain states, useful metonyms are needed. "Official English" and "English immersion" then become metonyms for the value of White domination. Thus language panics permit Whites to explore their moral dilemma without confronting the reasons it is experienced (since to admit to discomfort in the face of a challenge from the domain of color—that is, to admit to racism—is to challenge a sense of White "goodness" in a profound and unacceptable way). Interestingly, language panics yield precisely the same kind of sacrifice seen in White flight: the rich linguistic and cultural resources that racialized populations might bring to the American mix are reduced to impoverished fragments, circumscribed in time and space in ethnic restaurant menus, during school holidays, and at carefully circumscribed ethnic festivals (see Urciuoli 1996).

White fear of confronting and exploring racist culture is both a problem and an advantage for antiracist work. A problem, because anger at the mere mention of the "r" word, even in the technical sense I have used it here, makes it so difficult to initiate honest dialogue. Yet if Whites like Ronald K. Unz find an accusation of racism to be "vile," then the first step has been taken toward such a dialogue. Likewise, we can take the rhetorics of compassion and inclusion seriously, and show how their apparent intentions can be accomplished only if we grant members of racialized populations a respected voice in public dialogues rather than dismissing their claims on resources as evidence of corruption, or their concerns about living in a climate of racism as self-indulgent whining.

White fear of confronting racist culture is not the only problem in initiating antiracist dialogue. While for antiracists racist culture has obvious terrible social costs, we must still recognize that for many Whites the near-term advantages for individuals loom much larger than the long-term sacrifices for society and nation. These near-term privileges are, of course, justified by the sense of White virtue, so the two problems are tightly intertwined to make antiracist work extremely difficult.

Finally, we need to be especially alert to the penetration of racist culture into our own scholarly practice. If analysts such as David Theo Goldberg (1993) are correct, at least in general, then the entire system of modernity is so permeated by the presuppositions of racism that traps await us at every turn. We must demand of ourselves no less in the way of reflexivity than we ask of our opponents.

Notes

1. Exit polls conducted by major news organizations showed that Whites had voted for the initiative in "supermajorities" of over 60 percent, while Latino voters rejected it in the same proportion. The exit polls have been challenged by pro-227 spokespersons, who had proudly boasted of Latino support during the campaign (Unz 1997a; Crawford 1998).

2. My own view is that the division between "whiteness" and "color" is the most important project of racialization. Other scholars have suggested that the fundamental division is that between "Black" and "White," with groups such as Asians, Latinos, and Native Americans forming somewhat anomalous intermediate classes. I do not have space to argue for this position here, but I believe that evidence will show that Asians, especially those of Japanese, Chinese, and Korean descent, have joined the domain of whiteness. In contrast, all material indicators (rates of poverty, ill health, high infant mortality, relatively low levels of educational achievement) suggest that African Americans and Latinos are more similar to each other than either group is similar to Whites. The insistence of classifiers in the U.S. Bureau of the Census that Hispanics are an ethnic rather than a racial group is, of course, inconsistent with my position.

3. Here I have in mind phenomena such as the choice of the *New York Times Book Review* to feature a positive lead review of Murray and Herrnstein's (1994) *The Bell Curve*.

4. An excellent example is the 1997 report by anthropologist Antony Paredes that his own ambiguous appearance elicits comment and speculation from perfect strangers in public places. He concludes that Americans are obsessed with the appropriate classification of people by race.

5. One of the serious concerns of opponents of bilingual education in California was that children were often placed in bilingual education classes or classified as limited English proficient on the basis of such limited data as having a Latino last name. That such abuses in fact occurred has been verified by scholars who are in no way opposed to bilingual education (see Mendoza-Denton 1997). Such practices are, of course, in themselves evidence of the dominance of racist culture; they parallel the disproportionate tracking of minority children into "special education" classes. They

do not, however, have any bearing on the value of appropriately administered bilingual education programs for young children whose home language is not English.

6. I take the expression "language panic" from the idea of a moral panic proposed by Stanley Cohen (1972) and Stuart Hall (1978).

7. My source is the excellent archive on Ebonics maintained by linguistic anthropologist Jim Wilce, at jan.UCC.nau.edu/~jmw22.

8. The December 18 resolution included the following language: "African Language Systems are genetically-based and not a dialect of English." Scholars such as John Rickford and Leanne Hinton, who have talked to the school board members who framed the resolution, report that the framers always intended "genetic" in the historical-linguistic sense, meaning that Ebonics had a phylogenetic origin in African languages. But it was widely and falsely reported that the Oakland school board members believed that their students spoke Ebonics by biological endowment. The revised version of the resolution, issued January 15, 1997, changed this language to read "African Language Systems have origins in West [African] and Niger Congo languages and are not merely dialects of English." The term "Ebonics," a blend of "ebony" and "phonics," was apparently coined by Robert Williams, author of *Ebonics: The True Language of Black Folks*, at a conference in St. Louis in 1973.

9. John Rickford (1998/1999) states that linguists participated because they were afraid that Specter's committee would react to the Oakland resolution by eliminating Title I education funds that support programs for "standard English proficiency." Fortunately, Rickford reports, Senator Specter accepted the testimony of proponents and not only did not recommend eliminating SEP funding, but also proposed that an additional appropriation of $1 million be assigned to research the relationship between knowledge of African American English and achievement in standard English literacy.

10. At the time this chapter was written, Proposition 187 was moving through the federal courts, having been challenged on constitutional grounds. Proposition 209 was being implemented, resulting in a dramatic drop in non-Asian minority enrollment on the major campuses of the University of California.

11. The Web site for English for the Children, the sponsoring group for Proposition 227 (www.onenation.org), has a special page where people can post "stories"—about successful learning of English without bilingual education, about abuses of bilingual education, about struggles with

its unfeeling bureaucrats, and so forth. One of the favorite anecdotes for 227 supporters was the tale of how Latino parents boycotted Los Angeles's Ninth Street Elementary School to get English instruction for their children. James Crawford (1998) investigated this anecdote and decided that the boycott was completely engineered by a well-known conservative activist, Alice Callaghan, who constructed it as a bit of street theater in which the Latino parents may have been largely passive participants.

12. Krashen's "cavernous poolside home in Malibu" was featured, and its purported price—$700,000—characterized, in the kind of innuendo usually reserved for gangland figures, as "difficult to pay for on a simple professor's salary" (Stewart 1998, 9). Certainly, those who know Malibu will realize that Krashen's is, in its context, a modest residence.

13. Tuchman sat on the board of U.S. English, the principal advocate of Official English legislation. She apparently joined the board *after* the notorious remark by John Tanton, founder of U.S. English, that suggested that population growth and consequent immigration pressure from Latinos came because they could not control their sexual drive (Crawford 1998).

14. The only form of "evaluation" provided for in the initiative is the right of any parent or legal guardian to sue any level of the public school system right down to individual teachers if the parent feels that the terms of the initiative are being violated.

15. Unz once put his IQ (214) on his résumé (Bruni 1998, A24).

16. The children's language is never seen as a resource (Ruiz 1990).

17. One theme identified by Woolard, Uninformed Voter, was not salient in the discourses of either the Ebonics or the bilingual education language panics (it appeared in the texts she considered, which advocated eliminating bilingual ballots).

Works Cited

Bruni, Frank. 1998. "The California Entrepreneur Who Beat Bilingual Teaching." *New York Times*. June 14. A1, A24.

Chavez, Linda. 1998. "Keeping Bilingual-Education Programs Intact Makes for Lucrative Business." *Chicago Tribune* [Online]. May 27. Available: www.onenation.org/052798f.html

Cohen, Stanley. 1972. *Folk Devils and Moral Panics: The Creation of the Mods and Rockers*. London: MacGibbon and Kee.

Crawford, James. 1998. Language Policy Web site. Available: http://ourworld.compuserve.com/homepages/jwcrawford

Feagin, Joe R., and Hernán Vera. 1995. *White Racism: The Basics*. New York: Routledge.

Frankenberg, Ruth. 1993. *White Women, Race Matters: The Social Construction of Whiteness*. Minneapolis: University of Minnesota Press.

Goldberg, David Theo. 1993. *Racist Culture: Philosophy and the Politics of Meaning*. Oxford, U.K.: Blackwell.

González, Roseann D. 1989. "Bilingual Workers in the City of Tucson." *Renato Rosaldo Lectures VI*. Tucson: University of Arizona.

Hall, Stuart. 1978. *Policing the Crisis: Mugging, the State, and Law and Order*. London: MacMillan Press.

Herrnstein, Richard, and Charles A. Murray. 1994. *The Bell Curve: Intelligence and Class Structure in American Life*. New York: Free Press.

Hinton, Leanne, Birch Moonwomon, Sue Bremner, Mary Van Clay, Jean Lerner, and Hazel Corcoran. 1987. "It's Not Just the Valley Girls: A Study of California English." In Jon Ake, Natashe Beery, Laura Michaels, and Hana Filip, eds., *Thirteenth Annual Meeting of the Berkeley Linguistic Society*. Berkeley: University of California Department of Linguistics. 117–28.

Illich, Ivan. 1981. *Shadow Work*. Boston: M. Boyars.

Kozol, Jonathan. 1991. *Savage Inequalities*. New York: Crown.

Levine, Marc V. 1990. *The Reconquest of Montreal: Language Policy and Social Change in a Bilingual City*. Philadelphia: Temple University Press.

Luthin, Herb. 1989. "The Story of California (ow): The Coming of Age of English in California." In Keith Denning, Sharon Inkelas, Frances McNair-Knox, and John Rickford, eds., *Variation in Language, NWAV-XV at Stanford: Proceedings of the 15th Annual Conference on New Ways of Analyzing Variation*. Stanford, CA: Department of Linguistics, Stanford University. 312–24.

Mendoza-Denton, Norma. 1997. *Chicana/Mexicana Identity and Linguistic Variation: An Ethnographic and Sociolinguistic Study of Gang Affiliation in an Urban High School*. Unpublished doctoral dissertation, Stanford University.

Moonwomon, Birch. 1989. "Truly Awesome: ('open o') in California English." In Keith M. Denning, Sharon Inkelas, Frances C. McNair-Knox, and John R. Rickford, eds., *Variation in Language, NWAV-XV at Stanford: Proceedings of the 15th Annual Conference on New Ways of Analyzing Variation.* Stanford, CA: Department of Linguistics, Stanford University. 325–36.

Omi, Michael, and Howard Winant. 1994. *Racial Formation in the United States: From the 1960s to the 1990s.* New York: Routledge.

Paredes, Anthony. 1997. "Race Isn't What You See." *Anthropology Newsletter,* December.

Rickford, John. 1998/1999. "The Ebonics Controversy in My Backyard: A Sociolinguist's Experiences and Reflections." *Language and Society* [Special issue]. Available: http://www.stanford.edu/~rickford/papers/EbonicsInMyBackyard.html

Ronkin, Maggie, and Helen E. Karn. 1998. *Mock Ebonics: Linguistic Racism in Parodies of Ebonics on the Internet.* Paper presented at the Annual Meeting of the American Dialect Society, New York City. January 10.

Ruiz, Richard. 1990. "Official Languages and Language Planning." In Karen L. Adams and Daniel T. Brink, eds., *Perspectives on Official English: The Campaign for English as the Official Language of the USA.* New York: Mouton de Gruyter. 11–24.

Stewart, Jill. 1998. "KrashenBurn." *New Times LA* [Online], May 28. Available: www.onenation.org/052898e.html

Tuchman, Gloria Matta. 1992. "The Politics of Bilingual Education." *San Diego Union Tribune* [Online], Sept. 11. Available: www.onenation.org/tuchman 101192.html

Unz, Ronald K. 1994. "Immigration or the Welfare State." *Policy Review* [Online] (Fall). Available: www.onenation.org/unzprfall94.html

———. 1997a. "Bilingualism vs. Bilingual Education." *Los Angeles Times* [Online], Oct. 19. M6. Available: www.onenation.org/unz101997.html

———. 1997b. "Letter to the Editor." *La Opinion* [Online], May 27. Available: www.onenation.org/unzletter.html

Urciuoli, Bonnie. 1996. *Exposing Prejudice: Puerto Rican Experiences of Language, Race, and Class.* Boulder, CO: Westview Press.

van Dijk, Teun. 1993. *Elite Discourse and Racism.* Newbury Park, CA: Sage.

Wilson, Janet. 1997. "Audit of Hermandad Finds $500,000 Unaccounted For." *Los Angeles Times* [Online], May 22. Available: www.onenation. org/latherman.html

Winant, Howard. 1994. *Racial Conditions: Politics, Theory, Comparisons.* Minneapolis: University of Minnesota Press.

Woolard, Kathryn. 1989. "Sentences in the Language Prison." *American Ethnologist* 16: 268–78.

CHAPTER ELEVEN

Analyzing the Rhetoric of the English Only Movement

AMANDA ESPINOSA-AGUILAR
University of Wisconsin Oshkosh

The destruction of cultures and the loss of land through past colonization is familiar history to many. Most U.S. schoolchildren have heard the stories of Columbus arriving in the Caribbean, about the waves of colonizers who followed to rape the land, and about the people and cultures they encountered. We still live in a world where colonization takes place, but through very different means. Today, dominant groups see the minds of unsuspecting voters as fertile soil for planting their political agendas (i.e., government-endorsed statements, laws and practices concerning language use). Their goal now is not to colonize land, but to colonize minds through English-linguistic imperialism and xenophobic language policy, which establish English-linguistic hegemony, or through "the explicit and implicit values, beliefs, purposes, and activities . . . which contribute to the maintenance of English as a dominant language" in the United States (Phillipson 1992, 73).

In his book-length study of linguistic imperialism, Robert Phillipson (1992) explains that "the dominance of English is asserted and maintained by the establishment and continuous reconstitution of structural and cultural inequalities between English and other languages" (47). English Only (EO) and English Language Amendment (ELA) proponents employ discourses of fear to convince both Whites and minorities that multilingual U.S. citizens and immigrants, and their resistance to assimilation, are threats to the stability of the United States. Consequentially, English Only advocates are guilty of English-linguistic imperialism since they want voting Americans, in general, to support the idea that English should legally and officially become the dominant language of the United States.

The elevation of English above other languages by the government reinforces cultural inequalities representative of English-linguistic imperialism. Linguist Joshua Fishman (1988) has speculated that an ELA represents a simplistic response to "middle class Anglo fears and anxieties . . . rather than any mature grappling with the really monumental economic, social and political causes of conflict" in U.S. society (132). Many literacy experts and linguistics scholars see ELA and English Only activists as modern agents of colonialism and linguistic imperialism who rhetorically plant seeds of fear into the minds of mainstream and minority voters alike. Language educators can combat English Only rhetoric by unmasking the deceptive language used by proponents.

In the past, colonizers were blatant in their assimilation of the land, language, and cultures of the people they conquered. A colonizing mentality continues to be prominent in the United States, but now it is masked as language policy which convinces both dominant and language-minority groups of the need to legislate an official language.

To combat this insidious attempt at colonizing American minds, educators should publicly proclaim and train others to examine how the rhetoric of the ELA and English Only movement is intentionally deceptive. This essay examines the literature and influence of U.S. English, the largest, most organized special interest group that promotes an ELA. By comparing both older and more recent U.S. English literature, I will show how this group has learned to mask its rhetoric to gain support across demographic lines. Its rhetoric convinces many people, regardless of ethnicity, to accept and support legislation which promotes linguicism[1] and xenophobia, thereby devaluing ethnic cultural pride and identity. First, I explain how and why ELA advocates convince minorities and Whites to support them. In doing so, groups such as U.S. English can statistically claim that many Americans favor English-language legislation, regardless of their ethnicities. Second, I examine the rhetoric of U.S. English literature and documents found on its Web site. Next, by using U.S. House of Representatives and Senate bills, I demonstrate how U.S. English has imposed its agenda of xenophobia on unsuspecting politicians and voters. Finally, I discuss the future implications and the repercussions that imposing an official language policy will have and already has had on U.S. citizens, thereby demonstrating how Official English rhetoric promotes discrimination.

Who Supports English Only and Why Do They?

At first glance, ELA legislation appears to have national support across demographic lines. Among the reasons that mainstream Americans support this legislation are star power, nativism, and status preservation. While minorities are often convinced by these reasons, they are also concerned about being deported and feel obligated to appear patriotic toward the United States. I examine these factors in turn and conclude by looking at how gender, income, and education also play a role in who supports official language policies.

Many Whites and minorities in America seem to be swayed, whether or not we admit it, by star power. Many people will support a cause just because a popular figure does. Sponsoring organizations such as U.S. English highlight in their literature and on their Web site that they are supported by celebrities such as Arnold Schwarzenegger and Saul Bellow (U.S. English 1995b, 1). When ELA organizers ask for donations through biased pamphlets and misleading, statistic-filled bulk mailings, these successful stars have the extra money to make sizable contributions. According to James Crawford (1992), "U.S. English has spent upwards of $18 million since 1983 to promote English as the official language of the United States" (171). U.S. English is supported by solicited donations ranging from $15 to $250 per supporter. Meanwhile, scholars and educators have to face budget cuts and yearly calls by Republicans to shut down the U.S. Department of Education.

Minorities are also victims of star power. They too are convinced that if celebrities, especially minority ones, support a specific cause, they should as well. Minority attitudes are sometimes also influenced by the success of other people of color. It is no coincidence that U.S. English was founded by a person of color and has often been led by one. This sends a message that U.S. English must support people of color if "one of their own" runs it. For example, Linda Chavez was the executive director until 1988, when then-president John Tanton was unveiled as anti-immigrant and anti-Hispanic/Latino. Chilean immigrant Mauro Mujica is the current chair of U.S. English. When a person of power supports or promotes the EO movement, it is easy for ordinary citizens to accept these endorsements unquestioningly.

Nativism, or the favoring of "truly American" inhabitants over immigrants, also influences why Whites and minorities support English Only, but in a different way. Carol Schmid (1992) states, "Complaints about a breakdown in the process of assimilation seem to be especially prevalent during periods of high immigration, economic restructuring, and recession, providing fertile soil for the growth of nativism" (203). Members of ethnic groups who want to appear patriotic will demonstrate a nativist mentality, especially during key elections. A good example is the large number of people of color who voted in favor of the California citizens' initiative Proposition 187, which prevents illegal immigrants from receiving most forms of state-funded social services, including free public education, welfare, and medical care except in emergencies. According to Matloff (1994), in California's 1994 vote on Proposition 187, the rates of "yes" votes among African Americans, Asian Americans, and immigrants were near the overall statewide rate of 59 percent. Some legal immigrants support this kind of legislation because they feel they have an obligation to the country and its native inhabitants. This has led Schmid to note that, because they want to fit in, "immigrant groups [are] anxious to demonstrate their 'Americanism'" by supporting the status quo (1992, 203).

In the Proposition 187 vote, this was true especially among Latinos, the largest language minority in the United States. Fishman (1988) explains that middle-class Hispanics "must reject the charge of anti-Americanism or they must confirm it, and the only way they can reject the charge in today's climate of opinion is to vote for English Only far more frequently than do other Hispanics (29%)" (135). Over the past eighteen years, "Hispanics who were anxious to appear supportive of a popular majority group proposition" were the most likely to support ELA and anti-affirmative action legislation, such as California's Proposition 209 or Washington's Proposition 200 (Zentella 172). Under the guise of tax savings and patriotism, many states have been passing initiatives such as these which do away with bilingual education, affirmative action programs, and social services such as welfare, health care, and food stamps. The nativist desire to be seen as different and better than more recent immigrants causes some people of color to support ultimately xenophobic legislation.

Both mainstream and ethnic groups are also convinced to support EO to preserve the socioeconomic status they have developed. "Status preservation involves declining groups seek[ing] to maintain their eroding position by identifying with extremist causes" (Schmid 1992, 203). Whites are most worried that their position of dominance is slipping to the growing numbers of second-language speakers in the United States. Nativism affects Whites' status preservation because they often mistakenly believe that immigrants do not want to adapt to U.S. life. One of the more widely distributed U.S. English pamphlets claims that groups fighting the ELA represent an "anti-assimilation movement," comprising "those who would like to turn language minorities into permanent power blocs" (Wright 1992, 128). In 1996 the U.S. Bureau of the Census found that the number of non-Hispanic/Latino Whites in the United States had dropped by about 10 percent since 1990, whereas Hispanics/Latinos in the same period grew by 10 percent, Blacks by 1 percent, and Asians and American Indians by less than 1 percent. "By 2000, the non-Hispanic White proportion of the population is projected to decrease to less than 72 percent with just under 13 percent Black; over 11 percent Hispanic origin; 4 percent Asian and Pacific Islander; and less than 1 percent American Indian" (Spencer and Hollmann 1998, 8). One way to prevent Whites from losing so much status that they become minorities themselves is to approve legislation such as an ELA that will keep more minorities from taking their place. People of color will also be prevented from infringing on the status of Whites if they are prevented from voting for like-minded candidates who want to see minorities get ahead in the United States. By passing an ELA, basic democratic rights such as voting are threatened if a person has limited English proficiency. Whites maintain their dominance in U.S. society if they are the only ones with the literacy levels necessary to cast a vote.

Some minorities, who are also worried about status preservation and want to maintain their hard-earned status, will turn against each other during voting seasons. In 1994 this was demonstrated in the Latino community of California when Proposition 187 was being debated. According to a Hispanic/Latino magazine poll, up to 84 percent of Hispanics/Latinos say there are already too many immigrants coming into the United States (Laguna 1994). Some people of color are worried about losing their place in U.S. society to more recent immigrants, which makes them vote with the status quo.

Status preservation and nativism also come into play regarding bilingualism. The ideologies of those people who hold the power within a society readily influence the beliefs of those with little or none. Disempowered groups are comprised of people who very often just want to fit in, be accepted, or get ahead. In the United States, language minorities and immigrants are often disenfranchised. Those with power fuel the fears of the disempowered by bombarding them with rhetoric which suggests that if they maintain their native languages, cultures, and beliefs, they will not (and most definitely their children will not) "make it" in this country. Phillipson (1992) uses the term "apartheid inheritance" to describe Africans who believe that support for use of native languages is "intended to confine [their users] to an inferior position" in the colonized state (127). In the U.S. version of apartheid inheritance, many ethnic Americans mistakenly believe that achieving the American dream-myth implicitly requires them to support legislation that actually hurts them and requires them to give up their native language. Therefore, many of them follow the nativist idea of assimilation, which "[rejects] the contention that one [can] keep one's mother tongue, yet still be a good citizen of the United States. Learning English [is] not enough—committed immigrants [have] to cast off their alien tongues along with their alien status" (Leibowicz 1992, 105).

Besides race, gender, and income, education also affects who supports ELA legislation. Ana Celia Zentella conducted a study looking at these traits in polls and interviews conducted in 1986 and 1987 in New York City. When analyzing the data, Zentella found that in general women do not support the EO movement, noting that "there is some evidence that women are more sensitive to the social needs of language minorities" (1990, 171). Perhaps state-based ELAs have passed because female voices still lack equal representation in public arenas of power. This may be due in part to the fact that there are fewer women than men in positions such as judges, lawyers, politicians, and business leaders.

Education levels also seem to influence who supports an ELA. There is a myth in the United States that people who have more education are enlightened and concerned with civil rights and liberties. While this may have been true in the 1960s, in the current political and economic environment this is no longer the case. When it comes to education demographics, some people may be surprised to discover that Zentella's (1990) analysis of the data suggests that people who are highly educated and more financially secure are more likely to support the passage of an ELA regardless of their ethnicity:

> The level of education of those interviewed did not turn out to play its expected role, if it is assumed that those with more education would be more aware of the socio-political underpinnings of the language policy issues and the damaging repercussions of an English-only amendment. Instead, those with the least education, elementary or below, were most against the amendment (71%), and those with the most education, graduate school, were most in favor of it (57%). . . . In general, as the subjects' educational level increased, so did their pro-ELA sentiments. (171)

On a similar note, income in conjunction with race also creates division lines in the distribution of EO votes. Carol Schmid's (1992) analysis of voting trends regarding state-based ELAs in Texas and California demonstrates these trends:

> In California [in 1988], Hispanics with incomes below $10,000 [were] least likely to support Official English (19.9%), while those with incomes between $30–40,000 are most likely to do so (30.5%). By contrast, almost two in three Anglos support English as the sole official language; only California Anglos with incomes between $10–20,000 fall below the 50% mark. (204)

Significantly, people of color who are extremely poor do not seem as worried about status preservation as Whites in the same income bracket. In Schmid's (1992) study, over 60 percent of Whites with incomes under $10,000 favored an ELA. Therefore, race and income must be considered in tandem when determining who supports an ELA.

These findings regarding gender, education, and income are important to anti-ELA activists because they indicate groups of people that anti-ELA supporters can target. Educating these groups alone may result in the votes required to keep another state-based ELA, or a national one for that matter, from passing. In the next section, I show how learning to analyze the rhetoric used by groups such as U.S. English will help U.S. voters understand how an ELA promotes linguicism.

The Language and Literature of U.S. English

Because we live in a world that considers xenophobia irrational, modern colonialists such as members of U.S. English know they must mask their agenda in language that does not appear racist. In fact, the language they use has two purposes. First, the language of political correctness and diversity helps recruit support for their legislation from both in and outside ethnic communities. Ironically, politically correct rhetoric convinces some people of color to support racist agendas without realizing it. Second, EO groups use language that plays into mainstream fears of losing power and status in U.S. society to traditional minorities. As Phillipson (1992) points out, "Linguicism has taken over from racism as a more subtle way of hierarchizing social groups in the contemporary world" (241). In this section, I look at how U.S. English deliberately uses phrases and word choices which promote unfounded fear and xenophobia.

U.S. English uses polling as a propaganda tool to promote status preservation. Namely, it asks loaded questions to justify inequalities in access to government resources. In polls sent with donation requests, U.S. English asks questions such as, "Do you feel it is the U.S. taxpayer's obligation to pay for providing government services for everyone in the language of his choice?" Few Americans would answer "yes" to such a question simply because words like *obligation* and *providing* and the phrase "in the language of his choice" imply that some people are being forced to pay for services they do not use themselves. U.S. English uses these replies to create statistical percentages which suggest that 86 percent of Americans favor an ELA (U.S. English 1997, 2). Status preservation is often achieved through linguicism, which uses language as "the means for effecting or maintaining an unequal allocation of power and resources" (Phillipson 1992, 55). The rhetorical practices of groups such as U.S. English, especially in regard to language policy and planning, are designed to promote linguicism in the United States.

In the recent past, the fact sheets, pamphlets, and questionnaires distributed by U.S. English had an obviously anti-second-language-user and anti-immigrant tone. Memos, speeches, and internal correspondence released in 1986 demonstrated the bigotry of founder and one-time president of U.S. English, John Tanton, especially toward Latinos. Since then, U.S. English leadership has learned from past mistakes and toned down its language in an attempt to mask the message behind the diction. U.S. English writers spin their tarnished image by appropriating politically correct terminology. As a result, U.S. English has rallied support in even ethnic and traditionally liberal communities for passage of English Only language policies, first at the state and now at the federal level.

Yet the 1995 U.S. English fact sheets clearly demonstrate the organization's xenophobic message. They discuss almost exclusively issues of immigration, private business/employment, multilingualism, and national unity, each a sore point in the current political climate. Comparisons between the way U.S. English discussed these issues in 1995 versus in its 1997–98 online fact sheets demonstrate that the group has moved away from the previous policy of using explicitly bigoted comments to using language which masks and perpetuates myths and stereotypes about immigrants and second-language users.

One major issue discussed in the 1995 fact sheets is immigration, legal and illegal. The 1995 U.S. English pamphlet asks, "What in the world is happening to our country?" (U.S. English

1995b, 2), referring to the "fact" that too many people coming to the United States do not attempt to assimilate to "our" culture, language, and religion. Repetition of the comment "that the American taxpayer is obligated to pay for translations, teachers and multi-lingual services for immigrants who don't want to make the effort to learn our language" plays on middle-class fears. In fact, the 1995 fact sheet repeats this message four times in a pamphlet that is only five pages long! Such statements perpetuate the myth that immigrants are lazy and a burden on society, thereby creating support from bigoted and tax-frustrated Americans.

Ironically, these sentiments also gather minority support for an ELA in two ways. First, these statements criticize anti-ELA supporters for "fighting to make America officially multi-lingual" (U.S. English 1995b, 2), creating the impression that second-language users want the world to view the United States as a multilingual society. This claim has no supporting evidence and belies the many studies which show that opponents of the ELA do not necessarily support any specific language policy for the United States. It also perpetuates the fear that too many services and benefits go to ethnic people but not to mainstream Americans, resulting in reverse discrimination. Because they do not want to be seen as drains on U.S. resources, many immigrants and second-language users support an ELA.

These statements also garner ELA support from minorities by shaming non-English-speakers into abandoning their native languages in order not to become the burden they are accused of being. Minority immigrants abandon multilingualism because they are convinced by U.S. English claims that multilingualism "holds back immigrants from becoming productive citizens" and "is one of the key factors responsible for the growing chaos, disunity and disharmony festering in America today" (U.S. English 1995b). The original fact sheets went on to claim that "[t]his is bad for America, bad for our new citizens, and it's bad for you" (emphasis in original, U.S. English 1995b, 2). Since they do not want their native languages to hold them back, many minorities misguidedly support an ELA, naively believing that its passage will prove they want to succeed and fit in.

The problem with the U.S. English rhetoric highlighted above is that it assumes that all non-English-language-proficient users are new citizens, not native-born ones. Especially noteworthy in U.S. English literature is the constant use of the word *our,* because it designates immigrants and the non-English-proficient as not "us" but "them," or "the other." This of course raises the question, to whom is U.S. English referring when it uses *our* and *you?* The 1995 U.S. English pamphlet states, "the American people overwhelmingly feel that when you come to live in America, you have an obligation to learn our language" (1995b). The implication is of course that the *our*'s (the Real Americans) are pitted against the *you*'s (immigrants, anti-assimilationists, American Indians, and multilingual people), regardless of citizenship status. Left out of this picture are the millions of native-born Americans who may be monolingual in a language other than English. The use of the word *our* is plainly exclusionary.

Many native-born Americans grow up in bilingual families where English is not the primary language. My own grandmother, for example, was born in New Mexico Territory in 1903 and lived until 1996, never having learned a word of English. How was her inability to speak English "bad for you"? She raised two boys and two girls who not only spoke English but their native language as well. Of these children, two went on to serve in foreign wars such as the Korean War, one earning a Purple Heart. Clearly, my grandmother's inability to speak English was irrelevant to her loyalty and duty to family and country. Americans so easily forget that only 150 years have passed since most of Spanish-speaking southwestern America was colonized as a spoil of the Mexican-American War, with little or no regard for the linguistic, cultural, and social rights of the people already living there. The same can also be said of modern day Puerto Rico.

In the past, the language of U.S. English fact sheets was especially and explicitly biased against recent immigrants, claiming that "[i]mmigrants don't want to make the effort to learn our language." Yet, and quite ironically, this same pamphlet also claims that "English [is] the language of 97% of the people in this country" (U.S. English 1995b, 2). Does this mean that immigrants only make up 3 percent of the population? Why is U.S. English afraid of the power of so small a group? Linguistic studies show that by the third generation, immigrants have usually lost their native-language ability because the first-generation immigrants are shamed into not passing their language on to their children. Realizing the inconsistency in its message, U.S. English plays down the anti-immigrant tone in the 1997 fact sheet, claiming, "the melting pot assimilates new influences and is strengthened by them." This new language use is intended to portray U.S. English as a welcoming and sympathetic organization that has the interests of immigrants in mind. An examination of the congressional bills that U.S. English has drafted and sponsored, however, clearly demonstrates that it in fact does not have the interests of language minorities in mind. If it did, it would not be pushing for the elimination of bilingual education; instead, it would promote legislation that provided more funds to the Department of Education for more classes in English as a second language.

Another issue that U.S. English obsesses over is language use in the business sector. In its 1995 literature, for example, U.S. English uses language implying that companies whose business is conducted in more than one language were directly responsible for the excesses in illegal immigration. This naturally placed those businesses in an unpatriotic light. When asked how an ELA would affect private business, U.S. English responded that, "While private business would not be legally required to operate in English, an alternate language would clearly communicate who the business is seeking to serve" (1995a). Clearly, this language carries "us versus them" subtext and was modified in the 1997 literature to say that an ELA "does not affect the languages spoken in private businesses" (U.S. English 1997, 2). This alteration demonstrates that U.S. English continues to learn that it must be subtler in its language use if it wants to recruit support from a broader audience.

Another piece of U.S. English literature takes a negative tone in discussing the benefits of being multilingual. This fact sheet is designed as a set of questions and answers, one of which asks: "Does official English imply that there is something wrong with multilingualism?" (U.S. English 1995a). While the answer is listed as "no," it is followed by: "However, it is both inefficient and expensive for the government to be required to function in multiple languages." This response claims not to devalue the ability of individuals to "function" in many languages, yet in the same breath declares that for the government (which is made up of individuals) to do so is both inefficient and expensive. What could possibly be "right" about that? The way this question and answer are set up provides a clear message that those who are bilingual are a drain on the "rest of us." U.S. English likes to put the onus of excessive government spending at the doorstep of immigrants. The 1997 U.S. English fact sheet says, "the designation of official English will eliminate the needless duplication of government services in multiple languages. Government operations will be simplified" (U.S. English 1997, 1). It even goes so far as to claim that "[m]oney formerly spent on multi-lingual services can instead provide immigrants with the assistance they need—classes to teach them English." Doing away with multilingual services will not reduce the costs of funding English-proficiency classes. But what this comment fails to even address or acknowledge is that millions of native-born Americans are multilingual and use these services. Moreover, this strategy contradicts the received wisdom of teachers, scholars, and researchers of language use and civil liberties. The Linguistic Society of America, the National Council of Teachers of English, the Modern Language Association, and the College Composition and Communication's Language Policy Committee have not only passed anti-ELA resolutions, but they advocate multilingualism for all U.S. citizens. Yet ELA proponents claim that monolingualism is best despite many findings to the contrary.

U.S. English has also succeeded in perpetuating the myth that the unity of the United States is at stake if an ELA is not passed. This myth permeates the language of the actual bills H.R. 123 and H.R. 1005. EO activists claim that without an official language, the American people will become divided along language lines, causing "severe damage to our nation's unity" (U.S. English 1995b). They present this claim using fear tactics and logical fallacies that convince many uncritical people that racial problems in the United States come from being multilingual. Much of the research in applied linguistics, language planning, and literacy shows that this argument is specious at best (Phillipson 1992, 230). David F. Marshall and Roseann Dueñas González (1990), for instance, note that "attempts to force language homogeneity for reasons of national unity are doomed to be counterproductive, and will inevitably cause only increased disunity" (45). Among many other scholars, Kellman (1971) has shown that "the development or establishment of a common language . . . may well create inequities and meet with resistances and may hamper, rather than enhance, . . . unity" (37).

U.S. English's 1995 fact sheet is so bent on promoting this false unity that it writes that those fighting the ELA "are doing severe damage to the unity of our nation" six times in the four-page document (1995a). This is not a topic that U.S. English is willing to abandon. In fact, the 1997 fact sheet says that because of government-sponsored multilingual services, "immigrants fail to learn English and separate into linguistic enclaves. This division of the United States into separate language groups contributes to racial and ethnic conflicts." This paragraph further claims that "[d]esignating English as the official language will halt this harmful process," another fallacious statement. Study after study has found that "rather than preserving feelings of community, . . . the English Only movement is more likely to breed disharmony and intergroup tension" than solve or prevent it (Schmid 1992, 209).

While it is nice for U.S. English (1995b) to claim or wish that "a shared language is the common bond that promotes the understanding of racial and cultural differences," the fact remains that this is nothing more than an unrealistic dream. Where is the proof to contradict all of the academic studies to the contrary? African Americans and Euro-Americans, for example, have been speaking varieties of English in the United States for centuries, and how unified are they? Robert Phillipson (1992) makes this point best: "National unity is not something that any language can guarantee, just as proclaiming a single official language cannot wish away a multilingual reality" (283).

ELA legislation is no more than a Band-Aid applied to already existing ethnic tensions in an unequal society that likes to think it has made many strides, when it has not. Racial tensions in the United States will not go away by mandating legislation that makes the use of only one language acceptable and legally binding. All such legislation does is fan the flames of intolerance and lend legitimacy to the racist cries of "Speak English, this is America!" and "Go back where you came from." EO and ELA legislation only promotes greater polarization and increased interethnic hostility, just the opposite of what Official English advocates and H.R. 123 and H.R. 1005 claim are their primary goals.

Because U.S. English members helped draft the original version of H.R. 123, it is important to examine how pieces of this legislation may have convinced the public and politicians that no harm could come from its passage into law. The language of this and other proposed laws presents hegemonic arguments, which Antonio Gramsci once defined as dominant ideas "which can be presented plausibly as being in the interests of the whole people, of the nation" (qtd. in Phillipson 1992, 74). The next section of this essay examines only a few paragraphs of H.R. 123 and H.R. 1005 to demonstrate the appropriation of the language of inclusion to exclude multilingual citizens from public services in the United States.

English as the Official Language of the United States

In 1995, U.S. English helped sponsor the introduction of House Bill 123, which if passed would declare English the official language of the United States. Less than one year later, in August of 1996, H.R. 123, now named the English Language Empowerment Act, was passed in the House. Since most Americans do speak English, and because the name of the bill makes it sound positive, it should come as no surprise that the House voted in its favor. But a close examination of the ideas, wording, and organization of H.R. 123 demonstrates that it not only does not empower anyone, but in its new form, H.R. 1005, this bill also violates the constitutional rights of U.S. citizens who speak English as a second language.

Since members of U.S. English helped write both H.R. 123 and H.R. 1005, they easily managed to include in them the unity agenda. As a result, both bills repeat almost verbatim the 1995 U.S. English fact sheets' fallacious wording and rally of unity, which is no more logical now than it was then. Section 101, finding number 4 of the bill states, "in order to preserve unity in diversity and to prevent division along linguistic lines, the United

States should maintain a language common to all people" (H.R. 123, §101.[4]).

According to section 2, number 6 of the H.R. 123, "the purpose of this Act is to help immigrants better assimilate and take full advantage of economic and occupational opportunities in the United States." The bill contains no suggestions (or provision) for how assimilation will lead to jobs. This statement also assumes that immigrants are not assimilating on their own, and that mandating English-language use will help immigrants assimilate. Nothing in the bill, however, indicates how the act will help immigrants assimilate, unless forcing them to lose their native language is what is meant by *helping* or *assimilation.*

In 1995 U.S. English claimed that "foreign language instruction [would not] be affected in any way. . . . The purpose of bilingual education, that of teaching non-English proficient (NEP) children English, will be strengthened" (U.S. English 1995b, 2). H.R. 123 took up the U.S. English position to "support the use of effective, transitional bilingual education programs that quickly move LEP students into the mainstream." Both the 1997 U.S. English fact sheet and H.R. 123 claim that "any monetary savings derived from the enactment of this title should be used for the teaching of the English language to non-English speaking immigrants." Finding number eight, section two, of H.R. 123 also claims that "the use of a single common language . . . will promote efficiency and fairness to all people." But again, isn't it fallacious to claim that this act will broaden immigrants' economic and occupational opportunities, given that H.R. 1005 eliminates both the bilingual voters act (the Voting Rights Act of 1965) and bilingual education programs?

H.R. 123 is careful to note that it is not intended in any way "to discriminate against or restrict the rights of any individual in the [United States]." If this is true, why does H.R. 123 only "preserv[e] use of Native Alaskan or Native American Languages (as defined in the Native American Languages Act)?" Why does the more current bill, H.R. 1005, repeal the Bilingual Education Act, call for the termination of the Office of Bilingual Education and Minority Languages Affairs in the U.S. Department of Education, and repeal the Voting Rights Act of 1965? Isn't this discrimination? Why is one family of non-English languages protected and not the rest? Since H.R. 123 and 1005 also repeal the Voting Rights Act, citizens whose English proficiency is limited are denied the right of democratic participation. How can these bills not be discriminatory toward non-English-speakers when they repeal the most basic, fundamental right of people belonging to a democracy, the right to vote?

Unity, integration, prevention of discrimination, and equal opportunity are the key phrases repeated in both U.S. English literature and the bills it has sponsored and helped draft. Given the bill's language, the House may have approved H.R. 123 in order to be part of the politically correct bandwagon. But this democratic talk is a cover for an anti-immigration, xenophobic, linguistically imperialistic agenda. Ana Celia Zentella's (1990) study found that "[t]hose who [are] given the opportunity to consider the possible repercussions of official English amendments for education, voting rights, and public safety . . . are more likely to reject the ELA if they understand its negative implications" (167). It is our duty as citizens to inform ourselves, colleagues, friends, and legislators of the discrimination that results from passing this kind of bill. If voters had understood what their representatives were really voting on, they might have urged them not to support H.R. 123 or H.R. 1005. But the U.S. House of Representatives passed the English Language Empowerment Act on August 1, 1996, by a vote of 259–169.

Implications and Conclusions

Over six years ago, in the essay "Who Supports Official English, and Why?" Zentella (1990) made much the same case I have in this chapter—that it is up to teachers, scholars, parents, and voters to combat racist language-planning policies. She wrote, "The tactics, techniques, and wording of the proposed laws, and the associated campaign thrusts, must be analyzed and understood . . . . The challenge is fivefold: To clarify the wording, explain the repercussions, calm the fearful, uncover the hidden agenda, and unmask the bigots" (177). Unfortunately, her call to action has been largely ignored, as evidenced by the fact that when Zentella wrote those words only eighteen states had Official English laws;

as of 1998, that number has grown to twenty-three. When a modified version of H.R. 123 was sent up to the U.S. Senate (as S.R. 323) in February 1997, it was never voted on. If S.R. 323 and the newly revised H.R. 1005 pass, the entire country has only a presidential veto to prevent legislated discrimination from returning to the United States Constitution. S.R. 323 now has 110 cosponsors. While it is not expected to pass in the Senate, and President Clinton has promised to veto it if it does, this may be yet another empty promise, given the president's record for flip-flopping on politically charged issues.

A major problem with the Official English movement is that it is not led or informed by anyone trained in language planning, applied linguistics, cognitive psychology, TESOL, bilingual education or ESL, rhetoric, social science, or literacy/language theory. Too often politicians and the general public cast their votes and make decisions and legislation on issues they know nothing about. In January 1997, the National Council of Teachers of English (NCTE) reintroduced the English Plus Resolution, first introduced in 1995, back into the first session of the 105th Congress, and a similar resolution was passed in May 1998. The latter is the only legislative counter to measures such as the bills discussed above. Among its many claims, the House resolution "recognize[s] the importance of multilingualism to vital American interests and individual rights, and oppose[s] English Only measures and other restrictionist language measures" (M.Con.Res. 4. 1997). Ever since the Makerere Report was released in 1961, linguists have known that English is not best taught monolingually; that the ideal teacher of English is not a native speaker; that the more and earlier English is taught does not always produce better results; and that if other languages are used in instruction, standards of English will not drop (Phillipson 1992, 185). It is time to get these facts out to the general public.

A February 1997 issue of *The Council Chronicle* updates the NCTE membership on the fight in the U.S. Supreme Court on the constitutionality of the ELA passed in Arizona. Specifically, passage of any ELA contradicts the 1923 Supreme Court case *Meyer v. Nebraska,* which ruled, "The protection of the Constitution extends to all; to those who speak other languages as well as to those born with English on the tongue." In the *Chronicle* article, Geneva Smitherman, chair of the Language Policy Committee of the Conference on College Composition and Communication, says the interest in such legislation "in this country that touts itself as the seat of democracy" (qtd. in Coombs 1997, 3) is ironic at best. During her presentation at the 1996 NCTE Annual Convention, Smitherman noted that

> fear is partly behind the official English movement—fear among the White majority who are seeing their numbers decline while Latino, African American, American Indian, Asian, and Pacific Islander populations grow. . . . [T]he economic environment in the U.S., in which unemployment hits even the most highly trained, well-educated workers, has created a "fear that limited resources will make it impossible for everyone to have a slice of the American dream pie." (qtd. in Coombs 1997, 3)

In this environment, people of color become easy scapegoats, Smitherman says, "especially when their language marks them as 'the other.'" Although Latinos are often the target of these unsubstantiated fears, it is not only the linguistic traditions of Spanish speakers that are threatened by Official English. This point needs to be made clear to the voting public. ELA legislation is written so that no languages other than English will be supported, funded, or promoted by any sector of the U.S. government.

In one of its original pamphlets, U.S. English claimed, "When enough citizens stand together and speak out together on an issue, the politicians listen." We need to be like U.S. English supporters who contact their elected officials to sway their votes. We need to sign petitions and create sound bites that inform the public at large of the implications of a national ELA. We need to convince the public that English is not now, nor has it ever been, threatened by multilingualism. We need to promote the economic, social, and professional benefits of being a speaker of many languages. We need to be those citizens who let our politicians, colleagues, friends, family, students, and parents know that U.S. educators will neither support this legislation nor reelect those who do.

Note

1. *Linguicism* is defined by Phillipson (1992) as "ideologies, structures, and practices which are used to legitimate, effectuate, and reproduce an unequal division of power and resources (both material and immaterial) between groups which are defined as the basis of language" (47).

Works Cited

Coombs, Kate. 1997. "Technical Problems Derail English Only Case in Supreme Court." *The Council Chronicle* 6(3): 3.

Crawford, James. 1992. "What's Behind Official English?" In James Crawford, ed., *Language Loyalties: A Source Book on the Official English Controversy.* Chicago: University of Chicago Press. 171–77.

Fishman, Joshua. 1988. "'English Only': Its Ghosts, Myths, and Dangers." *International Journal of the Sociology of Language* 74: 125–40.

H.Con.Res.4. 1997. English Plus Resolution, Jan. 7.

H.R. 123. 1997. Bill Emerson English Language Empowerment Act of 1997, Jan. 6.

H.R. 1005. 1997. A bill to amend Title 4, United States Code, to declare English as the official language of the Government of the United States, Mar. 11.

Kellman, H. C. 1971. "Language as an Aid and Barrier to Involvement in the National System." In Joan Rubin and Bjorn H. Jernudd, eds., *Can Language Be Planned? Sociological Theory and Practice for Developing Nations.* Honolulu: University of Hawaii Press. 21–51.

Laguna, Jesse. 1994. "Latinos Want a Tighter Border, Too." *LA Times,* Sept. 23.

Leibowicz, Joseph. 1992. "Official English: Another Americanization Campaign?" In James Crawford, ed., *Language Loyalties: A Source Book on the Official English Controversy.* Chicago: University of Chicago Press. 101–11.

Marshall, David F., and Roseann Dueñas González. 1990. "Una Lingua, Una Patria? Is Monolingualism Beneficial or Harmful to a Nation's Unity?" In Karen L. Adams and Daniel T. Brink, eds., *Perspectives on*

Official English: The Campaign for English as an Official Language of the USA. Berlin: Mouton de Gruyter. 29–51.

Matloff, Norman. 1994. "How Immigration Harms Minorities." *LA Times*, Oct. 11.

Phillipson, Robert. 1992. *Linguistic Imperialism*. New York: Oxford University Press.

Schmid, Carol. 1992. "The English Only Movement: Social Bases of Support and Opposition among Anglos and Latinos." In James Crawford, ed., *Language Loyalties: A Source Book on the Official English Controversy*. Chicago: University of Chicago Press. 202–9.

Spencer, Gregory, and Frederick W. Hollmann. 1998. "National Population Projections." *Population Profile of the United States: 1997*. Current Population Reports, Series P23-194. U.S. Bureau of the Census. Washington: GPO.

S.R. 236. 1998. 105th Cong., 2nd sess. May 22.

U.S. English. 1995a. *Common Questions about Official English*. Flier.

———. 1995b. *Should English Be the Official Language of America?* Flier.

———. 1997. *Why Is Official English Necessary?* Flier.

Wright, Guy. 1992. "U.S. English." In James Crawford, ed., *Language Loyalties: A Source Book on the Official English Controversy*. Chicago: University of Chicago Press. 127–29.

Zentella, Ana Celia. 1990. "Who Supports Official English and Why? The Influence of Social Variables and Questionnaire Methodology." In Karen L. Adams and Daniel T. Brink, eds., *Perspectives on Official English: The Campaign for English as an Official Language of the USA*. Berlin: Mouton de Gruyter. 161–77.

IV

OFFICIAL ENGLISH, OFFICIAL LANGUAGE, AND THE WORLD

It has been a tradition in the literature on language policy to include comparison and analysis of the language policies of other multilingual communities in the world. Examples have been deployed on both sides: proponents of Official English cite examples of national division and ethnic conflict to argue that without a strong single language gluing them together, nations, as a rule, fall apart. Opponents of Official English also cite examples of how centralized and oppressive language policies, rather than multilingualism, cause division. To continue this tradition, we have included three essays that approach English Only from an international perspective. Each of these essays, however, is unique in that it does not simply follow the pattern of using examples from other countries.

Robert B. Kaplan and Richard B. Baldauf Jr. provide an excellent update on Official English legislation in the United States, and also present a host of valuable reasons why these policies, if adopted at the federal level, are likely to cause problems. They view languages as complex ecological systems that interact with their social environment in complex ways. Language use, just like living organisms, is hard to regulate or standardize. English is a language of many varieties that are spoken in the United States and all over the world. Some of these varieties respond to changes in English spoken in the United States; some of them do not. In addition, the United States is already a multilingual culture comprised of eclectic cities like Los Angeles, where more than one hundred communities of different languages coexist. To enforce any kind of standard or official English in the United States and in those parts of the world where U.S. English is already regarded as "standard" would take more than a presidential signature. Such legislation would place on the U.S. government the burden of defining what exactly standard official English is, and would include covering the costs of its enforcement through education and publication of guidelines.

Although English Only proponents do not usually consider the global impact of such policies, their ideas have already served as a model in Slovakia, where legislators, advised by Official U.S. English advocates, passed law on an official state language. It is ironic that the exceptionally stringent and oppressive restrictions on minority-language use in Slovakia, which hit the largest minority population—Hungarians—particularly hard, were justified on the grounds that they follow the U.S. example. Thus the United States has become an accomplice in facilitating policy that the United States is expected to condemn for its violation of civil rights. The Slovak government's statutes require that people change their names and that all foreign-language programs be banned from the media unless they are translated, just to name a few of the consequences of enforcing an official language in a multilingual region. Even more ironic, these restrictive measures are being implemented in eastern Europe, where the newly elected democratic governments are supposed to restore civil rights that the former communist regimes had disregarded.

The other two essays in this section focus on countries where the restoration of a democratic and free social order brought about policy that is extremely tolerant and supportive of multilingualism. Geneva Smitherman's chapter relates how South Africa reinstated local languages to official status after the oppressive apartheid regime was over. But she tells another interesting story, this one about the history of African American Vernacular English (AAVE) in the United States. Just like the languages of black communities in South Africa, the languages of the enslaved African population in the United States were suppressed, devalorized, and declared substandard. This phenomenon emerged as a concomitant of colonialization in both countries. The history of the black population in the United States is a history of internal colonialization that, after the end of slavery and the triumph of the civil rights movement, is still part of this country's social reality. The only difference is that now linguistic colonialization functions in place of the more brutal physical forms of deprivation and subjugation. Smitherman's chapter places the Ebonics debate in the context of internal colonialization, and her insightful parallels with South African history and language policy lead to the conclusion that the U.S. black community should continue its struggle for "linguistic democratization and empowerment for those on the margins" (p. 341).

Cynthia Miguélez tells another story of "linguistic normalization" following political democratization. After democracy replaced a forty-year period of dictatorship, Spain began working out the details of a language policy based on a sense of regional identity and pride in the diverse linguistic heritage of the country. The democratic Spanish government made significant efforts to support the regional languages and promote bilingualism by publishing its official documents in regional languages and subsidizing cultural events and activities performed in these languages. Finally, and most important, bilingual education and programs in both the official *castellano* and the regional dialects were established to promote bilingualism at all levels. Although government involvement in these programs may seem unusually high by U.S. standards, the Spanish example has some important lessons for the United States. First, the languages protected by language policy in Spain are regional languages whose usefulness is limited outside their regional boundaries. The languages that bilingual individuals in the United States speak are universal languages used in business, diplomacy, and travel all over the world. Yet in Spain the general sentiment is that bilingualism is an asset, whereas in the United States bilingualism is considered suspicious. If the policies adopted by Spain seem unrealistic in the United States, it is mostly because this country does not willingly recognize or respect those individuals who have accomplished the "significant and admirable" achievement of becoming bilingual. The United States may never have a language policy that actively promotes the maintenance of any language other than English, but neither should it adopt a language policy that would make the development of respect and recognition for bilingualism more difficult.

Chapter Twelve

Not Only English: English Only and the World

Robert B. Kaplan
University of Southern California

Richard B. Baldauf Jr.
University of Sydney

The end of the second decade of the English Only controversy is rapidly approaching; it was in 1981 the late Senator S. I. Hayakawa introduced the first resolution to amend the United States Constitution to designate English the official language of the United States (Senate Joint Resolution 72). For nearly twenty years, the Congress of the United States, some thirty-five individual states, a number of municipalities, many professional associations, as well as the general populace have all been engaged in trying to decide whether English should be declared the sole official language of the United States. Although twenty-one states (as of 1999) and some municipalities have enacted English Only legislation, with some going so far as to prohibit the state from doing business in any other language, a smaller number (six) have enacted "English Plus" legislation.[1] English Only legislation is also pending in other states. The matter remains open for continuing debate; indeed, there were at least four bills on the issue pending before the 105th Congress.[2]

The principal actor (though by no means the only one) on the English Only side of the debate has been an organization called U.S. English, founded in 1983. In 1995 that organization claimed 600,000 members and had an annual operating budget of $7 million. The stated goals of U.S. English are to make English the official language of the United States and to oppose bilingual education, the provision of a bilingual ballot, and bilingual services in the public and private sectors (see, e.g., Peña 1991). The other side of the debate has been less centrally organized, but critics of English Only have raised many counterarguments to the notion that there is a need for the enactment of an official language constitutional amendment (e.g., Crawford 1992; Daniels 1990; Thomas 1996). We outline here a few of the more obvious of these arguments to provide a context for what we believe are the largely overlooked wider implications of enacting English Only legislation on the status of English outside the United States. Some counterarguments advanced include:

1. It is unnecessary for the United States to designate a de jure official language since it already has a de facto official language. Nations declare de jure official languages because such languages are seen as powerful symbols of national unity, but no one in the United States seeks separation from the federal union, and thus no such symbol of national unity is needed beyond the unifying influence of de facto English-language hegemony.

2. In a polity as linguistically heterogeneous as the United States, the nation should—for economic, political, humanitarian, and social reasons—be exploiting its linguistic diversity, not trying to suppress it. Indeed, in a polity as linguistically heterogeneous as the United States, the declaration of a de jure official language would be oppressive, depriving speakers of languages other than English of the few rights they are guaranteed by enforcing an Official English linguistic hegemony.[3] Marshall (1986) argues that an English Only law might be more divisive than the alleged linguistic heterogeneity it seeks to suppress.

3. Crawford (1992, ix) has suggested that the English Only movement is merely a new guise for historical ethnic intolerance. It is already the case—in the areas of police activity and the judiciary—that the rights of non-native speakers of English are infringed, since police are not obligated to administer the Miranda rights in languages other than English,

and since presiding justices have the authority to decide whether an accused individual is entitled to an interpreter.[4] It is also the case that the civil service is not required to provide services in languages other than English[5] and that key sectors of society—for example, banking (Kaplan, Touchstone, and Hagstrom 1995; Touchstone, Kaplan, and Hagstrom 1996)— essentially operate monolingually in English.

4. English Only legislation creates important issues for geographers and mapmakers as well: what is to be done about states, cities, streets, and various geographic features which are named with words drawn from other languages—e.g., the states of *California* and *Connecticut*; the cities of *Los Angeles*, *San Francisco*, and *Pierre*; the geographic features *Abrazo* Drive, the *Hoh* River, and *Putah* Creek? Many more issues and examples could be adduced. As important and interesting as the lengthy and somewhat acrimonious discussion has been on the domestic scene, however, a number of significant factors have been largely overlooked, each having a direct bearing on the status of English outside the United States. These issues are related to the domestic impact of official status on the English language and to the global implications of adopting an English Only model.

The Domestic Impact of Official Status on the English Language

First, let us consider the implications of official status on the language itself. What has been lost in the domestic debate is that English is a world language, widely spoken as both a first and a second language, and really no longer the exclusive property of any one group of English-language speakers. It is conservatively estimated that there are 573 million speakers of English, about 235 million of whom are second-language speakers (Crystal 1997, 56–60; see also Crystal 1995), and that it is the latter group which is growing most rapidly. These figures understate the importance of English as a communicative medium since many of the second-language speakers are people of status in their own societies.

While British colonization (in the nineteenth century) and U.S. economic power (in the twentieth century) have underpinned the growth of English (Grabe and Kaplan 1986; Kaplan and Baldauf 1997), it can be argued that growth in English has also come about through successful competition with other languages (Wardhaugh 1987). A factor in this growth has been that English is not standardized in the same way that, for example, French is; that is, English is a pluricentric language: African American Vernacular English, Australian English, British English, Caribbean English, Indian English, Singaporean English, Southern U.S. English, and Zambian English, to name just a few, are all accepted as the same language. While some varieties have more prestige than others, the range of acceptable variation due to the lack of a central standard has meant that many peoples have claimed English as their own. The lack of a single national identity for English also makes what Crystal (1997) calls "world standard" English more acceptable as an international language (136–39). Thus there has developed a balance between "internationalism"—the need to keep the varieties of English mutually intelligible—and "identity"—the need for varieties to be different enough to represent national identities. Were American English to be standardized, it could seriously upset this balance.

This is not to say, however, that these varieties do not compete. Although it would be difficult to demonstrate beyond doubt, Great Britain and the United States have been engaged in a significant competition for regions of influence—regions in which either British English is emulated (largely in the former British Commonwealth, but increasingly in eastern Europe) or American English is emulated. More recently, Australia (e.g., in Hong Kong and Southeast Asia) and Canada have entered into this international competition. All of these English-speaking nations have competed through their agencies for international development—e.g., Britain's Overseas Development Administration (ODA) and the British Council, the U.S. Agency for International Development (AID) and the United States Information Agency (USIA—its overseas offices known as USIS), the Australian Overseas Service Bureau (OSB) and the Australian Agency for International Development (AusAID), the Canadian International Development Agency (CIDA),[6] and even some agencies of nations where English is not the first language, such as the Swedish Development Cooperation Agency (SIDA). By investing to varying degrees in development projects in less developed nations around the world, such initiatives almost always carry a component of teaching English as a foreign language (e.g., Ablin 1991; Crooks and Crewes 1995; Kaplan 1995, 1997; Kenny and Savage 1997).

The competition among the worldwide varieties of English forecasts a major question regarding the imposition of English as an official national language—that is, should English at some point become the official language of the United States, which English (or whose English) should it be? Once English is declared the official language of the United States, it will be necessary to specify which variety of English will be official and which variety will take precedence in matters of dispute. Will it be the English of Jimmy Carter, of Howard Cosell, of Walter Cronkite, of Lyndon Baines Johnson, of John F. Kennedy, or of some other famous speaker of "American" English? Will it be the dialect of New York, or of Texas, or of South Dakota, or of California? Will it be a variety of African American Vernacular English? Will it be some linguist's artificial creation? What indeed will be the "standard" English language?[7] It will be necessary not only to designate an official variety, which will take precedence any time a question of authority occurs, but also to designate an agency to adjudicate disputes. In other words, we will need a "language academy" charged to preserve the purity of the official variety; to develop spelling guides, dictionaries, and grammars of that variety (no more publisher competition for the dictionary market); and to rule on questions of authority. It may also be necessary to create a "linguistic police" to enforce the universal use of the approved standard variety.[8] As language change of this magnitude will take decades to fully implement, how will the United States deal with the long period of instability?

The designation of an official variety and of an agency to guard its official status will inevitably have an impact on how English as a second or foreign language is taught worldwide. The British agencies have been careful, even in the absence of a formal language agency, to promulgate "Oxbridge English" as the prestige variety—witness the English pronunciation and spelling of generations of East Indian speakers of English (who, incidentally, constitute only about one per cent of the Indian population). Once there is a standard variety in the United States, the dictionaries to be exported to non-English-speaking areas will have to represent the official version of the language, and a whole new generation of textbooks designed to promulgate that variety will need to be created. In the past, the standardization practices of publishers and broadcasters have sufficed, but that cannot be the case once an official variety is chosen. More important, since the English-language teaching community represents one of the major "exports" of the United States in terms of bringing in new money and helping with the balance of trade, which English will the United States export? Who will decide?

The cost of such an enterprise is potentially staggering, not only in terms of the direct expenditure on the creation and maintenance of an agency, but also indirectly in terms of the impact on the huge English-teaching, textbook publishing, and dictionary publishing industries. Undoubtedly, multitudes of new jobs will be created, but at the same time a multitude of existing jobs will be made redundant (as well as a multitude of teachers whose variety is "nonstandard"). It will require a team of economists to undertake appropriate cost-benefit analyses to determine whether the alternative represented by an official U.S. variety of English is really cost effective.

The Domestic Impact of English Only on Special Language Groups

English Only also raises questions with regard to special-language groups in places where the United States has international obligations. Coulombe (1993) points out that individual language rights are confirmed under the United Nations Charter in sections 26 and 27, which respectively guarantee civil and political rights without discrimination based on language and affirm the right of linguistic minorities to use their own language among themselves.

Therefore English Only raises interesting questions about the use of the indigenous languages of the United States. Obviously, there are implications for Native American languages such as Hopi, Mohawk, Navajo, Sioux, Zuni, and so on. Are these languages also to be prohibited? What are the treaty rights associated with each of these languages, and do they provide the basis for possible legal challenges before the Supreme Court? Some of the more recent legislative drafts exempt Native American languages, but the exemption is symbolic rather than substantive.[9] Navajo speakers can, for example, speak Navajo to each other, but with who else and in what registers will they be able to use their language? Will the civil service recognize Navajo? Will legislation in the state of Arizona? As Crawford (1992) observes, "In an English Only America, only English speakers would enjoy equal rights."(175).

Another interesting question deals with the languages of the hearing-impaired community. A segment of the hearing-impaired community in the United States advocates the use of American Sign Language (ASL), which is clearly not exclusively a variety of English. Will it be proscribed? Another segment of the hearing-impaired community in the United States supports the use of signed English. That segment has, perhaps mistakenly and in desperation, turned to U.S. English for support, though U.S. English has not really considered the needs of the hearing-impaired community. Even so, if English is the official language of the United States, will people with hearing impairments be required to sign only the standard variety of signed English? Alternatively, will they be forced to lip read and be taught to "speak" the new standard? These questions are not only about language, but also about the basic human rights of hearing-impaired individuals to practice their cultural heritage. Under an English Only regime, would the United States be guilty of what Phillipson (1988) has called linguacide?

The Domestic Impact on the English Ecological System

Languages are not isolates; rather, they constitute complex ecological systems (Kaplan and Baldauf 1997; Mühlhäusler 1995). Modifications of English in the United States will have significant ripple effects on the varieties of Englishes around the world—

even Australian, British, Canadian, and New Zealand Englishes. Already efforts to reduce sexism and other social problems in domestic usage have had worldwide effects and in some cases have spawned significant debates about whether to follow suit; for instance, the gender-neutralization of U.S. English has not been widely (or happily) accepted among some speakers of English in the Middle East, Africa, Southeast Asia, or East Asia. National (and local) borders—the borders of nation-states (or of ethnic communities)—have no reality in terms of language issues. Borders are arbitrary geopolitical demarcations; speakers of the same language live on both sides of virtually every border and create dialect border-bands, which frustrate language purists. What is to be done with speakers of Hungarian who live in Slovakia, speakers of German who live in Denmark (or Danish speakers in Germany), or speakers living in literally hundreds of other cross-border populations? That problem can be replicated across the multilingualism of the United States. Where is the precise border between Spanish speakers in East Los Angeles and the neighboring English-speaking, Korean-speaking, Black-English-speaking, Chinese-speaking, Japanese-speaking communities in Los Angeles? Los Angeles encompasses more than one hundred communities of speakers of languages other than English. What effort and what cost will be required to convert that multitude of people into monolingual English speakers of the correct variety?

The problem of establishing a "standard" variety, of maintaining that standard variety through multitudinous publications (indeed, of maintaining the "purity" of that variety), of the dissemination of that standard variety, of the training of teachers to teach that standard variety, of the implications of exporting that standard variety worldwide, of the impact of the existence of that standard variety on all the other indigenous Englishes that have developed around the world (e.g., Filipino English, Indian English, Hong Kong English, Japanese English, etc.)—these are complex issues not solved simply because the president signs a piece of legislation. Incidentally, it is unlikely that Congress will attach a large sum of money to any such legislation to enable its enforcement. How will the huge costs of implementation be met? Will a user-pays principle then have to be applied, meaning that the burden of cost will be put back on the states and on those whose English is nonstandard—often those who can least afford the costs?

The Global Implications of the English Only Model

The English Only movement has, however, had another global impact. Though not yet enacted as federal legislation in the United States, the model propounded by U.S. English has already been emulated elsewhere. On November 15, 1995, the National Council of the Slovak Republic enacted the Law on the State Language of the Slovak Republic.[10] This law took effect as of January 1, 1996 (except section 10, dealing with fines for violations of the law, which took effect one year later on January 1, 1997). Under the terms of this law, the citizens of the Slovak Republic no longer have the right to use a language of their choice in virtually any interaction between citizens and public officials—in local government, on buses, in teachers' meetings, in schools, in worship, in church bulletins, in street signs, in the presentation of cultural events, in legal documents, in employment, in verbal contacts with health care workers, and so forth. Foreign audiovisual works directed to children less than twelve years of age must be dubbed in the official state language. All broadcasts on local television and radio must be in the state language. Catalogs for museums, libraries, and art galleries and programs for movie houses, theatrical productions, concerts, and other public cultural events must be in the state language. All signs and advertisements (in shops, sports grounds, restaurants, etc.) must be in the state language. Place names of communities inhabited by Hungarians are to be immediately "Slovakized."[11] According to articles 9 and 10 of the 1995 Slovakian language law, enforcement is delegated to the Ministry of Culture, which has the right not only to enforce the conditions of the use of the state language but also to levy fines for violations. Fines are exorbitant; violations of the restrictions on signs in shops and restaurants may be levied to a maximum of 50,000 Slovak crowns, and violations of the broadcasting regulations may be fined at the level of half a million crowns.[12] Ironically, the fine for desecrating the Slovak flag is a mere 3,000 crowns (Kontra 1996, 357). What does all this mean? According to Nunberg (1997):

> Since Slovakia became an independent state a few years ago [1990], the Slovak majority has been imposing increasingly stringent language restrictions on the Hungarian minority. Hungarian place names must be changed to Slovak spellings, all official business must be transacted in Slovak even in districts that are almost entirely Hungarian-speaking, and so forth. It's a familiar pattern in that part of the world with its virulent ethnic antagonisms.
>
> But in this case, the Slovakians have insisted that their policies are in fact following the lead of the United States. The Slovak State Language Law cites the example of English Only legislation in America. But the similarities have to leave us wondering.[13] What if it's we who are becoming more like them. . . .
>
> The entire [English Only] movement comes to seem tainted with the defensive character we associate with linguistic nationalism in such places as Slovakia. Not that the two movements will ever be the same. But it gets harder to tell them apart. (A9)

To put the situation into context, over 10 percent of Slovakia's population—nearly 600,000 people—are ethnic Hungarians, indigenous largely to southern Slovakia.[14] They constitute the majority in hundreds of localities. Since 1990, under the previous law on the official language of the Slovak Republic, in communities having at least a 20 percent minority population, the minority language could be (and was) used in all official communications. The new 1995 law vacates the earlier law. In effect, the more than half a million Hungarians who have resided in what is contemporary Slovakia for a millennium[15] are now required immediately to become competent speakers of Slovak and to surrender their use of Hungarian. The Hungarians in Slovakia, the Hungarian Academy of Sciences in Budapest, the Hungarian government, and literally dozens of professional linguistic bodies across the world have protested the Slovak Republic's new language law.

Kontra (1996) documents direct contact between the drafters of the Slovak language law and U.S. English. A "justification" attached to an October 1995 draft of the Slovak language law states:[16]

In drafting the law on the state language, we took into consideration regulations having the force of law in several European states, primarily France, Lithuania, Belgium, and Holland.[17] The following information from the USA is characteristic: Republican Congressional Representative [Toby] Roth [R-Wisconsin][18] submitted a bill to Congress whereby the official language of the USA would be English. The law aims to simultaneously terminate bilingual education in elementary and secondary schools, as well as multilingual election materials. In his opinion, transactions related to obtaining American citizenship also have to be conducted in English. The proposal already has 150 supporters, and should be debated and voted still this year. [Didn't happen!] In addition to proclaiming English as the official language, the bill also states that English is the preferred form of contact for USA citizens, which the government will also support. Employee contact with citizens will also occur in English. It is the compulsory task of citizens to learn to write, read, and speak English to the best of their physical and intellectual abilities. Institutions dealing with naturalization will demand that applicants for citizenship have a standard knowledge of English. (cited in Kontra 1996, 359)

A delegation from U.S. English visited Slovakia to meet the drafters of the Slovakian law in September 1995. According to a story in the major Hungarian newspaper in Slovakia on October 5, 1995, the president of U.S. English, Mauro Mujica, tried to convince his audience that in the United States, "the academic performance of pupils in bilingual education programs is poor; such children are left behind in social competition and are stuck in ghettoes" (qtd. in Kontra 1996, 360)—a view quite at variance with much of the available bilingual and educational research. In all fairness, some of the ideas in the Slovak law were also borrowed from Quebec's Bill 101: Charter of the French Language (enacted in 1977 by the Quebec National Assembly).

It constitutes an interesting irony that while the European Community is busily engaged in promoting linguistic diversity, and while Australia in 1987 enacted a national policy on languages that recognizes the rights of linguistic minorities,[19] a few nations are still trying to create an environment in which the nation-state is defined in terms of linguistic homogeneity. In western Europe, as the European Community has taken cognizance of the linguistic diversity of Europe, the Treaty of Maastricht

(1992) has lent considerable support to cultural and linguistic diversity, which the treaty considers to be one of Europe's major assets:

> A general policy goal is to place the highest priority on educational mobility; the objective is to enhance the level of familiarity of as many European students as possible with other European cultures and languages as an element of quality in Education. Language learning remains a top priority, and to this end, member states are encouraged to promote trilingualism; they are advised to make language qualifications desirable for entry into, and compulsory for exit from, higher education; and they are requested to give particular attention to the learning of minority languages. (Baetens Beardsmore 1994, 94)

Not so in Slovakia, or for that matter in the Baltic states or in other areas of central Europe,[20] and not so in an English Only United States.

Conclusion

The English Only movement in the United States has important implications for the worldwide status of English as a language and important global implications in those instances where its views have been taken as a model for other polities. Slovakia has done everything necessary to impose linguistic homogeneity: it has enacted state language legislation (the Law on the State Language of the Slovak Republic and subsidiary laws such as the Law on Bilingual Place-name Signs and the Law on the Registration of Births, Marriages, and Deaths, both enacted in 1994); it has created a body to determine which language variety will prevail (the State Language Department of the Slovak Ministry of Culture); and it has created a "linguistic police" to enforce the law.[21] It has even urged the modification of personal names. As Jernudd (1994) observes:

> [H]uman rights are likely to be violated when the state intervenes in the relationship between individuals' names and group

identity. Mandatory adjustment of names is a means to deny a group's existence qua group . . . or to erode for significant numbers of individuals their ability to manifest their identity as members of a group. . . . States wishing to forcibly assimilate visible ethnic groups require names to be changed. (130)

The English Only movement in the United States presupposes that

> measures designed to coerce immigrants into learning the majority language will have the effect of enhancing their identification with the majority culture. The [English Only] movement has been successful because these assumptions are generally consistent with the commonsense understanding that most of the public brings to linguistic questions, so that well-meaning people find it easy to accept the English Only program as a plausible approach to the problem of bringing recent immigrants into the economic and social mainstream. (Nunberg 1989, 584)

What has happened, and is happening, in Slovakia is illustrative of what might happen in the United States if U.S. English and its supporters have their way. Clearly, events in Slovakia suggest the steps that must be taken to implement a national language law (as opposed to a rational language policy). We have suggested here that the machinations of proponents of English Only may have the most profound implications for the state of English as a language—both nationally and internationally. We have suggested further that the efforts of U.S. English and the proponents of English Only have had effects not only in the United States but elsewhere in the world. All of this activity offers poor treatment for a condition which is not in need of treatment in the first place. Donahue (1995) argues that the issue may be an empty one—both sides have made a purposeful attempt to paralyze all debate and to preclude the formation of any real policy alternatives.

In the end, "[t]he [ultimate] irony of all this [activity in defense of English] is that there was never a culture or a language so little in need of official support. A Frenchman I know describes the 'English-only' measure as akin to declaring crabgrass an endangered species" (Nunberg 1997, A9).

Notes

1. Legislation:

State	Date	Notes
Alabama	1990	EO constitutional amendment adopted by voter initiative
Arizona	1988	EO constitutional amendment adopted by voter initiative; ruled unconstitutional by federal district court and appellate courts; decision vacated March 3, 1997, by U.S. Supreme Court. Ruled unconstitutional by Arizona Supreme Court, April 1998; U.S. Supreme Court refused to hear final appeal January 11, 1999.
Arkansas	1987	EO statute
California	1986	EO constitutional amendment adopted by voter initiative
Colorado	1988	EO constitutional amendment adopted by voter initiative
Florida	1988	EO constitutional amendment adopted by voter initiative
Georgia	1986	EO nonbinding resolution
Hawaii	1978	EP constitutional amendment declaring the state officially bilingual, recognizing English and Native Hawaiian as official languages
Illinois	1969	EP statute repealing "American" as official state language
Indiana	1984	EO statute
Kentucky	1984	EO statute
Mississippi	1987	EO statute
Missouri	1998	EO statute
Montana	1995	EO statute
Nebraska	1923	EO constitutional amendment
New Hampshire	1995	EO statute
New Mexico	1989	EP resolution
North Carolina	1987	EO statute
North Dakota	1987	EO statute
Oregon	1989	EP resolution
Rhode Island	1992	EP resolution
South Carolina	1987	EO statute
South Dakota	1995	EO statute
Tennessee	1984	EO statute
Virginia	1981	EO statute; revised 1996
Washington	1989	EP resolution
Wyoming	1996	EO statute

Key: EO = English Only legislation; EP = English Plus legislation.

English Only legislation was pending in thirteen other states in 1997:

Connecticut	Iowa	Kansas
Massachusetts	Michigan	Missouri
New Jersey	New York	Ohio
Oklahoma	Utah	Washington
Wisconsin		

In Alaska an Official English initiative statute was approved on November 3, 1998; California and Virginia have legislation pending which can be described as anti-Ebonics. In Utah, on January 21, 1999, the state House of Representatives defeated an English Only initiative by a vote of 43 to 31. The initiative, introduced by Rep. Tammy Rowan (Oregon) and supported by U.S. English, came to the House, without passing through the committee structure, after 39,783 Utah voters signed a petition in support of the measure. (This information was accurate as of January 25, 1999, based on information on http://ourworld.compuserve.com/homepages/ JWCrawford/langleg.htm. See also *TESOL Federal Update*, September 1997 [Vol. 3, No. 3, p.4.])

2. The following pertinent bills were pending in the 105th Congress:

♦ H.R. 123 (initially introduced by Congressman Emerson; reintroduced in 1997 by Congressman Randy Cunningham, R-California, with 146 cosponsors; reintroduced by Barr in the 106th Congress)

♦ H.R. 622 (introduced by Congressman Bob Stump, R-Arizona, with 20 cosponsors; see also H.R. 1203, introduced by Congressman Stump)

♦ H.R. 1005 (introduced by Congressman Peter T. King, R-New York, with 22 cosponsors)

♦ S.R. 323 (introduced by Senator Richard Shelby, R-Alabama, with 20 cosponsors)

The full text of these bills may be accessed at any of the GPO Access sites; e.g., UNCLIB.LIB.UNC.EDU—log in as "Library."

There were, in addition, a number of resolutions and tangentially related bills:

♦ H.J. Res 37 (introduced by John T. Doolittle, R-California, with 3 cosponsors, calling for an EO constitutional amendment)

♦ H.Con.Res.4 (introduced by Jose Serrano, D-New York, with 37 cosponsors, a nonbinding EP resolution in opposition to English

Only—The full text of this resolution, endorsed by the executive committee of the Linguistic Society of America, can be found in *LSA Bulletin* 1995); (reintroduced in the 106th Congress, referred to Education and Workforce Committee)

◆ H.R. 28 (introduced by Peter T. King, R-New York, with 7 cosponsors, disapproving of use of federal funds for school programs that recognize Ebonics)

◆ H.R. 856 (introduced by Congressman Don Young, R-Alaska, with 87 cosponsors, the Puerto Rico plebiscite bill)

◆ H.R. 1203 (introduced by Congressman Bob Stump, R-Arizona, with 128 cosponsors, to prohibit the use of federal funds to promote the use of regional dialects—i.e., African American Vernacular English)

3. The repressive rules enacted by Congress in 1996 through the Illegal Immigration Reform and Immigration Responsibility Act (IIRAIRA) already impose some language restrictions and achieve others by implication. (See also Davies 1996; Davies 1997; and McNamara 1998.)

4. Except at the level of federal courts.

5. Except in some limited jurisdictions; e.g., the city of Pasadena, California.

6. In the past few years, however, Canada has dropped from being among the five most generous supporters of aid to eleventh place as the result of severe budget cutting at the national level.

7. A "standard" language generally results from a complex set of historical processes intended precisely to produce standardization; indeed, a "standard" language may be defined as a set of discursive, cultural, and historical practices—a set of widely accepted communal solutions to discourse problems. Additionally, a "standard" language is a potent symbol of national unity. If this definition of a "standard" language may be assumed to be viable, then the "standard" language is really no one's "first" language. On the contrary, the "standard" language must be acquired through individual participation in the norms of usage, and these norms are commonly inculcated through education (with the powerful assistance of canonical literatures and the print media). But the reality of most linguistic communities is marked by the normative use of a wide range of varieties in day-to-day communication—i.e., the use of slang, jargon, nonstandard forms, special codes, different varieties (e.g., in the U.S. context, Network, Northern, Midland, Southern, African American Vernacular , Gullah, Appalachian), even of different languages (as in code-switching). Consequently, a

"standard" language constitutes a purely ideological construct, although some proportion of the population may become native speakers of that construct variety. The existence of such a construct, however, creates an impression that linguistic unity exists, when reality reflects linguistic diversity. The notion of the existence and dispersion of a "standard" variety through a community suggests that linguistic unity is the societal norm; it also suggests a level of socioeconomic and sociopolitical unity which may be contrary to the reality of linguistic diversity. The legal obligation to use a codified standard is likely to cause frustration among minority-language speakers since the standardized language is for them a nondominant variety; minority-language speakers probably use a contact variety, likely to be at considerable variance from the standard variety. In the Slovakian situation, this phenomenon is a virtual guarantee that bilinguals will violate the language law as it has been enacted.

8. While it may be argued, as Black (1991) does for Australian Kriol (a language with 15,000 speakers), that standardization is not necessary for a language to grow and develop, the notion of standardization is central to the concept of having a de jure national language in a modern state (see Joseph [1987] for standardization of French, or Milroy and Milroy [1991] for a more English orientation). Moreover, if enforcement is not to be arbitrary, then a defined standard is necessary.

9. "First, there would be no practical way to exempt indigenous languages from all the legal effects of the English Only bills. . . . While it might be possible to shield some Native American programs, S. 356 and H.R. 123 would . . . seem implicitly to repeal the Bilingual Education Act. This could prove devastating to American Indian and Alaska Native schools, which rarely have alternative sources of support for native-language programs. . . . Second, there would be no way to exempt Native Americans from the political impact of an English-only law" (LMRI 1995, 2).

10. I am dependent on the English version of the law, published in Kontra (1996), which appears to be the clearest version available.

11. The law addresses the complex issue of personal names. Section 3, paragraph 6 states: "Every citizen of the Slovak republic has the right to have his/her first and last names adjudicated to the rules of Slovak orthography free of charge." This implies the addition of the suffix -*ova* (meaning "daughter of" or "wife of") to feminine names; it is important to emphasize that only women's names are implicated. Hungarian names do not normally carry such a suffix. (See Jernudd 1994 quoted on pages 304–5.)

12. Section 10 (paragraph 1, parts a-c) of the law establishes fines as follows: "up to 250,000SK for legal entities in breach of obligations" outlined in parts of sections 4 (concerning education) and 8 (concerning the

economy, services, and health care); 500,000SK for violations in parts of section 5 (concerning the mass media, cultural events, and public meetings); and 50,000SK for violations of other parts of sections 4 and 5. The official currency of the Slovak Republic is the Slovenska koruna (i. e., the Slovak "crown" [SK]). In mid-September 1997, 34 Slovak crowns equaled U.S.$1.00. As of the same date, the average monthly income in Slovakia was reported at around 8,000SK, equivalent to about U.S.$235.30. Fifty thousand SK represents about seven months of average income. The fine for desecrating the flag—3,000SK— is less than half a month's average salary. This information is provided courtesy of Dr. Peter Medgyes (personal communication); Dr. Medgyes was at the time of writing deputy state secretary for foreign affairs in the Ministry of Culture and Education, Budapest, Hungary. Actual research and verification were undertaken at the behest of Dr. Medgyes by Ms. Virág Denke, then deputy director general in the same ministry.

13. The discussion of the pertinence of the U.S. model ignores differences between indigenous people and immigrants. In the case of Hispanics/Latinos in the United States, for example, there is an obvious difference between legal and "undocumented" immigrants who arrived in the United States from Mexico yesterday and Hispanics/Latinos who, following the enactment in 1848 of the Treaty of Guadalupe Hidalgo, suddenly found themselves citizens of the United States.

14. According to the 1991 census, the population of Slovakia consists of:

Group	Number	Percentage*
Czechs	0,053,400	01.00%
Germans	0,005,600	00.10%
Gypsies (Romanies)	0,080,600	01.55%
Hungarians	0,566,000	10.75%
Poles	0,002,900	00.05%
Ruthenians	0,016,900	00.33%
Slovaks	4,500,000	85.60%
Ukrainians	0,013,800	00.25%
Others	0,017,100	00.35%
Total	5,256,300	99.98% (rounding error)

[All groups other than Slovak and Hungarian = 03.63%]

*Rounded to the nearest hundred

Source: Magocsi 1993.

These eight minorities (14.4 percent of the population = 756,300 individuals) are equally stripped of their language rights under the 1995 law.

15. The history of population relocation is very old in central Europe, certainly dating back as far as the post–World War I settlements. (At the end of World War I, when the Austro-Hungarian monarchy ceased to exist, peace treaties paid scant attention to Hungarian ethnic boundaries; something like two-thirds of historically Hungarian territory were ceded to the politically created multiethnic states of Czechoslovakia and Yugoslavia, to a reconfigured Romania, and to Austria.) Certainly, the post–World War II settlements, encoded in the Potsdam Conference (1945) and the Kosice Manifesto (1945), added to the problem by relocating populations "to their original pre-war homes" while actually serving largely to force population movement and inflict severe hardships on large numbers of people in alleged "repatriation"—in actuality, away from their traditional homes.

16. The quotation is drawn from an official English (authorized by the National Translation Agency) translation of the text.

17. This list of nations strikes us as odd; it would seem that the Balkan states and Canada might serve as better examples.

18. See also legislation introduced and supported by Senator Richard Shelby (R-Alabama) (S.R. 323) and Representative Bill Emerson (R-Missouri) (H.R. 123). Representative Roth was not returned to the House in the 105th Congress (see note 1.) It is important to note that none of these bills has yet been enacted.

19. Subsequent legislation has increased the focus on English literacy—by implication, one does not become literate in other languages (see Moore 1996). In 1997, within one segment of the Australian community, there was an increase in anti-immigrant and anti-Aboriginal sentiment. Were English Only to be enacted in the United States, it would undoubtedly strengthen the case for those advocating similar legislation in Australia.

20. The U.S. State Department, in its March 6, 1995, Human Rights Report, cited prejudice against the Roma (Gypsy) people as an area of major concern. See, for example, the recent immigration of Roma people from the Czech Republic and the Slovak Republic into Canada (Nickerson 1997). The U.S. State Department report also called attention to the problem of Hungarians in Slovakia.

21. Section 9 of the Law of the National Council of the Slovak Republic, of 15 November 1995 on the State Language of the Slovak Republic (to give it its official name) states, in full: "The Culture Ministry monitors the

observance of the obligations ensuing from this law. If it finds non-compliance, it alerts the legal entities or individuals in whose activities the non-compliance has occurred, and is authorized to call upon them to correct the illegal state of affairs." Although fines could not be imposed before January 1, 1997, four so-called "language consultants" were appointed to begin work on February 1, 1996, in three Slovak districts and in Bratislava to supervise the strict observance of the new language law. The qualifications of these language consultants are not absolutely clear. The Hungarian press in Slovakia is actually using the Hungarian neologisms for "language police" and "language policemen."

Works Cited

Ablin, David A. 1991. *Foreign Language Policy in Cambodian Government: Questions of Sovereignty, Manpower Training and Development Assistance.* Paris: UNICEF.

Baetens Beardsmore, Hugo. 1994. "Language Policy and Planning in Western European Countries." In William Grabe et al., eds., *Annual Review of Applied Linguistics, 14.* New York: Cambridge University Press. 93–110.

Black, Paul. 1990. "Some Competing Goals in Aboriginal Language Planning." In Richard B. Baldauf Jr. and Allan Luke, eds., *Language Planning and Education in Australasia and the South Pacific.* Clevedon: Multilingual Matters. 80–88.

Coulombe, Pierre A. 1993. "Language Rights, Individual and Communal." *Language Problems and Language Planning* 17(2): 140–52.

Crawford, James W. 1992. *Hold Your Tongue: Bilingualism and the Politics of English Only.* Reading, MA: Addison Wesley.

Crooks, Tony, and Geoffrey Crewes, eds. 1995. *Language and Development.* Jakarta: Indonesian Australian Language Foundation.

Crystal, David. 1995. *The Cambridge Encyclopedia of the English Language.* Cambridge: Cambridge University Press.

———. 1997. *English as a Global Language.* Cambridge: Cambridge University Press.

Daniels, Harvey A., ed. 1990. *Not Only English: Affirming America's Multilingual Heritage.* Urbana, Illinois: National Council of Teachers of English.

Davies, Alan. 1996. *Australian Immigrant Gatekeeping through English Language Tests: How Important Is Proficiency?* Paper presented at the annual Language Testing Research Colloquium, Tampere, Finland. August.

———, ed. 1997. *Ethics in Language Testing.* Special Issue of *Language Testing,* (14): 3.

Donahue, Thomas S. 1995. "American Language Policy and Compensatory Opinion." In James W. Tollefson, ed., *Power and Inequity in Language Education.* Cambridge: Cambridge University Press. 112–41.

Grabe, William, and Robert B. Kaplan. 1986. "Science, Technology, Language and Information: Implications for Language- and Language-in-Education Planning." *International Journal of the Sociology of Language* 59: 47–71.

Jernudd, Björn H. 1994. "Personal Names and Human Rights." In Tove Skutnab-Kangas and Robert Phillipson, eds., *Linguistic Human Rights: Overcoming Linguistic Discrimination.* Berlin: Mouton de Gruyter. 121–32.

Joseph, John Earl. 1987. *Eloquence and Power: The Rise of Language Standards and Standard Languages.* London: Frances Pinter.

Kaplan, Robert B. 1995. [Review of the book *Language and Development* by Tony Crooks and Jeoffrey Crewes, eds.] *ESP Journal* (17)3: 317–20.

———. 1997. [Review of *Language Development: Teachers in a Changing World* by Brian Kenny and William Savage, eds.] *Asian Journal of English Language Teaching* 7: 121–26.

Kaplan, Robert B., and Richard B. Baldauf, Jr. 1997. *Language Planning from Practice to Theory.* Clevedon, Avon: Multilingual Matters.

Kaplan, Robert B, Ellen E. Touchstone, and Cynthia L. Hagstrom. 1995. "Image and Reality: Banking in Los Angeles." *Text* 15: 427–56.

Kenny, Brian, and William Savage, eds. 1997. *Language Development: Teachers in a Changing World.* In Christopher N. Candlin, gen. ed., Applied Linguistics and Language Study series. London: Longman.

Kontra, Miklós. 1996. "'English-Only's' Cousin: Slovak Only." *Acta Linguistica Hungarica* 43(3-4): 345–72.

Linguistic Minority Research Institute. 1995. "Congress Hears English-Only Legislation." *LMRI* 5(4): 2.

LSA Bulletin. 1995. *LSA Bulletin No. 149*. Washington, D.C.: Linguistic Society of America. [Compiled by Geoffrey Nunberg, 1996. Reprinted in *New Language Planning Newsletter* 10(4): 6–8.

Magocsi, Paul R. 1993. *Historical Atlas of East Central Europe*. Seattle: University of Washington Press.

Marshall, David. 1986. "The Question of an Official Language: Language Rights and the English Language Amendment." *International Journal of the Sociology of Language* 60: 7–5.

McNamara, Tim. 1998. "Policy and Social Considerations in Language Assessment." In William Grabe et al., eds., *Annual Review of Applied Linguistics, 18*. New York: Cambridge University Press. 304–19.

Milroy, James, and Lesley Milroy. 1991. *Authority in Language: Investigating Language Prescription and Standardisation* (2nd ed.). London: Routledge.

Moore, Helen. 1996. "Language Policies as Virtual Realities: Two Australian Examples." *TESOL Quarterly* 30: 473–97.

Mühlhäusler, Peter. 1995. *Linguistic Ecology: Language Change and Linguistic Imperialism in the Pacific Region*. London: Routledge.

Nickerson, Colin. 1997. "Canadian Welcome Mat Frayed with Arrival of Czech Gypsies." *Seattle Post-Intelligencer*, Aug. 28. A12.

Nunberg, Geoffrey. 1989. "Linguists and the Official Language Movement." *Language* 65: 579–87.

———. 1997. "English-Only the Wrong Medicine for an Imaginary Disease." *Seattle Post-Intelligencer*, Aug. 26. A9.

Peña, Fernando de la. 1991. *Democracy or Babel? The Case for Official English in the United States*. Washington, D.C.: U.S. English.

Phillipson, Robert. 1988. "Linguicism: Structures and Ideologies in Linguistic Imperialism." In Tove Skutnabb-Kangas and James Cummins, eds., *Minority Education: From Shame to Struggle*. Clevedon: Multilingual Matters. 339–58.

Thomas, Lee. 1996. "Language as Power: A Linguistic Critique of US English." *Modern Language Journal* 80(2): 129–40.

Touchstone, Ellen E., Robert B. Kaplan, and Cynthia L. Hagstrom. 1996. "Home, Sweet Casa: Access to Home Loans in Los Angeles." *Multilingua* 15: 329–48.

Wardhaugh, Ronald. 1987. *Languages in Competition: Dominance, Diversity, and Decline.* Oxford, U.K.: Basil Blackwell/André Deutsch.

CHAPTER THIRTEEN

Language and Democracy in the USA and the RSA

GENEVA SMITHERMAN
Michigan State University

This chapter compares the struggles for language rights in the United States of America (hereafter USA) and the Republic of South Africa (hereafter RSA), focusing on parallels between the Black speech communities in these two nations. While there are, to be sure, distinct differences between the USA and the RSA, there are also formidable similarities in terms of political economy, issues of linguistic imperialism, and domination and subordination vis à vis the European settler population and African descendants. Using what he terms "comparative Black politics," Walters (1993) provides a brilliant analysis of the past and present condition of Black South Africans and Black Americans:

> Despite the dissimilarities of culture, history, demography, legal structure and other important elements of state between the United States and South Africa, there does exist a basis for the comparative analysis of Black politics in the two countries. It rests upon the similar characteristics of the internal political dynamics . . . between the white and Black community in each society. (246)

Presently, post-apartheid South Africa struggles to implement a constitutional provision that would elevate the status of its African languages. South Africa's is a policy of English Plus. By contrast, an influential element of post-apartheid, post-civil rights USA struggles to amend its Constitution to declare English the sole official language. This would be a policy of English Only. Since the USA currently has no de jure language policy at all, the movement to enshrine an English Only policy in the U.S. Constitution presents a fundamental challenge to all linguistic minorities, including speakers of USA Ebonics—also known as Black English (Vernacular), African American Language, and African American Vernacular English. (My use of the term "Ebonics" in this chapter, whether preceded by the designation "USA" or not, should be construed to refer to that variety of Ebonics spoken in the USA.)

Following Walters (1993), I take the perspective of what I term "Black language politics" to analyze the dynamic relationship between language and politics in both the USA and the RSA. This subsequent comparison employs a class analysis and is situated in the profound similarities in historical, educational, and linguistic experiences that link these two Black groups. (In fact, RSA and USA Blacks are, in some senses, linked in a more profound way than Black Americans are linked to West Africans, although West Africa is generally considered to be our ancestral homeland.)

Internal Colonialism in the USA and the RSA

In the USA, internal colonialism began with the conquest and near extermination of the indigenous peoples (so-called "Indians," after the Italian explorer Columbus's mistaken belief that he had "discovered" India when he landed on these shores in 1492). British settlers encountered these native peoples when they established the colony of what would become the new nation-state of America in the early years of the seventeenth century. Beginning with the introduction of African slavery into the British colony of America in 1619, early White settlers came to recognize the value of the African as human capital, unlike the "savage" Indian, who rebelled against the agrarian lifestyle of colonial America's farms and cotton plantations. These White settlers, themselves colonial subjects of the British Crown until the American Revolution in the late eighteenth century, in turn subjugated and colonized the Africans. For well over two centuries, this free African slave labor was expropriated to build a society that, according to Minister Louis Farrakhan in his 1995 Million Man March speech, "was to be a nation by white people and for white people. Native Americans, Blacks, and all other non-white people were to be the burden bearers for the real citizens of this nation" (Farrakhan 1996, 10).

In the RSA, the stage was set for internal colonialism with the conquest of South Africa by the Netherlands and Great Britain, beginning with the establishment of the Cape colony by Dutchman Jan van Riebeeck in 1652, followed by the British occupation of the Cape in 1795. Internal colonialism was solidified in 1910 with the consolidation of the White settler colonists, Boer and British, into the South African nation-state, essentially a "state of the white race" (Barnes, qtd. in Jaffe 1994). In this process, it was critical that all Whites, including workers, be elevated to a level above all Africans in order to maintain White minority rule and simultaneously secure "capital in the masses of cheap black labor" (Magubane and Mandaza 1988, 10). In the USA, similar White capitalist hegemony operated, despite Whites being the overwhelming majority of the population. Racism and appeals to White racial superiority effectively divided the working class and facilitated the capitalist exploitation of both Black and White workers.

In the RSA, as in the USA, the internal colonialist formation is not the classic polarization between an oppressor nation and a dominated colonized subject people, as was the case elsewhere in Africa (and in India, Mexico, the Sudan, etc.). Rather, RSA and USA colonialism—also deemed a "system of racial capitalism" (Alexander 1989, 20)—manifested itself as a fundamental contradiction between Europeans of all nations, socially constructed as a "superior" race, and Africans of all nations, socially constructed as an "inferior" race (see, e.g., Magubane and Mandaza 1988; Jaffe 1994; Walters 1993).

In order to make this internal colonialism work, the White ruling class in both countries created elaborate superstructural systems of law, education, politics, custom, and cultural belief sets to support the economic exploitation and domination of Blacks by the USA and RSA capitalist economies. Apartheid, whether in the RSA or the USA, via de jure policies and de facto practices, involved not merely the social segregation of the races, but also the segregation of "whites with superior material status and political rights from Blacks [with] inferior material status and political rights" (Walters 1993, 199). In both countries, then, Black participation (or lack of such) in the labor force was critical and remains so today. Walters (1993) states,

> in both countries, Blacks make up the largest proportion of the unskilled work force, and the economic projections for such labor are not bright because employers are adding technologically sophisticated capital equipment and trained employees. . . . [I]t is a modern feature of the workings of the American and South African capitalist economies that Africans suffer high levels of unemployment. . . . In the United States, the under-count of the Black population and the much higher rate of short-term unemployment for Blacks mean that the real rate could also be as high as 30% of the potential Black work force. . . . In South Africa, the only factor which makes possible the growth of the Black labor participation rate is the easing of the job reservation system, making possible the hiring of semi-skilled Blacks in jobs formerly reserved for whites. Nevertheless, South African economists admit that the economy is currently unable to generate the requisite jobs needed to keep pace with the expanding African population. (201)

The devastating material exploitation of Blacks was compounded by psychological subjugation. Not only were the colonized Black subjects relegated to an inherently "inferior" racial group, but their culture and historical past were devalued as well. According to Fanon (1963), "nothing has been left to chance. . . . [T]he total result looked for by colonial domination was indeed to convince the natives that colonialism came to lighten their darkness; . . . if the settlers were to leave, they would at once fall back into barbarism, degradation, and bestiality" (210–11). The resulting crisis in identity among Blacks, in both the RSA and the USA, created a sense of dual consciousness at war with itself. As Fanon (1963) put it: "Because it is a systematic negation of the other person and a furious determination to deny the other person all attributes of humanity, colonialism forces the people it dominates to ask themselves the question constantly: 'In reality, who am I?'" (250). The answer to Fanon's question was captured nearly a century ago by Du Bois, who coined the term "double consciousness" to refer to the ambivalent identity created in Black Americans. It is an ambivalence exacerbated in the lives of RSA and USA Black subjects forced to live daily in the midst of the colonizer. Du Bois (1961) elaborates:

> [T]he Negro is a sort of seventh son, born with a veil, and gifted with second-sight in this American world—a world which yields him no true self-consciousness, but only lets him see himself through the revelation of the other world. It is a peculiar sensation, this double-consciousness, this sense of always looking at one's self through the eyes of others. . . . One ever feels his two-ness . . . two souls, two thoughts, two unreconciled strivings; two warring ideals in one dark body. (16–17)

Linguistic Colonialism in the RSA and the USA

Similarities

Given the nature of internal colonialism as it adversely affected Black participation in the political economy of both countries, it follows that the languages and cultural-communicative practices of both groups would also be adversely affected. The colonizers' languages (English and Afrikaans in the RSA, English in the USA) were accorded more prestige than the African languages in the RSA and Ebonics in the USA. Further, the use of the non-African tongue affected the sociolinguistic construction of reality of the colonized Black subjects. What Marx called the "language of real life" became distorted among Blacks, whose own languages were suppressed and devalued. Ngugi wa Thiong'o (1986) argues:

> By imposing a foreign language and suppressing the native languages as spoken and written, the colonizer was already breaking the harmony previously existing between the African child and the three aspects of language as communication. Since the new language was a product reflecting the "real language of life" elsewhere, it could never, as spoken or written, properly reflect or imitate the real life of that community. This may, in part, explain why technology always appears to us as slightly external, *their* product and not *ours*. The word *missile*, for instance, used to hold an alien faraway sound until I recently learnt its equivalent in Gikuyu, *Ngurukuhi*. Learning, for a colonial child, became a cerebral activity and not an emotionally felt experience. (76–77)

While USA Blacks were stripped of their African languages (though not entirely, as we will see), RSA Blacks were allowed to retain theirs. British colonial language policy, however, relegated these languages to low status by considering them dialects rather than languages, and by establishing a system of material rewards for Africans who spoke English. According to Alexander (1989):

> For the colonised people . . . [British colonial language policy] meant that English language and English cultural traits acquired an economic and social value that was treasured above all else while their own languages and many of their cultural traits were devalued and often despised. . . . [B]uilt into the consciousness of black people (and of many whites) [was a] programme [that stressed that] all . . . one had to do was to climb up the socio-economic ladder which stood ready for every competent, abstinent and disciplined person to mount. If one had these attributes and was able to communicate in English, then—in the mythology of colour-blind individual rights—the sky was the limit! (20)

Although the African languages were not eradicated in the RSA, in one of the great ironies of linguistic colonialism the languages became the source of a viciously effective divide-and-rule strategy by South Africa's White minority elite. The establishment of Bantustans[1] and Verwoerd's[2] post-1948 blueprint for apartheid dictated that Africans who spoke different languages had to live in separate quarters (Alexander 1989, 21). Under the guise of promoting linguistic dignity and freedom for each and every group, the apartheid emphasis on African languages was, in reality, designed to "break up the black people into a large number of conflicting and competing so-called ethnic groups" (Alexander 1989, 21). The foundation for the division of RSA Blacks into ten ethnic "homelands" had already been established by Christian missionaries who "invented ethnicity" (Ranger, qtd. in Alexander 1989, 22) by cutting up the African linguistic continuum and erecting other boundaries in such a way as to "restructure the African world . . . to make it more comprehensible to Europeans" (23).

In addition to rewarding a small Black elite proficient in English, the RSA's internal colonialism privileged Whites through socioeconomic policies (e.g., job reservations) that led to the association of Afrikaans and English with high status since these were the languages spoken by Whites. This linguistic colonialism was reinforced by the devaluing of the indigenous languages by the RSA's Boer and British ruling elite—and, unwittingly, by the promotion of English over Afrikaans by the RSA's Black intelligentsia. Alexander notes that traditionally, Black intellectuals conceptualized the RSA's language conflict as being only between English and Afrikaans. While this "fragile class of people" was promoting "what to them represented 'liberty' as against enslavement," nonetheless, as Alexander (1989) notes, the result was that no "serious thought [was given] to the claims and rights of the African languages spoken in South Africa, beyond the issue of the medium of instruction in primary schools" (29).

Historical Overview of Ebonics

In this country, linguistic colonialism took a slightly different, but no less viciously effective, path. The seventeenth- and eighteenth-century empirical evidence on Ebonics is scant, in great part because the colonizer's interest was only in the African slave as a beast of burden. But certain factors about enslaved Blacks' sociolinguistic situation can be gleaned from the logic of linguistic processes. For instance, since it is linguistically impossible for any group of people to suddenly "lose" their native tongue and immediately begin speaking a foreign tongue, we can assume that enslaved Africans arriving in the British colony of America in the early seventeenth century brought their African languages with them (e.g., Turner 1949; Vass 1979). In addition, given what we know about the European and American slave trade, we can also assume that some brought a pidginized form of English acquired during their often lengthy imprisonment in the slave fortresses ("castles") in West Africa and during the long middle passage across the Atlantic. Because it was the practice of their White captors to mix up Africans from different linguistic backgrounds on the same plantation so as to foil communication and thwart escape plans, those who did not know pidgin English soon learned it in order to be able to communicate with their fellow slaves. Thus pidgin English became a lingua franca among the enslaved and was added to their multilingual repertoire (see, e.g., Dillard 1972, 1977).

The slave trade was a dangerous and costly proposition, made so particularly by the long, treacherous journey from West Africa to America. As an economic alternative, slavers instituted the practice of growing their own slaves on American soil. It became common practice for "Ole Massa" to designate certain male slaves as "breeders," nurturing their promiscuity on the plantation so that they might impregnate as many female slaves as possible (Bennett 1961). Over time, the linguistic impact of this new enslavement practice meant that as fewer slaves were imported from Africa, African languages were heard less and less, pidgin English was used more and more, and newer generations who were born into enslavement learned the pidgin English as their primary language. Thus the pidgin English became a creole English. (A pidgin becomes a creole when it is the first and only language of a speech community.) Within a hundred years after the introduction of American enslavement, this creole English had become the lingua franca of the enslaved speech community. This historical USA Ebonics began to lose its creole character with the movement for emancipation and enfranchisement in the nineteenth century, an optimism that was soundly trounced by the inscribing of "separate but equal" laws toward the end of that century. Also halted was the decreolization (de-Africanization) of the language that had begun as a corollary to the nineteenth-century Black freedom movement.

Forced to use the colonizer's language, enslaved Africans appropriated the foreign tongue and reconstructed it as a counterlanguage by superimposing their own linguistic rules and practices on the White man's speech. Ebonics provided a code for Africans in America to talk about Black business, publicly or privately, and even to talk about Ole Massa himself right in front of his face. When the enslaved African said, "Eveybody talkin bout Heaben ain goin dere," the phrase not only reflected the Africanized phonetics of West African languages, but it was also a double-voiced register of English which conveyed two meanings simultaneously, one the literal surface meaning, the other the ironic subtext. For those in the enslaved community, the statement was understood as a style of speaking known as "signifying," an indirect commentary on or critique of someone. In this instance, it was slaveholders who were being signified on because they professed Christianity but practiced slavery—hence "Eveybody talkin bout Heaben ain goin dere."

Given the White colonizer's linguistic hegemony, neither the African languages nor the older form of Ebonics (i.e., pidgin-creole English) was valued. Harrison, author of the first "scientific" study of Ebonics, attributed the development of "Negro English" to a pathological Africanness. Writing in 1884, he stated:

> The humor and naivete of the Negro are features which must not be overlooked in gauging his intellectual calibre and timbre; much of his talk is baby-talk. . . . [T]he African, from the absence of books and teaching, had no principle of *analepsy* in his intellectual furnishing by which a word, once become obscure from a real or supposed loss of parts or meaning, can be repaired, amended, or restored to its original form. . . . Negro speech organs are becoming slowly and with difficulty accustomed to the sound th. (232–33)

Notwithstanding that enslaved Africans spoke a different language, i.e., the African-derived pidgin-creole English, their status depended to a great extent on their competence in the variety of English spoken by colonial Whites. Advertisements for runaway slaves generally cited the slave's degree of competence in English as a badge of identification, using descriptors such as "bad English," "tolerable English," or "good English." For instance:

> Ran away . . . a new Negro Fellow named Prince, he can't scarce speak a Word of English. Ran away from the Subscriber, living near Salisbury, North Carolina. . . . [A] negro fellow named JACK, African born . . . about 30 years of age . . . speaks bad English. Run away . . . a Negro Man named Jo Cuffy, about 20 Years of age . . . speaks good English. (Smitherman 1977, 12–13)

In the system of USA internal colonialism, just as the older form of Ebonics was devalued, the same holds true for the contemporary variety. Because this language resembles English and does not reflect a preponderance of words from African languages;

because it does not have a wholly different grammatical system from European American speech, or "White English"; and because it is spoken by racially oppressed descendants of slaves from an "inferior" race—for these reasons, Ebonics today, as in the past, is often labeled a broken, bastardized form of English, by both colonizers and some members of the colonized. Viewed through the lens of linguistic science, however, it is clearly a systematic, rule-governed language which fuses elements of American English with deep structural syntax and linguistic-cultural practices derived from West African languages.

Ebonics and the Oakland, California, Resolution

The language spoken by USA Blacks shares a number of patterns with European American English, but it also has a number of unique patterns of syntax, pronunciation, lexicon, discourse practices, and rhetorical and semantic strategies. Space will not permit an extended presentation and analysis of features of Ebonics, so in addition to the signifying example noted earlier, two other examples will have to suffice.

Consider "He been married" versus "He *been* married." The unstressed verb pattern means that the man in question is divorced, i.e., he has been married before, but that is no longer the case. The stressed *been* pattern means that the man in question married at some point in the remote past and is still married, i.e., he has been married for a long time.

Consider the statement, "The Brotha be looking good; that's what got the Sista nose open." "Brother" and "Sister," both of which would be pronounced without the post-vocalic *r* sound, are Ebonics for an African American man and woman, respectively. The terms have less to do with biological kinship than with the African-derived custom of using familial terms to denote racial, ethnic kinship. "Looking good" (both words would be pronounced with softened final consonants and/or final vowel sounds) refers to the "Brotha's" appealing essence; in the lexicon of Ebonics, this is not necessarily the same as being physically handsome. "Sister" (or, in Ebonics, "Sista") exhibits the use of adjacency to convey possession in Ebonics, i.e., the redundancy of the -s morpheme is not obligatory as is the case in European

American English. The Sista passionate feeling for the Brotha is conveyed by the Ebonics phrase "nose open," suggesting the kind of love that leaves one vulnerable to exploitation. The use of "be" means that the quality of "looking good" is not a one-time occurrence, limited to the present moment only. In Ebonics, that would be expressed as "He looking good," rather than "He be looking good." The "be" suggests the Brotha's past, present, and future essence, i.e., how he looks on a regular basis; thus, as in the case of Efik and other West African languages, Ebonics uses a verb pattern to convey iterativity, i.e., to distinguish static from continuous events.

To date, the U.S. government has refused to recognize Ebonics as a separate and distinct language, although it has, for instance, recognized Hawai'i Creole English as a language. Further, in the scholarly community there is a lack of consensus on the question of whether Ebonics is a language in its own right or merely a dialect of USA English. (But we should be reminded of linguist Weinreich's admonition that the difference between a language and a dialect is who's got the army and the navy!) Given the ambiguous status of Ebonics, coupled with the ever-problematic issue of race in the United States, a firestorm of national controversy was set off when the Oakland, California, school board issued its resolution in December 1996 declaring Ebonics the primary language (not dialect) of its Black students and asserting that this language would be the medium of instruction to teach these students "standard American English."

The term and the concept of "Ebonics" have actually been around for over twenty-four years, coined by clinical psychologist Dr. Robert L. Williams at a conference on language and the Black child held in St. Louis, Missouri, in January 1973. With this term, Black scholars sought to capture the Africanized quality of various African-European language mixtures which had developed throughout the African diaspora. Williams, who convened the conference and in 1975 published the proceedings in the book *Ebonics: The True Language of Black Folks*, writes in the book's preface:

> A significant incident occurred at the conference. The Black conferees were so critical of the work on the subject done by white

researchers, many of whom also happened to be present, that they decided to caucus among themselves and define Black Language from a Black perspective. It was in this caucus that the term **Ebonics** was created. (1)

In the book's introduction, Williams goes on to amplify this terminology, defining Ebonics as

> the linguistic and paralinguistic features which on a concentric continuum represent the communicative competence of the West African, Caribbean, and United States slave descendant of African origin. It includes the various idioms, patois, argots, ideolects, and social dialects of black people, especially those who have been forced to adapt to colonial circumstances. **Ebonics** derives its form from ebony (black) and phonics (sound, the study of sound) and refers to the study of the language of Black people in all its cultural uniqueness. (vi)

Despite the massive body of research on USA Ebonics over the past two decades that attests to its rule-governed dynamism and demonstrates that its speakers do not have cognitive-linguistic deficiencies as had been charged in earlier times; despite the tremendous crossover of this variety of Ebonics into the public discourse of the United States; despite its creative use by writers such as Alice Walker, who won the Pulitzer Prize for her 1982 novel *The Color Purple,* written almost entirely in Ebonics; despite the emancipation of African slaves in the mid-nineteenth century and the subsequent assignment of citizenship status to them; despite the dismantling of USA-style apartheid in the civil rights-Black Power era of the 1960s and 1970s—despite these tremendous sociopolitical changes, the status of Ebonics and its speakers remains problematic. Given the extremely high Black unemployment rate, and given an economy of rapidly declining industrialized ("blue collar") jobs, the White-controlled political economy continues to disprivilege Ebonics speakers by requiring European American English as a condition to compete for employment for scarce technical and "white collar" jobs.

Ambivalent and/or negative attitudes toward Ebonics reflect deep generational and class conflicts in the national Black community. These contradictions were strikingly and painfully showcased for the entire nation in the Oakland Ebonics controversy.

Younger Blacks—intellectuals, rappers, writers, students, and others—embrace Ebonics. For instance, Bill Stephney of Stepsun Records argued that

> [m]ost of the people who have been opponents of Ebonics are the same ones who have been dismissive of Hip-Hop. There is a segment of the older Black generation, the middle class, civil rights leadership, that is anti-youth. Most of them have no idea if Ebonics works as a method of reaching Black students. But because they are so busy being reactive to anything that mainstream white politicians are against, once again they are speaking out. And they haven't scratched the surface in understanding how the Hip-Hop Generation views the issue. (qtd. in Kelly 1997, 26)

On the other hand, older, established Blacks—some of whom, such as Reverend Jesse Jackson, are perceived as leaders—rejected Ebonics and condemned the Oakland school board for its resolution. Kweisi Mfume, president of the National Association for the Advancement of Colored People (NAACP), was quoted in the national press as calling the Oakland decision a "cruel joke" (Leland and Joseph 1997, 78) and asserting that folk in the hood need to shape up and speak "correctly" (Simmons 1997, 5). Reverend Jesse Jackson, Reverend Al Sharpton, and Maya Angelou attacked the Oakland school board decision, arguing that this language policy would "build barriers between the races" and "insult the Black community" (qtd. in Boyd 1996). On the national television program *Meet the Press,* Jackson went so far as to call the use of Ebonics as the medium of instruction "unacceptable surrender borderlining on disgrace." He later recanted. Meanwhile, in addition to the hip-hop generation, the Black working and un-working classes continue to speak Ebonics. As a linguistic minority, the Black masses are continuously exposed to European American English—in schooling, in the mass media, and elsewhere. Further, they have the cognitive-linguistic capacity to eradicate Ebonics in favor of the English spoken by the European American majority—if they desired to do so. Clearly, current Black American leadership is out of touch with what is happening on the ground.

Ebonics and the USA English Only Movement

In the 1920s, the following pledge was standard recitation for schoolchildren throughout the United States:

> I love the United States of America. I love my country's flag. I love my country's language. I promise:
>
> 1. That I will not dishonor my country's speech by leaving off the last syllable of words.
>
> 2. That I will say a good American "yes" and "no" in place of an Indian grunt "um-hum" and "nup-um" or a foreign "ya" or "yeh" and "nope."
>
> 3. That I will do my best to improve American speech by avoiding loud rough tones, by enunciating distinctly, and by speaking pleasantly, clearly, and sincerely.
>
> 4. That I will learn to articulate correctly as many words as possible during the year. (qtd. in Gawthrop 1965, 9–10)

This pledge represents an accurate linguistic snapshot of language attitudes that continue to persist in the American body politic.

Over half a century after this pledge was developed, a list of what New York public schools chancellor Dr. Richard Green termed "speech demons" was printed in the *New York Times* and endorsed by then-Mayor Edward Koch as a set of "offending" speech patterns that the chancellor was determined to eliminate from the speech of New York's students. The list included such forms as the following:

> May I <u>axe</u> a question?
>
> Hang the <u>pitcher</u> on the wall.
>
> He's <u>goin</u> home.
>
> I <u>ain't</u> got none.
>
> <u>Can</u> I leave the room? (Lewis 1989, 5B)

The U.S. sociolinguistic condition is such that not only does U.S. culture devalue Ebonics, Spanish, Native American languages, and even, to some extent, other European languages, but it also devalues varieties of White working- or lower-class English, as this list and the schoolchildren's pledge demonstrate. Thus, while the English Only movement would hit Blacks, Latinos, and other people of color hardest, it would also suppress all varieties of American English other than the economically dominant White middle- and upper-class version.

The roots of English Only can be traced back to colonial America. In the eighteenth century, for example, large groups of Germans immigrated to America, settling in the Pennsylvania colony, where they established their own schools to promulgate their traditions and the German language. Benjamin Franklin, however, a major figure in the American Revolution and one of the drafters of the U.S. Constitution, expressed concern that the Germans would soon outstrip the English in Pennsylvania and that "we . . . will not . . . be able to preserve our language, and even our government will become precarious" (Franklin 1992, 19). As a countermove, Franklin, together with other leading Anglos, established English schools in the German-speaking areas under the auspices of the Society for the Propagation of Christian Knowledge, a plan which failed when the Germans discovered that it had to do with language, not religion (Castellanos 1992, 17).

The contemporary English Only movement—also known as the Official English movement—dates back to 1981, when the late U.S. Senator S. I. Hayakawa, a Republican from California and an American of Japanese ancestry, introduced the first English Language Amendment (ELA) to the U.S. Constitution. Resolution 72 contained six short sections, which read as follows:

Section 1. The English language shall be the official language of the United States.

Section 2. Neither the United States nor any State shall make or enforce any law which requires the use of any language other than English.

Section 3. This article shall apply to laws, ordinances, regulations, orders, programs, and policies.

Section 4. No order or decree shall be issued by any court of the United States or of any State requiring that any proceedings, or matters to which this article applies, be in any language other than English.

Section 5. This article shall not prohibit educational instruction in a language other than English as required as a transitional method of making students who use a language other than English proficient in English.

Section 6. The Congress and the States shall have the power to enforce this article by appropriate legislation. (Hayakawa 1992, 112)

Over the ensuing years, an additional fifteen ELAs have been introduced into the U.S. Congress, although none have yet to come to a vote. In the meantime, individual states have taken up Hayakawa's cause and passed such amendments at the state level. And in March 1997, the U.S. Supreme Court, with conservatives and moderates now composing the majority of the Court, overturned a lower court ruling which had declared that the state of Arizona's English Only law was unconstitutional. The Supreme Court returned the case to the Arizona Supreme Court to decide exactly how that state's ELA law should be interpreted and implemented.

The English Only movement is well financed. One organization, U.S. English, has spent upwards of $18 million since 1983 to promote English as the official language of the United States (Crawford 1992, 171). It currently has an annual budget of $6 million, a membership of over 400,000, and a broad-based following.

The USA is often erroneously perceived to be a wholly English-speaking nation. Yet there are 35 million Blacks, at least 80 to 90 percent of whom understand and speak Ebonics some or all of the time (notwithstanding that some of these speakers also speak European American English). In addition to the speakers of Ebonics, there are nearly 32 million other American citizens who speak a language other than English, as indicated in Table 13.1 (p. 332), constructed from the 1990 census.

Threatening to (and undoubtedly motivating) English Only advocates is the rapidly shifting demographics of the United States. The population growth of people of color is outstripping that of Whites, and projections are that this trend will continue (see Table 13.2). Already in some areas of the United States—e.g., major cities such as Detroit, Atlanta, and Washington, D.C.—African Americans range from 80 to 85 percent of the population, and in

TABLE **13.1.** Language Spoken at Home, Persons Five Years of Age and Older

German	1,547,987
Yiddish	213,064
Other West Germanic language	232,461
Scandinavian	198,904
Greek	388,260
Indic	555,126
Italian	1,308,648
French or French Creole	1,930,404
Portuguese or Portuguese Creole	430,610
Spanish or Spanish Creole	17,345,064
Polish	723,483
Russian	241,798
South Slavic	170,449
Other Slavic language	270,863
Other Indo-European language	578,076
Arabic	355,150
Tagalog	843,251
Chinese	1,319,462
Hungarian	147,902
Japanese	427,657
Mon-Khmer	127,441
Korean	626,478
Native North American languages	331,758
Vietnamese	507,069
Other and unspecified languages	1,023,614
Total speaking language other than English	31,844,979
Total speaking only English	198,600,798
Total U.S. population over five years old	230,445,777

Source: 1990 U.S. census.

some counties of the western United States, Latinos constitute over 50 percent of the population. What has been called the "browning of America" is threatening to the dominant White elite.

As Gramsci taught, "Whenever the language question surfaces, in one way or another, it means that another series of problems is imposing itself" (qtd. in Nunberg 1992, 480). In the USA economic crisis—evidenced in an unresolved federal deficit crisis that caused Congress to shut the government down twice in the 1995–96 legislative year; citizens' anxiety about social deterioration; Whites' fears about loss of power and status; accelerating unemployment exacerbated by increased technological capitalist (over)development; limited resources that will make it impossible for everyone to have a slice of the traditional American (materialist) pie—African Americans and other people of color become ready scapegoats, especially when their language marks them as different. English Only can be used to accomplish what America's internal colonialist apartheid once did: outlaw resources for Blacks (and other people of color) to learn the language and literacy skills needed for them to participate in the USA political economy. They will thus be kept out of competition in the marketplace and "will always be a ready pool of laborers for the dead-end, risky, low-paying jobs that 'true' Americans do not want. At the same time they will be easily expendable in the marketplace" (Davis 1990, 76).

TABLE **13.2.** U.S. Population—1980, 1990, 2000 (Projection)

RACE	1980	1990	2000 (Projection)
African American	26,104,173	29,216,293	33,568,000
Spanish/Hispanic Origin	14,608,673	22,354,059	31,366,000
White	180,256,366	188,128,296	197,061,000
American Indian Eskimo, or Aleut	——————	1,793,773	2,054,000
Asian or Pacific Islander	——————	6,968,359	10,584,000
Other	5,576,593	249,093	1,000
Total	226,545,805	248,709,873	274,634,000

Source: U.S. Bureau of the Census 1996

In the classic divide-and-rule fashion employed by the masters of internal colonialism, the USA English Only movement threatens the developing political alliance of Blacks, Latinos, and other people of color. For instance, if there is a repeal of the Voting Rights Act, which mandates the printing of multilingual election ballots, Blacks would still be able to cast their vote, since most know enough written English to decipher a ballot. But Latinos who are not fluent in English would be unable to vote, thereby jeopardizing the fragile political unity between Blacks and Latinos and their potential to determine or influence election outcomes. Another possible threat to the unity of people of color would be if the current version of the Language of Government Act (essentially an English Only bill) should pass the U.S. Congress. The revised version of this bill now excludes Native American languages, thereby siphoning off opposition to English Only from Native Americans and the liberals who support their cause.

Yet another internal colonialist scenario would be a policy change in the requirements and a diminution in the funding for bilingual educational programs. Generally, these programs operate on a language maintenance, rather than language shift, model, seeking to make non-native English speakers bilingual and multilingual. English Only legislation would call for a reduction in funding for such programs. Further, such legislation would mandate that all bilingual education programs be geared toward the eradication of the native language and the shifting of non-English speakers toward the monolingualism of English Only.

In the *Martin Luther King Junior Elementary School Children v. Michigan Board of Education* federal court ruling of 1979 (also known as the Black English Case), Judge Charles C. Joiner's decision recognized the legitimacy of Ebonics (referred to as "Black English" in the court ruling), and mandated that the Ann Arbor, Michigan, school district had to "take [it] into account" in the teaching of standard English. (I was the chief advocate for the Black single mothers who brought the lawsuit against Ann Arbor; for an analysis, see Smitherman 1981; Labov 1982). In the wake of *King* (1978), which was actually filed in 1977 and set off a firestorm of national controversy for quite a few years after that, the federal government quickly issued an edict declar-

ing that Black English was only a dialect, and that language programs for speakers of Black English were not eligible for bilingual funding. Now, nearly twenty years later, the Oakland,
California, school board's resolution implicitly calls such edicts
into question. By employing the conceptual framework of
"Ebonics" rather than "Black English," the Oakland board introduced a new perspective into the debate, one which contends
that the speech of Africans in America constitutes a *language*,
not a *dialect*. Further, the Ebonics framework opens up the possibility of Black school districts applying for bilingual funds. If
bilingual education funding is not expanded to accommodate this
new demand, however, and if such funding is reduced as a result
of English Only legislation, then we would have a situation of
African and Latino Americans competing for the crumbs from
the colonial master's table—a situation not very different from
the historical conflict and competition among the RSA's internally colonized linguistic ("ethnic") groups under apartheid.

Finally, English Only would undoubtedly have an adverse
impact on the development and maintenance of Ebonics, which
enjoyed a positive period of creative and dynamic development
during the Black Pride-Black Power era (roughly 1966–1980).
The title of one educator's article sums up the language attitudes
of the pre-Black Power era: "Negro Dialect, the Last Barrier to
Integration" (Green 1963). The Black Power movement ushered
in new attitudes among African Americans about their language.
Black Power-Black Pride leaders, activists, intellectuals, and writers freely and defiantly employed Black language and Black communicative practices, cognizant of the need for linguistic
decolonization of Africans in America. They took a language that
was in the throes of decreolization (de-Africanizing) and
recreolized it. What I call the Recreolization movement was captured in the words of poet Haki Madhubuti (1968): "black poets
[will] deal in . . . black language or Afro-American language in
contrast to standard english . . . will talk of kingdoms of Africa,
will speak in Zulu and Swahili, will talk in muthafuckas and 'can
you dig it'" (56).

Although there was a hiatus in the Recreolization movement
with the election of President Reagan in 1980, toward the end of
that decade and especially in the 1990s, hip-hop culture and rap

music—the Ebonics of Black youth and of the Black un-working class—have regenerated the widespread use and creative development of Ebonics. English Only legislation would mandate standard White English in public discourse, the mass media, the schools, governmental affairs, and other institutional contexts. Such a language policy would serve to intensify the class and generational conflicts among African Americans, as well as hamper progressive educational efforts to use Ebonics as a medium of literacy acquisition for Blacks.

Language and Democracy in the RSA

Roman scholar Pliny the Elder, speaking about Africa, stated: "Ex Africa semper aliquid novi": there is always something new out of Africa—in this case, out of South Africa. At a time when the USA is experiencing a movement to amend its Constitution to declare English the sole, official language, newly democratic RSA has adopted a Constitution that mandates eleven official languages: the nine major Black languages (Sepedi, Sesotho, Setswana, siSwati, Tshivenda, Xitsonga, isiNdebele, isiXhosa, and isiZulu) and the two former official languages, English and Afrikaans. Speakers of these eleven languages comprise the overwhelming majority of the South African population (see Table 13.3).

The democratic need for such a language policy was perhaps foreshadowed by President Nelson Mandela, before he was president. In his autobiography, *Long Walk to Freedom,* he recounts a significant historical moment which symbolizes for him the sober recognition that "without language one cannot talk to people and understand them; one cannot share their hopes and aspirations, grasp their history, appreciate their poetry or savour their songs." Mandela (1994) writes:

> I recall on one occasion meeting the queen regent of Basutoland, or what is now Lesotho. . . . The queen took special notice of me and at one point addressed me directly, but spoke in Sesotho, a language in which I knew few words. Sesotho is the language of the Sotho people as well as the Tswana. . . . She looked at me

with incredulity, and then said in English, "What kind of lawyer and leader will you be who cannot speak the language of your own people?" I had no response. The question embarrassed and sobered me; it made me realize my parochialism and just how unprepared I was for the task of serving my people. (96–97)

In establishing eleven official languages, the Constitution mandates that "conditions shall be created for their development and for the promotion of their equal use and enjoyment. . . . A person shall have the right to use and to be addressed in his or her dealings with any public administration . . . of government in any official South African language of his or her choice." Further, the Constitution calls for provisions to promote multilingualism, for translation facilities, and for the "prevention of the use of any language for the purposes of exploitation, domination or division."

There are three significant points to note about language and democracy in the RSA's language policy. First, the Constitution sets forth a policy not of *English Only*, but of *English Plus*—that is, English plus ten other languages as the national official languages of the new democracy. Second, although Blacks constitute 75 percent of South Africa's population, the new Constitution

TABLE 13.3. Official Languages of South Africa

Language	Percent	Number of Speakers (in million)
isiZulu	21.95%	8.8
isiXhosa	17.03%	6.8
Afrikaans	15.03%	6.0
Sepedi	9.64%	3.8
English	9.01%	3.6
Setswana	8.59%	3.4
Sesotho	6.73%	2.7
Xitsonga	4.35%	1.8
siSwati	2.57%	1.0
Tshivenda	2.22%	0.9
isiNdebele	1.55%	0.6

Source: From "Some of the Metaphors about Language, In Language Planning Discourses in South Africa: Boundaries, Frontiers and Commodification," by Sinfree Makoni, 1995, *ELTIC Reporter,* 19(1), p. 21.

protects the language rights of the English-speaking minority, the descendants of the British colonizers, as well as the rights of speakers of Afrikaans, the language developed by Dutch colonizers and associated with the architects of apartheid. Third, in implementing the national language policy in the schools, the language in education policy mandates that in *all* schools, White as well as Black, from primary school on the curriculum must offer two of the official languages as the language of learning and instruction, and at least one of these must be a home language among large numbers of the students in a given school. Further, all students are to be encouraged to add a third language as a subject. Thus the RSA is promoting *additive*, not *subtractive*, multilingualism. The Project for Alternative Education in South Africa (PRAESA), under the leadership of Neville Alexander, summed up South Africa's multilingual education policy with this headline in its 1996 newsletter: "The Power of Babel."

I applaud South Africa's national language policy and see it as a major step forward in the decolonization of the minds of Black South Africans. Like many other USA Blacks, I enthusiastically look forward to the unfolding of democracy in the RSA. Nonetheless, it would be the height of irresponsibility to espouse uncritical and unquestioning acceptance of the policies of the new South Africa. In the spirit of political responsibility and Black camaraderie, I respectfully offer the following observations about efforts to promote language and democracy in South Africa.

First, the eleven-languages policy represents a compromise on the part of the African National Congress (ANC) to secure the National Party's agreement to the constitutional negotiations hammered out at Kempton Park in 1993. The policy elevated the nine major Black languages to national official status in recognition of the need for linguistic decolonization of South African Blacks; on the other hand, the policy left untouched the hegemonic status of English and Afrikaans. Especially in the case of English, this poses a particular problem for the elevation of the Black languages because South African Blacks still seek English-medium schools, "pressurize for English," promote "straight for English" patterns of education, and resist the curricular inclusion of languages other than English—including isiXhosa, the language of the then President Mandela (personal interview with

Marie Louise Samuels 1995). That the hegemony of English is problematic was forcefully brought home in 1996 when the ANC-dominated Joint Standing Defense Committee issued an order that only English (rather than Afrikaans—or isiZulu, isiXhosa, etc.) be used as the language of military command and instruction. President Mandela rebuked the Defense Committee and informed the South African Defense Force to ignore the order (*Christian Science Monitor* 1996).

An alternative language policy would have been to establish the nine African languages at the national level and English and Afrikaans as official provincial languages. Another option would have been a policy with two of the major African languages at the national level, English as a link language at the national level, and the other languages as official provincial languages. There are a number of possibilities, all of which were undoubtedly considered but rejected in the art of compromise that constitutes politics. One can only hope that this compromise does not come back to haunt the ANC.

Second, the language in education policy requires only *two* instructional languages and leaves it to local schools to select those two languages. This leaves open the possibility that the two languages will be English and Afrikaans. At present, only about 7.5 percent of those formerly classified as White, Coloured, or Indian can speak a Black language (Human Sciences Research Council, cited in Desai 1994, 21). If these groups and the Black elite do not embrace the African languages, there is a distinct possibility that we will witness the reinscribing of the apartheid linguistics of the past.

Third is the persistent problem of ambivalent, if not outright negative, attitudes toward the African languages (e.g., Gough 1996; Kamwangamalu 1996)—even among members of the Black intelligentsia (e.g., Phaswana 1994). If the status of these languages is to be elevated, their use must be aggressively promoted among both the Black majority and the White minority (as well as among former "Coloureds" and "Indians"). Serious thought needs to be devoted to creative ways to advance the African languages, above and beyond using them as media of teaching and learning. One idea might be massive public displays of these languages in signs and on billboards, and encouraging and rewarding their pervasive use throughout the mass media such as radio and television programs and advertisements.

In the first parliamentary session of newly democratic South Africa, 87 percent of the speeches were given in English (Quirk 1995). Hopefully, this will not become a pattern. Rather, Black members of Parliament should take leadership in using the languages of their nurture in parliamentary deliberations and discussions. University students might be encouraged to major in translation of these languages with language internships in Parliament.

With its eleven-languages policy, the RSA has embarked on a bold new course in which it can and should take pride. But it has to be made real. Continued adherence to what Nigerian author Chinua Achebe once referred to as the "fatalistic logic of the unassailable position of English" could result in South Africa going the way of other postcolonial African countries, with the emergence of a Black elite, highly fluent in English, and the continued oppression of the Black working and underclass, who lack English fluency.

Conclusion

Among both USA and RSA Blacks, the lingering legacy of internal colonialism continues to characterize Black language politics and to pose a barrier to the full flowering of linguistic democratization. In the USA, the linguistic manifestation of this colonialism is the historical division of the African enslaved community into those who speak "good" English or "bad" English, the devaluing of African languages, the denigration of past and present forms of USA Ebonics, and the awarding of jobs and material benefits to speakers of European American English. In the RSA, the linguistic manifestation is the historical apartheid policy of using African languages to divide the Black community into competing ethnic enclaves, the devaluing of these languages as dialects and gibberish, and the awarding of jobs and material benefits to speakers of English and Afrikaans.

In both the RSA and USA, linguistic colonialism and material deprivation are still the order of the day for everyday people.

As a result of the civil rights-Black Power movement of the 1960s and 1970s, the USA Black community has at last produced a substantive, critical mass of what Du Bois foreshadowed as the "Talented Tenth": the upper 10 percent of Blacks, who would get education, skills, and training, then return to their communities and uplift the masses. At the same time, the conditions of the Black masses have worsened, a fact which the Talented Tenth has thus far either ignored or dealt with ineffectively. USA Ebonics enjoys crossover status, and American public culture, fueled by the energy and dynamism of African American linguistic-cultural production, is a multi-billion-dollar business. It remains to be seen whether the African American community will resolve its internal contradictions and unite (as it has done effectively in the past) to push the dominant White elite toward linguistic democratization and empowerment for those on the margins.

As for RSA Blacks, their country entered a new democratic era in 1994, instituting a Constitution designed to elevate its African languages. It remains to be seen whether the material conditions and sociolinguistic status of the masses of Black South Africans will be fundamentally altered. As of this writing, this is not yet the case, although it is important to remember that the new South Africa is still young.

Walters (1993) concluded the following about Blacks in the RSA and the USA:

> The United States accepted full legal status for Blacks and afforded a modest amount of racial integration and economic, political and social mobility. However, while there has been some absolute change in the status of Blacks, the dominant material conditions and the pattern of social stratification between them and whites has remained largely unchanged. . . . [T]here is in each society [i.e., the RSA and the USA] an enduring pattern of race stratification based on the white dominance-Black subordinate model. . . . [T]his pattern owes its maintenance to such factors as the persistence of institutionalized race prejudice and capitalism. (210, 213)

All of this is, as the saying goes in the USA, the bad news. The good news, and what provides hope for the future of Blacks in both countries, is the fact that Black South African languages and USA Ebonics are alive and well, with no prognosis of linguistic demise in sight. What Du Bois called the "dogged strength" of Black consciousness has continued to resist the linguistic imperialism of internal colonialism. I conclude with the words of Ngugi wa Thiong'o (1986)—words which capture the dogged linguistic spirit of both USA Ebonics speakers and speakers of Black South African languages:

> [African languages] would not simply go the way of Latin to become fossils for linguistic archaeology. . . . [T]hese national heritages of Africa were kept alive by the peasantry [who] saw no contradiction between speaking their own mother-tongues and belonging to a larger national or continental geography. . . . These people happily spoke Wolof, Hausa, Yoruba, Ibo . . . Kiswahili . . . Shona, Ndebele . . . Zulu or Lingala without this fact tearing the multi-national states apart. . . . African languages refused to die. (23)

Notes

1. Bantustans were ethnic "homelands" established under South Africa's apartheid system, whereby Blacks were forced to live in separate areas called "homelands" or "Bantustans." These areas were considered separate "states" even though they were located in the same geographical territory as the White "states" of South Africa and even though the Blacks/Africans were indigenous people and the Whites were English and Dutch settlers. The Bantustans made it easier to discriminate against Black South Africans because they were considered citizens of separate states by the rulings of the South African party.

2. Hendrik Frensch Verwoerd (1901–1966) is considered the chief architect of apartheid.

Works Cited

Alexander, Neville. 1989. *Language Policy and National Unity in South Africa/Azania*. Cape Town: Buchu Books.

Bennett, Lerone. 1961. *Before the Mayflower: A History of Black America*. Chicago: Johnson.

Boyd, Herbert. 1996. "Karenga on Jackson Criticism: 'Jesse is versed in Ebonics.'" *Daily Challenge*. Dec. 27–29. 198.

Castellanos, Diego. 1992. "A Polyglot Nation." In James Crawford, ed., *Language Loyalties: A Source Book on the Official English Controversy*. Chicago: University of Chicago Press. 13–18. (Original work published 1983)

Christian Science Monitor, The. 1996. News article. Feb. 29.

Crawford, James, ed. 1992. *Language Loyalties: A Source Book on the Official English Controversy*. Chicago: University of Chicago Press.

Davis, Vivian. 1990. "Paranoia in Language Politics." In Harvey Daniels, ed., *Not Only English: Affirming America's Multilingual Heritage*. Urbana, IL: National Council of Teachers of English. 71–76.

Desai, Zubeida. 1994. "Praat or Speak but Don't Theta: On Language Rights in South Africa." *Language and Education* 8(1-2): 19–29.

Dillard, Joey Lee. 1972. *Black English*. New York: Random House.

———. 1977. *Lexicon of Black English*. New York: Seabury Press.

Du Bois, William E. B. 1961. *Souls of Black Folk: Essays and Sketches*. New York: Fawcett Edition. (Original work published 1903)

Fanon, Frantz. 1963. *The Wretched of the Earth*. New York: Grove Press.

Farrakhan, Louis. 1996. "Day of Atonement." In Haki R. Madgubuti and Maulena Karenga, eds., *Million Man March/Day of Absence: A Commemorative Anthology*. Chicago: Third World Press.

Franklin, Benjamin. 1992. "The German Language in Pennsylvania." In James Crawford, ed., *Language Loyalties: A Source Book on the Official English Controversy*. Chicago: University of Chicago Press. 18–19. (Original work published 1753)

Gawthrop, Betty. 1965. "1911–1929." In Raven I. McDavid Jr., ed., *An Examination of the Attitudes of the NCTE Toward Language*. Urbana, IL: National Council of Teachers of English. 7–15.

Gough, David. 1996. "Black English in South Africa." In Vivian deKlerk, ed., *Focus on South Africa*. Amsterdam: Benjamins.

Green, Gordon C. 1963. "Negro Dialect, the Last Barrier to Integration." *Journal of Negro Education* 32: 81–83.

Harrison, James A. 1884. "Negro English." *Anglia* 7: 232–79.

Hayakawa, S. I. 1992. "The Case for Official English." In James Crawford, ed., *Language Loyalties: A Source Book on the Official English Controversy.* Chicago: University of Chicago Press. 94–100. (Original work published 1981)

Jaffe, Hosea. 1994. *European Colonial Despotism: A History of Oppression and Resistance in South Africa.* London: Karnak House.

Kamwangamalu, Nkonko M. 1996. *Multilingualism and Education Policy in Post-Apartheid South Africa.* Paper presented at the Fifth Conference of the International Society for the Scientific Study of European Ideas, Utrecht, Netherlands. August 19–24.

Kelly, David. 1997. "Native Tongues." *The Source* (April): 26–27.

King. 1978. *The Martin Luther King Junior Elementary School Children v. The Michigan Board of Education, the Michigan Superintendent of Public Instruction, and the Ann Arbor School District Board.* Civil Action No. 77-71861, U.S. District Court, Eastern District of Michigan, Southern Division.

Labov, William. 1982. "Objectivity and Commitment in Linguistic Science: The Case of the Black English Trial in Ann Arbor." *Language in Society* 11: 165–201.

Leland, John, and Nadine Joseph. 1997. "Education: Hooked on Ebonics." *Newsweek* 129(1): 78–79.

Lewis, Neil. 1989. "Chancellor Aims to Purge 'What-Cha's' and Ain't's." *New York Times.* Feb. 28. 5B.

Madhubuti, Haki (formerly Don L. Lee). 1968. "Directions for Black Writers." *Black Scholar* (December): 53–57.

Magubane, Bernard, and Ibbo Mandaza, eds. 1988. *Whither South Africa?* Trenton: Africa World Press.

Mandela, Nelson. 1994. *Long Walk to Freedom.* Randburg, South Africa: Macdonald Purnell.

Nunberg, Geoffrey. 1992. "The Official English Movement: Reimaging America." In James Crawford, ed., *Language Loyalties: A Source Book on the Official English Controversy.* Chicago: University of Chicago Press. 479–94.

Phaswana, Nklebehni E. 1994. *African Language Planning Policies at the University of Venda and the Medium of Instruction Question.* Unpublished master's thesis, University of Cape Town, South Africa.

Quirk, Randolph. 1995. Keynote address. English in Africa Conference, Grahamstown, South Africa. September 11–14.

Samuels, Marie Louise [Headmistress, Battswood Educare Center]. 1995. Interview by Geneva Smitherman and Ezra Hyland. Cape Town, August 22.

Simmons, Judy D. 1997. "Ebonics Plagues Policymakers." *Daily Challenge*, Jan. 3–5.

Smitherman, Geneva. 1977. *Talkin' and Testifyin': The Language of Black America*. Detroit: Wayne State University Press.

———. 1981. "'What Go Round Come Round': King in Perspective." *Harvard Educational Review* 51: 40–56.

Tollefson, James W. 1991. *Planning Language, Planning Inequality: Language Policy in the Community*. London: Longman.

Turner, Lorenzo D. 1949. *Africanisms in the Gullah Dialect*. Chicago: University of Chicago Press.

U.S. Bureau of the Census. 1990. *Languages Spoken at Home, Persons Five Years of Age and Older*. Washington, D.C.: Census Population Statistics.

Vass, Winifred K. 1979. *The Bantu Speaking Heritage of the United States*. Los Angeles: University of California Center for Afro-American Studies.

Walker, Alice. 1982. *The Color Purple*. New York: Harcourt Brace Jovanovich.

Walters, Ronald W. 1993. *Pan Africanism in the African Diaspora*. Detroit: Wayne State University Press.

wa Thiong'o, Ngugi. 1986. "The Politics of Language in African Literature." In Lou Turner and John Alan, eds., *Frantz Fanon, Soweto and American Black Thought*. Chicago: News and Letters.

Willams, Robert L., ed. 1975. *Ebonics: The True Language of Black Folks*. St. Louis: Institute of Black Studies.

Chapter Fourteen

The "Normalization" of
Minority Languages in Spain

Cynthia Miguélez
Universidad de Alicante, Spain

Official language policy and the actions of governmental and regulatory institutions serve as excellent indicators of the political climate and general acceptance of linguistically different groups in areas where two or more languages, and therefore two or more culturally different groups, coexist. The struggle to create a social and political atmosphere in which cultural and linguistic diversity are not only accepted but truly valued is a difficult one. This is certainly true in the United States, where many of the advances made over the last few decades in the number and kinds of services available to non-English-speaking or limited-English-proficient individuals have been reversed by the English Only movement and the positioning of immigrants—and, by extension, all those within the United States who seem "foreign"—as the new national "enemy" since the fall of the Soviet Union and communism. One of the programs that has been the object of severe criticism and serious derailment efforts is bilingual education. Educational programs are the cornerstone of language maintenance and enrichment, and without them, other efforts to create an atmosphere of acceptance for all ethnic and linguistic groups often suffer and fail.

Spain is a country which enjoys a great deal of linguistic diversity within its borders, with several regionally based languages in use along with Spanish, the national language. The struggle to maintain or enhance the use of these regional languages is similar in some aspects to the struggle in the United States to protect and promote the rich linguistic pluralism that exists unofficially within its borders. Some clear parallels are interesting to note.

For example, regional languages in Spain are considered "historical." This means they were spoken in areas that at some point in the past were recognized political entities that did not belong to what we now call Spain. These areas have had a separate and independent history; significant cultural manifestations in literature, music, folklore, and so on; and even well-defined legal and administrative systems. At different points in time, and through different historical processes, each of these regions became part of what is today the nation called Spain. In the United States, a similar situation can be found in relation to the country's major second language, Spanish. The entire southwestern section of the country was part of Mexico until the mid-nineteenth century, when the Tratado de Guadalupe Hidalgo and the Tratado de la Mesilla (the Gadsden Purchase) provided for the transfer of these lands to U.S. territorial status. The peoples who inhabited these lands already had a culture, a language, a shared history, and an identity as a community when they were ushered into a new political reality, the result of events over which they themselves had little control. Given these facts, Spanish would qualify as a "historical" language, at least in certain parts of the United States, according to the definition of that term as used in Spain.

Another point of commonality between Spain and the United States is that minority or regional languages in both countries have been the object of empassioned support and bitter attack by various segments of society at different points in time. The pendulum has swung in both directions in terms of approval for programs designed to assist linguistically different individuals. Legislation has been introduced establishing the rights of linguistic minorities and mandating services for them such as the Bilingual Education Act in the United States and the various *Estatutos de Autonomía* in Spain. The difference lies in the tenor of the debate in each country, especially surrounding bilingual education. In the United States, the focus has been almost exclusively remedial and transitional, while in Spain it has been maintenance and enrichment. In Spain strong legislative, institutional, and societal support has been given to what is called the "normalization" of regional languages. This term refers to both the reestablishment of these languages so that their use is considered "normal" once again and to efforts to standardize some of them for educational development purposes because they had fragmented into many oral variants and dialects during the almost forty years of neglect and repression they were subject to during the middle of this century. The proactive and positive approach Spain has taken to enrich its linguistic reality through bilingualism has proven to be a key element in the resurgence of these languages. In contrast, bilingualism in the United States is not considered high prestige, school districts often only begrudgingly offer bilingual education programs and then only to correct what is considered a deficiency, and there is constant questioning of the validity of promoting bi- or multilingualism instead of focusing on how best to produce well-prepared young people who can speak two or more languages fluently and in an educated manner. The Spanish experience offers a positive approach to creating respect and appreciation for the many languages that coexist within a country's borders and can shed some light on the role of the government and societal institutions in creating an atmosphere of tolerance and acceptance.

Background

Within Spanish borders, *castellano* is the name given to the language which in English-speaking countries is called Spanish. In addition to this language, several others are spoken in different regions of the peninsula. Four of the most widely used are *galego*, spoken in Galicia in the northwestern corner of Spain; *euskera* or Basque, spoken in the three Basque Country of Spain (Vizcaya, Guipúzcoa, and Álava) and in some of the northern parts of Navarra; *català*, spoken along the eastern Mediterranean seaboard and in the Balearic Islands; and *bable*, spoken in Asturias in northern Spain. Some of these languages have regional variants or dialects, referred to in Spanish administrative parlance as *"modalidades lingüísticas."*

In the early part of this century, Spain was basically a rural agrarian society. During this period, regional language use was widespread. A large percentage of the population in some areas of Spain did not speak *castellano*. Travel was limited, and for many there was virtually no contact with people from outside their own language community. The Spanish Civil War drastically altered the linguistic reality of Spain. Franco's monolithic vision of a united and homogeneous country had as its goal a monolingual country in which all citizens shared a common language. Speaking the regional languages was considered divisive, therefore subversive, and laws were passed prohibiting their use in public. Speakers of these languages were criticized and ridiculed. When Francoist forces entered Barcelona after the Civil War, for example, they put up signs that said, *"Catalán, no ladres, hable castellano"* (People of Catalonia, don't bark, speak Castellano), equating speaking the home language of that city to barking and the people who spoke it to dogs (Bellón Carabán 1995, 16).

The language of all instruction, of all institutional and governmental activity, and of all publishing and media was officially *castellano*. Use of the term *español* to refer to the language began to be heard more often. *Español* was the language of *España* and of all *españoles*, including the *catalanes, gallegos, asturianos y vascos*. Some analogies can be drawn with the concept of the "melting pot" in the United States and with the general mood that prevailed during the 1950s and McCarthyism, when an exaggerated emphasis was placed on being "American," as defined by a few who felt they alone knew what it meant to be American. This spirit of promoting homogenization of the population and forging a single and universally applicable definition of an American has been kept alive by groups such as those supporting the English First and English Only movements.

In many regions of Spain in the 1930s, 1940s, and 1950s, diglossia was the rule, not the exception. *Castellano/español* was used outside the home, and the regional languages were used inside the home, and all Spaniards educated during these decades did indeed learn *castellano*. In spite of this, the Francoist regime failed in its efforts to eradicate regional languages, which survived, albeit in a clandestine way and to varying degrees depending on the geographical area and the language in question.

Other events had a strong impact on language usage as well, especially from the 1950s on. Both the advent of television and the beginning of a period of extensive internal migration greatly affected the linguistic reality of Spain. Television and radio have been the chief standardizers of languages and cultures. In Spain during the Franco regime, television, radio, and the print media were all controlled by the government. The arrival of state-controlled, monolingual television to small rural communities in the 1960s brought *castellano* into many homes where it had not previously been heard, much less used as a tool of communication. People's passive acceptance and subsequent knowledge of *castellano* grew, and soon after so did their active use of this language. Franco used the visual media aggressively and effectively to mold public opinion and to "standardize" national values and attitudes in his efforts to make Spain the unified and indivisible entity he had envisioned, a nation he called *"una, grande y libre."*

The change from a rural agrarian society to a more industrialized urban society brought great shifts in population as speakers of *castellano* moved into Catalonia and the Basque Country, two areas where regional languages had a strong base. Within the different regions themselves, many people moved from a rural setting, where it was difficult for the government to monitor and control language use, into urban areas, where the language of school, the workplace, and officialdom was dictated from above and was always *castellano*. Although each region experienced and reacted to these phenomena in its own way, it can be said that in all linguistically diverse areas of Spain, the years of Franco's rule were oppressive, and the retention of regional languages presented a formidable challenge.

The Transition to Democracy

In Spain the period immediately after Franco's death until the first democratic national elections and the promulgation of the 1978 Constitution is known as *"la transición."* A forty-year period of dictatorship was replaced by a fully functioning democracy in which previously outlawed political parties representing a wide range of political ideologies freely participated. The fact that this transition took place smoothly and nonviolently in a relatively short period is a great source of pride for the Spanish people. The Spanish model has been admired and imitated in other regions of the world where similar situations have existed.

The resurgence of regional nationalism after Franco's death in 1975 can be compared in some ways to the explosion of ethnic and racial pride that came about in the 1960s in the United States during the civil rights movement. There was in both situations a sense of urgency about gaining respect for "different" groups and ensuring their proper place within the broader society. In the United States, laws were passed and programs were established to promote tolerance and raise awareness of the multicultural and multilingual nature of the country. While acceptance was not complete nor tolerance perfect, advances were made. Bilingual education programs and ethnic studies departments in universities were part of the process.

In Spain similar efforts were made to recover a sense of regional identity and to promote pride in the heritage and language of the different peoples of Spain. As in the United States, a language, a common history, and a shared culture are the elements that identify a specific community within a larger entity. Laws were passed in Spain to promote the use of regional languages, and educational programs were developed. This governmental and institutional support contributed greatly to the success that was achieved in returning Spain to its pre–Civil War level of linguistic and cultural diversity.

Legal Foundations for Language Recovery

Spain is currently a constitutional or parliamentary monarchy comprising seventeen *comunidades autónomas*. This denomination is given to the first level of political division of Spain as a nation. Roughly speaking, a *comunidad autónoma* in some ways can be compared to a state in the United States. It is important to be aware of these divisions in order to understand the legal foundations for linguistic diversity in Spain.

The current Spanish Constitution dates back to December 1978, three years after Franco's death. The Constitution is made up of 169 articles that set out the rules by which Spanish society is to function. The preamble states the philosophy and principles of the new democratic nation, among which we find constitutional protection for culture, traditions, and language:

> La nación española . . . proclama su voluntad de: . . . Proteger a todos los españoles y pueblos de España en el ejercicio de los derechos humanos, sus culturas y tradiciones, lenguas e instituciones. [The nation of Spain . . . proclaims its will to: . . . protect the human rights, culture, traditions, languages and institutions of all the citizens and peoples of Spain.]

Article 2 of the Constitution recognizes that while Spain is indivisible as a nation, it is made up of several regional communities. Although solidarity is stated as the basis for the relationship between the different communities, this article also guarantees them "autonomy":

> La Constituticón se fundamenta en la indisoluble unidad de la Nación española, patria común e indivisible de todos los españoles y reconoce y garantiza el derecho a la autonomía de las nacionalidades y regiones que la integran y la solidaridad entre todas ellas. [The Constitution is based on the permanent unity of the Spanish nation, the common and indivisible homeland of all Spaniards, and it recognizes and guarantees the right to autonomy of the nationalities and regions that form part of the nation and the solidarity that exists between them.]

Article 3 addresses the issue of language and linguistic diversity head-on. It first establishes *castellano* as the official language of Spain, stating that all citizens have the duty to know it and the right to use it. It then immediately recognizes the regional languages as co-official in the autonomous communities where they are spoken in accordance with whatever the regional law on the subject may be. The article ends by making a philosophical statement to the effect that the linguistic diversity of Spain is a national treasure which should be respected and protected:

> Art.3.1.El castellano es la lengua española oficial del Estado. Todos los españoles tienen el deber de conocerla y el derecho de usarla.2. Las demás lenguas españolas serán también oficiales en las respectivas Comunidades Autónomas de acuerdo con sus

Estatutos.3. La riqueza de las distintas modalidades lingüísticas de España es un patrimonio cultural que será objeto de especial respeto y protección. [Art. 3.1. *Castellano* is the official Spanish language of the State. All Spaniards have the obligation to know it and the right to use it. 2. The other Spanish languages are also official in the respective Autonomous Communities [in which they are spoken] according to their statutes. 3. The wealth of languages that exists in Spain is a part of our cultural heritage that merits special respect and protection.]

Articles 137 and 143 of the Spanish Constitution more fully develop the geopolitical organization of the Spanish state and confer a certain degree of autonomy on the different regions. This sets the basis for each *comunidad autónoma* to develop a set of laws and regulations by which to govern itself. Shared governance of this kind is new to Spain but suits Spanish reality well because it recognizes the *"nacionalidades históricas"* which have long existed within Spain, and allows other regions with a strong sense of regional identity to gain a degree of self-rule. One of the results of this quasi-federal system, however, is that language policy varies from one region to another since it is based—as the Constitution provides—on regional legislation and statutory provisions.

The first two regions to promulgate a type of regional constitution called *"Estatutos de Autonomía"* were the Basque Country and Catalonia in 1979. All the other regions of Spain followed suit in the next few years, and the geopolitical map of Spain, as it exists today, was drawn by 1983. Because each of the seventeen regions wrote and negotiated its own *estatutos* with the central government, the division of power and assignation of competencies varies to some extent from one area to another. Some of the regional governments, for example, have control over the educational system (Catalonia, the Basque Country, Andalucia, and Galicia, to name a few), while in other *comunidades*, education is still controlled by the central government's Ministry of Education. In terms of linguistic diversity, a total of seven of the seventeen regional *estatutos* grant co-official status to a language other than *castellano*. These include Catalonia and the Balearic Islands, where the co-official language is *català*; Valencia, where *valenciano* is spoken; Galicia, the area where the regional language, *galego*, is spoken by a higher percentage of the population than any of the other regional languages in their respective areas; the Basque Country, in which *euskera* is recognized as the regional language; and Navarra, where a variant of Basque known as *vizcaino euskera* or *vascuence* is spoken in a small part of the *comunidad*. The first census taken after the current regional divisions were created shows that in 1986, 42 percent of the population of Spain resided in these two-language areas (Siguan 1992, 80).

Each of these regions has a unique linguistic reality, and each provides an interesting case study. Catalonia, a prosperous and dynamic region of Spain, has experienced a high level of immigration from other economically more depressed areas. Approximately half of its inhabitants were born outside of the region itself. Nevertheless, the *catalán* language enjoys great prestige and is widely used in Catalonia, with those whose mother tongue is *castellano* stating that they can understand and often even speak it. More than six million people are reported to speak *català*. This represents approximately 74 percent of the population. Another 22 percent say they understand the language although they do not speak it, and only 4 percent state that they neither speak nor understand it (Meyer 1998).

The case of the Balearic Islands is also quite interesting. Variants of *català* are spoken in Ibiza (*ibicenco*), Mallorca (*mallorquín*), and Menorca (*menorquín*). Speakers of these dialects and of *català* are mutually understandable. The inhabitants of these islands were somewhat isolated for many years, so their language usage was less affected by the pressures brought to bear on the peninsula. But the growing popularity of these islands as tourist destinations in the last twenty years has produced an influx of seasonal workers from other areas as well as many foreign residents, all of which has had an influence on language usage. Use of *mallorquín* in Mallorca is reported at 50 percent of the population in the capital city and up to 80 percent in outlying areas.

Valencia is located immediately to the south of Catalonia and comprises three provinces, all bordering the Mediterranean. The case of *valenciano* is an interesting one. Regional groups were strongly in favor of its reestablishment but could not agree on the correct denomination for this language. *Valenciano* is grammatically similar to *català*, so the *catalanistas* consider it simply a dialect of that language. There are appreciable lexical and phonetic differences between the two languages, however, and a vocal and active group defends the position that *valenciano* is a separate language. This faction cites the rich history, including its literature, of the language as spoken in areas of Valencia, which they feel should not be considered part of Catalonian history or literature. Additionally, areas of Valencia are not traditionally *valenciano*-speaking, and this is one of the reasons that the "historical" language has fallen into disuse here more than in some of the other regions of Spain. Since the efforts to recover regional languages has been in place, however, *valenciano* has steadily gained in prestige and usage.

The Basque Country maintains a strong nationalist movement, but knowledge of *euskera* is relatively low. Approximately 630,000 people, only about one in four, still speak the language in one of its eight recognized dialects. This may be due to the fact that *euskera* is a difficult language to master and one that does not share many features with *castellano*, as most of the other regional languages do. In parts of the provinces, *euskera* has not been spoken for centuries (Siguan 1992, 83). *Euskera* is still considered the home language in only a small area of northern Navarra, but the recovery projects continue to identify individuals throughout the Navarran region who speak it.

Finally, the case of Galicia merits special attention because in many ways it shares the most points in common with the situation of Spanish in the United States. As mentioned earlier, Galicia is the area in which the highest percent of inhabitants list the regional language, *galego,* as their mother tongue. Eighty percent of this population speaks the regional language, with comprehension reaching 90 percent, a figure that represents 2.5 million people. Galicia also has a rich literary tradition. These facts could be interpreted as a sign of high prestige and effective conservation of the language, but the reality is that this region traditionally has had a lower level of economic prosperity, less schooling and access to the media, and more emigration than immigration. Consequently, regional language use has remained high, especially in rural areas, but until recently it was generally associated with poverty and ignorance. There was little social pressure to use *galego* as a language of instruction and study in the schools. *Castellano* was seen as the language of the rich and powerful, the language of upward social mobility. Even though most adults spoke *galego* among themselves, they would often speak to their children in *castellano*, even if they did not speak it well. This phenomenon is one that many Latinos in the United States can relate to. When bilingual programs were first implemented in the United States, it was sometimes difficult to convince Spanish-speaking parents to allow their children to participate. Many felt that the best way to help their children survive and prosper in the United States was to have them become as much like the majority as possible, and if this meant shedding home and ancestral languages and culture, so be it. No one seemed bothered by the irony: these same children who were pushed to become monolingual in English in elementary school were later required to study a "foreign" language (often their home language) under the tutelage of a non-native speaker. Although some progress was being made in the United States in creating respect for bilingualism, in the last several years bilingual programs and the maintenance of languages other than English have once again come under attack. In Galicia great strides have been made in restoring prestige to the regional language. Much of the pressure for change is coming from above, from the government and institutions of higher education. The effort to reestablish the regional language in Galicia has not been so much a process of recovery as one of status building.

Regarding regional language policy, these seven areas share some common features and yet also differ in significant ways. The common points are that all of the *estatutos* have established the co-official status of their respective regional language and *castellano*, prohibit discrimination based on language, and explicitly state that people living in the region have the right to speak their "own language" even though the Spanish Constitution stipulates that all citizens have the duty to learn *castellano* and the right to use it anywhere in Spain.

Catalonia, the Basque Country, Valencia, and Galicia set a legal foundation for governmental and institutional action in laws that stipulate that the government will create the conditions and provide the means needed to promote and protect the regional language. In Valencia and Navarra, specific mention is made in the *estatutos* of educational programs designed to recover and promote these languages. In the Basque Country, the *estatutos* recognize the sociolinguistic diversity of the region and create an official academy of the Basque language (*Real Academia de la Lengua Vasca-Euskaltazaindia*) along the lines of Spain's Royal Academy of the Spanish Language (*Real Academia de la Lengua Española*), the function of which is to oversee from a descriptive, not prescriptive, perspective the use of the Spanish language (i.e., *castellano*), not only in Spain but also throughout the world. The official body in Asturias called the *Academia de la Llingua Asturiana* (*bable*) and the *Instituts de Estudis Catalans* in Catalonia are similar in some of their functions to an academy of the language. In the Balearic Islands, the dialects or *"modalidades"* of *català* spoken are recognized and protected, and are the object of study without that fact affecting in any way the acceptance or recognition of *català* as the "mother" language of these island variants. And finally, the *estatutos* of Navarra and Valencia recognize that there are zones within their regional borders in which the regional language is not used.

In addition to the seven regions that have negotiated a co-official status for their languages with the central government, other regions include in their regional statutes a lesser degree of formal language recognition. In Asturias the regional language of *bable* is granted protection, promotion, and respect. In Aragon the linguistic diversity of the region is protected as part of the region's cultural and historic legacy. And in Andalucía, where many would argue that *castellano* is the only language spoken, the *estatuto autonómico* states that an awareness of Andalusian cultural identity will be encouraged through research and the dissemination of knowledge about the rich and varied historical, cultural, and linguistic values of the Andalusian people.

Where there is no formal or legal recognition of a regional language, there are often attempts at some level to promote a variant or seek institutional recognition for it. Such is the case in León, where two associations—*Facendera pola Llingua* and *La*

Academia de Llingua Lleunesa—have been created in the last three or four years to defend *"lleonés"* as a regional language. The Asturian language is often called *"astur-leonés,"* but defenders of both *bable* and *leonés* emphasize the differences between the two. Many believe that if León had remained a separate region during the process of drawing the geopolitical map of Spain instead of being administratively connected to Castilla, there would be more institutional and societal attention paid to the distinct linguistic characteristics of the region.

Finally, it is important to point out that there are also laws for the "normalization" of regional languages that develop the precepts found in the *estatutos*. The way in which language is spoken of in these laws is a good indicator of the reverence the Spanish have for language. In the Basque Country, language is recognized as the *"elemento integrador de todos los ciudadanos del País Vasco"* (the element that unites all of the citizens of the Basque Country). In the Balearic Islands, *català* is considered the *"vehículo de expresión y principal símbolo de nuestra identidad como pueblo"* (the means of expression and the most important symbol of our identity as a people). In Galicia *galego* is described as *"el núcleo vital de nuestra identidad"* (the vital nucleus of our identity) and *"la mayor y más original creacion colectiva de los gallegos, la verdadera fuerza espiritual que le da unidad interna a nuestra Comunidad"* (the greatest and most original collective creation of the Galician people, the true spiritual force that gives us our sense of community). In Navarra the law reads, *"Aquellas Comunidades que, como Navarra, se honran en disponer en su patrimonio de más de una lengua están obligadas a preservar este tesoro y evitar su deterioro o su pérdida"* (Those regions that are privileged to have more than one language as part of their cultural heritage, as is Navarra, have an obligation to protect this treasure and keep it from deteriorating or disappearing.) The unequivocal wording of these statutes clearly demonstrates that language diversity is considered a positive aspect of the cultural identity of a community, something worthy of protection. Nowhere in Spain is linguistic pluralism seen as a threat or described as a divisive factor in society, as it is often depicted in the United States by some factions.

From Legal Precepts to Practice

Having a strong legal foundation for action is all well and good, but it is not a guarantee that useful, practical programs will be designed and put into practice. Clearly, laws cannot magically change public opinion, immediately reform longstanding institutional practices, or right the wrongs that have been perpetuated for decades, nor can they produce an overnight change in individual linguistic practices. They can, however, mandate that efforts be made to address the problems in ways that do not produce a backlash or create new problems to replace the old ones. In Spain proactive attempts were made to entice people who were reluctant to return to the regional languages to make the effort. Assurances had to be given that there would be no negative repercussions for doing so after forty years of linguistic repression. Those who were able and willing to reactivate their use of the regional languages were rewarded, and resources were dedicated to providing attractive cultural events and leisure activities in the "lost" languages. All of these efforts were coupled with strong educational programs designed to provide children and adults with a solid base in the historical language and culture of their area, and the opportunity to become bilingual again while strengthening their biculturalism.

One of the main areas of activity was in public administration, the way in which government employees interacted with the everyday citizen. New legislation mandated that all laws and legal provisions were to be published and all official documents and information were to be made available in both languages. Either language could be used in administrative and legal proceedings of any kind, and means had to be provided to ensure that citizens could interact with the administration in whichever language they preferred. One of the practical outcomes of this legal mandate was that a certain number of government employees in each department or division had to speak both languages. In most two-language communities, incentives were instituted to promote bilingualism among government employees. Extra points were given to candidates applying for posts who could prove proficiency in the regional language, and monolingual workers who were already employed were given the opportunity to attend language classes often provided free of charge or at a very low fee by the government. Work schedules were sometimes adapted to accommodate participation in these language classes, and in certain cases comp time was granted for attendance, sending a clear message to employees that becoming functional in the regional language was highly valued. These programs came to be known as "recycling" programs, a kind of inservice effort to provide employees with new skills that were not stipulated as requirements when they were first employed. In Catalonia a directive was issued stating that the internal operating language of public entities was to be *català*, another means of encouraging government employees to learn the language which actually gave them an opportunity to practice on the job.

Another effort made by regional administrations was to carry out social research and provide statistical information to the private sector in order to encourage regional language use in ad campaigns and business interactions. In this way, the regional languages would grow in social prestige and functional value.

Regional languages were also promoted through government subsidies of cultural events and activities that made use of the regional language. These subsidies came not only from regional governments but also from the central government. Theater groups that wrote and performed in regional languages were funded. Efforts to produce publications written in the regional languages were supported, be they literary magazines, comic books, or student or community newspapers. Daily and weekly newspapers and news publications can now be found in all of the major regional languages. Radio and television programs were developed and aired on government-run channels. Time was blocked out of daily programming on national state-controlled television channels for regional newscasts and documentaries. Eventually, separate regional television and radio stations were created which broadcast 100 percent of their programming in the regional language. Special attention was given to programs aimed at children. Popular cartoon series dubbed in the regional language were quite successful in attracting preschoolers and exposing them to a language to which they might not otherwise have had access before entering school. These kinds of efforts encouraged language acquisition by making it fun and attractive.

The final and perhaps most important area in which the government and institutions of Spain played a significant role in the recovery of regional languages was through the educational system. School programs are without a doubt the most effective way of achieving this type of societal goal. The educational effort encompasses many facets of the recovery and reestablishment of an endangered language including identifying the state of affairs that exists before recovery programs are instituted, setting policies for action and designing specific projects to implement those policies, and developing curricula and designing appropriate materials for all levels of schooling, from preschool to the adult education programs sponsored by the government. They also include what might be called public relations efforts to inform the public of the nature of the programs to be offered, the options available, and the expected outcomes, in order to raise awareness and make the programs attractive. Finally, they include proposals for ways in which educational institutions would integrate parents and the public in the general process and mechanisms for addressing problems that arise.

In Spain bilingual education was implemented to meet these goals. Different types of programs were proposed. In all regions involved in these efforts, the laws governing the educational programs recognized a child's right to be educated at the outset in his or her home language, be that *castellano* or the regional language. The parents of children from homes in which both languages were spoken had the right to decide in which language they wished their children to receive instruction. In addition, it was mandated that children study the other language, and that by the time they finished elementary school, they be proficient in both languages. This recognition of the desirability of producing proficient bilinguals is of special interest. Only Catalonia has moved beyond this desire for proficient bilinguals to one of monolingual proficiency in *català*. In other words, what started out as enrichment bilingual programs has evolved into early childhood immersion programs and transition to *catalán* programs for *castellano*-speaking children. This approach, however, is meeting with a great deal of criticism and resistance from a large sector of society which supports proficient bilingualism but not transitional monolingualism.

How has this desire to produce bilingual students translated into real programs? The efforts made by the departments of education throughout the regions of Spain to encourage students to participate in bilingual programs range from incentives to obligatory studies. At a minimum, students in most regions are required to study the regional language as a school subject from the time they enter kindergarten until they finish their preuniversity education. Exercises in the regional language form part of the university entrance exam procedures, although once at university, students in most major areas are not required to continue formal study of the regional language. They are, however, entitled to study in the regional language and present their papers and take their exams in either of the official languages recognized in the region.

Other programs at the preuniversity level include bilingual schools where, for example, there is a *"línea valenciana"* alongside a *"línea castellana."* Incentives are in place to entice students into the regional language programs. Some of these include free or subsidized books and school materials, free transportation to a school where there is a full bilingual program, generally smaller classroom size, and so on. Of course, these incentives and the actual programs offered vary from region to region and from community to community. In Catalonia the immersion approach is more popular. In Euskadi or the Basque Country, *ikastolas*, or Basque schools, were created in the Franco era as a clandestine attempt to forestall the demise of the Basque language. With great effort, they were established as a parallel alternative to the school system which provided only Spanish-language instruction. These schools are now being incorporated into the public school system. In Valencia the bilingual school approach is the most frequently encountered. As for instruction, the "recycling" approach described earlier for government employees was also instituted for teachers who were not proficient in the regional language. Once again, language acquisition or improvement courses were offered at convenient times and at low or no cost, and teachers were awarded points that could be used when seeking promotion and mobility within the system. Furthermore, proficiency in the regional language was an important require- ment for new hires, no matter what the level or the subject. Teach- ers were also sometimes awarded grants and release time to develop materials not only for language acquisition but also for cultural activities programs. Emphasis was not placed exclusively on learning the language, but rather on learning the language as part of the broader culture, with its history, literature, music, customs, and values. All of these elements were incorporated into Spain's educational programs.

Conclusions

It is certainly true that governmental or institutional action alone cannot ensure the success of a given linguistic policy. There must be popular support for the basic underlying principles and phi- losophy of the policy, and societal forces must be involved in the creation, development, implementation, and modification of the programs that develop the policy. The policies themselves must be based on a solid understanding of the sociolinguistic realities of a community, region, or country so that appropriate and real- istic decisions can be made. There is, however, a symbiosis be- tween policy and public opinion, and the old question of which came first, the chicken or the egg, is applicable. Does public opin- ion dictate governmental policy, or does governmental action form public opinion? It is most certainly a little of both. Spain pro- vides a good example. While it is true that there was broad pub- lic support for drastic change after forty years of dictatorial rule under Franco, it is also true that lawmakers and those in posi- tions of power were able to interpret the social atmosphere of the time correctly, put the desire for more freedom and tolerance into eloquent words that guaranteed equal rights and recogni- tion for all, and then translate those words into real programs that would produce tangible results.

Language policies in Spain are not free of controversy. The goals set for the "normalization" or reestablishment of regional languages have not yet been universally met, and those involved in the process are still grappling with problems such as how to equitably distribute funds earmarked for language normalization, how to best promote bilingualism without mandating it, and how to improve educational programs designed to give students and adults alike an opportunity to become bilingual. Errors have been made, some due to a lack of experience in bilingual efforts, some to a lack of consensus, some to overzeal-ousness. In Catalonia, for example, there is a movement afoot to replace monolingualism in *castellano* with monolingualism in *català*. While this approach is supported by some of the more radical social and political sectors of Catalan society, it is rejected by many and has become the subject of intense social debate at all levels. Currently, there seems to be less support for *català* monolingualism than for bilingualism.

As is to be expected, social response has not been uniform. Unanimous support does not exist for any of the approaches being tried, and the social debate about the desired final outcome of these experiments continues. One of the most interesting problems related to language normalization at present has to do with the fact that Spain is becoming an increasingly mobile country internally, and issues related to exactly who should be required or expected to study or master a regional language and how to strike a balance between "natives" and "newcomers" still have not been resolved. One approach has been to exempt the children of families that move into a region due to employment opportunities or work assignments from studying the regional language for two years if the parents so desire, especially if the assignment is a temporary one. Many parents do not choose this option, however, especially if they consider their move to the area to be permanent.

In spite of these ongoing problems, there is a general acceptance of the concept of endangered languages and of the need to ensure the survival of Spain's regional languages. There is a general consensus that individuals should be allowed to speak these languages in a wide range of situations, at least in the regions where they have a historical base, and that the government and institutions are the social agents that should provide the means by which these goals can be achieved. Finally, there is a great respect for bi- and multilingualism that is not limited to these regional languages, a fact which contributes to the prestige they enjoy.

Spain's proactive approach to the reestablishment of its regional languages, its appreciation and understanding of the benefits of having a population that is proficient in more than one language, its ongoing debate on how to achieve the final goal without continually questioning the goal itself, and the government-sponsored programs that have been instituted to achieve the goal all serve as a positive example. Serious issues still need to be resolved and there are still dangers to be avoided, but the steps taken up to this point have proven productive, as can be seen by turning on the television or radio, or walking up to a newsstand or striking up a conversation on the street in Barcelona, San Sebastián, Valencia, Santiago de Compostela, or any of the hundreds of cities, towns, and villages where the reestablishment of regional languages is underway. The flow of two languages in coexistence and the acceptance of a natural bilingualism are enviable.

The question remains, what does the Spanish experience have to offer the United States? The situation in the United States varies in one significant way from the Spanish situation, and that is that the minority languages fighting for survival in the United States are universal languages that are used on a daily basis in business, diplomacy, travel, and personal relations by people in many parts of the world. The regional languages of Spain cannot make this claim, and it is unlikely in the foreseeable future that any of them will become major world languages. This limits their usefulness outside of the regions in which they are spoken, but in spite of this, there is clear recognition of their instrinsic worth and support for their survival. Perhaps this is one of the most important lessons to be learned, that linguistic pluralism is an asset, not a threat. If this can be achieved, it logically follows that bilingual education programs should be conceived and instituted as enrichment, not transition, programs. These can only be implemented if society recognizes that being bilingual is always beneficial. If this is the case, it then makes no difference what the student's first language is when he or she enters school. All children should be given the opportunity to acquire a second language, and this means ongoing education in both languages, even when a certain level of proficiency is reached. Designing bilingual programs that have built-in exit criteria at the outset doom those programs to failure because they are seen as remedial, and those who participate in them are stigmatized and held in low esteem by others. Educational psychology tells us this is a recipe for disaster. Language is not a quantifiable construct, not a corpus that can be easily measured, and proficiency is a difficult concept to define. When a student is moved from a bilingual program to a monolingual program, a disservice is done, because that student will no longer have the opportunity to develop in one of the two languages, and it is a well-known fact that language needs development through study. If this were not true, there would be no language requirements for students in their native tongues. It makes little sense to work so hard to acquire a second language and then let the first one falter.

Becoming bilingual is a significant and admirable achievement and a fully satisfying personal experience. Those who have gone from being monolingual to being bilingual know this to be true. The fear some people feel when confronted with individuals who are different physically or who speak a different language is irrational and based on ignorance rather than understanding.

In some of the linguistically diverse regions of Spain, bilingual education is available to every child and is held in high esteem, not seen as a transitional remedial program for children who are somehow deficient. If this seems unrealistic in the United States, at the very least there should be a recognition and acceptance of those individuals who, due to their life circumstances, depend on two languages to negotiate their daily lives. These people should not be feared or shunned, but respected, admired, and accommodated. Individuals, community groups, institutions, and governmental agencies can work together to create an atmosphere of tolerance and to confer on bilingualism and multilingualism the prestige they deserve.

Bibliography

Aymá Aubeyzon, Josep M. 1992. *Allò que no se sol dir de la normalització lingüística* [*What Is Not Usually Said about Language Standardization*]. Barcelona: Editorial Empúries.

Bassa, Ramón. 1991. *El catalá a l'escola (1936/39–1985): Crónica d'una desigualtat* [*Catalán in School from 1936/39 to 1985: A Case of Inequality*]. Barcelona: La Llar de Llibre.

Bastardas, Albert, and Emili Boix, dirs. 1994. *¿Un estado, una lengua? La organización política de la diversidad lingüística* [*One State, One Language? The Political Organization of Linguistic Diversity*]. Barcelona: Ediciones Octaedro, S.L.

Bellón Carabán, J. A. 1995. "Política lingüística y política educativa" [Linguistic Policy and Educational Policy]. In F. J. García Marcos, ed., *Actas de las I Jornadas Almerienses sobre Política Lingüística*. Almería: Universidad de Almería. 15–20.

Gaitero, Ana. 1998. "El leonés oculto" [The Hidden Language of León]. *Diario de León,* Apr. 20: 9–10.

Meyer, Daniela. 1998. "Lenguas minoritarias en España" [Minority Languages in Spain]. *Al Norte. Revista del Instituto Cervantes de Bremen.* Sept. 6.

Mollá, Toni. 1994. "Opciones de política lingüística: Models i vies" [Options for Linguistic Policy. Models and Approaches]. *III Jornadas de Sociolingüística. Normalització i Planificació Lingüístiques.* Alcoy: Ayuntament d'Alcoi.

Ninyoles, Rafael L. 1994. "España como país plurilingüe: Líneas de futuro" [Spain as a Multilingual Country: Approaches for the Future]. In Albert Bastardas and Emili Boix, eds., *¿Un estado, una lengua? La organización política de la diversidad lingüística* [*One State, One Language? The Political Organization of Linguistic Diversity*]. Barcelona: Ediciones Octaedro, S.L. 141–54.

País Vasco, Gobierno. 1990. *La normalización del uso del euskera en las administraciones públicas: normativa básica* [*The Standardization of the Use of Basque in Government Offices: Basic Rules and Regulations*]. Vitoria: Servicio Central de Publicaciones del Gobierno Vasco.

Perez de Lama, Ernesto, ed. 1994. *Manual del estado español, 1994.* Madrid: Editorial Lama. 13–45.

Reniu i Tresserras, Miquel. 1994. *Planificació lingüística: estructuras i legislació* [*Language Planning: Structures and Legislation*]. Barcelona: Dpto. de Cultura, Generalitat de Catalunya.

Salvador, Gregorio. 1992. *Política lingüística y sentido común* [*Language Policy and Common Sense*]. Madrid: Istmo Editorial.

Siguan, Miquel. 1992. *España plurilingüe* [*Multilingual Spain*]. Madrid: Alianza Editorial.

Verney i Llobet, Jaume. 1994. "La regulación del plurilingüismo en la Administración Española" [Regulating Multilingualism in Government Offices in Spain]. In Albert Bastardas and Emili Boix, eds., *¿Un estado, una lengua? La organización política de la universidad lingüística* [*One State, One Language? The Political Organization of Linguistic Diversity*]. Barcelona: Ediciones Octaedro, S.L.117–40.

Lessons, Caveats, and a Way Forward

THOMAS RICENTO
University of Texas at San Antonio

Understanding the Official English (OE) movement in the United States can be both a simple and a complex matter. If we were to ignore for the moment the more than five hundred year history of ethnolinguistic contact on the North American continent and consider only the last twenty years of U.S. history, the explanation for the apparently widespread support for Official English is simple. A well-intentioned (although misinformed) politically liberal analysis of the current situation might yield the following syllogism:

1. A relatively large percentage of people living in the United States either do not speak English, or they speak English with strong accents.

2. Speaking and writing standard English provides access to education and employment for all Americans.

3. All Americans should be required to speak and write standard English.

The deceptiveness of this simple and seductive reasoning is difficult to counter with mere facts that render the underlying premise false. Polls suggest that most Americans believe English already is the official national language. For many Americans unaware of the complex history of languages and cultures in the United States, the OE movement is a benign, if perhaps slightly provocative, symbol to which frustrations of various sorts might be attached. In educational settings, there is often even less concern about any negative effects of the OE movement. After all, English *is* the language of instruction in all fifty states: teachers teach in English, students are tested in English, their diplomas are in English, their college curricula is in English, and English is the language of the workplace. What, these educators ask, is all the fuss about?

The essays in this volume explain what the fuss is about. But the information and analyses they contain are complex. The liberal myths of an egalitarian U.S. society are deeply ingrained and reinforced by the major media. Recent data indicate, for example, that a majority of U.S. families have seen no rise in real income (i.e., adjusted for inflation) over the past twenty years; yet it is more convenient for some to blame immigrants (documented or otherwise) for "taking away jobs" from "Americans" than to engage in uncomfortable discussions about the causes of the growing gap in income and wealth between the top 10 percent and the bottom 40 percent of the U.S. population.[1]

The best and most accurate response to "What is the problem with declaring English the official language of the United States?" does not fit into one sentence or a paragraph. While this is unfortunate, and there is no obvious remedy for this problem, it is not all bad. It is, in fact, symptomatic of the problem of the OE movement itself. It took many generations of lived history to arrive at a point where, incredibly, nearly half of the fifty states have laws "protecting" the status of English, the preeminent world language. The OE movement is part of a continuing and, in my view, troubled thread in our collective histories as peoples on this continent (see Ricento 1996). It will take a while for these tangled histories of languages, people, and cultures in contact and conflict to be resolved in a way that will benefit all citizens. As a first step, however, we need to unpackage this history (and this volume achieves that aim nicely), bring it to light, and expose it to *informed* and dispassionate debate. At the same time, we need to understand our own histories, how they are interwoven in the larger sociohistorical fabric, and how our thinking on these matters continues to be influenced by events and discourses which affect us, and of which we ourselves partake.

Let me briefly rehearse the main themes presented in this volume. I will add caveats where appropriate, refer to some of my own research findings on U.S. language policies, and conclude with some thoughts on the future.

1. *English continues to be the language of the workplace, but this does not give employers unlimited license to prohibit the use of other languages.*

The evidence presented in the essays by Edward Chen (Chapter 2), Juan Perea (Chapter 5), and Randy Lee and David Marshall (Chapter 7) suggests that "English Only laws are unnecessary, patronizing, and divisive" (Chen, p. 31). While the federal courts have found that private sector employers may require English Only rules in the workplace (*Garcia v. Gloor* 1980; *Garcia v. Spun Steak Co.* 1993), Official English laws that attempt to regulate speech in governmental settings have been viewed with less favor. In *Gutierrez v. Municipal Court* (1988) the U.S. Court of Appeals for the Ninth Circuit found that California's Official English amendment did not require an English Only policy for employees. The court found the Official English provision to be "primarily a symbolic statement" and irrelevant in deciding the case. In *Yñiguez v. Mofford* (1990), District Court Judge Rosenblatt ruled Arizona's Official English statute unconstitutional. He found the law so broadly worded that it would prohibit all officers and employees of all political subdivisions from using any language other than English while performing their official duties. Although these decisions were appealed to the U.S. Supreme Court, in both instances the lawsuits were ruled moot because the employees had left their jobs. The decision in *Ruiz v. Hull* (1998) by the Arizona Supreme Court invalidating the Official English provisions of the Arizona Constitution is a hopeful sign but not the last word on the constitutionality of Official English legislation. Statutes that are less restrictive and that do not appear to target a particular language or ethnic group could pass constitutional muster. In all of these cases, it is important to remember that the courts are not interested in protecting *language* rights per se, but rather free speech and political participation. In one of the most famous cases of the twentieth century dealing with language—*Meyer v. Nebraska* (1923)—the U.S. Supreme Court's majority affirmed the right of the state to make reasonable regulations for all schools, including a requirement that they shall give instruction in English. Indeed, in his dissenting opinion, Oliver Wendell Holmes argued that all citizens of the United States should be required to speak a common tongue (Murphy 1992). Thus, despite the setbacks to Official English statutes, the issue of *positive* language rights—that is, the right to use a language other than English in the workplace, the right to receive education in a language other than English, or the right of bilingual or even non-English-speaking individuals to serve on juries,[2] is an underdeveloped area of the law in the United States.

2. Laws that attempt to regulate language behavior and attitudes usually do not work.

Randy Lee and David Marshall (Chapter 7) warn of the unintended consequences of "going to law." Efforts to manage language behavior through legislation, official government policies, or the courts rarely achieve intended results. There is no evidence to show that Official English laws in the United States have changed *language* behavior. Since legislation typically provides no funding for English-language education, there is no way to quantify whether the objective of "encouraging the acquisition of English" has been met. Language shift to English occurs because of the obvious economic and social benefits, and Official English laws have no impact in this regard (see Robert Williams and Kathleen Riley, Chapter 3). On the other hand, the availability of public services and voting materials in languages other than English *does* offer measurable benfits.[3] It enables U.S. residents to access health, safety, and other public services to which they are entitled and fosters political participation for persons who may not yet be proficient in English or who, for various reasons, have missed the opportunity to acquire English.

While attempts to protect dominant languages that need no protection have negative consequences, attempts to protect minority languages and the rights of their speakers are not always successful either. A brief consideration of the language situations in Switzerland, Canada, and South Africa demonstrates this point.

Switzerland is often cited as an example of a successful multilingual country in which the inhabitants speak, read, and write all four Swiss national languages on an equal basis. In reality, only a minority of Switzerland's inhabitants are bi- or multilingual on an equal basis. German is the primary language of 63.6 percent of the national population, followed by French (19.2 percent), Italian (7.6 percent), and Rumantsch (0.6 percent) (Weil and Schneider 1997, 289). German speakers enjoy economic superiority, and this greatly influences patterns of language use and shift within cantons, as well as language attitudes between minority- and majority-language groups. In a project conducted by the Research Center for Multilingualism at the University of Berne, Weil and Schneider (1997) found that language attitudes of French speakers (7.8 percent of the Bernese population) toward German speakers (83.8 percent of the Bernese population) were more negative than the attitudes of German speakers toward French speakers. The Latin regions of Switzerland deplore the presence of the Swiss German-speaking members of the population (289). Recent parliamentary discussions about the revision of article 116 of the Swiss Constitution, which concerns the status of the German, French, Italian, and Rumantsch languages, have increased minority concerns about the German influence on their territory. Weil and Scheider conclude that "[t]he attempt to find a solution that would combine the principle of freedom of language and the principle of territoriality in favor of a more diversified vision of a multilingual state has failed" (289).

The situation in Canada is, if anything, more complex than that in Switzerland. Although aggressive language legislation and policymaking over the past thirty years has benefited the status of French and Francophones in Quebec Province, shift to English by Francophones outside Quebec continues. Data show that the net Anglicization rate of the overall Francophone population has increased in each province outside Quebec; in all areas except New Brunswick and portions of the Bilingual Belt in Ontario, 50 percent or more of Francophones have adopted English as the main home language by the time they reach mature adulthood (Castonguay 1998). Even though laws were passed to protect the rights of minority-language speakers in the workplace and to access government services, the reality is that differences in psychological climate and the working environment have combined to maintain English in Ottawa and French in Montreal as the normal, preferred, expected, and thus dominant languages of work in these two cities. Thus a gap exists between the formal policy of free choice and the more complex social reality of everyday language contacts (Hay Management Consultants 1993; Veltman 1998).

In South Africa, sociolinguistic behavior will not be determined by constitutional protections and provisions for the eleven named official languages. Although English is the first language of only 9 percent of the South African population, it is still indisputably the dominant language (Ridge 2000). Given the role of English in the liberation of South Africa from apartheid and as the de facto lingua franca of Parliament (see Geneva Smitherman Chapter 13), English will likely retain its preeminent status for the foreseeable future. The promise of a truly mulitlingual South Africa depends greatly on the ability of the education system to promote and develop the nine official African languages. Ridge warns that "unless significant work is possible in teacher in-service education, including the production of suitable materials and engaging the support of the community, English will not only be dominant but dominating in its effect" (2000, 169–70).

The lessons from Switzerland, Canada, and South Africa, while cautionary, should not be used to dismiss serious and long-standing efforts to ensure the economic, social, human, and political civil rights of bilinguals and minority-language speakers. Rather, they exemplify the dangers of expecting too much from laws and policies that attempt to significantly modify existing sociolinguistic and sociopolitical relationships. As Cynthia Miguélez notes in Chapter 14, "It is certainly true that governmental or institutional action alone cannot ensure the success of a given linguistic policy. There must be popular support for the basic underlying principles and philosophy of the policy, and societal forces must be involved in the creation, development, implementation, and modification of the programs that develop the policy" (p. 363).

3. *Ideologies play a role in language policies; the underlying ideologies, or even the motives, for a particular language policy are not always transparent.*

After investigating the discourse surrounding the Ebonics controversy of 1996–97 and California's antibilingual Proposition 227 of 1997–98, Jane Hill concludes that "language panics [such as Ebonics and Proposition 227] are not really about language. Instead, they are about race" (see Chapter 10, p. 245). She notes that this perspective on language panics is not widely shared by linguists and language educators. In the case of both the Ebonics and bilingual education panics, linguists assumed the problem was the public's ignorance about "scholarly understanding of these phenomena." They reasoned that if the public could only come to understand what linguists already know—that bilingualism can be an important national resource in the global economy and that African American English is a fully "grammatical" language variety—the public would change its mind on these issues. Linguists and educators rarely mentioned race as a factor. The importance of Hill's research is that it focuses our attention on the social and cultural ideologies that are inevitably linked to attitudes about language.

Lynn Goldstein (Chapter 9) achieves a similar goal in her essay, which demonstrates the benefits of investigating folk linguistic beliefs about the Official English movement. Just as important, she acknowledges that opponents of OE—as she herself is—no less than supporters have ideologies about languages and linguistic diversity which inform their research and policy positions. Goldstein argues that we should acknowledge our own positions and try to understand the thinking of those whose views we disagree with. It is crucial that researchers and scholars not succumb to the "false consciousness" view of ideology, which presupposes "the possibility of some unequivocally correct way of viewing the world" (Eagleton 1991, 11). This can lead to solutions as bad as the problems they seek to cure.

Alastair Pennycook develops the idea that in order to understand language policies, it is necessary to examine them in broader sociohistorical contexts. He notes that "languages are not mere media but instead stand at the very core of major cultural and political questions" (Chapter 8, p. 217). In his analysis of colonial language policies within the British Empire—particularly in India, Singapore, Malaya, and Hong Kong—he finds that the competing demands and interests of the colonizers and the colonized led to contradictions in language policies, with Anglicists supporting English and Orientalists supporting the use of native languages in education. Although the underlying goals of

Anglicists and Orientalists were similar—economic efficiency and social control of native populations—different ideologies led to different language policies. In the contemporary context, Pennycook warns that language policies that appear to be diametrically opposed—for example, linguistic diversity versus English Only—may in fact be complicit with each other and with a broader politics.

The view that language "panics," policies, or debates are not primarily about language is, of course, not new. In the 1960s and 1970s, Arnold Leibowitz developed the thesis that language is primarily a means of social control. In a series of careful analyses of language policies from the colonial period through the civil rights era in the United States, in the areas of the school system, citizenship and voting, and the economic life of the country, Leibowitz found that

> language designation in the three areas followed a marked, similar pattern so that it is reasonably clear that one was responding not to the problems specifically related to that area (i.e., job requirements in the economic sphere) but to broader problems in the society to which language was but one response. Language designation was almost always coupled with restrictions on the use of other languages; it was also coupled with discriminatory legislation and practices in other fields. (1976, 450)

What are the implications for English teachers? Supporters of Official English tend to deny the associations of racism, exclusion, and negative stereotyping that attach to their movement, and often claim that it is the opponents whose views are "ideological." Opponents believe their fight for the underdog and for linguistic human rights is morally superior. The first step in the education process, then, is to understand that *all* positions are undergirded by a complex set of assumptions, or ideologies; there is no such thing as a neutral, or nonideological, position with regard to the Official English movement.

An important task for opponents of OE is to unpackage the ideologies and hidden agenda associated with that movement. At the same time, some of the positions advocated by supporters of linguistic diversity and language rights should be critically evaluated. For example, support for English Plus (the idea that everyone should acquire English plus another language), on closer examination, could be viewed as a utopian universalist dream, one that is unwittingly complicit with the goals of the Official English movement because of the enormous asymmetry in prestige between English and minority languages (especially in English-dominant countries). In diglossic situations, it is usually the case that one language (the high variety) is used for high-status functions, while other languages (the low varieties) are used for more limited, lower-prestige functions. In these contexts, monolingual speakers of the low variety continue to be socially and economically disadvantaged; the "remedy" for them is usually assimilation into the dominant high language or variety, if that is an option, and in the case of minority languages in the United States, the eventual loss of the low variety by succeeding generations. This surely is not the image supporters of English Plus have in mind if they truly support linguistic and cultural diversity; in some ways, this policy is more pernicious than English Only because it is supported by liberals and advocates of linguistic diversity. The antidote to this outcome, at least in the United States, is the development of full biliteracy through effective bicultural-bilingual programs from kindergarten through grade 12. This legitimizes the minority language—and its speakers—by providing institutional support and social recognition. The problem with English Plus is that minority languages (such as Spanish in the United States) are usually viewed as "foreign" languages to be "studied," and usually forgotten, in what remains an essentially monolingual society.

Conclusion

The Official English movement has suffered legal setbacks in recent years. With the rising importance of Latinos and Asians in national politics, it has become less likely that Official English will be embraced by the major political parties or candidates for high office. Yet the agendas which OE encompasses continue in force. These include (1) the movement to eliminate bilingual education, which began with the passage of Proposition 227 by the voters of California on June 2, 1998, and which has now moved to Arizona, where a ballot initiative (English Language Education for Children in Public Schools) will appear on the November 2000 ballot (Ricento 2000); (2) continuing attempts to dismantle affirmative action, which, like bilingual education, is viewed as an illicit "ethnic entitlement" by OE activists; and (3) the continued stigmatizing of so-called nonstandard varieties of English, including African American Vernacular and Chicano English, with negative consequences for those who use these varieties (see Smitherman Chapter 13; Lippi-Green *Volume 1*, Chapter 10; and Lippi-Green 1997). Thus, whether or not English is ultimately declared the official language of the United States, issues which attach to language(s), education, and ethnicity will persist. If English is declared the official language, additional problems (as noted by Robert Kaplan and Richard Baldauf Jr. in Chapter 12) will emerge. These include deciding which variety of English will be chosen as the standard; what will happen with Native American languages, now protected by federal legislation; and what will be the fate of various languages for hearing-impaired individuals, including American Sign Language (ASL)? These concerns are already with us today; an Official English declaration would merely add to current tensions while providing nothing in the way of solutions.

Recent events in El Cenizo, a small town on the U.S. side of the Texas-Mexico border, provide some indication of the volatility of language matters in the United States. In August 1999, city officials in this former colonia of 1,500 residents, which was incorporated in 1989, declared Spanish as the municipality's official language. They also declared that they will fire any municipal employees who help the U.S. Border Patrol apprehend undocumented immigrants (Schiller 1999a). City council sessions and other official functions will be conducted in Spanish, notices will be posted in Spanish, and English translations will be provided within forty-eight hours' notice. To conform with state and federal regulations, ordinances will be created in English but will be translated into Spanish. As might be expected, hate mail and death threats soon followed. According to Mayor Rafael Rodriguez, who speaks little English and who has no plans to retreat from implementing the ordinances, "They say they will kill us and burn City Hall" (Schiller 1999b). The response from the major group supporting Official English was predictable and telling. Tim Schultz, spokesperson for the Washington, D.C.-based U.S. English, said, "We essentially predicted we would have a dropping out—a linguistic ghettoization of the country; we did not know it would happen this soon" (Schiller 1999a). A small, impoverished border town that only recently obtained water and electricity, all of whose residents speak Spanish, declares Spanish the official language of the municipality, and all hell breaks loose. The obvious lesson, missed by U.S. English, is that policies that favor one language or language variety (viz., standard English) usually create negative feelings in speakers of other languages or varieties. In the case of El Cenizo, the desire to increase civic interest and participation in local government justified a policy that facilitates communication in a language everyone understands. If a legitimate goal of a language policy is to improve access to the political culture while not excluding anyone, then El Cenizo's policy makes sense. The comments by U.S. English provide clear evidence that for them, at least, the only acceptable policy is one which demands absolute conformity to English Only in the public domain for all Americans, regardless of the needs or feelings of the people affected by such a policy, or even whether it is in the long-term best interest of the nation. As David Corson notes: "The 'English Only' movement is . . . sadly out of touch with the real world" (Chapter 4, pp. 103–4).

My opposition to the Official English movement rests not on a narrow, ideological commitment to linguistic diversity as inherently good, but on a range of issues having to do with human rights and social justice[4] that spreads well beyond the narrow interests of protecting or promoting one or another language. Declaring English the official language will surely make matters in the United States worse (see Ricento 1998), but I am concerned that the attention this movement has garnered since 1981 distracts us from developing alternative discourses and strategies in public space. Educators need to take to heart their responsibilities to understand the underlying agendas which are attached to the OE movement and to discuss them openly with their students, just as they should examine the underlying beliefs and goals which inform alternative policies. Such dialogues encourage new thinking and self-reflection about who we are as individuals and our roles as participants in and creators of U.S. culture. It is time that we, individually and collectively, create alternative and liberatory discourse in place of the tired English Only versus English Plus debate. The future of the United States may depend on it.

Notes

1. One indicator is the growing wage gap between CEOs (chief executive officers) of U.S. corporations and workers. In 1980, CEOs earned 42 times the pay of average workers; in 1998, they made 419 times more in salary. In contrast, a worker earning $25,000 in 1999 would have made about $3,400 *more* in 1973, adjusting for inflation (Sklar 1999).

2. In October 1999, state District Judge Robert Robles (New Mexico) threw out a jury pool of several hundred, declaring that it had been illegally impaneled because non-English-speakers were excluded. Robles cited the 1911 New Mexico Constitution, which states that residents cannot be restricted from sitting on juries because of an "inability to speak, read, or write the English or Spanish languages." In the first trial affected by the ruling, Luis Escobedo, a Spanish-speaking juror, was provided a translator, who also accompanied Escobedo into the jury deliberation room. The many issues raised by this ruling remain unsettled ("New Mexico Wrestling" 1999). (See Guadalupe Valdés [Chapter 6] for a discussion of language-based discrimination as it affects bilingual groups.)

3. Based on surveys conducted in San Antonio and East Los Angeles between 1981 and 1982, Brischetto and de la Garza (1983) concluded that "the availability of bilingual ballots and coordinated voter registration drives may account for . . . unexpectedly high levels of voting-related participation among older Spanish monolinguals" (29; also cited in Ricento 1998, 325).

4. I concur with David Corson, who notes:

> Social justice has to do with ideas about legitimacy, about fairness and impartiality, about welfare and mutual advantage, and about political and social consensus. The fair treatment of speakers of language varieties that are not the dominant dialect is one key concern of social justice theorists. . . . The question of who is entitled to decide which language varieties should be used in public domains in the United States is at the heart of the English Only debate. (Chapter 4, p. 96)

Works Cited

Brischetto, R. Robert, and Rodolfo O. de la Garza. 1983. *The Mexican American Electorate: Political Participation and Ideology.* The Mexican American Electorate Series, Occasional Paper No. 3. San Antonio, TX: Southwest Voter Education Project/Hispanic Population Studies Program of the Center for Mexican American Studies, University of Texas at Austin.

Castonguay, Charles. 1998. "The Fading Canadian Duality." In John Edwards, ed., *Language in Canada.* Cambridge: Cambridge University Press. 36–60.

Eagleton, Terry. 1991. *Ideology.* London: Verso.

Hay Management Consultants. 1993. *Negotiating Language Choice in the Federal Civil Service.* Toronto: Hay Management Consultants.

Leibowitz, Arnold H. 1976. "Language and the Law: The Exercise of Political Power through Official Designation of Language." In William O. O'Barr and Jean F. O'Barr, eds., *Language and Politics.* The Hague: Mouton. 449–66.

Lippi-Green, Rosina. 1997. *English with an Accent: Language, Ideology, and Discriminatin in the United States.* London: Routledge.

Murphy, P. L. 1992. "Meyer v. Nebraska." In K. L. Hall, ed., *The Oxford Companion to the Supreme Court of the United States.* New York: Oxford University Press. 543–44.

"New Mexico Wrestling with Language, Juries." 1999. *San Antonio Express News*, Dec. 15. 3B.

Ricento, Thomas. 1996. "Language Policy in the United States." In Michael Herriman and Barbara Burnaby, eds., *Language Policies in English-Dominant Countries: Six Case Studies.* Clevedon: Multilingual Matters. 122–58.

———. 1998. "Partitioning by Language: Whose Rights Are Threatened?" In Thomas Ricento and Barbara Burnaby, eds., *Language and Politics in the United States and Canada: Myths and Realities.* Mahwah, NJ: Lawrence Erlbaum. 317–30.

———. 2000. "The Implementation of Proposition 227 and the Future of Antibilingual Education Legislation in the U.S." *The Multilingual Educator* 1(1): 30–33. [Los Angeles: California Association for Bilingual Education.]

Ridge, Stanley G. 2000. "Mixed Motives: Ideological Elements in the Support for English in South Africa." In Thomas Ricento, ed., *Ideology, Politics, and Language Policies: Focus on English*. Amsterdam: John Benjamins. 151–72.

Schiller, Dane. 1999a. "No Ingles in Border Town of El Cenizo, Spanish Is In and the INS Is Out." *San Antonio Express News,* Aug. 11. 1A.

———. 1999b. "Ordinance Draws Fire from Afar: Spanish-speaking Town Gets Threats." *San Antonio Express News,* Aug. 29. 1B.

Sklar, Holly. 1999. "For CEOs, a Minimum Wage in the Millions." *Z Magazine* 12 (7-8): 63–66. [Cambridge, MA: The Institute for Social and Cultural Communications.]

Veltman, Calvin. 1998. "Quebec, Canada, and the United States: Social Reality and Language Rights." In Thomas Ricento and Barbara Burnaby, eds., *Language and Politics in the United States and Canada: Myths and Realities*. Mahwah, NJ: Lawrence Erlbaum. 301–15.

Weil, Sonia, and Hansjakob Schneider. 1997. "Language Attitudes in Switzerland: French and German along the Language Border." In Martin Pütz, ed., *Language Choices: Conditions, Constraints, and Consequences*. Amsterdam: John Benjamins. 287–304.

Index

EDITORS

Roseann Dueñas González is currently professor of English, the first Mexican American woman to attain such distinction at the University of Arizona. She has been a faculty member and administrator at the University of Arizona for twenty-five years, working in the areas of minority education, second-language acquisition, language policy, and interpreter training and testing. She is founder and director of the Writing Skills Improvement Program and the Summer Institute for Writing and Thinking, two programs dedicated to supporting the intellectual and writing development of minority students. After directing the graduate program in English Language and Linguistics for ten years, González co-founded and developed the Second Language Acquisition and Teaching (SLAT) doctoral program at the University of Arizona. She is currently director of the National Center for Interpretation Testing, Research and Policy and directs the Federal Court Certification Program that certifies Spanish-English interpreters for use in federal courts throughout the United States, providing due process for non-English-speaking Hispanic Americans. She has written and lectured widely in the areas of minority education, language policy, language discrimination, and judicial interpreter training and testing, and has held a variety of posts in NCTE.

Ildikó Melis is currently a doctoral student in the Rhetoric, Composition, and the Teaching of English (RCTE) program of the University of Arizona, where she also teaches first-year composition classes and works on language policy–related research projects. She earned her M.A. in English and Hungarian at Eötvös Loránd University (ELTE), Budapest, Hungary, and an M.A. in ESL in 1989 at the University of Arizona. From 1990 to 1996, she was director of the first-year composition program and assistant professor of English applied linguistics in ELTE's School of English and American Studies, teaching courses in applied linguistics and academic writing. She has also coauthored two course texts on writing in English, *The Joy of Reading* (1994) and *The Little Red Writing Book* (1996), both published by the Hungarian National Educational Publisher Company.

CONTRIBUTORS

Richard B. Baldauf Jr. is associate professor and director of the University of Sydney Language Centre and president of the Applied Linguistics Association of Australia. He has published numerous books, as well as articles in refereed journals. Baldauf is co-editor of *Language Planning and Education in Australasia and the South Pacific* (1990) and co-editor with Robert Kaplan of *Language Planning in Malawi, Mozambique and the Philippines* (1999), principal researcher and editor of *Viability of Low Candidature LOTE Courses in Universities* (1995), co-author with Robert Kaplan of *Language Planning from Practice to Theory* (1997), and executive editor of the new journal *Current Issues in Language Planning*.

Dennis Baron is professor of English and linguistics and head of the Department of English at the University of Illinois at Urbana-Champaign. He has written extensively on language policy, gender and language, and language history and reform. He received an NEH fellowship in 1989 to work on his book *The English-Only Question: An Official Language for Americans?* (1990). He is currently working on a book on the new technologies of literacy.

Edward M. Chen is staff attorney with the American Civil Liberties Union Foundation of Northern California. He co-chairs the Language Rights Project jointly sponsored by the ACLU of Northern California and the Employment Law Center in San Francisco. Chen has written and spoken widely on language discrimination and the English Only movement and has litigated numerous language-rights cases including challenges to English Only workplace rules, accent discrimination, language barriers to business and governmental services, restrictions on bilingual education, and Official English laws.

David Corson is professor at the Ontario Institute for Studies in Education in Toronto. He has taught in universities in Canada, England, Australia, and New Zealand, and has been a teacher at primary and secondary levels, a curriculum officer, and a school and system administrator. Author or editor of twenty books, he is founding editor of *Language and Education: An International Journal*, and general editor of the *Encyclopedia of Language and Education*. His Web site is http://www.oise.utoronto.ca/~dcorson.

Amanda Espinosa-Aguilar is assistant professor of English and director of the writing center at the University of Wisconsin Oshkosh. She teaches classes in rhetorical theory, composition, and ethnic American literature; her research interests are varied but center on autobiography, ethnic literature, sociolinguistics, and literacy theory. Espinosa-Aguilar is working on a number of articles that look at the uses of anger as a rhetorical device in the autobiographical writings of ethnic Americans. She was a recipient of the Conference on College Composition and Communication Scholars for the Dream Travel Award in 1996.

Henry A. Giroux holds the Waterbury Chair Professorship at Pennsylvania State University and is currently director of the Waterbury Form in Education and Cultural Studies at Penn State. He has published extensively; his books include *Schooling and the Struggle for Public Life* (1988), *Teachers as Intellectuals* (1988), *Postmodern Education: Politics, Culture, and Social Criticism* (1991, co-authored with Stanley Aronowitz), *Border Crossings: Cultural Workers and the Politics of Education* (1992), *Living Dangerously: Multiculturalism and the Politics of Difference* (1993), *Disturbing Pleasures: Learning Popular Culture* (1994), *Fugitive Cultures: Race, Violence, and Youth* (1996), *Channel Surfing: Racism, the Media and the Destruction of Today's Youth* (1997), *Pedagogy and the Politics of Hope* (1997), *The Mouse That Roared: Disney and the End of Innocence* (1999), *Stealing Innocence: Youth, Corporate Power, and the Politics of Culture* (2000), and *Impure Acts: The Practical Politics of Cultural Studies* (2000). Giroux is also on the editorial and advisory boards of numerous national and international scholarly journals and serves as the editor or co-editor of four scholarly book series. He was selected Kappa Delta Pi Laureate in 1998 and was recently the recipient of a Getty Research Institute Visiting Scholar Award. He lectures frequently both in the United States and abroad on a variety of issues including cultural studies, youth, critical pedagogy, democratic theory, public education, social theory, and the politics of higher education.

Lynn M. Goldstein is professor of TESOL and applied linguistics at the Monterey Institute of International Studies, where she also directs the campus writing program. She has published in the areas of second-language acquisition and sociolinguistics and in second-language writing. Her current research includes an examination of how the Oakland Ebonics resolution was addressed in newspapers across the United States, with a particular focus on the use of linguistics in these discussions. She was the 1987 recipient of the TESOL/Newbury award for distinguished research.

Jane H. Hill is Regents Professor of anthropology and linguistics at the University of Arizona. A specialist in the sociolinguistics of the languages of Native Americans, she has recently been working in the area of language and racism, emphasizing mock Spanish—a mainstream culture usage that constructs covert racist discourses. Currently, she is president of the American Anthropological Association, and she has served as president of the Society for Linguistic Anthropology.

Robert B. Kaplan is emeritus professor of applied linguistics at the University of Southern California. He has published numerous books and articles and written several special reports to governments, in the United States and elsewhere. He is founding editor in chief of the *Annual Review of Applied Linguistics* and a member of the editorial board of the Oxford International Encyclopedia of Linguistics. He has served as president of the National Association for Foreign Linguistics and has served as president of the National Association for Applied Linguistics.

Randy H. Lee is North Dakota Bar Foundation Professor at the School of Law, University of North Dakota. He is admitted to practice in Maryland and North Dakota, and is a member of the bar of the United States Supreme Court. A law professor for the last twenty-five years, Lee previously engaged in full-time private practice and has served as an assistant attorney general in Maryland. He has also served the U.S. District Court as a special master.

David F. Marshall is currently professor of English, linguistics, and peace studies at the University of North Dakota. He has published extensively, including comprehensive monographs, on language laws and their effects on ethnolinguistic minorities, and is well known for his *The Question of an Official Language: Language Rights and the English Language Amendment*. He has been Fulbright professor Eötvös Loránd University, Budapest, Hungary, and Nanjing University in the People's Republic of China, as well as visiting professor at the University of Arizona, Visiting NEH Scholar at Stanford University and the University of Wisconsin Madison, and Lilly Visiting Scholar at Duke University.

Cynthia Miguélez has been a member of the faculty of the Universidad de Alicante since 1990. Prior to taking up her current post in Spain, she was actively involved in efforts to promote bilingual education in Arizona, where she taught in a pilot program at the secondary level and sat on several steering committees for the development of bilingual programs for elementary and junior high schools. Once in Spain, Miguélez complemented her interest in bilingualism and language equivalency with teaching and research in the area of translation and interpretation. She is currently in charge of the interpreting component of both the undergraduate and graduate degree programs in translating and interpreting at the Universidad de Alicante, and she also speaks and writes on topics related to this field for audiences in the United States, Latin America, and Europe.

Alastair Pennycook is professor of language in education at the University of Technology, Sydney, Australia. He formerly taught critical applied linguistics at the University of Melbourne. He has worked widely as an English teacher in Germany, Japan, Canada, China, and Hong Kong, and has lectured on critical applied linguistics in North and South America, Europe, Asia, and Australia. Pennycook is author of *The Cultural Politics of English as an International Language* (1994) and *English and the Discourses of Colonialism* (1998). His many interests include the global spread of English, colonialism, plagiarism, poststructuralism, language policies, and language rights. His new book, *Critical Applied Linguistics: A Critical Introduction,* is currently in press.

Juan F. Perea is University of Florida Research Foundation Professor of Law at the University of Florida College of Law. He is editor of and contributor to *Immigrants Out! The New Nativism and the Anti-Immigrant Impulse in the United States* (1997) and author of *Race and Races: Cases and Resources for a Diverse America* (with Richard Delgado, Angela Harris, and Stephanie Wildman) (2000). He has written extensively on the law and history of language regulation in the United States, and on immigration and citizenship law. Perea has testified before the United States Senate as an opponent of Official English legislation, and before the United States Commission on Civil Rights with regard to proposed modifications of Title VII of the Civil Rights Act of 1964.

Thomas Ricento is associate professor of applied linguistics in the Division of Bicultural-Bilingual Studies at the University of Texas at San Antonio. He was Fulbright professor at four universities in Colombia (1989) and at the University of Costa Rica, School of Modern Languages (2000). His research focuses on language policies, politics, and ideologies. Ricento is editor of *Ideology, Politics, and Language Policies: Focus on English* (2000) and co-editor (with Barbara Burnaby) of *Language and Politics in the United States and Canada: Myths and Realities* (1998). He is also co-editor (with Nancy Hornberger) of a special topic issue of *TESOL Quarterly*

(*Language Planning and Policy*, 1996). Recent articles include "Unpeeling the Onion: Language Planning and Policy and the ELT Professional" (with Nancy Hornberger), *TESOL Quarterly* (1996), and "Historical and Theoretical Perspectives in Language Policy and Planning," *Journal of Sociolinguistics* (2000).

Kathleen C. Riley teaches linguistics and anthropology at Johnson State College, Vermont, and is managing editor of the *Green Mountains Review*, a literary magazine. She is presently completing her doctorate in linguistic anthropology at the Graduate Center, CUNY, for which she conducted research on language socialization in the Marquesas, French Polynesia. Since 1997 she and Robert Williams have been conducting an ethnographic study of language shift and cultural identity among French Canadians in northern Vermont.

Geneva Smitherman is an internationally recognized scholar-activist who has been at the forefront of the struggle for Black language rights for more than two decades. Presently, she is University Distinguished Professor of English and director of the African American Language and Literacy Program at Michigan State University. Her current research focuses on language-planning policy in South Africa. She has served on the NCTE Commission on Language and chairs the Language Policy Committee of the Conference on College Composition and Communication. Smitherman is author (or editor) of ten books and over one hundred articles and papers on the language, culture, and education of African Americans, most notably the classic work *Talkin' and Testifyin': The Language of Black America* (1977). She has two forthcoming books: *Talkin' That Talk: Language, Culture, and Education in African America* (2000) and a new edition of *Black Talk: Words and Phrases from the Hood to the Amen Corner* (2000).

Guadalupe Valdés is professor in the School of Education and in the Department of Spanish and Portuguese at Stanford University. Working in the areas of sociolinguistics and applied linguistics, she is concerned with discovering and describing how two languages are developed, used, and maintained by individuals who become bilingual in immigrant communities. Her recent books include *Bilingualism and Testing: A Special Case of Bias* (1994) and *Con Respecto: Bridging the Distance between Culturally Diverse Families and Schools* (1996). Recent articles include "Chicano Spanish: The Problem of the 'Underdeveloped' Code in Bilingual Repertories," *Modern Language Journal* (1998); "The Construct of the Near-Native Speaker in the Foreign Language Profession: Perspectives on Ideologies about Language," *ADFL Bulletin* (1998); "Bilinguals and Bilingualism: Language Policy in an Anti-immigrant

Age," *International Journal of the Sociology of Language* (1997); and "The Teaching of Minority Languages as 'Foreign' Languages: Pedagogical and Theoretical Challenges," *Modern Language Journal* (1995).

Robert S. Williams is assistant professor of TESL/applied linguistics at Saint Michael's College in Colchester, Vermont. He previously taught ESL and linguistics at UCLA, Southern California Institute of Architecture, and Los Angeles City College. He is presently engaged in research on ancestral language and cultural identity, language and public opinion, and second-language acquisition.

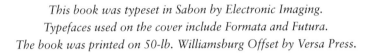

This book was typeset in Sabon by Electronic Imaging.
Typefaces used on the cover include Formata and Futura.
The book was printed on 50-lb. Williamsburg Offset by Versa Press.